AF605983

AMERICAN ETHNIC AND CULTURAL STUDIES

John C. Walter and Johnnella E. Butler, Series Editors

AMERICAN ETHNIC AND CULTURAL STUDIES

The American Ethnic and Cultural Studies series presents critical interdisciplinary, cross-disciplinary, and comparative studies of cultural formations and expressions of racialized peoples of North America. Focusing on African Americans, American Indians, Asian Americans, Chicanos/as, and Latinos/as, and on comparative works among these groups and racialized Euro-Americans, the series also explores new and changing configurations of race and ethnicity as shaped by gender, class, and religion in global and domestic contexts. Informed by research in the humanities, arts, and social sciences; transnational and diasporic studies; film studies; legal studies; public policy, environmental, urban, and rural studies, books in the series will aim to stimulate innovative approaches in scholarship and pedagogy.

Color-line to Borderlands: The Matrix of American Ethnic Studies
Edited by Johnnella E. Butler

Being Buddhist in a Christian World:
Gender and Community in a Korean American Temple
Sharon A. Suh

Complicating Constructions:
Race, Ethnicity, and Hybridity in American Texts
Edited by David S. Goldstein and Audrey B. Thacker

Writing Off the Hyphen: New Critical Perspectives
on the Literature of the Puerto Rican Diaspora
Edited by José L. Torres-Padilla and Carmen Haydée Rivera

Writing Off the Hyphen

NEW CRITICAL PERSPECTIVES ON THE LITERATURE OF THE PUERTO RICAN DIASPORA

EDITED BY

José L. Torres-Padilla and Carmen Haydée Rivera

UNIVERSITY OF WASHINGTON PRESS SEATTLE AND LONDON

THIS BOOK IS PUBLISHED WITH THE ASSISTANCE OF A GRANT FROM THE STROUM BOOK FUND, ESTABLISHED THROUGH THE GENEROSITY OF SAMUEL AND ALTHEA STROUM.

Printed in the United States of America
Designed by Pamela Canell
13 12 11 10 09 08 5 4 3 2 1

University of Washington Press, PO Box 50096, Seattle, WA 98145-5096 U.S.A.
www.washington.edu/uwpress

Library of Congress Cataloging-in-Publication Data
Writing off the hyphen : new critical perspectives on the literature of the Puerto Rican diaspora / edited by José L. Torres-Padilla and Carmen Haydée Rivera.
p. cm. — (American ethnic and cultural studies)
Includes bibliographical references and index.
ISBN 978-0-295-98813-9 (hardback : alk. paper)
ISBN 978-0-295-98824-5 (paperback : alk. paper)
1. American literature—Puerto Rican authors—History and criticism.
2. Puerto Ricans—United States—Intellectual life. 3. Puerto Rican literature—History and criticism. 4. Puerto Ricans in literature. I. Torres-Padilla, José L.
II. Rivera, Carmen Haydée.
PS153P83W75 2008 810.9'97295—dc22 2007040823

The paper used in this publication is acid-free and 90 percent recycled from at least 50 percent post-consumer waste. It meets the minimum requirements of American National Standard for Information Sciences—Permanence of Paper for Printed Library Materials, ANSI Z39.48–1984. ♾ ♲

I respectfully dedicate this book to my parents, Luis F. Rivera and Carmen D. Vega, for their conscientious choice to create a home full of Puerto Rican tradition in diaspora and for always supporting and nurturing my diasporic spirit in constant *vaivén*, now resettled in Borinquén.

To my husband—Axel I. López—for our migrations and return migration, for his loving companionship and support.

CARMEN HAYDÉE

To my mother, Marcelina Padilla, who worked in sweatshops to knit my dreams, *con mucho amor y aprecio.*

To my wife, Lee, and sons, Alex and Julian, who anchor me in *el vaivén*, with my deepest love.

JOSÉ LUIS

CONTENTS

ACKNOWLEDGMENTS

To our contributors, our deepest gratitude for trusting us with your work, for your thought-provoking essays, and for your patience throughout the process.

To Guarionex Loran, whose beautiful photography adorns our cover and captures the multiple perspectives and palimpsest layers of diasporic experience.

Thanks to the University of Washington Press, especially Johnella Butler, Jacquie Ettinger, and Mary Ribesky, for believing in this project and helping us hone it to its finest completion.

We also wish to pay our respects to the critical/theoretical voices that have influenced our research and understanding of diasporic Puerto Rican Studies: Edna Acosta-Belén, Virginia Sánchez-Korrol, Clara Rodríguez, Juan Flores, Frances Aparicio, Efraín Barradas, Arnaldo Cruz-Malavé, Frances Negrón-Mutaner, Ramón Grosfoguel, Jorge Duany, William Luis, Lisa Sánchez-González, and the late Eugene Mohr, among others. Your groundbreaking scholarship has paved the way for this anthology, which we respectfully put forth to join the evolving critical conversations and debates in the field.

Thanks to Arte Público and *Centro Journal* for permission to publish the essays by Lisa Sánchez González and José Torres-Padilla, respectively.

Due to the scope and nature of this project, the works of several diasporic Puerto Rican authors were unfortunately left unattended. Nevertheless, as editors, we feel the need and the responsibility to point out that authors such as Luz María Umpierre, Gloria Vando, Martin Espada, Giannina Braschi, and Edward Gallardo, among others whom we cannot name due to space restraints, have all made important contributions to Puerto Rican literature in the United States and continue to be the best reason for further research and critical studies in forthcoming projects.

Our sincere thanks to these and every other diasporic Puerto Rican writer whose life and work *son la razón de ser de esta antología.*

Heartfelt thanks to my co-editor, colleague and friend—José Luis Torres-Padilla—for bringing the idea of this project to my attention and for persevering through its publication.

To my "home-camp" colleagues and friends at UPR, Río Piedras: Mirerza González, Nadjah Ríos, María Cristina Rodríguez, Lowell Fiet, María Soledad Rodríguez, Maritza Stanchich, Tony Bethell, Diane Accaria, Jorge Duany, and Johanna Díaz, among others: thanks for your encouragement and support.

CARMEN HAYDÉE

Carmen Haydée, thanks for joining me on the wonderful journey that represents the production of this anthology. Your enthusiasm, optimism, and commitment made it easier to persevere.

JOSÉ LUIS TORRES-PADILLA

Writing Off the Hyphen

INTRODUCTION

The Literature of the Puerto Rican Diaspora and Its Critical Practice

JOSÉ L. TORRES-PADILLA AND CARMEN HAYDÉE RIVERA

To fully appreciate the literature of Puerto Rican diaspora writers involves understanding the process of transnationalism,[1] questioning the ideas that underpin concepts such as "nation," "national," and "cultural identity," and scrutinizing the merging of histories and linguistic hybridity. It implies coming to terms with the works of writers who form part of a "commuter nation,"[2] of communities in constant transition and evolution, where the concepts of emigration and migration at once reflect and perplex the literary representation of Puerto Rican experience. Critical analysis of the literary works produced by Puerto Rican writers in the United States must, therefore, minimally include an examination of the migratory patterns that, to a large extent, shape significant characteristics of the writing and influence the authors' perspectives. These patterns shed light not only on years of political, social, and economic ties between the island and the United States but also on the ways in which, historically, these relationships have complicated notions of cultural identity and national affiliation, two prominent topics in the literary works of Puerto Ricans writing in the United States. A more profound critical inquiry of this literature would also necessarily have to focus on how the diasporic condition continues to influence these and other important literary themes associated with gender, class, race, and sexuality.

An appropriate starting point for the examination of Puerto Rican migration is Clara Rodríguez's insightful sociohistorical and demographic study[3] charting the stages of an increasing Puerto Rican exodus from the island to the United States after the U.S. takeover in 1898.[4] The analysis contained in this study in many ways parallels the development of a diasporic Puerto Rican literary history, which in turn gives way to a rich array of critical and theoretical scholarly discussions of the literature. Therefore, this introduction relies on the framework set forth by Rodríguez's study while introducing and interweaving important critical discussions by major scholars in the fields of diasporic Puerto Rican studies, cultural studies, and postmodern and postcolonial theory.

Rodríguez classifies the waves of Puerto Rican migration into three specific periods that illustrate the historical context and causes for leaving the island as well as the political and economic relationships between Puerto Rico and the United States that prompted this move.[5] During the first period (1900–1945), Puerto Ricans migrated mainly for socioeconomic and political reasons. Many workers were affected by a deteriorating economic infrastructure because of the collapse of the sugarcane industry on the island, by the aftermaths of the 1899 San Ciriaco Hurricane, and also by the lure of foreign job recruitment, especially to the sugarcane fields of Hawaii, where the first migrant Puerto Rican farmers went to work. Others (such as Ramón Emeterio Betances, Eugenio María de Hostos, Lola Rodríguez de Tió, Pachín Marín, Sotero Figueroa, Arturo Alfonso Schomburg) suffered political persecution that resulted in exile during the late nineteenth and early twentieth centuries. This group of early migrants, known as the *pioneros*, settled mainly in New York City. They began to form Puerto Rican communities bonded by a common historical and geographical past, by traditions, customs, and language, and by their social struggles and efforts to obtain the coveted benefits of the "American Dream."

The author who best captures the crude realities and contradictions of this historical era with detailed precision is Bernardo Vega in *Memoirs of Bernardo Vega*.[6] Migrating to the United States in 1916 at the age of thirty, Vega carefully delineates his encounter with an alien and often hostile society, which he refers to as the "Iron Tower of Babel." His writing reflects the first stage of the awakening of a cultural consciousness, discussed by Juan Flores ("the state of abandon"),[7] in which the newly arrived migrant is confronted with an environment totally different from the one he or she left on the island. This leaves a lasting imprint and develops in the newcomer a desire to return to Puerto Rico. Getting over this initial stage of cultural and linguistic disruption marks the beginning of an adaptation process that enables the migrant to exist within the hostility and limitations of the new environment.

Vega's *Memoirs* contain the most detailed and politically coherent account of Puerto Rican life in New York from 1916 to the aftermath of World War II. The work also reveals Vega's efforts to construct a historical and cultural legacy of the Puerto Rican migrant experience that would counteract the defamatory depiction of Puerto Ricans in the media.[8] Vega was an erudite intellectual *tabaquero* (cigar maker), adhering to the ranks of the Socialist Party and actively involved in the unionization of the working class. As a self-proclaimed Puerto Rican *jíbaro* (Puerto Rican peasant) from the highlands of Cayey, he valued his cultural heritage as he forged his way toward a metropolitan, proletariat, global perspective and lifestyle within a multicultural society. His work is an indictment of the era's racism, discrimination, and classism but also a celebration of the early Puerto Rican migrants' tenacity, courage, organization, and cultural pride.

Though Vega originally wrote his *Memoirs* in Spanish in the 1940s, it was not until the 1970s, after his death, that his friend and partner in social causes César Andreu Iglesias, edited the manuscript for publication. Since Andreu Iglesias died in 1976, the project was taken up by Puerto Rican writer and critic José Luis González, who finally saw the book through publication in 1977 under Ediciones Huracán. Juan Flores's 1984 translation exposed Vega's story to a wider, English-speaking audience and helped consolidate the work's reputation as a seminal contribution that fills many critical voids in conventional assessments of the Puerto Rican experience in the United States.

Jesús Colón is another important writer who charts the history of struggle, solidarity, and cultural unity of the early working-class Puerto Rican migrants. His work, *A Puerto Rican in New York and Other Sketches* (1961), much like Vega's writing, engages in a literary representation of the historical and cultural development of the Puerto Rican community in New York during the first three decades of the twentieth century.[9] His writing brings to the forefront discussions of the lack of opportunities and the difficulties brought about by exclusionary and discriminatory labor tactics in the United States. Colón's sketches cut to the core of the idealism of the American Dream, the driving force behind many migrants' initial inclination to leave their homelands.

Other, less-known but equally important writers who form part of this first wave of Puerto Rican migration were the radical feminist and anarchist Luisa Capetillo, the librarian and children's book author Pura Belpré, the renowned historian and archivist Arturo Alfonso Schomburg, and the advocate of Puerto Rican independence Graciany Miranda Archilla. Pedro Juan Labarthe's novel, *The Son of Two Nations: The Private Life of a Columbia Student* (1931), was among the first literary works written in English to focus on the experience of Puerto Ricans and their integration process.[10] These works provide valuable insights into migrant realities by exposing the nature of the authors' relations to their country of origin and their distinctiveness from the rest of the Anglo-American community.

From these early writers we know that the first wave of Puerto Ricans constituted an active community, the *colonia*, "where intellectual pursuits and sociopolitical activism often came hand in hand."[11] We also know that several Spanish-language newspapers flourished during that period.[12] In *Memoirs*, Vega cites various periodicals published during the 1880s when he mentions the intensification of cultural and artistic activity in New York (89). Founded or operated by political exiles, such as Sotero Figueroa and Pachín Marín, most of these newspapers devoted much of their editorial content to the revolutionary struggles for independence. However, like the Hispanic immigrant newspapers, these political periodicals also saw a wider obligation to serve the cultural and social needs of their readership. In this regard, "during the nineteenth and the first half of the twentieth century, they were the primary publishers of creative literature in the Spanish language, including poetry, literary prose, serialized novels and even plays."[13] They also included book reviews, so that the earliest record of literary criticism written by Puerto Ricans is in newspapers such as the *Puerto Rican Herald* (1901–1904), published by Luis Muñoz Rivera, and *Gráfico* (1926–1931) or in magazines like *Artes y Letras* (1933) and *La Revista Ilustrada de Nueva York* (1882) that would eventually appear to cater to the educated tastes of the Puerto Rican bourgeoisie and intelligentsia.[14] These illustrated magazines tended to espouse a pan-Hispanic worldview. *Artes y Letras* contained within its pages works by some of the most renowned writers and literary critics from the island, including Isabel

Cuchí Coll, Enrique Laguerre, and Luis Palés Matos. A thorough examination of these periodicals is required to fully comprehend the extent of coverage devoted to literary topics and the nature of the critical discourse. It is clear, however, that the earlier periodicals view the diasporic subject from a strictly island perspective, which started to change only sometime in the forties and fifties when newspapers such as *La Defensa* (1941) and *El Diario* (1948) began to chronicle the lives of those Puerto Ricans destined to remain in the United States.[15]

The second period in the process of Puerto Rican migration discussed in Clara Rodríguez's article corresponds to the years from 1946 to 1964. This stage marks the aftermath of World War II up to the civil rights era. It also encompasses the period known as "the Great Migration," when, in the 1950s, the largest number of Puerto Ricans left the island and settled in the United States. The new settlers not only enlarged the existing Puerto Rican communities formed by the first wave, or *pioneros*, but also began to disperse and establish themselves in other states of the country such as New Jersey, Connecticut, Massachusetts, and Illinois.[16] Increased migration to the United States solidified the presence of Puerto Ricans as a social group and helped promote the concept of a cultural citizenship marked by new denominations (Nuyorican, Diasporican, Latinos/as), the establishment of defined social spaces, and the rejection of racist and/or stereotypical images that ignored Puerto Rican communities' numerous contributions to society.

Writings of "sojourners"[17] emerged during this second period of migration. These authors initially wrote in Spanish, but their works have since been translated and constantly studied for their vivid portrayals of migrant realities. Such authors and works include René Marqués's play *La carreta*, whose production in New York City in 1953 marked the "birth of the modern Puerto Rican drama in New York";[18] José Luis González's *Paisa*; Pedro Juan Soto's *Spiks* and *Ardiente suelo, fría estación*; Guillermo Cotto-Thorner's *Trópico en Manhattan*; Emilio Díaz Valcárcel's *Harlem todos los días*; some of Julia de Burgos's poetry; and Jaime Carrero's collection of poetry, *Jet neorriqueño: Neo-Rican Jet Liner*,[19] which not only, as Juan Flores aptly claims, "foreshadowed the onset of Nuyorican literature in New York" but probably also looked forward to Luis Rafael Sánchez's "flying bus" metaphor.[20] This corpus of writing, for the most part, presents a bleak and desolate picture of Puerto Rican life in New York City and is marked by a strong sense of nostalgia and yearning for return to the island. Conditions of hostility and exclusion are set against a romanticized view of the island. Songwriters and singers of the period, such as Noel Estrada, Rafael Hernández, and Bobby Capó, also reiterate this longing for the "island paradise" in their music.

This period marks a significant turning point in the history of Puerto Rican diasporic consciousness that José Luis González would analyze eloquently in his landmark essay "El escritor en el exilio." First published in 1976, the essay describes González's own experience as an exiled Puerto Rican writer and goes on to acknowledge the diaspora as a significant factor in the formation of "the national Puerto Rican experience."[21] González is also the first to validate the literary production of those Puerto Ricans in the United States writing in English. In many ways visionary, this essay marks the beginning of the Diasporican era for Puerto Rican literary production, as González contemplates questions of hybridity, "national" literature, and identity within a sphere of growing globalization.

If there were Puerto Rican writers considered sojourners, then we may consider Efraín Barradas a "sojourner critic." In the introduction to *Herejes y mitificadores*, an anthology of Puerto Rican diasporic poetry, the Puerto Rican scholar and literary critic, who has taught Latin American and Puerto Rican literature in the United States for many years, argues, from an island perspective, for the incorporation of diaspora literature into the Puerto Rican literary canon as part of its "immigrant literature." As did José Luis González, Barradas cites the historical significance of the diaspora and the necessity of considering its impact when analyzing literature produced by Puerto Ricans living away from their "homeland." Barradas's essay is the first to ponder the complexity of situating this literature within a diasporic context. His critical analysis identifies a difficulty in labeling all diasporic production as "Nuyorican" and sees the lack of "categorias criticas apropriadas para el estudio de estas creaciones" (appropriate critical categories to study their creations).[22] He struggles to find a theme or motif that can unite the respective works, finally deciding that it is the literature's thematic variety that best exemplifies its unity. He also comments on the creation of myths that attempt to connect diasporic Puerto Rican writers to the island and to a sense of *puertorriqueñidad* (Puerto Ricanness). In some ways, Barradas's ideas here evoke Benedict Anderson's concept of "imagined community."[23]

The third period of Puerto Rican migration to the United States included in Clara Rodríguez's discussion begins in 1965 and continues to this day. The most important historical events to mark this period of Puerto Rican migration are those related to the struggles for civil rights and social justice during the late 1960s and 1970s. Puerto Ricans, united with other minority groups (Chicanos/as, African Americans, Native Americans, Asian Americans), fought against segregation and discrimination and, through social activism and organization, demanded respect for their civil rights, social equality, and wider recognition of their contributions to a multicultural American society.[24] These struggles resulted in increased visibility, attention to their social needs, the formation of interdisciplinary academic areas in major universities, and, eventually, the publication of literary works that formerly would have been ignored or bypassed.

The autodenominated Nuyorican poets' incursion onto the literary scene during this period was initially marked by explosive social protest poems (e.g., Pedro Pietri's "Puerto Rican Obituary") that were influenced by political unrest but gradually developed other concerns related to issues of identity and language. What began as casual yet energetic conversations and poetry readings at Miguel Algarín's house gave way to live performances—the precursors of today's poetry slams—at the Nuyorican Poets Café, founded in 1974 by Algarín and Miguel Piñero in Manhattan's Lower East Side (better known to denizens as "Loisaida"). The poetry, rooted in and emerging from the streets of New York's urban barrios, had an important oral-performance and consciousness-raising character. The poets stressed the importance of oral traditions and audience participation while at the same time emphasizing and showcasing the immediacy of their civil rights struggles. The works of Algarín, Piñero, Sandra María Esteves, and Pedro Pietri, among others, capture the essence of this social protest.[25]

In 1975, a year after the founding of the Nuyorican Poets Café, Algarín and Piñero edited *Nuyorican Poetry*, the first anthology of its kind.[26] In the introduction, Algarín establishes the first critical commentary concerning Puerto Rican diasporic sensibility and its literary expression. Algarín's principal focus is language and the Nuyorican poets' need to "invent a new language, a new tradition of communication," that fits their diasporic condition. The poets must harness this new idiom to the political necessities of their people: "The Nuyorican poet fights with words" (24). Despite its aimless political posing, the reductive rendering of the Nuyorican as a "street" subject, the sometimes-obscure allusions, and the masculinist views, this introduction, as critical text, contributes to the consideration of Spanglish (the Spanish-English hybrid) as the poetics of an evolving Puerto Rican diaspora, a topic widened and refined in Frances Aparicio's essay "*La vida es un Spanglish disparatero*: *Bilingualismo* in Nuyorican Poetry."[27] Algarín also emphasizes poets' sociopolitical responsibility to their people; the poet "tells the tale of the streets to the streets" (11). In a later essay, Algarín sharpens some of these ideas into a "nuyorican esthetic" that again accentuates orality, language, discourse, and their use for survival. Equally important for Algarín is the political activity of creating spaces for artistic expression.[28]

Similarly, other poets, such as Tato Laviera in works like *AmeRícan* (1985) and *La Carreta Made a U-Turn* (1979) and Willie Perdomo in *Where a Nickel Costs a Dime* (1996), celebrate and reaffirm the bilingual, bicultural self as a proud contributing member of American society.[29] The ever-evolving work of poet Victor Hernández Cruz focuses on recuperating Taíno, Spanish, and African heritage in ways that reveal continuity and connection to the contemporary multicultural experience of Puerto Ricans living in the United States. The poems "Areyto," "African Things," and "Geography of the Trinity Corona," along with others collected in *Maraca: New and Selected Poems*, explore the contextual implications of a Puerto Rican historical and cultural legacy.[30] His current ongoing commute between Puerto Rico and Morocco (residing for six months of the year in each place) gives way to a convergence of cultures—Moorish, Spanish, African, Indian, Puerto Rican, American—in his most recent work, *The Mountain in the Sea* (2006), which is full of his characteristic use of rhythm, color, and local voices.[31] The legacy of these influential poets lives on in the works of a new generation of diasporic Puerto Rican writers, such as María "Mariposa" Fernández, Caridad "La Bruja" de la Luz, Urayoan Noel, Emmanuel Xavier, and Jaime "Shaggy" Flores, among others.[32]

The dramatic and performative quality of Nuyorican poetry may have been influenced by the emerging theater scene. Miguel Piñero, a

Nuyorican poet, was also the most widely recognized and critically acclaimed of Nuyorican playwrights. His play *Short Eyes* (1974), winner of the New York Drama Critics Circle Award for Best Play of the Year (1973–1974), won him many accolades and placed him on the map of influential American dramatists. Other attempts to create visibly Puerto Rican characterizations and settings in playwriting include Miriam Colón's Puerto Rican Traveling Theater, a group founded in 1967 with the intention of taking theatrical pieces to inner-city areas where the possibilities of seeing live performances, and particularly Puerto Rican performers, were very scarce. In the 1980s Rosalba Rolón's Teatro Pregones focused on dramatic productions portraying Puerto Rican traditions, stories, and historical events and was geared toward youths in public schools and universities. The concern with political and social issues continues to the present and is emblematic of such productions as José Rivera's *Marisol* (1994) and Carmen Rivera's *Julia* (1992).[33]

Other diasporic Puerto Rican writers rely on the use of autobiography and memoir in dealing with racism, poverty, marginality, and intergenerational and intercultural clashes. Following the bildungsroman model, or the coming-of-age story, their works highlight relevant gender differences between male and female writers and the respective subaltern experiences and conditions that shape these differences. Piri Thomas's writing, for instance, illustrates the complexities of a Puerto Rican boy's experience before and during the civil rights era. Born in Spanish Harlem, Thomas focuses on his violent New York City upbringing in *Down These Mean Streets* (1967) and *Savior, Savior, Hold My Hand* (1972).[34] Contrary to Bernardo Vega's and Jesús Colón's stylistic use of language in their works, Thomas brings forth an explosion of idiomatic expressions and unconventional syntax. His writing is characterized by the use of slang, cursing, and code switching between English and Spanish that reflects the turbulent life of some inner-city youth. Where Vega's tone is formal and didactic, Thomas's tone is informal and conversational, luring the reader into the complications of a life plagued by drug abuse, armed robbery, and prison time.

Thomas's preoccupation with race and identity is intensified by the concept of perceptual dissonance: the incongruity between how he identifies himself (as Puerto Rican) and what others perceive him to be (a black man). Interaction with his African American friend Brewster Johnson and their travels through the segregated South as merchant marines bring to the forefront the underpinnings of racism and discrimination that gave way to tumultuous struggles for civil rights. In a similar vein, in his novels *Carlito's Way* (1975) and *Q & A* (1978), Edwin Torres portrays fictional re-creations of street life loosely based on his upbringing in the same neighborhoods that Piri Thomas describes.[35] The violence and crudeness depicted in Torres's descriptions of urban ghetto life rival those of Thomas's autobiographical scenes. In *Family Installments* (1983), Edward Rivera charts his migration from the island to New York and then, like Thomas and Torres, focuses on the difficulties of growing up in an environment that demands street-smart, instinctual methods of survival in the barrio.[36] Nicholosa Mohr represents the strongest woman's voice of this generation, rendering the barrio experience from the perspective of young and mature women in her fiction: *Nilda* (1973), *El Bronx Remembered* (1975), *In Nueva York* (1977), and *Rituals of Survival: A Woman's Portfolio* (1985).[37]

Abraham Rodríguez continues the Nuyorican urban narrative tradition with his collection of short stories, *The Boy without a Flag* (1999), and his two novels, *Spidertown* (1994) and *The Buddha Book* (2001).[38] Ernesto Quiñonez's *Bodega Dreams* (2000) represents another contemporary addition, most notable for its metafictional understanding and appreciation of its predecessors.[39] Ed Vega's fiction offers another vision of Latino urban life.[40] His work, which continues to develop and change, focuses more on the consequences of bicultural life in the city and less on crime and violence. Likewise, Honolulu-based author Rodney Morales further broadens and complicates the parameters of diasporic Puerto Rican writing, as his works—*The Speed of Darkness* (1988) and *When the Shark Bites* (2002)—explore twentieth-century Puerto Rican, Japanese, and Native Hawaiian cultural interaction linked to the history of Puerto Rican migration to Hawaii, which can be traced back to the late nineteenth and early twentieth centuries.[41]

The works of these writers also illustrate how elements of both Puerto Rican culture and Anglo-American culture thrive and merge in both Puerto Rico and the United States. The Latinization of American society is increasingly visible in the popularity of Puerto Rican customs, traditions, food, music, and celebrations, as well as those from other Caribbean and Latin American countries.[42] Likewise, Puerto Rico has undergone a social and cultural metamorphosis produced by over a hundred years of contact and interaction with the United States. Contemporary Puerto Rican life and society are very different from those Bernardo Vega left behind when he migrated. Transnational ties, once attenuated by time and space, are now enhanced and prosper through the use of telecommunications, air travel, and other technological advances.

Aurora Levins Morales, Judith Ortiz Cofer, and Esmeralda Santiago are among the writers who capture this bicultural, bilingual, evolving nature of the Puerto Rican experience during the latter part of the third period of settlement mentioned in Clara Rodríguez's article. Levins Morales's collaborative collection *Getting Home Alive* (1986), which she cowrote with her mother, Rosario Morales, presents the authenticity and acceptance of a hybrid self, one that celebrates cultural heritage while also welcoming new elements and possibilities of multicultural existence.[43] Ortiz Cofer's writing, *Silent Dancing: A Partial Remembrance of a Puerto Rican Childhood* (1990) and *The Line of the Sun* (1989), artistically evokes incidents in her life as a "cultural chameleon" learning to adapt and coexist in two different cultural contexts and linguistic codes.[44] Ortiz Cofer also questions antiquated expectations and patterns of behavior, particularly those related to gender, in essays such as "The Story of My Body" and "The Myth of the Latin Woman: I Just Met a Girl Named María," which appear in her prose and poetry collection *The Latin Deli: Telling the Lives of Barrio Women* (1995).[45] Santiago's autobiographical works, *When I Was Puerto Rican* (1994), *Almost a Woman* (1999), and *The Turkish Lover* (2004), delineate the stages of her life in and after Puerto Rico, her experience of migration to the United States, and her acculturation process into Anglo-American society.[46] Taking on a more mature narrative perspective and voice, Luisita López Torregrosa explores her troublesome relationship to the island in her memoir, *The Noise of Infinite Longing* (2004).[47] Writing with disarming honesty and lyrical prose, López Torregrosa delves into the stories of painful family ruptures produced by migration and family dispersal. At the same time, she reveals her rejection of and confrontation with a dominant patriarchal social and family structure. She also questions her nationality and cultural hybridity while coming to terms with her gendered experience.

With these writers' exploration of topics closely related to diaspora, it is not surprising that the criticism of this literature has recently initiated forays into how its literary production operates within its present socioeconomic matrix, what theorists have labeled late or global capitalism. Critics are now increasingly interested in how Puerto Rican writers represent the diasporic subject across gender, class, racial, and sexual lines. Critical foci continue to be hybridity, especially the linguistic type, questions related to identity, and the importance of location in constructing it. In short, the criticism of the literature of the Puerto Rican diaspora has entered, like the literature itself, into the discursive space of postcolonialism and postmodernism. Any literature will breed a body of critical work that usually parallels significant developments in its primary texts, and the literature of the Puerto Rican diaspora is no different.

We can see how far we have arrived critically with this body of literature when we look at the first book-length critical study of it, Eugene Mohr's *The Nuyorican Experience.*[48] Mohr's work is valuable in that he maps out the existing literary terrain, renders some fine analysis and interpretation, and also provides the study of this literature with some needed critical terminology. Mohr's primary critical approach to the literature is to situate it within the immigration literature of U.S. literature. This is understandable, even seemingly logical at first glance, given that most of the texts were written in English and contain themes similar to those in U.S. immigrant literature. This strategy, however, leads to a bifurcation of the writers, so that Mohr clearly delineates between those who provide "views from the island" and those, like Thomas, with "no umbilical cord to the island" (43). Mohr's impulse to group the writers of the Puerto Rican diaspora with those of other immigrants demonstrates a reliance on a theoretical framework that eventually cannot serve to explain the complexity of the circular migration that characterizes the Puerto Rican diaspora. Mohr's final pronouncement that Nuyorican literature will disappear, just like other ethnic literatures (except, he argues, the Jewish American novel) (127), sounds way off the mark when we consider the explosion and renaissance of multiethnic literature in the United States toward the end of the twentieth century. Mohr's miscalculation here can be attributed to what many could not see at the time: the emergence of a global economic and geopolitical condition that is currently referred to as "globalization," among other things, and that has engendered attendant theorizations grouped under "postmodernism" and "postcolonial" that attempt to explain the cultural consequences of global capitalism.

The early critical work of José Luis González, Miguel Algarín, Efraín Barradas, and Mohr acknowledges the significance of the migration process to literary production, but these authors seem determined to situate the literature within one national literary canon, be it Puerto Rican or U.S. Two essays which exemplify this critical tendency are Juan Flores's "Puerto Rican Literature in the U.S.: Stages and Perspectives" and Yanis Gordils's "Island and Continental Puerto Rican Literature: Cross-Cultural and Intertextual Considerations."[49] In *Boricua Literature*, her breakthrough literary history of the Puerto Rican diaspora, Lisa Sánchez González launches a critical analysis of these two essays as a way to enter the wider metacritical discussion of "scholarship on Boricua cultural intellectual history."[50] Sánchez González views the two essays as demonstrative of "the reluctance to deal with the diaspora as a distinct constituency in the United States" (17) and accurately notes that, although both critics claim the existence of a diasporic Puerto Rican literature, formed by unique political and economic conditions, they ultimately argue for "tethering Boricua literature to either 'Puerto Rico' or 'America' as an act of 'nationalist signification'" that, in her opinion, "does not serve the best interests of Boricua literary scholarship" (20). Both essays advance discussion of these issues initiated by José Luis González that, in the contemporary critical climate, have become central to the study of this literature. But Sánchez González's reading of their critical work represents a current perspective that is influenced by postmodernist theory and that appears to be reshaping ideas and approaches to Puerto Rican diasporic literary production. Her views argue for a consideration of "in-betweenness" as one among other postmodernist and postcolonial concepts that operate as crucial elements in the creation and critical interpretation of this literature. The constant flux of the writers' lived experience, which they attempt to represent through their words, must be taken into account, not as a process with an end result, but precisely as an ongoing, indeterminate one. Such a critical view allows for a reading of the literary text that suspends nationalist urgency and that, in turn, opens up areas sometimes not approached critically because they do not easily fall into the framework established by a particular "nationalizing agenda."

It is within such a postcolonial and postmodernist critical position that William Luis frames his study of Caribbean literature written in the United States, *Dance between Two Cultures*, which contains several chapters on Puerto Rican diaspora literature. Luis sees the newer critical theories as excellent hermeneutic tools for analyzing these literatures. "Latino," as an identity, is in itself "an identity postcolonial people have developed within the colonizing country—an identity that does not extend outside its geographic borders."[51] However, with Latinos and Latinas, postcoloniality takes on a unique dimension because they live within the colonizing country (286). This state of affairs makes the study of Latino/a culture and its literary production from a postcolonial and postmodern perspective more relevant. Another important point made by Luis is that postmodernist and postcolonial theories allow for an opening of topics and issues that form basic areas of study—such as race, gender/sexuality, ethnicity, and class—but are undertheorized or completely neglected within the existing critical corpus of Puerto Rican diaspora literature. A good example of this development is Miriam Jiménez Román's essay "*Allá y acá*: Locating Puerto Ricans in the Diaspora(s)," in which she notes how literature of the diaspora tends to assimilate the island's racist view that somehow Nuyoricans become "black" once they leave Puerto Rico and enter the "really" racist mainland U.S. society.[52] In response to Thomas's statement about being "caught up between two sticks," Jiménez Román retorts that these writers "are actually stuck between the myth of racial democracy [in Puerto Rico] with its implicit preference for mestizaje, and the reality of African descent and racism" (4). This type of analysis and discussion can only come from a profound understanding of the interplay between the concept of "race" and the historical consequences of diaspora on Puerto Ricans and their cultural production.

A cursory glance at the critical work devoted to the literature of the Puerto Rican diaspora during the last two decades shows definite postmodernist leanings. We can see this development most clearly in established critics like Edna Acosta-Belén and Juan Flores, who have consistently contributed to the critical conversation on the literature. In an essay published in 1992, Acosta-Belén expands on an earlier essay written seventeen years ago. The later essay is actually a deft appropriation and application of many postmodernist and postcolonial concepts—diaspora, the malleable nature of identity and culture, translocation, cultural syncretism, multiple levels of consciousness, global capitalism, "imaginary nation"—to explain the impetus for the literary production of the Nuyorican school and to delineate those "diverse elements that characterize" it.[53] In "Life off the Hyphen," a chapter from his book *From Bomba to Hip-Hop*, Flores focuses on the classist and racist perceptions and constructions of "Latino" literature as it grows and becomes "mainstream." Flores sees differences in how each of the various literatures that constitute "Latino literature" represents its individual take on U.S. society. In the case of Puerto Rican writers in the United States, Flores argues that their absence of cultural capital has much to do with their "in-betweenness." Puerto Ricans stubbornly refuse to accept the hyphenation that characterizes other ethnic identities: "Rather than embracing the hyphen . . . Puerto Ricans typically challenge that marker of collusion or compatibility and erase it as inappropriate to their social position and identity."[54] From Flores's comments, we can ascertain that Puerto Ricans in the United States live "off the hyphen."

Evidently, postmodernist and postcolonial ideas have filtered into the criticism that claims Puerto Rican diasporic literature as its domain. Flores's metaphor for the Puerto Rican diasporic condition in the United States is also apt for how critics can approach the literary production of those writers of Puerto Rican ancestry who share that experience and attempt to express and represent it within what Homi Bhabha calls the "third space."[55] The title of the present volume, *Writing Off the Hyphen*, tweaks Flores's phrase to comment on the critical intention of the included essays. The critics in this collection have approached the literature of the Puerto Rican diaspora from current theoretical positions, with provocative and insightful results. Acutely aware of the unique diasporic lived experience of Puerto Ricans, they have sought to analyze how this experience is played out in the context of the ever-present and pressing issues of class, race, gender, and sexuality and how other themes emerging from postcolonialism and postmodernism come into play. Their critical work also demonstrates an understanding of how the process of migration and the relations between Puerto Rico and the United States complicate the rendition of hegemonic notions of cultural and national identity as the writers confront their bilingual, bicultural, and transnational realities. These essays also underscore the notion that reading the works of Puerto Rican diaspora writers entails a movement away from insular conceptions of nationality toward a more integrated awareness of a hybrid self constantly shifting between historical time and geographic spaces, a movement that perpetuates the "flying bus" metaphor so accurately coined by Luis Rafael Sánchez[56] and restated in Jorge Duany's book title *The Puerto Rican Nation on the Move*.

The critics in this volume, like other contemporary critics, analyze these issues across the widening body of work available to them, including the works of forgotten, neglected, or minimally studied early writers. Indeed, one of their goals is to discover, reclaim, and revisit those writers who came to the United States in the early waves of migration. In part I, "Earlier Voices," three critics explore the work of these earlier writers with an eye to how it connects to present critical and literary production. José Irizarry Rodríguez's essay outlines the prominent ideas formulated by four *pioneros*—Vega, Colón, Labarthe, and Schomburg—and argues that the traditionalist and modernist tendencies found in these authors' works establish theoretical and strategic positions dealing with identity for future writers. We can consider the "modernizing" perspective as the precursor of the present diasporic position. Important to the formation of these evolving identities were the still-conflicted issues of race, national identity, class, and the colonial relationship between the United States and Puerto Rico.

Lisa Sánchez González elaborates on the Boricua experience of modernity at the turn of the twentieth century and focuses on Luisa Capetillo—the radical feminist and anarchist ignored and reviled in and after her time—as one of the earliest and most pivotal Boricua literary figures. By situating Capetillo's work among the writings of the "transnationalist agitators" who labored in print and public to incite a social revolution, Sánchez González points to a politically contiguous recovery and analysis of Boricua cultural intellectual history. José Torres-Padilla's essay takes a semiotic approach to texts written by three early diasporic Puerto Rican writers: Jesús Colón, Pura Belpré, and Graciany Miranda Archilla. Torres-Padilla shows how the production of ethnic signs in these texts demonstrates that each writer has a different view of, and rhetorical purpose for, Puerto Rican ethnicity. That the ethnic project differs in the case of each writer, and seems to downplay "nationalism," affirms the idea that ethnic and national identities, as social and textual constructs, are perceived and valued differently.

In part II, "Political and Historical," three critics contemplate the interplay between these areas from diverse, yet profoundly postmodernist, critical approaches. Ferdâ Asya employs a threefold theoretical approach in her essay to discern the individualist, communist, and ecological ideology of anarchism as an important element in Aurora Levins Morales's writing. William Burgos traces the etymological transformation of "Nuyorican" to "Diasporican" and the respective historical significance of each as identity marker. Burgos uncovers the deeper meanings of these terms as they unfold in the selective literary texts he analyzes. In his analysis, we can observe how the texts contain the development of postmodernist and postcolonial concepts such as hybridity, *mestizaje*, and transculturation within strategies to resist the older modernist paradigm's notions of binarism and essentialization, among others. Trenton Hickman discusses the activist origins and influences of Nuyorican poetry's political base. He starts from a consideration of the diasporic conditions that form alterity and, in the case of Puerto Ricans, that have nurtured the political resistance against hegemonic culture that informs the poetry.

Postcolonial theory has a fascination with ideas related to location and dislocation, especially as it contemplates the various consequences of diaspora and the shaping of identity. The essays in part III, "Identity and Place," explore these themes. Antonia Domínguez Miguela looks at how two Puerto Rican writers "tropicalize" the urban landscape within the narrative literary space as a function of their own understanding of Puerto Rican translocation and transculturation. In his essay, Víctor Figueroa argues that, despite the celebration of diverse ethnicities in our seemingly multicultural age, a careful reading of Pedro Pietri's collection *Puerto Rican Obituary* suggests that ethnic pride was not always a priority in the agenda of a significant number of immigrants, particularly Puerto Ricans. Maritza Stanchich discusses how the fiction of Rodney Morales historicizes and complicates the diasporic literary canon by avoiding reductive, essentialist categories, and she reveals broad and sometimes-contradictory agendas among diasporic writers. John Waldron's essay offers a different take on the postcolonial concept of mimicry. Waldron's analysis of Tato Laviera's parodic handling of René Marqués's *La carreta* reveals the unique subject positions of Nuyorican writers responding to the island's established colonial elite and their literary representations. Waldron argues that Laviera's intertextual work is an act of agency that undermines Marqués's colonial canonical text and its establishment of "docility" as trope. As in most acts of mimicry, Laviera's rhetorical maneuver plays a subversive role in its opening of space within Puerto Rican diasporic literature to voices and traditions formerly excluded.

Within diaspora and postcolonial studies, the term "home" has received much critical attention. Diaspora leads to displacement and dislocation that, in turn, make the construction of signs such as "home" problematic. The essays in part IV, "Home," focus precisely on the complexity behind that construction for the diasporic Puerto Rican subject and its literary representation. Kelli Lyon Johnson argues that with her first English-language novel, *The House on the Lagoon*, Rosario Ferré develops a historical consciousness by claiming Puerto Rico and its collective memory for Puerto Ricans and their families both on and off the island while she creates a new center of Puerto Rican identity independent of history and geography—the narrative space of the novel. According to Johnson, Ferré's publications transmit collective memory to fill the void left by displacement and migration. By employing an anthropological lens focusing on "translating cultures," Joanna Barszewska Marshall explores cultural practices associated with "home" as constituted through contact with the "outside" and also through travel and dwelling elsewhere in two works by Judith Ortiz Cofer (*The Line of the Sun* and *Silent Dancing*). Marshall examines how translation may be reclaimed as a strategy for resistance since it can serve to disrupt notions of what is natural in both the "source" culture and the culture into which these practices are translated. Solimar Otero discusses the shared tropes of journey, home, and resettlement found in Yoruba and Puerto Rican diasporic literary traditions. Her essay provides a much-needed critical reading of the "African roots" often mentioned in relation to Nuyorican literature and Diasporican literature in general but rarely analyzed in depth. By revisiting this literature from an acutely off-center position—off the hyphen—we are invited to see not only the concept of "home" in a very different light but the literature itself.

The three essays in part V, "Gender," explore the interstices of sexuality, gender, and ethnicity in the Diasporican subject. Analyzing three gay Diasporican writers, Enrique Morales-Díaz points to the resisting strategies that they utilize as they attempt to confront the ethnic and sexual pressures and demands placed on them by the diasporic condition. Morales-Díaz's discussion opens up issues related to totalizing "national identities" that tend to disregard and even oppress other identity formations. In her essay, Betsy Sandlin posits that Manuel Ramos Otero participates in a "queering" of his literary precursor, Julia de Burgos, a woman who has been transformed into a mythical figure and cultural icon, as an oppositional strategy that manipulates the past in order to infiltrate and critique dominant homophobic notions of Puerto Ricanness and Puerto Rican literary history. Mary Jane Suero-Elliott examines how two Puerto Rican women writers—Alba Ambert and Esmeralda Santiago—deploy female agency and cultural resistance against dominant Anglo discourses within a mainland context influenced by Puerto Rico's commonwealth status to highlight how the history of U.S. involvement with Puerto Rico makes the act of establishing a successful home on the continent an act of resistance. Instead of critiquing U.S. hegemony through a self-defining return to the nation of origin, Suero-Elliott contends that in their writing these authors "return" to a culture of origin by importing it to the host culture, thereby challenging hierarchies within the "global village" and restructuring transnational imaginaries.

As these essays demonstrate, current theoretical ideas and approaches create exciting opportunities and possibilities for the study of Puerto Rican diasporic literature. However, we understand that pursuing these ideas is not without problems. Critics must apply postcolonial and postmodernist concepts and ideas cautiously and critically. For example, anyone familiar with Puerto Rico's political status would agree with the irony, and the inherent problems, of applying "postcolonial" theory to literature produced by people essentially still colonized. We also have to be wary—as we become more involved with theorizations derived from these new critical perspectives—not to become part of a "postcolonial intelligentsia" that Arif Dirlik claims loses sense of its own class position in global capitalism and, in the process, integrates itself into the very system that creates the ideology and conditions that their people still struggle to resist.[57] With these caveats in mind, we still believe that postmodernist and postcolonial theory, especially when the latter is "engaged together" with U.S. border studies, as suggested by Amritjit Singh and Peter Schmidt, can enrich and deepen the critical discourse dedicated to the study of Puerto Rican diasporic literature.[58] We hope that this collection will provide one more step toward that goal.

NOTES

1. Jorge Duany defines "transnationalism" "as the establishment of frequent and intense social, economic, political, and cultural links between two or more countries." He goes on to add that one must consider Puerto Rico's lack of sovereignty when using this definition, and "therefore the analytic distinction between state and nation must be made carefully." See his *Puerto Rican Nation on the Move: Identities on the Island and in the United States* (Chapel Hill: University of North Carolina Press, 2002), 216.

2. For in-depth analysis of how Puerto Rico's social, economic, and political relationship with the United States uniquely positions the island as a "commuter nation," see Edna Acosta-Belén et al., *"Adiós, Borinquen Querida": The Puerto Rican Diaspora, Its History, and Contributions* (Albany, NY: CELAC, 2000).

3. Clara Rodríguez, "A Summary of Puerto Rican Migration to the United States," in *Challenging Fronteras: Structuring Latina and Latino Lives in the U.S.*, ed. Mary Romero, Pierrette Hondagneu-Sotelo, and Vilma Ortiz (New York: Routledge, 1997), 101–113.

4. Another examination of the historical process of Puerto Rican migration to the United States can be found in Virginia Sánchez Korrol's *From Colonia to Community: The History of Puerto Ricans in New York City* (Berkeley and Los Angeles: University of California Press, 1994). For a pictorial presentation of the first wave, see Félix V. Matos-Rodríguez and Pedro Juan Hernández, eds., *Pioneros: Puerto Ricans in New York City, 1896–1948* (Charleston, SC: Arcadia/Tempus Publishing, 2001). See also Edna Acosta-Belén, "The Building of a Community: Puerto Rican Writers and Activists in New York City (1890s–1960s)," in *Recovering the U.S. Hispanic Literary Heritage*, ed. Ramón Gutiérrez and Genaro Padilla (Houston: Arte Público Press, 1993), 1:179–195. For a full study of the Puerto Rican diaspora that focuses on the most important communities that emerged in the United States, see Carmen Teresa Whalen and Victor Vázquez-Hernández, eds., *The Puerto Rican Diaspora: Historical Perspectives* (Philadelphia: Temple University Press, 2005).

5. Although Rodríguez provides us with a very convenient structure for analyzing the various waves of Puerto Rican migration to the United States, we are indebted to Juan Flores for providing an earlier framework of the development of Puerto Rican literature of the diaspora in his seminal essay "Puerto Rican Literature in the United States: Stages and Perspectives," *ADE Bulletin* 91 (Winter 1988): 39–44, which we will discuss further on.

6. *Memoirs of Bernardo Vega: A Contribution to the History of the Puerto Rican Community in New York*, ed. César Andreu Iglesias, trans. Juan Flores (New York: Monthly Review Press, 1984). Hereafter cited in text.

7. Juan Flores, "'*Qué assimilated, brother, yo soy asimilao*': The Structuring of Puerto Rican Identity in the US," in his *Divided Borders: Essays on Puerto Rican Identity* (Houston: Arte Público Press, 1993).

8. In *"Adiós, Borinquen Querida,"* Acosta-Belén et al. provide extensive discussion and examples of what came to be known as "models of cultural deficiency" that portrayed

Puerto Ricans as uncultured, uneducated, economically disadvantaged, and nonassimilationists with deficient traditions, customs, and family structure. The main purpose of Acosta-Belén et al.'s study (and those of many other scholars, writers, sociologists, and historians) is precisely to debunk the myths of an unorganized and culturally weak Puerto Rican migrant community.

9. Jesús Colón, *A Puerto Rican in New York and Other Sketches,* 2d ed. (New York: International Publishers, 1982) (originally published 1961).

10. Pedro Juan Labarthe, *The Son of Two Nations: The Private Life of a Columbia Student* (New York: Carranza, 1931).

11. Acosta-Belén, "Building of a Community," 183.

12. See Nicolas Kanellos, with Helvetia Martell, *Hispanic Periodicals in the United States, Origins to 1960: A Brief History and Comprehensive Bibliography* (Houston: Arte Público Press, 2000).

13. Ibid., 7.

14. On the *Puerto Rican Herald,* see ibid., 19; on *Gráfico,* 53–57; on *Artes y Letras,* 70 (see also 132n100); on *Revista Ilustrada de Nueva York,* 66–69.

15. On *La Defensa*, see ibid., 107–108; on *El Diario*, 58–60.

16. Data included in Acosta-Belén et al., *"Adiós, Borinquen Querida,"* indicate that by the 1980s, Puerto Ricans resided in every state of the United States, including Alaska and Hawaii. Population demographics currently vary from approximately 1.5 million in New York City to approximately 325 in Wyoming. "The Hispanic Population Census 2000 Brief" corroborates these projections and updates the statistical information contained in "*Adiós, Borinquen Querida.*" Other demographic studies, such as the one conducted by the Puerto Rican Federal Affairs Administration, *Atlas of Stateside Puerto Ricans*, in 2004, indicate that, for the first time in history, the number of Puerto Ricans living in the United States surpasses the number living on the island.

17. In *The Nuyorican Experience: Literature of the Puerto Rican Minority* (Westport, CT: Greenwood Press, 1982), Eugene Mohr uses this term to refer to those writers who spent short periods of time in the United States but did not permanently establish themselves there. Many of them returned to the island and became celebrated national authors.

18. John Antush, ed., *Nuestro New York: An Anthology of Puerto Rican Plays* (New York: Signet, 1994), xi.

19. José Luis González's *Paisa* (Mexico: Fondo de Cultura, 1950) was later included in the collection *Viente cuentos y paisa* (Río Piedras, PR: Editorial Cultural, 1973); Pedro Juan Soto, *Spiks* (Mexico: Presentes, 1956); Pedro Juan Soto, *Ardiente suelo, fría estación* (Mexico: Editorial Veracruzana, 1961); Guillermo Cotto-Thorner, *Trópico en Manhattan* (San Juan: Editorial Cordillera, 1960); Emilio Díaz Valcárcel, *Harlem todos los días* (San Juan: Ediciones Huracán, 1978); Jaime Carrero, *Jet neorriqueño: Neo-Rican Jet Liner* (San German: Interamericana, 1964).

20. Flores, *Divided Borders*, 150; Luis Rafael Sánchez, *La guagua aérea* (Río Piedras, PR: Editorial Cultural, 1994).

21. José Luis González, "El escritor en el exilio," in his *El pais de cuatro pisos y otros ensayos* (Río Piedras, PR: Ediciones Huracán, 1980), 101.

22. Efraín Barradas and Rafael Rodríguez, eds., *Herejes y mitificadores: Muestra de poesia puertorriqueña en los Estados Unidos* (Río Piedras, PR: Ediciones Huracán, 1980), 17.

23. Benedict Anderson, *Imagined Communities: Reflections on the Origin and Spread of Nationalism* (London: Verso, 1983).

24. For a comprehensive, detailed account of these events, see Andrés Torres and José Velázquez, eds., *The Puerto Rican Movement: Voices of the Diaspora* (Philadelphia: Temple University Press, 1998).

25. Important early works include Miguel Algarín and Miguel Piñero, eds., *Nuyorican Poetry: An Anthology of Puerto Rican Words and Feelings* (New York: William Morrow, 1975); Sandra María Esteves, *Yerba Buena: Dibujos y poemas*, Greenfield Review Chapbook 47 (Greenfield Center, NY: Greenfield Review Press, 1980); Pedro Pietri, *Puerto Rican Obituary* (New York: Monthly Review Press, 1973); Miguel Piñero, *La Bodega Sold Dreams* (Houston: Arte Público Press, 1980); José Angel Figueroa, *East 110th Street* (New York: Broadside, 1973); and José Angel Figueroa, *Noo Jork*, trans. Victor Fernández Fragoso (San Juan: Instituto de Cultura Puertorriqueña, 1981). A more recent sampling of "Nuyorican" poetry is Miguel Algarín and Bob Holman, *Aloud: Voices from the Nuyorican Poets Café* (New York: Owl Books/Henry Holt, 1994).

26. Hereafter cited in text.

27. Frances Aparicio, "*La vida es un Spanglish disparatero*: *Bilingualismo* in Nuyorican Poetry," in *European Perspectives on Hispanic Literature of the United States*, ed. Genevieve Fabre (Houston: Arte Público Press, 1988), 147–160.

28. Miguel Algarín, "Nuyorican Literature," *MELUS* 8, no. 2 (Summer 1981): 92.

29. Tato Laviera, *AmeRícan* (Houston: Arte Público Press, 1985); Tato Laviera, *La Carreta Made a U-Turn* (Gary, IN: Arte Público Press, 1979); Willie Perdomo, *Where a Nickel Costs a Dime* (New York: W. W. Norton, 1996).

30. Victor Hernández Cruz, *Maraca: New and Selected Poems* (Minneapolis: Coffee House Press, 2001).

31. Victor Hernández Cruz, *The Mountain in the Sea* (Minneapolis: Coffee House Press, 2006).

32. The writings of these "neo-Nuyorican poets" have received wide attention and critical acclaim not only through publication but also through school and university tours and workshops, poetry readings in and out of the United States, Web sites, HBO programming like *Russell Simmons Presents Def Poetry*, *Def Poetry Jam* on Broadway, and CDs such as *Yemayá y Ochún*.

33. José Rivera, *Marisol and Other Plays* (New York: Theatre Communications Group, 1997); Carmen Rivera, *Julia*, in Antush, *Nuestro New York*, 133–178. For further information on Puerto Rican drama, see John Antush, *Recent Puerto Rican Theater: Five Plays* (Houston: Arte Público Press, 1991); and Antush, *Nuestro New York*.

34. Piri Thomas, *Down These Mean Streets* (New York: Knopf, 1967); Piri Thomas, *Savior, Savior, Hold My Hand* (New York: Doubleday, 1972).

35. Edwin Torres, *Carlito's Way* (New York: Dutton, 1975); Edwin Torres, *Q & A* (New York: Avon, 1978).

36. Edward Rivera, *Family Installments* (New York: Penguin, 1983).

37. Nicholosa Mohr, *Nilda* (New York: Harper, 1973); Nicholosa Mohr, *El Bronx Remembered* (New York: Harper, 1975); Nicholosa Mohr, *In Nueva York* (New York: Dial, 1977); Nicholosa Mohr, *Rituals of Survival: A Woman's Portfolio* (Houston: Arte Público Press, 1985).

38. Abraham Rodríguez, *The Boy without a Flag* (Minneapolis: Milkwood, 1999); Abraham Rodríguez, *Spidertown* (New York: Penguin, 1994); Abraham Rodríguez, *The Buddha Book* (New York: Picador, 2001).

39. Ernesto Quiñonez, *Bodega Dream* (New York: Vintage, 2000). Quiñonez's *Chango's Fire* (New York: Rayo, 2005), his second novel, is not as well crafted or accomplished.

40. Vega's work to date includes two collections of stories, *Casualty Report* (Houston: Arte Público Press, 1991) and *Mendoza's Dreams* (Houston: Arte Público Press, 1987); and the novels *The Comeback* (Houston: Arte Público Press, 1985), *Blood Fugues* (New York: Rayo/HarperCollins, 2005), among others.

41. Rodney Morales, *The Speed of Darkness* (Honolulu: Bamboo Ridge Press, 1988); Rodney Morales, *When the Shark Bites* (Honolulu: University of Hawai'i Press, 2002).

42. The effects are most dramatic in the urban areas increasingly inhabited by Latinos. Various books have analyzed and discussed this phenomenon; most notable are Agustín Laó-Montes and Arlene M. Dávila, eds., *Mambo Montage: The Latinization of New York* (New York: Columbia University Press, 2001); Mike Davis, *Magical Urbanism: Latinos Reinvent the U.S. City* (London: Verso, 2000); Victor M. Valle and Rodolfo Torres, *Latino Metropolis* (Minneapolis: University of Minnesota Press, 2000); Raul Villa Romero, *Barrio Logos* (Austin: University of Texas Press, 2000). For an excellent collection of essays on Latinos and popular culture, see Michelle Habell-Pallan and Mary Romero, eds., *Latino/a Popular Culture* (New York: New York University Press, 2002), and, more specifically, on Puerto Rican pop culture, Frances Negrón-Muntaner, *Boricua Pop: Puerto Ricans and the Latinization of American Culture* (New York: New York University Press, 2004).

43. Aurora Levins Morales and Rosario Morales, *Getting Home Alive* (Ithaca, NY: Firebrand Books, 1986).

44. Judith Ortiz Cofer, *Silent Dancing: A Partial Remembrance of a Puerto Rican Childhood* (Houston: Arte Público Press, 1990); Judith Ortiz Cofer, *The Line of the Sun* (Athens, GA: University of Georgia Press, 1989).

45. Judith Ortiz Cofer, *The Latin Deli: Telling the Lives of Barrio Women* (New York: W. W. Norton, 1995).

46. Esmeralda Santiago, *When I Was Puerto Rican* (New York: Vintage, 1994); Esmeralda Santiago, *Almost a Woman* (New York: Vintage, 1999); Esmeralda Santiago, *The Turkish Lover* (New York: Perseus Books, 2004).

47. Luisita López Torregrosa, *The Noise of Infinite Longing: A Memoir of a Family and an Island* (New York: HarperCollins, 2004).

48. Hereafter cited in text. See n. 17.

49. These two essays appeared in *ADE Bulletin* 91 (Winter 1988). Flores's essay was later published in A. LaVonne Brown Ruoff and Jerry W. Ward, eds., *Redefining Ameri-*

can Literary History (New York: MLA, 1990); in Gutierrez and Padilla, eds., *Recovering the U.S. Hispanic Literary Heritage*, vol. 1; and in Flores, *Divided Borders* (1993).

50. Lisa Sánchez Gonzalez, *Boricua Literature: A Literary History of the Puerto Rican Diaspora* (New York: New York University Press, 2001), 17. Hereafter cited in text. "Boricua" refers "to the Puerto Rican diasporan community at large" (1).

51. William Luis, *Dance between Two Cultures* (Nashville, TN: Vanderbilt University Press, 1997), 280. Hereafter cited in text.

52. Miriam Jiménez Román, "*Allá y acá*: Locating Puerto Ricans in the Diaspora(s)," *Dialogo* 5 (Winter/Spring 2001), Center for Latino Research, DePaul University, Chicago, IL, 19 Feb. 2004, *http://condor.depaul.edu/~dialogo*. Hereafter cited in text.

53. Edna Acosta-Belén, "Beyond Island Boundaries: Ethnicity, Gender, and Cultural Revitalization in Nuyorican Literature," *Callaloo* 15, no. 4 (Autumn 1992): 996.

54. Juan Flores, *From Bomba to Hip-Hop: Puerto Rican Culture and Latino Identity* (New York: Columbia University Press, 2000), 180.

55. Homi Bhabha, "The Commitment to Theory," in his *The Location of Culture* (London: Routledge, 1994).

56. Sánchez, *La guagua aérea*.

57. Arif Dirlik, "The Postcolonial Aura: Third World Criticism in the Age of Global Capitalism," in *Dangerous Liaisons: Gender, Nation, and Postcolonial Perspectives*, ed. Anne McClintock, Aamir Mufti, and Ella Shohat (Minneapolis: University of Minnesota Press, 1997), 501–528.

58. Amritjit Singh and Peter Schmidt, "On the Borders between U.S. Studies and Postcolonial Theory," in *Postcolonial Theory and the United States: Race, Ethnicity, and Literature*, ed. Amritjit Singh and Peter Schmidt (Jackson: University Press of Mississippi, 2000), 3–69.

BIBLIOGRAPHY

Acosta-Belén, Edna. "Beyond Island Boundaries: Ethnicity, Gender, and Cultural Revitalization in Nuyorican Literature." *Callaloo* 15, no. 4 (Autumn 1992): 979–998.

———. "The Building of a Community: Puerto Rican Writers and Activists in New York City (1890s–1960s)." In *Recovering the U.S. Hispanic Literary Heritage*, ed. Ramón Gutierrez and Genaro Padilla, 1:179–195. Houston: Arte Público Press, 1993.

Acosta-Belén, Edna, et al., *"Adiós, Borinquen Querida": The Puerto Rican Diaspora, Its History, and Contributions*. Albany, NY: CELAC, 2000.

Algarín, Miguel. "Nuyorican Literature." *MELUS* 8, no. 2 (Summer 1981): 89–92.

Algarín, Miguel, and Bob Holman. *Aloud: Voices from the Nuyorican Poets Café*. New York: Owl Books/Henry Holt, 1994.

Algarín, Miguel, and Miguel Piñero, eds. *Nuyorican Poetry: An Anthology of Puerto Rican Words and Feelings*. New York: William Morrow, 1975.

Anderson, Benedict. *Imagined Communities: Reflections on the Origin and Spread of Nationalism*. London: Verso, 1983.

Antush, John, ed. *Nuestro New York: An Anthology of Puerto Rican Plays*. New York: Signet, 1994.

———. *Recent Puerto Rican Theater: Five Plays*. Houston: Arte Público Press, 1991.

Aparicio, Frances. "*La vida es un Spanglish disparatero: Bilingualismo* in Nuyorican Poetry." In *European Perspectives on Hispanic Literature of the United States*, ed. Genevieve Fabre, 147–160. Houston: Arte Público Press, 1988.

Barradas, Efraín, and Rafael Rodríguez, eds. *Herejes y mitificadores: Muestra de poesia puertorriqueña en los Estados Unidos*. Río Piedras, PR: Ediciones Huracán, 1980.

Bhabha, Homi. "The Commitment to Theory." In *The Location of Culture,* by Homi Bhabha, 18–28. London: Routledge, 1994.

Carrero, Jaime. *Jet neorriqueño: Neo-Rican Jet Liner*. San German: Interamericana, 1964.

Colón, Jesús. *A Puerto Rican in New York and Other Sketches*. 2d ed. New York: International Publishers, 1982. (Originally published 1961.)

Cotto-Thorner, Guillermo. *Trópico en Manhattan*. San Juan: Editorial Cordillera, 1960.

Dávila, Arlene M., and Agustín Lao, eds. *Mambo Montage: The Latinization of New York*. New York: Columbia University Press, 2001.

Davis, Mike. *Magical Urbanism: Latinos Reinvent the U.S. City*. London: Verso, 2000.

Díaz Valcárcel, Emilio. *Harlem todo los días*. San Juan: Ediciones Huracán, 1978.

Dirlik, Arif. "The Postcolonial Aura: Third World Criticism in the Age of Global Capitalism." In *Dangerous Liaisons: Gender, Nation, and Postcolonial Perspectives*, ed. Anne McClintock, Aamir Mufti, and Ella Shohat, 501–528. Minneapolis: University of Minnesota Press, 1997.

Duany, Jorge. *The Puerto Rican Nation on the Move: Identities on the Island and in the United States*. Chapel Hill: University of North Carolina Press, 2002.

Esteves, Sandra María. *Yerba Buena: Dibujos y poemas*. Greenfield Review Chapbook 47. Greenfield Center, NY: Greenfield Review Press, 1980.

Fabre, Genevieve, ed. *European Perspectives on Hispanic Literature of the United States*. Houston: Arte Público Press, 1988.

Falcón, Angelo. *Atlas of Stateside Puerto Ricans*. Washington, DC: Puerto Rican Federal Affairs Administration, 2004.

Figueroa, José Angel. *East 110th Street*. New York: Broadside, 1973.

———. *Noo Jork*. Trans. Victor Fernández Fragoso. San Juan: Instituto Cultura Puertorriqueña, 1981.

Flores, Juan. *Divided Borders: Essays on Puerto Rican Identity*. Houston: Arte Público Press, 1993.

———. *From Bomba to Hip-Hop: Puerto Rican Culture and Latino Identity*. New York: Columbia University Press, 2000.

———. "Puerto Rican Literature in the United States: Stages and Perspectives." *ADE Bulletin* 91 (Winter 1988): 39–44.

The 4th Annual Voices for the Voiceless Poetry Contest, *Yemayá y Ochún*, Dark Souls Records and Press. Springfield, MA: Dark Souls Enterprises, 2003.

González, José Luis. *En Nueva York y otras desgracias*. Mexico: Siglo XXI, 1973. Repr., Río Piedras, PR: Ediciones Huracán, 1981.

———. *El pais de cuatro pisos y otros ensayos*. Río Piedras, PR: Ediciones Huracán, 1980.

———. *Veinte cuentos y paisa*. Río Piedras, PR: Editorial Cultural, 1973.

Gordils, Yanis. "Island and Continental Puerto Rican Literature: Cross-Cultural and Intertextual Considerations." *ADE Bulletin* 91 (Winter 1988): 52–55.

Guzmán, Betsy. "The Hispanic Population Census 2000 Brief." U.S. Department of Commerce, Economics and Statistics Administration. Washington, DC: U.S. Census Bureau, 2001.

Habell-Pallan, Michelle, and Mary Romero, eds. *Latino/a Popular Culture*. New York: New York University Press, 2002.

Hernández Cruz, Victor. *Maraca: New and Selected Poems*. Minneapolis: Coffee House Press, 2001.

———. *The Mountain in the Sea*. Minneapolis: Coffee House Press, 2006.

Jiménez Román, Miriam. "*Allá y acá*: Locating Puerto Ricans in the Diaspora(s)." *Dialogo* 5 (Winter/Spring 2001). Center for Latino Research, DePaul University, Chicago, IL. 19 Feb. 2004. *http://condor.depaul.edu/~dialogo*.

Kanellos, Nicolas, with Helvetia Martell. *Hispanic Periodicals in the United States, Origins to 1960: A Brief History and Comprehensive Bibliography*. Houston: Arte Público Press, 2000.

Labarthe, Pedro Juan. *The Son of Two Nations: The Private Life of a Columbia Student*. New York: Carranza, 1931.

Laó-Montes, Agustín, and Arlene M. Dávila, eds. *Mambo Montage: The Latinization of New York*. New York: Columbia University Press, 2001.

Laviera, Tato. *AmeRícan*. Houston: Arte Público Press, 1985.

———. *La Carreta Made a U-Turn*. Gary, IN: Arte Público Press, 1979.

Levins Morales, Aurora, and Rosario Morales. *Getting Home Alive*. Ithaca, NY: Firebrand Books, 1986.

López Torregrosa, Luisita. *The Noise of Infinite Longing: A Memoir of a Family and an Island*. New York: HarperCollins, 2004.

Luis, William. *Dance between Two Cultures: Latino Caribbean Literature Written in the United States*. Nashville, TN: Vanderbilt University Press, 1997.

Marqués, René. *La carreta*. Río Piedras, PR: Editorial Cultural, 1955.

Matos-Rodríguez, Félix V., and Pedro Juan Hernández, eds. *Pioneros: Puerto Ricans in New York City, 1896–1948*. Charleston, SC: Arcadia/Tempus Publishing, 2001.

Mohr, Eugene. *The Nuyorican Experience: Literature of the Puerto Rican Minority*. Westport, CT: Greenwood Press, 1982.

Mohr, Nicholosa. *El Bronx Remembered*. New York: Harper, 1975.

———. *Nilda*. New York: Harper, 1973.

———. *In Nueva York*. New York: Dial, 1977.

———. *Rituals of Survival: A Woman's Portfolio*. Houston: Arte Público Press, 1985.

Morales, Rodney. *The Speed of Darkness*. Honolulu: Bamboo Ridge Press, 1988.

———. *When the Shark Bites*. Honolulu: University of Hawai'i Press, 2002.

Negrón-Muntaner, Frances. *Boricua Pop: Puerto Ricans and the Latinization of American Culture*. New York: New York University Press, 2004.

Ortiz Cofer, Judith. *The Latin Deli: Telling the Lives of Barrio Women*. New York: W. W. Norton, 1995.

———. *The Line of the Sun*. Athens, GA: University of Georgia Press, 1989.
———. *Silent Dancing: A Partial Remembrance of a Puerto Rican Childhood*. Houston: Arte Público Press, 1990.
Perdomo, Willie. *Where a Nickel Costs a Dime*. New York: W. W. Norton, 1996.
Pietri, Pedro. *Puerto Rican Obituary*. New York: Monthly Review Press, 1973.
Piñero, Miguel. *La Bodega Sold Dreams*. Houston: Arte Público Press, 1980.
———. *Short Eyes*. New York: Wang and Hill, 1975.
Quiñonez, Ernesto. *Bodega Dreams*. New York: Vintage, 2000.
———. *Chango's Fire*. New York: Rayo, 2005.
Rivera, Carmen. *Julia*. In *Nuestro New York*, ed. John Antush, 133–178. New York: Signet, 1994.
Rivera, Edward. *Family Installments*. New York: Penguin, 1983.
Rivera, José. *Marisol and Other Plays*. New York: Theatre Communications Group, 1997.
Rodríguez, Abraham. *The Boy without a Flag*. Minneapolis: Milkwood, 1999.
———. *The Buddha Book*. New York: Picador, 2001.
———. *Spidertown*. New York: Penguin, 1994.
Rodríguez, Clara. "A Summary of Puerto Rican Migration to the United States." In *Challenging Fronteras: Structuring Latina and Latino Lives in the U.S.*, ed. Mary Romero, Pierrette Hondagneu-Sotelo, and Vilma Ortiz, 101–113. New York: Routledge, 1997.
Ruoff, A. LaVonne Brown, and Jerry W. Ward, eds. *Redefining American Literary History*. New York: MLA, 1990.
Sánchez, Luis Rafael. *La guagua aérea*. Río Piedras, PR: Editorial Cultural, 1994.
Sánchez Gonzalez, Lisa. *Boricua Literature: A Literary History of the Puerto Rican Diaspora*. New York: New York University Press, 2001.
Sánchez Korrol, Virginia. *From Colonia to Community: The History of Puerto Ricans in New York City*. Berkeley and Los Angeles: University of California Press, 1994.
Santiago, Esmeralda. *Almost a Woman*. New York: Vintage, 1999.
———. *The Turkish Lover*. New York: Perseus Books, 2004.
———. *When I Was Puerto Rican*. New York: Vintage, 1994.
Singh, Amritjit, and Peter Schmidt. "On the Borders between U.S. Studies and Postcolonial Theory." In *Postcolonial Theory and the United States: Race, Ethnicity, and Literature*, ed. Amritjit Singh and Peter Schmidt, 3–69. Jackson: University Press of Mississippi, 2000.
Soto, Pedro Juan. *Ardiente suelo, fría estación*. Mexico: Editorial Veracruzana, 1961. Trans. Helen R. Lane as *Hot Land, Cold Season* (New York: Dell, 1973).
———. *Spiks*. Mexico: Presentes, 1956. Trans. Victoria Ortiz as *Spiks* (New York: Monthly Review Press, 1973).
Thomas, Piri. *Down These Mean Streets*. New York: Knopf, 1967.
———. *Savior, Savior, Hold My Hand*. New York: Doubleday, 1972.
Torres, Andrés, and José Velázquez, eds. *The Puerto Rican Movement: Voices of the Diaspora*. Philadelphia: Temple University Press, 1998.
Torres, Edwin. *Carlito's Way*. New York: Dutton, 1975.
———. *Q & A*. New York: Avon, 1978.

Valle, Victor M., and Rodolfo Torres. *Latino Metropolis*. Minneapolis: University of Minnesota Press, 2000.

Vega, Bernardo. *Memoirs of Bernardo Vega: A Contribution to the History of the Puerto Rican Community in New York*. Ed. César Andreu Iglesias. Trans. Juan Flores. New York: Monthly Review Press, 1984.

Vega, Ed. *Blood Fugues*. New York: Rayo/HarperCollins, 2005.

———. *Casualty Report*. Houston: Arte Público Press, 1991.

———. *The Comeback*. Houston: Arte Público Press, 1985.

———. *Mendoza's Dreams*. Houston: Arte Público Press, 1987.

Villa Romero, Raul. *Barrio Logos*. Austin: University of Texas Press, 2000.

Whalen, Carmen Teresa, and Victor Vázquez-Hernández, eds. *The Puerto Rican Diaspora: Historical Perspectives*. Philadelphia: Temple University Press, 2005.

PART I *Earlier Voices*

1 EVOLVING IDENTITIES

Early Puerto Rican Writing in the United States and the Search for a New Puertorriqueñidad

JOSÉ M. IRIZARRY RODRÍGUEZ

Jesús Colón, Pedro Juan Labarthe, Arturo Alfonso Schomburg, and Bernardo Vega were among the first Puerto Rican writers in the United States to feel an urgency, and to assume the authority, to record their recollected experiences as exemplars. Due to various circumstances, they were writing after prolonged separation from their native land. Indeed, exile was their state of being. It is, therefore, understandable that in their narratives these writers attempted to invoke a critical awareness that warned against rooting one's sense of identity, culture, and values solely in the materialism and hegemonic racial paradigms of the United States. After their arrival, each writer realized that most cultural constructs that sustained Puerto Rican identity in Puerto Rico could not sustain them in their new home. It is this insight that leads Vega early in his *Memoirs* to exclaim: "What a difference between our customs back home and the behavior of Puerto Rican men and women in New York!"[1]

These writers believed that the tribulations experienced by Puerto Ricans in the United States and the self-doubt instilled in them by the negative beliefs about and images of Puerto Ricans permeating U.S. society and culture, in conjunction with the U.S. racial paradigms, necessitated Puerto Ricans to protect and promote their cultural character and value systems in order to ensure survival as a healthy community. Vega and the others wrote to resist the alterations that would be forced upon the Puerto Rican community and its value systems if U.S. culture and consumerism were to determine its identity. Throughout their texts, the four writers attempt to challenge and curtail this threat by negotiating and reinforcing an autonomous Puerto Rican identity and sense of dignity. Through storytelling *testimonios* of success, they hoped to guide their compatriots through perilous new circumstances and to strengthen community. Under these conditions, it is understandable why these writers foregrounded Puerto Rican identity rather than succumbed to an identity imposed by U.S. beliefs and images that promoted the eradication of Puerto Rican uniqueness. As Puerto Ricans, their race, expectations, and values differed from those of the United States, and this did not facilitate their integration. The only ways for Puerto Ricans to fit within the imposed conditions in the United States were to "pass" or, if skin color did not permit, to accept the socioeconomic limitations and barriers imposed upon them due to race. These writers understood that Puerto Ricans, through the negotiations of self presented in their works, could surpass this imposed marginal status and maintain their identity and sense of dignity as Puerto Ricans.

The works of these early Puerto Rican writers promoted a form of political cultural criticism similar to that suggested by Cornell West in his *Race Matters*. According to West, "Self-love and love of others are both modes toward increasing self-valuation and encouraging political resistance in one's community."[2] Their texts focus on generating a sense of agency and increasing self-valuation of what is Puerto Rican. By offering their experiences as exempla, these writers engaged in a politics of conversion that provided new models for an oppositional, collective Puerto Rican politics. To their non–Puerto Rican readers, these texts offered an understanding and an alternative construction of Puerto Ricans—as a people who in the face of adversity were a potential force to be reckoned with and equally rational and resourceful. Through their narratives, Schomburg, Colón, Vega, and Labarthe offered Puerto Ricans the chance to believe that there was hope for the future and meaning in identifying as Puerto Rican. As Susan Willis suggests, "While traditional society defines the subject in terms of community, advanced capitalism has generated a society in which subjects are isolated individuals. If the struggle against oppression (which involves the struggle for selfhood) is waged for the sake of the individual, it will necessarily end in the isola tion of the subject and the fragmentation of social relationships."[3] These writers perceived that the major peril confronting Puerto Ricans in the United States was the alienation of the individual Puerto Rican caused by promises of material success through stoic individualism. Therefore, through their work they resisted the tendency of U.S. ideology to isolate and racialize minority individuals from their community and thereby strip them of their identity. Consequently, these early Puerto Rican writers in the United States focused on the individual within the larger context of the collectivity; but each approached this problem from a different standpoint. This difference in approach and purpose, as noted in their narratives and historical reenvisioning, consolidates and foregrounds a sense of community.

Traditionalist versus Modernist Rhetoric

Although their particular outlooks present the social demands, hopes, and aspirations of Puerto Ricans in the United States, each writer pursued a distinct predilection for viable solutions. Their ideological perspectives can be best described as that of traditionalists or modernizers. Both of these stances negotiate the acceptable limits of Americanization or assimilation allowed with minimum risk to *puertorriqueñidad* (Puerto Ricanness).

Colón and Vega fall into the category of traditionalist political and cultural critics. Throughout their narratives, they promote a bicultural way of life that emphasizes the maintenance of an authentic Puerto Rican national and popular culture and that seeks to preserve these in the face of industrialization, urban settings, and other external influences. Throughout Vega's *Memoirs* and Colón's *Sketches*,[4] there is a resolve to maintain and preserve Puerto Rican values and customs while accommodating those elements of the U.S. mainstream ethos concerning political democracy and equality needed for the continuance of their singular and consolidated communities. Community, for both Vega and Colón, consists primarily of Puerto Ricans, with a lesser inclusion of other Hispanics, Americans, and other political allies with similar political ideals. Through the establishment of community, they strive to resist the negative images of Puerto Ricans while at the same time promoting a separatist sentiment for this community. In their depiction of the Puerto Rican community, they foreground the struggle for independence of the community in diaspora and of the island as founded on the right of self-determination. Therefore, their concept of community centers on Puerto Ricans and their need for cohesion. Consequently, this centering also permits the non–Puerto Rican reader to view these texts as pluralistic manifestations that legitimate the further ghettoization of Puerto Ricans within U.S. culture.

While Colón and Vega were writing, and when their texts were finally published, the place—the community they described—no longer existed as they understood it. Modern modes of production and the accommodation of U.S. individualism by Puerto Ricans had long eroded the camaraderie and ideals of the socialist workers and the *tabaqueros* (tobacco workers). Their descriptions of community make Puerto Ricans scrutinize the community as it existed in the past and make them face the reality of its present and future existence. As is consistent with autobiography, both Colón and Vega associate the existence of community with their youth and past. As traditionalists they see themselves as struggling and writing against the devastating influence of modern life in the United States, particularly as it erodes the traditional cultural identity of the Puerto Rican community.

Schomburg and Labarthe, on the other hand, assume a modernizer's perspective in their narratives. As modernizers, they conceive of knowledge for knowledge's sake, without territorial borders, and entrust their understanding of progress to autonomous experimentation and innovation in their sense of community. The ultimate goal for these modernizers is transculturation, the creation, through a more dynamic concept of *puertorriqueñidad,* of a new Puerto Rican. This experimentation allows a more culturally inclusive character for the community. Although both writers agree on the creation of a new Puerto Rican character that incorporates a new worldview or global community, each arrives at a different conclusion on the final character for the new Puerto Rican. Unlike the traditionalists, the modernizers view their willingness to incorporate U.S. culture and values not as separatist, but rather as assimilationist.

Schomburg promotes the incorporation of Puerto Ricans into the brotherhood of global Pan-Africanism on revisionist historical grounds. Working within the confines of U.S. racial paradigms, Schomburg advocates the political integration of Puerto Ricans as American Puerto Ricans. He does this by associating Puerto Ricans racially with the more militant and outspoken New Negro movement and globally with the empowered world community of the Pan-African movement. For instance, in his historical essays, Schomburg views all Puerto Ricans regardless of skin color as members of the colored race. He portrays many light-skinned Puerto Rican artists as notable representatives of the colored race. In his essays "West Indian Composers and Musicians" and "José Campeche, 1752–1809: A Puerto Rico Negro Painter," Schomburg categorizes very light-skinned Puerto Ricans as "negroes" because they are Puerto Ricans and not Spaniards, thereby establishing a historical Pan-African kinship among the colored races.[5] Like his North American black colleagues who actively participated in the New Negro movement, he never renounced his U.S. citizenship because of race. Rather, as demonstrated in "Masonic Truths: A Letter and a Document," he promotes his race as worthy in participating equally in pursuit of the American Dream and the nation's democratic ideals: "We believe men, no matter what race, can respect each other without the hobby of raising the dust of social equality before the law."[6] In his youth, Schomburg's view of history's purpose was influenced by his teacher José Julian Acosta. Acosta founded La Sociedad Recolectora de Documentos Historicos in 1851 with the goal of reclaiming Puerto Rico's historical roots unknown to Puerto Ricans. Influenced by this "mythmaker" while in Puerto Rico, Schomburg, the historian, in the United States reclaimed what he viewed as the global historical roots of Puerto Ricans. Again in "Masonic Truths," Schomburg makes clear his concept of the purpose of history: "There is no denying the fact that the whites today enjoy the higher level, but they will have to keep pegging away at it. In the past others were on the top rung of the ladder. History will absolutely and unqualifiedly repeat itself, and others in the human procession may succeed the whites just as unerringly as the day follows the night."[7] Schomburg's view of history clearly promotes the equality of humankind within the set parameters of European history. Further on in the essay, he comments on the proposed separation along racial lines within the Masonic order, reflects on the restrictions placed on his race, and promotes his view of an expanded community.

Much like Schomburg, Labarthe also expands his sense of community by broadening the Puerto Rican ethos concerning personal relationships to include non–Puerto Ricans: educated and accomplished Euro-Americans, South and Central Americans, and Europeans of all social classes on an equal basis. His enlightened principles—acquired from personal reading and the liberal humanist education that he received in Puerto Rico and at Columbia University—are the means for justifying this inclusion. This encompassing perspective allows Labarthe to expand upon the more parochial traditional Puerto Rican notions of community and to incorporate all those who accept and are worthy of his friendship into a society while retaining his own version of *puertorriqueñidad.*

From Labarthe's perspective, he and other Puerto Ricans benefit from this extended community, intellectually and socioeconomically. In *The Son of Two Nations*, he embraces the U.S. work ethic and rebukes and transcends what he considers limiting traditional and cultural Puerto Rican values associated with nationalism, language, religion, sexual mores, and kinship.[8] This inclusive and open perspective accounts for Labarthe's extensive catalog of celebrities whom he meets or with whom he corresponds during his college years and his emphasis on the establishment of friendships outside the Puerto Rican community in diaspora. This also explains Labarthe's meticulousness in detailing and rationalizing the concepts and lessons acquired throughout his academic career. More significantly, for his readers' edification, he validates this newly acquired knowledge by juxtaposing it against the cultural assumptions and knowledge learned previously in Puerto Rico.

In short, Schomburg, Vega, Colón, and Labarthe all set out to redefine *puertorriqueñidad*, whether as traditionalist or modernizer, and each (based on his understanding of the world) resists the wholesale absorption of Puerto Ricans into the U.S. melting pot. Each writer found an agreeable middle ground that allowed for a concept of Puerto Rican community to insinuate itself into the matrix of U.S. culture rather than lose its uniqueness and existence. Through their stances they reflect their own agendas with regard to the unresolved status of Puerto Rico's political relationship with the United States, a question frequently debated by Puerto Ricans in diaspora as well as those living on the island.

Outside Looking In

Due to their autobiographical nature, the works written by Vega, Colón, and Labarthe share similar structures and posturing, although each arrives at a distinctly different conclusion. Aside from the motif of race or ethnicity, which is a primary determinant of the Puerto Rican experience in the United States, one must consider the anecdotal construction of the works. In an interview, Judith Ortiz Cofer, a contemporary Puerto Rican writer in the United States, discusses the importance of *cuentos*, or stories, in Puerto Rican culture: "I was fascinated by the power of the *cuentos* to influence people, to move them and keep their attention, so in most of my stories there is a storyteller and I use a frame story. . . . Immigrants transfer culture by oral transmission. . . . They passed on not only culture but yearning."[9] The use by Vega, Colón, and Labarthe of the *cuentos* format is due to the persuasive power of this form, as observed by Ortiz Cofer. In addition, as Puerto Ricans, they were aware of a cultural preference and tradition for oral transmission and reception of information in which the unassuming *testimonio* is held in high regard. This format gives the texts an easy-to-understand narrative that by U.S. literary standards may seem unsophisticated. Nevertheless, for Puerto Ricans in transition these narratives provide powerful and thought-provoking stories of shared experience through which to reconsider and rationalize their condition.

A closer examination of the texts reveals other similarities. In the first sections of each work, Colón, Labarthe, and, to a lesser degree, Vega justify their right to speak for Puerto Ricans. They attempt to set themselves apart as impartial spokesmen, for they criticize their homeland's ideologies and abuses. Therefore, they are not inclined to challenge only the ideologies and injustice of the United States, but they reveal Puerto Rico as being just as flawed. Through this critical stance, they become an "other" even within their own communities. As each begins his narrative by placing himself in this marginal position, he attempts to lend credibility to his claims as spokesperson. This decentering is crucial and is achieved through the description of certain formative experiences that serve to validate and motivate their participation in the community as its representatives. The retellings of these selected experiences serve both to introduce the reader to the conditions that led to their inevitable departure from the island and to establish their right to speak as Puerto Ricans.

It is feasible to focus on Colón and Labarthe, because in their works they focus directly on the formulation of ideologies and also detail their own critical development prior to their arrival in the United States. Although Vega mentions his participation in founding a socialist cell in his hometown of Cayey, he speaks of the *tabaquero* tradition in the context of the United States and notes that the main reason he left Puerto Rico was his unrequited love for a woman. As mentioned earlier, all these writers had particular agendas meant to achieve different outcomes for the Puerto Rican community in the United States. Colón, as a traditionalist, and Labarthe, as a modernizer, differ essentially in their new conceptions of *puertorriqueñidad*. Vega and Schomburg tend to focus on events that shape the Puerto Rican experience in the United States and therefore write as chroniclers. Colón and Labarthe go beyond the mere detailing of events and explore, through the use of literary invention and their life experiences, the underlying structure of the ideological changes needed to accommodate *puertorriqueñidad* and the consequences of these changes.

Sketches comprises fifty-five independent accounts that Colón says were written and published to compensate for the scarce and predominantly negative body of works written about Puerto Ricans in New York. He states that this collection aims to correct the record and present Puerto Ricans from a Puerto Rican perspective. In the first four sketches, Colón sets out to establish his credentials and his *puertorriqueñidad*. In "A Voice through the Window," Colón introduces the reader to the *tabaquero* legacy, a major influence during his formative years. These descriptions of the *lector* tradition help explain his awareness of the world, which in turn legitimates his belief in and hope for the triumph of "the prisoners of starvation" and the "wretched of the earth" (19).

In the following sketch, "My First Literary Venture," Colón notes that as a child he was gifted with the leadership skills that allowed him to accurately express the sentiment of a group when, as a grade school student, his letter was selected to express the condolences of his classmates. In the third sketch, "My First Strike," Colón recounts how his understanding of the earlier experiences and lessons learned recounted in his first two sketches evolved and developed as he experienced his first important life lesson in group solidarity and representation: his first participation in a successful strike, which he led. Through these first sketches, Colón emphasizes his natural leadership and the fundamental traditional value system used in his decision making.

Colón's development and coming of age are the subjects of "The Way to Learn." This fourth sketch culminates in defining Colón's legitimacy as an activist and spokesman for the Puerto Rican workers' cause at home and abroad. At the center of this sketch is an eventful day in Colón's senior year of high school: Friday, March 23, 1917. On that day, in front of the school playground, the students witnessed a peaceful protest by the wives of striking dock workers turn into a violent riot when police opened fire and killed a protester and wounded a student. Colón notes, "Nothing in those schoolrooms of old Barracones has taught me as much as that encounter between the workers and the police that eventful day" (21).

Colón does not detail the circumstances leading to his departure from Puerto Rico as a sixteen-year-old stowaway on the S.S. *Carolina*. We can infer that he left due to economic reasons, as did many Puerto Ricans at the time: "I think I don't have to explain that I did not carry a valise or other bundles with me. Just myself" (22). Shortly after the ship left San Juan, Colón was discovered and made to work hard for his passage in the ship's kitchen and dining room. Although he was a good worker and was offered a job on the ship before he arrived on U.S. soil, the allure of the adventure in the United States led him to go "ashore as unobtrusively as I had come into the boat in San Juan Bay in Puerto Rico" (24).

Labarthe devotes the first two chapters of *The Son of Two Nations* to his critical development and emigration to the United States. His thinly disguised autobiography is divided into five parts—"Part I: Genesis," "Part II: Development," "Part III: Stimuli," "Part IV: Struggles," and "Part V: Results." The headings suggest that the protagonist's life is the subject of an empirical study. In fact, Labarthe's table of contents reveals his objectification of self as an attempt to understand his subject. Later we see that the experiment is the Americanization of Pedro Juan Labarthe. Like Colón, the factors involved in his preparation as spokesperson begin long before his physical presence on U.S. shores. The quotation from Saint Benedict that serves as the book's epigraph, "Often it is to a young person that God reveals what is best" (i), supplies a means of access to Labarthe's book. Labarthe's belief that an educated youth is best equipped to understand and decide which path to take is a persistent theme throughout this novel. The educated youth is open to change, not limited by old-fashioned traditions, and can therefore adapt and succeed. *The Son of Two Nations* is the autobiography of a young person written scarcely a year after his graduation from Columbia University and, therefore, contains much youthful idealism and hope and a triumphant sense of invincibility.

The first part, "Genesis," begins with its main character, Pedro Juan Labarthe, standing on a ship's deck describing his disillusioning first view of New York. In a series of flashbacks, we are told of conditions before his birth. At this point, the narrative centers on life in Puerto Rico, with his parents' social background, beliefs, romance, and eventual mismatched and short-lived marriage as representative of the state of the island. Labarthe notes that his mother married his father because "seeing that Mr. Labarthe was the wealthier [of her suitors, she] decided to marry him to help her poor mother and brother" (22). Through these flashbacks describing the educational system and working conditions in Puerto Rico, he highlights the socioeconomic inequality and decadence of Puerto Rico as a Spanish colony and even as a U.S. colony in the early 1900s through the 1920s. Labarthe also takes the opportunity to clarify the reasoning behind the anti-Yankee sentiment in Puerto Rico: the fear of losing the Spanish language and heritage under the pressure of the American presence on the island, and U.S. colonial administrative disregard and abuses.

In the second part, "Development," Labarthe personalizes the ideological instability during his youth, and he describes breaking away from the emotional ideological quagmire in which he was raised by first seeking and creating an intellectual space which allowed his questioning of the world through observation; secondly, by actively participating in youth groups of both political persuasions; and finally, through reading books and researching outside sources from which to form his eventual opinion. Arriving at a final decision was difficult. The dilemma of whether to be pro- or anti-Yankee is resolved before leaving the island based on the actions of U.S. citizens, such as "beloved President Wilson and . . . President [T.] Roosevelt," who "always tried to help the Porto Ricans and talked highly of the island," and "many American teachers [who] were so devoted to the Porto Rican students and tried their best in their teaching" (35, 36, 37). Actions, not words, eventually led Labarthe to the acceptance of a limited Americanization and the economic and cultural potential it offered Puerto Rico. For Labarthe, *puertorriqueñidad*, as promoted by his father and Puerto Rican nationalist groups, involved romantic confabulations that recalled a mythic past far from the harsh realities in Puerto Rico. Puerto Rican and U.S. political and economic association was an undeniable reality; so therefore, Americanization offered a palpable opportunity for prosperity if one were receptive to change. Before he left Puerto Rico, he was certain of his understanding, as demonstrated by the discussion he had with his father on the merits of Americanization (39).

Once Labarthe had made his mind up about the promising aspects of Americanization, he was open to change under its influences. His major influence in Puerto Rico was an American history and civil government teacher, a North American, who dubbed him "the Son of Two Nations." Miss Bosworth encouraged Labarthe in his development and taught him an important life lesson through her teachings and actions. She helped create the space for Labarthe's conceptualization of his version of *puertorriqueñidad* because she recommended that "Porto Rico should keep its characteristics; there were many good things in the Porto Rican students, they were bright, ambitious and above all very gentle" (44). She encouraged Labarthe to keep certain traits, but she warned that to become better he and his classmates had to go beyond the boundaries of the island to study and then return with newly acquired knowledge that would benefit not only Labarthe but also Puerto Rico. One can easily see how Labarthe began to reconceptualize a dynamic version of *puertorriqueñidad*. For the young Labarthe, Miss Bosworth represented the America to be admired and emulated. It is evident from these episodes that Labarthe was influenced by U.S. colonialism. In his study of the psychology of the colonized, *The Wretched of the Earth*, Fanon declares that "the intellectual who has followed the colonialist with regard to the universal abstract will fight in order that the settler and the native may live together in peace in a new world."[10] This condition helps in understanding Labarthe's critical development and stance. For the modern reader, Labarthe is either a naïve, quintessentially colonized subject, or a pragmatic and impressionable young man; nevertheless, it is evident from these episodes that he wholeheartedly embraced the concepts of U.S. individualism and its value system. It can be argued that although Miss Bosworth's counsel leads Labarthe toward his colonization, it is Labarthe's inclination toward the belief in knowledge, as revealed in books, that determines his final decisions. Possibly the most influential advice by Miss Bosworth concerned her suggested readings, especially *The Americanization of Edward Bok*.[11] The power of the American Dream, personified through Edward Bok, became the object of Labarthe's admiration. The 1922 bestseller (and winner of the Pulitzer Prize) is the autobiography of a Dutch immigrant who, after fifty years in the United

States, became the rich and powerful editor of the most widely circulated magazine at the time, the *Ladies Home Journal.*

In addition to serving Labarthe as a model life, Bok's popular tale of immigrant success, with its "rags to riches" plot and the protagonist's eventual social acceptance through hard work, served Labarthe as a model for *The Son of Two Nations*, ideologically, stylistically, and thematically. Reading *The Americanization of Edward Bok*, Labarthe readily identified with the immigrant experience and learned important lessons on individualism, Americanization, and the opportunity for success in the United States that would prepare him for his own attempts at succeeding abroad. Bok placed importance on the individual, a basic U.S. value. Labarthe's belief in the American Dream is sustained by this and other immigrant stories. He struggles at achieving the U.S. ideal of the self-made man as presented in these texts. At one point in *The Son of Two Nations*, after receiving a letter from Bok, he reaffirms his trinity for success as being "Ambition, Fight and Work." In chapters 38, "Where America Fell Short with Me," and 39, "What I Owe to America," Bok reflects on the process of Americanization and his success. These are lessons that Labarthe took to heart and preached at every given opportunity. For example, Bok notes that what makes an American is not birthplace: the American "seems to take it for granted that because he is American-born, he is an American in spirit and has a right understanding of American ideals." "Their Americanization consists of lip service; the real spirit, the only factor which counts in the successful teaching of any doctrine, is absolutely missing" (445, 446). These words rang true to Labarthe, a Puerto Rican, who wanted to live with that spirit. Throughout his narrative, Labarthe is always an ardent practitioner of that universal abstract, the American spirit.

Robert F. Sayre comments, "From the times of Columbus, Cortéz, and John Smith, America has been an idea or many ideas," and these "Ideas . . . have organized the lives that Americans have lived and the stories they have written and how they have changed and progressed."[12] So it is with Labarthe: he took ideas that were taught to him, such as the "spirit of America," and chose to live by them. To succeed, his sense of *puertorriqueñidad* did not need to be erased, just as Bok's Dutch origins had not been. Miss Bosworth advocated the transitional change, and Bok confirmed that it could be done. Bok was abundantly clear on this point: "into the best that the foreign-born can retain, America can graft such a wealth of inspiration, so high a national idealism, so great an opportunity for the highest endeavor, as to make him the most fortunate man of the earth today" (447). Shortly after reading Bok, the young Labarthe wrote to the author lauding his book. Bok's text offered so much insight that Labarthe sincerely believed that every young man in Puerto Rico should have a copy. It is evident that Bok's narrative establishes many important frames of reference that would later serve Labarthe in the United States.

Another important theme in Bok's text, which prepares Labarthe for the situations he will confront, is that the United States is not flawless and not exceptionally receptive to the needs of immigrants. Bok is very straightforward about his country's shortcomings when it comes to its treatment of foreigners. "I did not succeed by reason of these shortcomings," he writes, "it was in spite of them, by overcoming them—a result that all might not achieve" (446–447). Bok assures his readers that regardless of the ill-treatment and the hardships of immigrant experience, U.S. ideology serves its purpose: "however America may have failed to help my transition from a foreigner into an American, I owe to her the most priceless gift any nation can offer, and that is opportunity" (449).

Labarthe took to heart these lessons from Edward Bok and Miss Bosworth and lived his life by them. At the center of these lessons, and most important for Labarthe, is the confirmation of his belief that *puertorriqueñidad* is enhanced by the addition of the enlightened ideas and principles that are at the heart of the so-called greatest nation in the Western Hemisphere. Bok's influence is also apparent in Labarthe's writing style in *The Son of Two Nations*. In the preface to his book, Bok discusses the use of the third person in autobiography. He states: "I had always felt the most effective method of writing an autobiography, for the sake of a better perspective, was mentally to separate the writer from his subject by this device" (vii–viii). In *The Son of Two Nations*, Labarthe objectifies his experiences and assumes the position of an objective viewer by narrating the tale, very much in Bok's style.

The above-mentioned formative experiences in Puerto Rico prepared Labarthe for his emigration and success in the United States. He was receptive toward the U.S. value system and was prepared to work hard to succeed, but he was not prepared for the race factor. Labarthe, unlike Colón, did not emigrate specifically for economic reasons; rather, he left

Puerto Rico with his mother and with the promise of a university scholarship from the Puerto Rican government. For both Labarthe and Colón, the bulk of their work deals with their arrival and experiences in the U.S and how they overcame them. Yet, their mere retelling of their U.S. experiences would provide little understanding if they did not justify their position as Puerto Rican spokespersons to their readers. This relating of relevant formative experiences served to legitimate their claims as spokespersons for their community and substantiate their point of view and interpretations of the experience.

Living in a Bicultural World

From Labarthe's and Vega's reminisces of their first walks through the streets of New York City to Colón's impassioned plea for others not to emigrate but to stay in Puerto Rico, many topics are detailed in these works. These experiences present day-to-day living as Puerto Ricans in the United States, but more significantly they treat the possibility of Puerto Ricans changing those factors that work against them.

It has been said that first impressions are long lasting, and the adage runs true with these writers. The limited prospects for work, food, and shelter in this land of millions were disheartening. Even the open-minded, idealistic, and ever-hopeful Labarthe found his first impression of New York City rather disillusioning: "Seeing the poor neighborhood of that section, the dirty street full of noise coming from a crowd of Italian youngsters, he felt downhearted. . . . The New York of his dreams held no such spectacle; it was full of gayety everywhere, cabarets, dancing halls, fashionable ladies and gentlemen, rows of fifty story skyscrapers bordering the streets and tickling the clouds. Pedro was disillusioned" (15). Although Labarthe was prepared by Miss Bosworth and by Bok's book for his Americanization process, it was still rather disillusioning to become invisible in the crowd. To further add to Labarthe's disillusionment, shortly after his arrival he was denied a promised scholarship from the insular auditor in Puerto Rico due to a lack of money. Labarthe then wonders, "What was he going to do in a country so big as the United States without money?" (54). Vega had a similar blow to his expectations: "The further along we moved, and as the dingy buildings filed past my view, all the visions I had of the gorgeous splendor of New York vanished. The skyscrapers seemed like tall gravestones. I wondered why, if the United States was so rich, as surely it was, did its biggest city look so grotesque? At that moment I sensed for the first time that the people of New York could not possibly be as happy as we used to think they were back home in Cayey" (7). As a *tabaquero* with experience he felt sure he would be able to find a job and survive, but he quickly realized that in the land of opportunity, opportunity was not easy to come by: "On my first day in New York I didn't go out at all. There was a lot to talk about, and Ambrosio and I had lengthy conversations. . . . He talked about the city, what life was like, what the chances were of finding a job. . . . To put it mildly, an utterly dismal picture" (7–8).

Colón does not write of his impressions concerning his first days, but the six sketches that follow "Stowaway" reveal the ordeal and economic hardship experienced by the unskilled. In these early sketches he describes scraping labels from bottles with his thumbnail at twenty-three cents an hour ("Easy Job, Good Wages"); sharing his work pants with his brother, so that these were constantly in use ("Two Men with But One Pair of Pants"); working in the dockyards with a black Panamanian foreman ("On The Docks It Was Cold"); working in the depths of ship cargo holds cleaning out excess oil by throwing cement at the oily walls ("I Heard a Man Crying"). In "I Heard a Man Crying," Colón investigates the sound of moaning and wailing, and much to his horror he discovers a man who "was actually starving, gradually dying of hunger" (37–38). This overpowering image drives home the reality of living in the United States without knowing the language or the laws. This scene, which occurred in 1918, summarizes for Colón the paradox of the American ethos and the sheer neglect of the welfare of the foreigner. It moves Colón to ask his readers to reflect on the painful scene and on the injustice.

As noted previously, racism was prevalent throughout the Puerto Ricans' daily life, but as noted by Labarthe, Colón, and Vega, it is more conspicuous and disheartening when one is attempting to find meaningful employment. In Labarthe's case, neither Ms. Bosworth's lessons nor Bok's autobiography informed him of the race barriers that existed in every aspect of U.S. culture. Labarthe's dealings with race occurred at two levels: while working at part-time jobs with uneducated coworkers to help finance his studies and at Columbia with classmates and professors. Labarthe described his first job as a stock boy at "Gimbal [*sic*] Brothers" department store: "Everybody tried to boss him. All gave him orders . . . gave him the hardest work and many times did nothing while [coworkers] watched Pedro carrying casks of china and sweating like a negro slave" (57–58). Later, at Columbia, Labarthe found himself combating prejudice and stereotypes in the college classroom, causing him to spend much time trying to present a true picture of Puerto Ricans to his classmates. In "Hiawatha," Colón recounts how, when looking for employment as a translator, he was refused the position once his employer saw that he was black.

Although all the authors deal with the effects of racism against Puerto Ricans, Colón excels in providing graphic descriptions of the acts and their effects on its victims. Colón portrays the racialization of Puerto Ricans and their submission into a subordinate socioeconomic class. In the sketch "Carmencita," a story about Colón's elderly mother-in-law's move to New York, we find through the embodiment of Carmencita the ways in which Puerto Rican culture clashed with U.S. mainstream culture. Originally, in Puerto Rico, Carmencita is doubtful of her son-in-law's socialist political affiliations and beliefs, as she understood them. She believes faithfully both in the U.S. idealistic ethos and in the cultural traditions of Puerto Rico. Colón is aware of her distrust of him and decides not to push his views upon her; rather, he prefers that she discover the detrimental paradoxes for herself. He was sure that as she adapted to living in the United States, she would begin to acquire firsthand experiences that would validate his worldview. It was Colón's reasoning that as questions arose he, with the help of a friend, would attempt to explain and rationalize them. The differences between U.S. and Puerto Rican cultures that Carmencita experienced in this sketch were familiar to most emigrating Puerto Ricans. This sketch serves a dual purpose in that it deals with conflicts that prevented Carmencita from accepting U.S. culture, and at another level it shows that there were also communal Puerto Rican customs that prevented Americans from accepting the Puerto Rican community in general. The first lesson to be learned for a greater understanding was the need to overcome the rather limited parochial vision of the world of the islander and gain a more sophisticated, global awareness. This Colón tried to teach his mother-in-law directly: "Joe and I sat down with Carmencita to explain that there was something greater than nationality and so-called race—and that is the conscious feeling and understanding of belonging to a class that unites us regardless of color and nationality" (105).

Colón promotes an expanded viewpoint in which Puerto Ricans

belong to a greater fraternity that is determined by class and transcends political, geographic, and biological boundaries. This ideological stance is similar to Labarthe's, but it foregrounds race and prevalent racial attitudes in the United States. By doing so, Colón emphasizes race as the factor in the United States that is the basis for the socioeconomic disadvantage experienced by Puerto Ricans. Throughout "Carmencita," we note the Americanization of his mother-in-law, and that race and its connotations in the United States become paramount in defining Puerto Ricans' status and existence in their new homeland. In one incident, when Colón and Carmencita are admiring a symbol of U.S. greatness—the great Prometheus statue near Radio City—Colón found the occasion to comment that at the Radio City Café Negroes and Puerto Ricans would not be served because they were looked upon as inferior (104). The paradox of a nation ideologically professing equality and democracy but in reality practicing racial discrimination and segregation prominently affected the daily lives of many Puerto Ricans. This major factor can be understood as conditioning their lives and economic progress, especially for those individuals who could not "pass."

As the sketch develops, Colón presents consumerism as the second factor affecting the daily lives and the socioeconomic development of Puerto Ricans in the United States. His mother-in-law soon discovers that callous consumerism penetrates every aspect of daily life and desecrates even the most sacred religious rites. As noted earlier, Carmencita embodies the cultural traditions of the island. In the United States, she finds that she must confront many of the set truths that governed her youth and adult life in Puerto Rico. Such was the case with her belief in the infallibility of her religious faith and its rituals. In Puerto Rico, Carmencita was a devout Catholic and especially devoted to the practices surrounding the cult of the Virgin Mary (particularly the praying of the rosary). Colón noted that after a time in the United States and participating in her local church, Carmencita "objected very strenuously to the fiesta character that has developed in New York around this religious ceremony. We pointed out to her the influence of the money-concept of life and culture that those who control everything have forced on even the most revered customs and traditions of the people" (107). Once the very foundations of her lifelong religious beliefs are shaken, her confidence in other beliefs begins to weaken. Eventually, much that Carmencita believed becomes doubtful to her.

This sketch provides Colón with a forum to instill new beliefs and political hope to ameliorate the sense of loss experienced by Carmencita and the Puerto Rican community at large. The subsequent experiences described in the sketch serve to validate Colón's perceptions, as they demonstrate to his mother-in-law the racist and materialistic nature of U.S. society. The racial issue is a noteworthy point made by Colón, because he clearly accepts African Americans as sharing similar experiences of marginalization with Puerto Ricans; but with his emphasized distinction of each group, he maintains that each is separate. Puerto Rican ethnicity and *puertorriqueñidad* sets them apart. This attitude toward the African American community is noted by Labarthe, in whose narrative African Americans are nonexistent, and by Vega, whose reference to interaction with the African American community is casual and rather superficial.

All three writers conclude their works with a summary and an evaluation of their U.S. experience. One would expect that closure would reveal a glimmer of hope for the future that could serve as the major tone for these texts. However, quite to the contrary, we find a conspicuous lack of closure. Colón finishes his *Sketches* with "A Puerto Rican in New York." This final sketch echoes many of the earlier ones, such as "Jose," which ends on a note of despair: "how many Joses are lost in basements and the top floors of New York City, with nobody telling them that they have talent, that they are perhaps geniuses. That they are a product of that ever self-renewing admirable mass of beauty and ugliness, enthusiasm and frustration we call the people" (89). For Colón, the plight of the Puerto Rican cannot be resolved, nor is there hope of a suitable solution to the Puerto Rican problem. Assimilation into U.S culture leads only to further marginalization, in turn further problematizing the very essence of Puerto Rican identity. Race and its consequent socioeconomic subordination of the community are major barriers that cannot be overcome in a land of paradox.

As Labarthe concludes his narrative, we find him signing up with several agencies to help him search for a Spanish-teaching position after a highly successful academic career. Although he spent much time presenting Puerto Ricans in a positive light in the classrooms of Columbia, upon graduation as he attempted to find employment he was confronted with the ever-present images of Puerto Rican inferiority in the real world. "You don't speak Spanish but Porto Rican," an employer tells him (173).

After correcting him, he is offered a position to teach Spanish. By finishing his novel with a recognition of his mother's support, Labarthe is clearly acknowledging and finding solace in traditional Puerto Rican culture and its idealization and devotion to the mother. Yet, there is a realization that although he does find a job as a result of his assimilation of the Bok work ethos for immigrant success, which is individualistic in nature, the racial misinformation about Puerto Ricans will always be present.

Vega's account ends in an unfinished chapter in which he is torn between returning to Puerto Rico and staying to work on the Henry Wallace presidential campaign "to help our people." The fact that he does not stay says much about his faith in the democratic process as practiced in the United States. In actuality, Vega returns to Puerto Rico and becomes a vanguard figure in the founding of the modern-day Partido Independentista Puertorriqueño and its youth organization Federación Universitaria Pro Independencia, never to return to New York.

It can be argued that none of these works achieve any real sense of closure because of the unresolved Puerto Rican–U.S. political situation—nor has there been closure in any Puerto Rican texts written in the United States while the question of Puerto Rican sovereignty is being resolved. The innocence with which these pioneers faced their new lives offers a perspective on and an inside view of Puerto Rican life in the United States. Confrontation with different values and customs made Schomburg, Vega, Colón, Labarthe, and the other Puerto Ricans in diaspora undergo marked changes. Their writings reflect choices made by Puerto Ricans to ensure their survival. Although their choices ultimately conditioned their adaptation to their new U.S. environment, at the same time they tragically separated them from their fellow countrymen in Puerto Rico. Their experiences in the United States made these writers acutely aware of and self-conscious about their ethnicity, their racial identity, and led them to adopt a dynamic sense of *puertorriqueñidad*, which ultimately evolved into a new identity—the Nuyorican. It is through the works of these four writers that we can document the beginnings of a Puerto Rican literary tradition that continues in the United States and to this day strives for recognition both in the United States and in Puerto Rico.

NOTES

1. Bernardo Vega, *Memoirs of Bernardo Vega: A Contribution to the History of the Puerto Rican Community in New York*, ed. César Andreu Iglesias, trans. Juan Flores (New York: Monthly Review Press, 1984), 9. Hereafter cited in text.

2. Cornell West, *Race Matters* (New York: Vintage Books, 1994), 29.

3. Susan Willis, *Specifying: Black Women Writing the American Experience* (Madison: University of Wisconsin Press, 1987), 213.

4. Jesús Colón, *A Puerto Rican in New York and Other Sketches*, 2d ed. (New York: International Publishers, 1982). Hereafter cited in text.

5. Arturo Alfonso Schomburg, "West Indian Composers and Musicians" and "Jose Campeche, 1752–1809: A Puerto Rico Negro Painter," ed. Flor Piñero de Rivera (San Juan: Centro de Estudios Avanzados de Puerto Rico y el Caribe, 1989).

6. Schomburg, "Masonic Truths: A Letter and a Document" (San Juan: Centro de Estudios Avanzados de Puerto Rico y el Caribe, 1989), 102.

7. Elinor Des Verney Sinnette, *Arthur Alfonso Schomburg: Black Bibliophile and Collector—a Biography* (New York: New York Public Library; Detroit: Wayne State University Press, 1989), 106.

8. Pedro Juan Labarthe, *The Son of Two Nations: The Private Life of a Columbia Student* (New York: Carranza, 1931). Hereafter cited in text.

9. Carmen Dolores Hernández, "Judith Ortiz Cofer," in *Puerto Rican Voices in English: Interviews with Writers* (Westport, CT: Praeger, 1997), 99–100.

10. Frantz Fanon, *The Wretched of the Earth* (New York: Grove Press, 1963), 45.

11. Edward W. Bok, *The Americanization of Edward Bok: The Autobiography of a Dutch Boy Fifty Years After* (New York: Scribner's, 1922). Hereafter cited in text.

12. Robert F. Sayre, "Autobiography and the Making of America," in *Autobiography: Essays Theoretical and Critical,* ed. James Olney (Princeton: Princeton University Press, 1980), 150.

BIBLIOGRAPHY

Acosta-Belén, Edna. "Beyond Island Boundaries: Ethnicity, Gender, and Cultural Revitalization in Nuyorican Literature." *Callaloo* 15, no. 4 (Autumn 1992): 979–998.

Andrews, William L., ed. *African American Autobiography: A Collection of Critical Essays*. Englewood Cliffs, NJ: Prentice-Hall, 1993.

———. *To Tell A Free Story: The First Century of Afro-American Autobiography, 1760–1865*. Urbana: University of Illinois Press, 1988.

Beverley, John. "The Margin at the Center: On Testimonio (Testimonio Narrative)." *Modern Fiction Studies* 35, no. 1 (1989): 11–28.

Bok, Edward W. *The Americanization of Edward Bok: The Autobiography of a Dutch Boy Fifty Years After*. New York: Scribner's, 1922.

Colón, Jesús. *A Puerto Rican in New York and Other Sketches.* 2d ed. New York: International Publishers, 1982. (Originally published 1961.)

———. *The Way It Was, and Other Writings.* Ed. Edna Acosta-Belén and Virginia Sánchez Korrol. Houston: Arte Público Press, 1993.

Fanon, Frantz. *The Wretched of the Earth.* New York: Grove Press, 1963.

Flores, Juan, ed. *Divided Arrival: Narratives of the Puerto Rican Migration, 1920–1950.* 2d ed. New York: Centro de Estudios Puertorriqueños, Hunter College, CUNY, 1998.

Hernández, Carmen Dolores. *Puerto Rican Voices in English: Interviews with Writers.* Westport, CT: Praeger, 1997.

Labarthe, Pedro Juan. *The Son of Two Nations: The Private Life of a Columbia Student.* New York: Carranza, 1931.

Locke, Alaine, ed. *The New Negro (1925).* New York: Touchstone/Simon and Schuster, 1997.

Piñero de Rivera, Flor. *Arthur Schomburg: A Puerto Rican's Quest for His Black Heritage.* San Juan: Centro de Estudios Avanzados de Puerto Rico y el Caribe, 1989.

Rodríguez, Clara E., and Virginia Sánchez Korrol, eds. *Historical Perspectives on Puerto Rican Survival in the U.S.* Princeton: Markus Wiener, 1996.

Rodríguez-Morazzani, Roberto P. "Beyond the Rainbow: Mapping the Discourse on Puerto Ricans and 'Race.'" *Centro* 8, nos. 1–2 (1996): 128–149.

Said, Edward W. *Culture and Imperialism.* New York: Vintage, 1993.

———. *Representations of the Intellectual: The 1993 Reith Lectures.* New York: Vintage, 1996.

Saldívar, Ramón. *Chicano Narrative: The Dialectic of Difference.* Madison: University of Wisconsin Press, 1990.

Sánchez Korrol, Virginia. *From Colonia to Community: The History of Puerto Ricans in New York City.* Berkeley and Los Angeles: University of California Press, 1994.

Sayre, Robert F. "Autobiography and the Making of America." In *Autobiography: Essays Theoretical and Critical,* ed. James Olney, 146–168 (Princeton: Princeton University Press, 1980).

Schomburg, Arturo Alfonso. "West Indian Composers and Musicians." Ed. Flor Piñero de Rivera. San Juan: Centro de Estudios Avanzados de Puerto Rico y el Caribe, 1989.

———. "Jose Campeche, 1752–1809: A Puerto Rico Negro Painter." Ed. Flor Piñero de Rivera. San Juan: Centro de Estudios Avanzados de Puerto Rico y el Caribe, 1989.

Sinnette, Elinor Des Verney. *Arthur Alfonso Schomburg: Black Bibliophile and Collector—a Biography.* New York: New York Public Library; Detroit: Wayne State University Press, 1989.

Vega, Bernardo. *Memoirs of Bernardo Vega: A Contribution to the History of the Puerto Rican Community in New York.* Ed. César Andreu Iglesias. Trans. Juan Flores. New York: Monthly Review Press, 1984.

West, Cornell. *Race Matters.* New York: Vintage Books, 1994.

Willis, Susan. *Specifying: Black Women Writing the American Experience.* Madison: University of Wisconsin Press, 1987.

2 FOR THE SAKE OF LOVE

Luisa Capetillo, Anarchy, and Boricua Literary History

LISA SÁNCHEZ GONZÁLEZ

La instrucción se adaptará sin banderas ni en
determinado estado o nación; el respecto absurdo
e idolátrico de los gobiernos será abolido . . .
La fraternidad como ley suprema, sin fronteras
ni divisiones de razas, color e idiomas,
será el ideal religioso . . .
El interés común como divisa, y como lema la verdad.

—LUISA CAPETILLO

love
    knows
        no
            compromise

—TATO LAVIERA

The very notion of Boricua literature is indebted to a body of scholarship in American literary history that has emerged in the past thirty years, one engaged in a recuperation of literature by and about people of color in tandem with a critique of elitist tenets tacitly at work in the formation of the U.S. literary canon, a canon that has, until recently, all but excluded nonwhite writers.[1] This new scholarship, which includes the work of critics such as Toni Morrison, Elaine Kim,

Ramón Saldívar, Houston Baker, Lisa Lowe, Paula Gunn Allen, and Clara Lomas, illustrates what Baker terms a "contiguity" of dissent, that is, the way that demands for radical institutional change in the States, historically articulated by communities of color in popular political mobilizations, should translate into parallel agendas in scholarship concerning these communities.[2] Yet Boricua literary studies has been slow to realize its potential in this new academic milieu; with a few notable exceptions, like the recovery work of historian Virginia Sánchez Korrol, scholarship on Boricua cultural intellectual history simply has not enjoyed the same kind of critical momentum that has fostered the development of African American and other United States–based critical race and gender studies in the late twentieth century.

Why this lag? Certainly the difficulties of garnering mainstream institutional support are a substantial part of the problem, as well as the obstacles that effectively bar the vast majority of Boricuas—a full 99 percent of the Nuyorican population and 88 percent of Boricuas nationally—from access to or success in higher education.[3] However, there is a related difficulty within university-based Puerto Rican studies itself: the reluctance to deal with the diaspora as a distinct constituency in the United States, one that has self-consciously *produced its own body of knowledge, based on its own specific assessment of its own unique predicament as a U.S. community of color.* In lieu of recuperating a cultural intellectual tradition organic to the Boricua experience, Puerto Rican studies in the United States (as its name clearly implies) has pivoted around insular Puerto Rican disciplinary canons, especially the social sciences, and the concerns raised in the consolidation of these canons. This orientation makes it virtually impossible for critics to systematically explore the diaspora as an integral community with its own political, aesthetic, and philosophical agency and agendas. Although at moments the existing scholarship may express an idealistic desire to bridge the divide between the colonial diaspora and Puerto Rico, it can ultimately function to displace the diaspora's self-articulation in an important realm of representational struggle in the U.S. public sphere—academia—with Puerto Rico's nationalist imaginary and the institutions that shore up this imaginary.

Though the humanities constitute a relatively minor area of mainland Puerto Rican studies, still the priorities of Boricua literary scholarship, which is almost entirely authored by scholars trained and/or teaching outside literary disciplines, tend to follow suit with the social sciences. A prime example of this tendency is a set of essays included in the 1988 bulletin of the American Departments of English (ADE). As the first and, to date, last extended scholarly English-language discussion of "Puerto Rican" literature published by a major U.S. academic journal, this special issue of the *ADE Bulletin* is as much a milestone as it is a touchstone for illustrating how Boricua literary history can be introduced as a topic only, in the final instance, to be supplanted by insular canonical concerns.

Indeed, according to one of this issue's contributing authors, Yanis Gordils, the "literature of the United States Puerto Rican communities, whether in English or Spanish, never totally detaches itself from the national literature of Puerto Rico."[4] This argument deploys rhetorical devices common in Puerto Rican studies concerning the diaspora, devices that appear to broach but actually overlook the particular cultural intellectual tradition organic to this community in its most precise U.S. contexts. Gordils contends that "any serious consideration of United States Puerto Rican literature requires extrapolations, sociohistorical contextualizations, and intertextual analyses" (52), ostensibly in exclusive concert with insular Puerto Rican literary history. Yet, in her discussion of these imbrications, the supposed literary dialogue between the islands and the diaspora never surfaces; while she can cite a number of island-based authors who have appropriated the Nuyorican experience as subject matter for their fiction—often in highly problematic ways—Gordils does not offer evidence of any sustained and substantive Boricua engagement with the insular experience.

Furthermore, though Gordils argues that a certain intertextual relationship obtains between these distinct literary traditions, two of the texts she cites to corroborate this claim, Tato Laviera's chapbook of poetry, *La Carreta Made a U-Turn* and Sandra María Esteves's poem "A Julia de Burgos," both subtly censure the islands' canonical project; the first is a satiric response to a modern work of Puerto Rican dialect literature; the second is a poetic expression of empathy with a women poet who, though posthumously reclaimed by the insular canon, exiled herself from Puerto Rico and died friendless, broke, and drunk on a New York City street corner.[5] While Gordils duly notes that insular Puerto Rican literary scholars by and large simply ignore Boricua literature, and that many Boricua authors have absolutely no interest in the insular literary tradition, she still insists that it is "extremely difficult, if not impossible, to draw a clear-cut line between" Boricua literature and "the national literature of Puerto Rico" (52).

Gordils's desire to append the diaspora's literature to the Puerto Rican canon resembles another article in this special ADE issue, Juan Flores's "Puerto Rican Literature in the United States: Stages and Perspectives."[6] This essay opens with a polemic about why U.S. students and scholars should read the Puerto Rican canon, then eventually segues into a discussion of Nuyorican writing as a liminal creature that retains its association to Puerto Rico's national literature and, by extension, to Latin American literary concerns. "In fact, it is Nuyorican literature's position straddling two national literatures and hemispheric perspectives that most significantly distinguishes it among the American minority literatures" (39). Yet, like Gordils, the evidence Flores offers of this "straddling" effect is primarily the work of insular authors who have, again, exploited the Boricua experience as thematic material. While Flores is highly critical of this insular appropriation, and distinguishes it as "a literature *about* Puerto Ricans in the United States rather than *of* that community" (42), still the bulk of his article concerns these and other outsider perspectives.

Flores and Gordils both intimate that there is a distinct body of mainland Puerto Rican literature, produced under a unique set of colonial diasporan circumstances and absent in or marginalized by both the Puerto Rican and the U.S. literary canons. Thus, the question arises: should the field of Boricua literature be annexed by the Puerto Rican canon and, if so, why this colonization in reverse? Flores's closing argument may offer some hints. Coming full circle to his opening polemic, Flores's conclusion articulates what seems to be less a concern with the diaspora's literary "stages" and "perspectives" than an explicit anxiety over protecting the status of Puerto Rico's national canon: "Despite the sharp disconnections between Island- and United States–based traditions, and between stages of the literary history here, it is still necessary to talk about modern Puerto Rican literature as a whole and of the emigrant literature—including the Nuyorican—as an extension or manifestation of that national literature. . . . After all, if Tato Laviera and Nicholasa Mohr are eligible for canonical status [in the States], why not José Luis González or Julia de Burgos, or, for that matter, Manuel Zeno Gandía, the author of the great Puerto Rican novel *La charca*?" (44).

Thus, expressing solidarity with the islands' national literary project by proposing its inclusion in the U.S. canon is the article's ultimate, if paradoxical, concern. This also entails narrating Boricua literature as a mere "extension or manifestation" of the Puerto Rican canon, despite the obvious and profound differences between these two literary histories.

But why is the anxiety over the Puerto Rican canon's relative obscurity triggered by the fact that black and women writers from the diaspora's working class, such as Laviera and Mohr, are garnering a legitimate place, albeit in the wings, on the stage of American letters? Flores's rationale for including insular "greats" like Manuel Zeno Gandía in the American canon is that their work would serve to mitigate the narrow nationalist and ethnocentric tendencies of this canon. Yet, if the goal is genuine sensitivity to and appreciation of writers from marginalized communities, would merging Boricua literature into the Puerto Rican national canon, then merging this canon into the U.S. national canon, really level the playing field for those from underrepresented groups in *either* national context? This is an especially pressing question where Boricua authors are concerned, since, as Flores and Gordils agree, they constitute one of the most under- and misrepresented groups in *both* the Puerto Rican *and* the U.S. literary traditions.

Given the neglect of Boricua literature in both national canons, alongside the habitual expulsion of Boricuas from both national identities, we might well argue that tethering Boricua literature to either "Puerto Rico" or "America" as acts of nationalist signification simply does not serve the best interests of Boricua literary scholarship. Clearly, the work of Boricua writers and cultural intellectuals is an equally valuable and vulnerable legacy that is routinely highjacked and/or disappeared on either side of the San Juan–New York divide. Reclaiming Boricua literature therefore means attending to this perpetual sequestration and invisibility in a context of forced exile from *dual* national identities and nationalist intellectual traditions. More important, however, it also means tracking and analyzing the diaspora's unique tradition of contiguous dissent and self-articulation, speaking not only of or about but *with* a community facing its own specific challenges in its own creatively stylized and politicized ways. For Boricua literary historians, this further entails the invention of a preliminary frame of reference that helps historicize Boricua narrative experimentation in its unique moments and milieus.

Flores's article proposes that the mainland Puerto Rican community's oldest extant literature will be found among an early migratory circuit of island-based intellectuals agitating for independence, such as Ramón Emeterio Betances and Eugenio María de Hostos, who spent time in New York as political exiles in the mid- to late nineteenth century. But while the travel writings of these figures may be extremely important for Puerto Rican literary and social historians, *Boricua* cultural intellectual history does not begin with these bourgeois revolutionaries' intellectual activities and sojourns in the United States. Rather, the first chapter of Boricua social and literary history begins at the turn of the twentieth century with the nomadic trek of humble exiles and activists jettisoned to New York after their involvement in Puerto Rico's more popular social movements of the 1890s. Many of these migrants were fairly young (in their late teens, twenties, or early thirties), highly politicized, usually underemployed, and keenly autodidactic; among them were Bernardo Vega, Jesús Colón, Arturo Schomburg, and Luisa Capetillo. All four of these figures left behind significant bodies of published work and archival materials attesting to the specific struggles and achievements of the first working-class emigrant enclave in New York City, a community defined in its literature by radical and mutually implicated aesthetic and political agendas. But while Vega's *Memorias* and Colón's *A Puerto Rican in New York*[7] have been reclaimed, republished, and taught by Puerto Rican scholars and educators as the pioneer emigrant generation's most representative texts, Schomburg and Capetillo have been all but completely ignored[8]

No doubt this elision is related to how both Schomburg and Capetillo struggled *within* the Puerto Rican and Cuban nationalist organizations of their time.[9] In this political engagement, Schomburg refused the tendency to put aside questions of internalized and structural racism in the Caribbean and its diasporas, and Capetillo insisted on the eradication of sexism as the sine qua non of genuinely revolutionary praxis.[10] Their work consequently attests to inner contradictions that would mitigate the arguably heroic masculinist-nationalist fabrication of Boricua social and literary history as an insular postscript.[11] And it is precisely this mitigation, this elaborate and elaborated threat *from below* to sacrosanct narratives of national and nationalist signification—not only of Puerto Rico but of the United States as well—that distinguishes their work as the earliest extant corpus to critically speak from, with, and of the

Boricua community. The fin-de-siècle working-class migrant generation's most avant-garde texts, therefore, in this critic's assessment, comprise the foundational narrative enterprise of Boricua literary history.

This essay proposes Luisa Capetillo, an anarcho-feminist effectively exiled to the New York Boricua community, as one of the earliest and most pivotal Boricua literary figures. The works Capetillo produced as an exile from Puerto Rico during a time of tremendous political upheaval, along with the work of this entire pioneer generation, should be read in light of the islands' pre- and post-1898 military regimes—first the Spanish, then, with the support of the insular elite, the United States—under which the very act of writing was, for working-class women and men of color, a highly subversive tactic. Describing this repressive ambient in Puerto Rico at the turn of the century, Julio Ramos explains that

> la escritura—en el sentido amplio, que incluye, más allá de la literatura, la administración misma de las leyes y los discursos estatales—era un dispositivo de control y subordinación social. . . . la escritura—más que un simple marcador del prestigio de los sujetos—era una tecnología . . . que posibilitaba la administración de la vida pública y que decidía, en el campo de la producción "simbólica" y cultural, la legitimidad de cualquier discurso con expectativas de representatividad y hegemonía.[12]
> [writing—in the broadest sense of the word, which in addition to literature includes the administration of state laws and discourses—was a mechanism of social control and subordination. . . . writing—more than a simple marker of subjects' prestige—was a technology . . . that made it possible to administrate public life and, in the field of "symbolic" and cultural production, to decide the legitimacy of any and all discourses that aspired to be representational and hegemonic[13]

Ramos adds that the "entry" of Capetillo and other voices into the "technology" of Puerto Rican writing was difficult and usually dangerous. These subjects, who were part of a constituency that had never enjoyed any self-representational power in Puerto Rican history, forced themselves into the sociosymbolic fray, one of the "most jealously protected realms," where "power produced the fictions of its law."[14] Consequently, these discursive agitators often suffered reciprocal—though usually more literal—violence at the hands of both Spanish and American colonial authorities and their agents.

Ramos portrays Capetillo as a radicalized product of the period's anarchist movement in Puerto Rico, Cuba, and Ybor City (Florida), and his introduction to her work offers a sketch of the more specific movement among tobacco workers, focusing on their workshops' unique political and intellectual culture. But what are we to make of Capetillo's specific role as an anarcho-*feminist*, as a working-class woman vying for a position as a "new discursant" in this transnational context and in what she and her anarchist colleagues considered a *supra*national movement? As an audacious and committed woman activist and writer, Capetillo ultimately found herself in the most peripheral and clearly dangerous discursive and physical spaces allotted her within the marginalized and imperiled workers' movement. This plight ultimately compelled her to leave the islands, after being harassed by both colonial regimes in Puerto Rico and becoming discontented with the workers' movement, which quickly transformed into a quasi-nationalist mobilization after 1898. Capetillo, with her demonstrated commitment to radical anarchist and feminist ideals, did not fit the part scripted for her in this emergent nationalist drama; or perhaps more accurately, despite proving the strength of her convictions in Puerto Rico's highly politicized field of discursive and institutional struggle, she was exploited, then ejected, by the islands' hegemonic and counterhegemonic technologies, which were owned and operated by opposing groups of men whose exclusive interests, she argued, were negotiated vis-à-vis these technologies. And as she moved farther away from this dangerous locus of utter discomfiture and contradiction, her life and work became more and more emblematic of the working-class experience of exile and political reengagement in the United States.

Capetillo was scandalously anomalous for her times, not merely as an anarchist but as a very well educated working-class Puerto Rican woman. Luisa Capetillo Perón was born in 1879 in Arecibo, Puerto Rico.[15] Her mother, Margarita Perón—a French national, probably from another Caribbean colony—apparently migrated to Puerto Rico as a young woman. Perón worked for one of Arecibo's wealthier families, first as a governess and later as a laundress. Capetillo's father, Luis Capetillo, was a Spanish immigrant worker who also settled in Arecibo.

According to Capetillo's biographer, Margarita frequented a neighborhood café called *La Misisipí* (The Mississippi) and was the only female participant in the *tertulias* (group discussions) that were regularly held there. Margarita Perón had a reputation for her liberal views and congenial temperament, characteristics that Luisa eulogized in the dedication to her penultimate text.

Capetillo's parents were autodidacts whose education was stimulated within the progressive circles of Puerto Rico's fledgling socialist movement. Luisa was their only child and although education was scarcely available at that time to women—and even less readily available to working-class children—her parents gave her a rather extensive education, primarily at home. Luis and Margarita were determined to nurture Luisa's intellectual growth. Although it seems that insular Puerto Rican literature was not part of this project, they had a library that included texts of literary vanguards in Russia, France, England, and the United States. Luisa read the work of Tolstoy, Hugo, Zola, Turgenev, Kropotkin, and Mill, among others. She learned French from her mother, while her father taught her the basics of reading, writing, and mathematics in Spanish.

Beyond this rather rough sketch, we know very little about Capetillo's childhood and adolescence. By her eighteenth birthday in 1897, Capetillo's father had apparently abandoned the family, and she had become involved in an amorous relationship with the son of her mother's employers; between 1898 and 1900 Luisa gave birth to two children, but soon afterward the couple separated.[16]

To support herself and her children, Capetillo became a garment worker in 1905. As early as 1904 she was writing newspaper articles in Arecibo.[17] In 1906 she began her post as a *lectora* (reader) in one of Arecibo's tobacco workshops. These kinds of "readings" were common in Puerto Rico, particularly among tobacco workers; for a minimal fee, designated readers would provide workers with the latest news and fiction in circulation—usually materials related to current events and socialist politics—by reading out loud and facilitating discussions while the employees had their hands and eyes occupied with the day's labor.[18] Finally, according to her biographer, Capetillo formally joined the Federación Libre de Trabajadores's (FLT) Arecibo organization in 1907.[19]

For women workers at the turn of the twentieth century, both on the islands and in the States, the practice of reading aloud in workshops provided a rare educational opportunity. Only a few critics have discussed the ways Puerto Rican women, who were also a significant part of the tobacco industry's workforce (not to mention the workers' movement overall), took advantage of this type of education.[20] Although Capetillo's early and extremely liberal studies at home certainly set her apart from most working-class women of her time, her coming to consciousness as a political activist and her subsequent literary contributions began with her post as a workshop reader. Her contributions may therefore provide an important inroad for understanding the specifically feminine concerns of her epoch.

My primary interest here is to analyze Capetillo's last surviving collection, *Influencias de las ideas modernas* (The Influences of Modern Ideas), published in 1916, which includes most of her fiction and experimental prose. This text also contains her ultimate thoughts on feminism, anarchism, and other related topics and was written primarily during her stays in the United States, beginning around 1912. But in order to make sense of her work at that juncture, I will begin with her literary career in Puerto Rico.

All of Capetillo's earlier texts reflect her formative involvement as an anarchist organizer and agitator. These texts, published between 1907 and 1911, pivot around three major issues: an outline of daily practice for women; the course of current politics, primarily the socialist agenda in Puerto Rico; and the development of a global workers' social movement. Her early work demonstrates how Capetillo analyzed and promoted the anarchist project in light of Puerto Rico's specific structures of social inequalities, especially those that contravened working-class Puerto Rican women's basic human dignity and rights. While crafting her ideas in these texts, Capetillo critiques a number of deeply entrenched institutions, especially the Catholic Church and, more emphatically, what she argues is the morally corrupt dogma promulgated by Christian institutions. She also offers numerous critical examples of the corruption of the elite classes and works through the complexities of working-class oppression and resistance, all the while critically engaging the political discourses of her time.

In her earlier texts, Capetillo's explication of a liberatory daily practice for women is like a spider's web; her diverse observations, commentaries, and polemics concerning the plight of working-class Puerto Rican women take irregular shape, but as she weaves them together, a single overall pattern becomes clear. Within this web, Capetillo captures for critique the most emblematic scenes of women's everyday life. We have no record of how she engaged her audience in her public speeches, but we can assume that the performative moment would have added an even more sprawling dimension to her analytical method.

The stylization of this method, which evolves in her later writing, is rudimentary in her first collection, *Ensayos libertarios* (Libertarian Essays).[21] At this early moment in her development as a social critic, Capetillo insists that people are good by nature but that this goodness is slowly but surely tainted by the imposition of nationalist and other bourgeois- or elite-identified structures of thought. Long before Althusser would garner credit for calling our attention to "ideological state apparatuses,"[22] Capetillo, in solid anarchist form, was already interpreting the maintenance of state-sponsored ideologies in commonsense attitudes and daily practices. Progressive education, in Capetillo's analysis, provides the best antidote to this manipulation of human will, since it can help working-class women identify and evaluate for themselves the belief systems and everyday customs that can otherwise coerce them into compliance with an oppressive social order and sexist culture. For Capetillo, the basis of this education should be philosophically grounded in liberatory Christianity—her rendition of an alternative conceptual space for elaborating a new feminist theory—which she references in exhorting even privileged women to change their ways:

> [El bien] no consiste en . . . dar ropa gastada, teniendo escaparetes repletos de lujosos trajes, como si hubieran algunos con más derechos a usar trajes nuevos y lujosos. Se me dirá: que los trabajen si los desean iguales. Continuamente están trabajando y continúan rotos, descalzos y hambrientos. ¿Y acaso trabajan las esposas e hijos de los explotadores? ¿Se llaman cristianos? ¿Dónde están las prácticas? hechos y no fórmulas. ¿Dónde el desinterés y abnegación por el prójimo? entonces ¿qué derecho tienen á llamarse cristianos, si son vanidosos, indolentes, egoístas, indiferentes y soberbios? Son vanidosos, porque nada hacen oculto; todo con la trompeta del anuncio y el halago; por eso hacen caridad o algún bien mal hecho al prójimo.
>
> Son indolentes, porque para todo tienen un ser humano para todos sus caprichos y no la hacen por sí mismos.
>
> Egoístas e indiferentes, porque luego de cubrir sus necesidades y vicios, no creen a los demás con derecho para hacerlo y tratan de mermar el mezquino

salario de sus sirvientes, y guardan todas las monedas que pueden, siéndole indiferente que sus hermanos, sirvientes, estén descalzos y duerman en el suelo; y se llaman cristianos.[23]

[[Goodness] does not consist . . . of giving away worn-out clothes, while keeping closets full of extravagant outfits, as if some people were more entitled to wear new and luxurious clothes. You will tell me, "let them work for it if they want such nice clothes." But they are continually working and yet continue to dress in torn clothes, to go barefoot and hungry. And do you think that the exploiters' wives and children work? And they call themselves Christians? Where are the daily practices, in deeds not formulas? Where's their selflessness and abnegation when their fellow human beings are concerned? By what right do they call themselves Christians, if they are vain, lazy, selfish, indifferent, and arrogant? They are vain, because they do nothing [good] in secret; everything they do is heralded with announcements and self-flattery—that's why they do charity work or some good deed, poorly, for their fellow humanity.

They are lazy, because they keep other human beings around for their caprices, and don't do a thing for themselves.

They are egotistical and indifferent, because after taking care of their own needs and vices, they don't believe that others have the right to do the same thing, and they try to lower their servants' measly salaries, and they hoard all the coins they can, feeling indifferent to the fact that their brothers and sisters, their servants, are barefoot and sleep on the floor; and they call themselves Christians.]

Not uncoincidentally, Puerto Rico's first published working-class feminist is also the first to insist on elaborating class divisions between women, which she argues are habitually rationalized in Puerto Rican culture. Capetillo was especially intolerant of those women who feel entitled to their relative luxury while seeing others in their immediate vicinity—even women working long hours in their own homes—suffer for lack of the most basic necessities. It is likely that her childhood experiences growing up as the daughter of a domestic servant of one of Arecibo's wealthiest families galvanized the indignation of her first published text. In this passage, Capetillo analyzes emblematic, everyday signs of more general inequalities between women. Shuttling between ruling-class privilege and working-class deprivations, while analyzing the most basic material and communicative contradictions they entail,

Capetillo depicts the broad outlines of social stratification without ever losing sight of everyday reality. And like prose poetry, her clauses test and transgress the limits of standard grammar and syntax. Yet her paragraphs are forged together with a liturgical urgency that makes each idea and phrase move confidently and logically into the next.

Ensayos libertarios, published in 1907, marks Capetillo's entry into the public scene of politics and includes work she wrote between 1904 and the date of publication. Her next text, *La humanidad en el futuro* (Humanity's Future), published in 1910, is a hastily prepared monograph exploring an ideal society. Her third work, *Mi opinión: Sobre las libertades, derechos y deberes de la mujer como compañera, madre y ser independiente* (My Opinion: Concerning Women's Liberties, Rights and Duties as Partners, Mothers and Independent Beings), published on the eve of her exile to the United States in 1911, is a wide-ranging exploration of the female condition.[24]

Mi opinión is introduced in the preface as a humble effort to illustrate how, in Capetillo's words, "Desire is power!" (¡Querer es poder!) (vii). The preface concludes with the premise that "the present social system, with all of its errors, is sustained by ignorance and the enslavement of women" (El actual sistema social, con todos sus errores, se sostiene, por la ignorancia y la esclavitud de la mujer) (viii). Capetillo furthers this compelling argument in the opening selection, "La mujer en el hogar, en la familia, en el gobierno" (Women in the Home, in the Family, in Government). This essay proclaims marriage the most culpable ritual in the perpetuation of women's bondage and urges women to reconceptualize love in ways that make desire a productive force in their lives rather than a naturalized obligation—sanctioned, codified, and enforced by the institutions of formal and common-law marriage—that reduces them to objects of exchange between men.

Subsequent pieces in *Mi opinión* include an edited translation of French anarchist Madeleine Vernet's essay "L'amour libre" (Free Love). One of the segments Capetillo emphasized in her representation of Vernet's original argues that depriving a woman of sexual pleasure is a deformation of her spiritual, physical, mental, and moral well-being; in fact, it means robbing her of a full fourth of her very existence and can actually kill her (43–44). In tandem with this reading of the quintessential necessity for women's sexual liberation *and* satisfaction, this essay also avers that women must learn to make the necessary distinctions between marriage, love, and sexual desire:

> He dicho al principio que no debe confundirse el amor con el matrimonio. Pues bien; antes de salir del terreno fisiológico iré más lejos, y diré que no debe confundirse el amor con el deseo.
>
> El amor es la comunión completa de dos cerebros, de dos corazones, de dos sensualidades. El deseo no es más que el capricho de dos seres que una misma voluptuosidad reune. Nada es tan pasajero que ó poco estable como el deseo; no obstante, ninguno de nosotros se escapa de él. . . .
>
> Nosotros no podemos ser dueños del deseo carnal, como tampoco lo podemos ser de la tiranía de nuestro estómago. Los dos son inherentes a nuestro ser físico; ellos son el resultado de dos necesitades naturales y también legítimas así la una como la otra. (44–45)
>
> [At the beginning I said that love shouldn't be confused with marriage. Well, enough said; but before I finish with the topic of physiology, I'll take it one step further and say that love and desire should not be confused either.
>
> Love is the complete communion of two minds, of two hearts, of two sensualities. Desire is nothing more than the whim of two beings united by the same voluptuousness. Nothing is as ephemeral or as unstable as desire; yet no one can escape it. . . .
>
> We cannot control carnal desire, just as we cannot control the tyranny of our stomachs. Both are inherent to our physical being; they are the result of natural necessities, and one is as legitimate as the other.]

Furthermore, it seems that anarcho-feminists were pressed not only to insist on sexual equality among their male peers but also to quell fears that it would foster some sort of hedonistic epidemic among women. In response to these fears, this article proposes that more sexually active women *should* be able to explore their pleasure without social censure, while the less erotically inclined should likewise be free to remain abstinent when and if they like:

> La libertad en amor así para la mujer como para el hombre, no es más que una gran justicia. Eso no forzará nunca a las "frías" a ser apasionadas, pero permitirá á las apasionadas no sufrir más la cautividad de leyes convencionales y sociales. (44)

[Free love for women as well as men is simply and purely justice. It would never force "frigid" women to be passionate, but it would free passionate women from their suffering under conventional and social laws.]

Thus, the anarcho-feminist agenda promoted freedom of choice for women in the most intimate aspect of their lives, though, in a sort of playful and sarcastic tone, the article also contends that "there is absolutely no doubt that if woman lived normally, if she weren't deformed by the physical and moral contract, the number of 'frigid' women would be greatly reduced" (no hay ninguna duda que si la mujer viviese normalmente, que si no hubiese sido también deformada por la contrata física y moral, el número de mujeres "frías" sería muy reducido) (43–44).

Other pieces Capetillo included in this collection contest the common contradictions bearing on women's lives and urge women to take control of their public and domestic situations by exhorting them to demand their "natural" rights in everyday life as well as the sociosymbolic order. Building from the basic premise that the oppression of women is at the root of all oppressions, the individual pieces that Capetillo published in *Mi opinión* elaborate the more general argument that sexual sovereignty for both women and men is the necessary first step for any genuine social revolution.

For Capetillo, the anarcho-syndicalist agenda seemed to offer the best blueprint for revolutionary action, and we see in her first texts a tremendous faith in the ideals of Puerto Rico's anarchist movement and the Federación Libre de Trabajadores (FLT) in particular. Yet her work suggests that she was under constant attack for her radical anarcho-feminist perspective. Already in *Mi opinión*, Capetillo is speaking as if she assumes her audience will be skeptical and outright dismissive of her ideas. She directly confronts her detractors in the opening lines of the book's preface:

Al publicar estas opiniones, lo hago sin pretender, recojer elogios, ni glorias, ni aplausos. Sin preocuparme de la crítica de los escritores de experiencia.

El único móvil que me impulsa a dar a la publicidad este tomo, es decir la verdad; la cual, aún aquellos que están en mejores condiciones y con más talento para decirlo no lo hacen. ¿Por qué? Por susceptibilidades de opinión, por no apoyar conceptos de una idea, cuya doctrina, la consideran utópica. Ese modo de juzgar no es suficiente para no publicar las verdades que encierra. (v)

[I publish these opinions without expecting to receive praise, glory, or applause. Without worrying myself with the criticisms of experienced writers.

The only thing compelling me to promote this book is telling the truth; which others with more resources and talent do not tell. Why? Because they are sensitive to public opinion, because they won't support the concepts of an idea whose doctrine they consider utopian. This kind of judgmental thinking is hardly grounds for not publishing the truth all around us.]

She argues that these so-called utopian projects are, in her opinion, as realistic as any nascent venture. She also condemns the politicos of her time as a self-interested and unenlightened bunch. In her words:

Los que vivían y viven de la ignorancia del pueblo trabajador, ¿Dijeron la verdad? ¡No, falsearon los hechos, calumniaron a sus apóstoles! ¿Qué conceptos tenemos de los que se oponen a todas las ideas de igualdad y libertad humana? . . . Todos los que juzgan una idea llevada a la práctica, utópica, son obstáculos, y los obstáculos deben empujarse a un lado. Son los que entorpecen las grandes iniciativas, las obras de bien. Y aun así, se llaman patriotas y padres de la patria.

¿Qué concepto de la patria tendrán? Un concepto egoísta, que empieza en ellos y termina en ellos. Ellos lo son todos. (vi)

[Those who lived and live off the ignorance of the working-class community; have they ever told the truth? No, they lied about events and slandered the community's apostles! What concept should we have of those who oppose every idea of equality and human liberty? . . . All those who pass judgment against putting a utopian idea into practice are obstacles, and obstacles should be shoved aside. Such men obstruct great initiatives, the works toward the common good. And still, these men call themselves patriots and the nation's fathers.

What conception will they have of the nation? A conceited conception, which begins and ends in them. All of them are like this.]

From around 1910 on, Capetillo perpetually argued that Puerto Rico's self-appointed "patriots" were frauds, and she never ceased to condemn what she considered the opportunistic and misinformed maneuvers of both Puerto Rico's political elite and the socialist leadership. We do not have a clear idea of how her polemics were received or who precisely posed as her antagonists. Perhaps comments such as the above would have resonated with men like Manuel Zeno Gandía, who was elected legislative representative of Arecibo, Luisa's hometown, shortly after he helped negotiate the U.S. invasion. Or perhaps she was alluding to Santiago Iglesias and his retinue, the exclusively male leadership of the FLT. Bernardo Vega reports a heated debate in the New York community, spurred by a polemic in which Luisa Capetillo participated, citing her argument that "tyranny, like liberty, has no fatherland, just as workers and exploiters have none" (la tiranía, como la libertad, no tiene patria, como tampoco la tienen los explotadores ni los trabajadores) (134–135).

What we do know is that Capetillo was clearly under attack in all these circles simultaneously because of her public, anarcho-feminist critique of nationalism. Politically, it seems she was caught between the proverbial rock and a hard place. To the right, many of those within Puerto Rico's propertied and professional classes were actively supporting U.S. rule on the islands. To the left, the anarchist leadership made a series of concessions after the U.S. invasion, particularly with the various national parties that were preparing themselves for the autonomy promised but never granted by the U.S. government. They also negotiated formal ties with the American Federation of Labor (AFL), under the leadership of Samuel Gompers.[25] All of these gestures toward becoming part of the insular institutional apparatus and the most centrist U.S. labor union of the time arguably compromised the anarchist tenets that had once made the FLT so appealing to Puerto Rican workers. The significance of these maneuvers was not lost on Capetillo and the organization's membership at large,[26] and also ignited the major debate among Boricua workers in New York City in which Capetillo participated.[27]

Like the other figures of the *pionero* generation, Capetillo never lost faith in Puerto Rico's working-class causes, despite the Far Left's political mistakes and compromises in the wake of the Spanish-American War. She continued her work with the FLT, however, amid a serious crisis in the anarchist movement.

Under pressure, the FLT leadership justified its bids to form official ties with the islands' paranational political parties and the AFL as inevitable steps, given what they assumed was Puerto Rico's imminent independence. But by 1908, two local elections had been held on the islands affirming the populace's desire for national sovereignty, and neither was recognized by the U.S. Congress as a legitimate "democratic" vote. Finally aware that the Puerto Rican people had been duped by the empty promises of the U.S. government, the FLT decided to redefine the organization's platform in an effort to reconcile its original anarchist program of action with its new syndicalist agenda, targeting two internal priorities: (1) propagating union organization and (2) promoting working-class solidarity via the development of an alternative proletarian culture.[28] The new platform's second project reaffirmed the early anarchist program, which fully rejected party politics and institutional reform and opted instead for educating and supporting workers in projects they designed and implemented for themselves, especially cooperatives and mutual aid societies. As part of the new program of action, the FLT launched the "Cruzada del Ideal" (Crusade of the Ideal), delegating worker "crusaders" to agitate and educate other workers on the concepts of a new, socialist world order in which, in the words of a writer well circulated among Puerto Rican anarchists, "each individual is a producer of both manual and intellectual work."[29] In what seemed a perfect project for her at the time, Capetillo joined the ranks of the Crusaders in 1909.

Working in the Cruzada should have been invigorating for Capetillo, whose education and idealism, after all, resonated with the program's timbre. The texts and ideas in circulation that were discussed and evaluated by Puerto Rican workers in their workshops and during the events sponsored by the Crusaders and the FLT came from all over the world. Anarchist newspapers and pamphlets arrived from places like Brazil, Panama, Argentina, and of course Spain, while some of the most popular polemics and novels were translations from Russian and French, such as the work of Tolstoy, Bakunin, Chernyshevsky, Zola, Diderot, and Balzac, with which Capetillo was already familiar. But despite this seemingly perfect match between her personal philosophies and political activities, Capetillo, again, became disillusioned and critical. Like so many of her contemporaries, she decided to leave Puerto Rico in the hope of finding better situations for her life and life's work in the United States.

This turning point in Capetillo's life—her disappointment with the vagaries of insular politics and politicos, her feeling of solitude as a working-class activist, and her self-imposed yet still politically forced exile—is what makes Capetillo such an important figure for understanding the dilemmas that the first avant-garde of Boricua writers and activists faced in their lives and explored in their work. Her engagements with broad revolutionary concepts like anarchism, socialism, and feminism had been, by this juncture in her life, tempered by her very personal recognition of their limits, not as discourses in and of themselves but rather as ideals that, in the translation into practice, were bogged down by too many real-life, real-time contradictions.

Capetillo's earlier published collections are self-conscious meditations focused primarily on the predicament of working-class women during the latest stage of Spanish colonialism and the earliest stage of U.S. colonialism and imperialism in the Caribbean. Her later narrative experiments, which she wrote mainly in the United States, evince her effort to elaborate in fiction her vision of the trajectories of her life and work as a political activist and theorist. In both phases of her writing, narrative devices of various genres provide her with a wide range of tools that she unapologetically manipulates (regardless of their conventional uses) to craft provocative new images, ideas, and social identities. Although Capetillo recognized the formidable challenge of constructing a conceptual landscape uninterrupted by sexual, class, and geopolitical borders, she never gave up hope in making this ideal a reality. In her last text, hope and love are foremost in her thought as she reaffirms the imperative of social revolution in the fullest and necessarily *creative* sense.

If we use the standard Euro-American literary historical categories, we can only describe Capetillo's final work, *Influencias de las ideas modernas*, as a naïvely postmodern piece, anachronistically published during Latin and North America's modernist periods.[30] But although her experimental prose challenges the limits of traditional generic structure and metanarrative conventions—two of the commonly definitive characteristics of postmodern literary expression—the postmodern label does not really fit the context or content of Capetillo's work. Fredric Jameson's reading of postmodern pastiche, for example, as "blank parody, a statue with blind eyeballs," converts it into a "neutral practice" of parody, a "blank irony" that is "devoid of laughter and of any conviction."[31] But the pastiche effect of Capetillo's final text is not an experiment in emptying aesthetic form of life and humor, nor is her tone plagued with the exasperated despair or cynical pleasure of finding the parts not fitting the whole. Rather, her writing is inspired by, and saturated with, a political and philosophical conviction that serves as its textual and extratextual logic. Furthermore, though we might read Capetillo's work as a particular type of poetic bricolage or rearrangement, the fragmentation and disjuncture of her text may also be simply due to the fact that a working-class woman of her times may not have had the luxury of revising and editing, of composing longer, more integrated narratives, or the resources (including editorial support) for publishing more extensive and polished volumes of prose.

Influencias de las ideas modernas, which includes plays, letters, journal entries, short stories, and a number of genre-defying fictional and quasi-fictional pieces, was composed primarily in New York City and Ybor City, Florida, during 1912–1916, although the title play was composed in Puerto Rico in 1907. Three years after beginning her work in the Cruzada, publishing in the magazine *Unión Obrera* (Workers' Union), and founding a feminist magazine, Capetillo traveled to the continental United States in 1912 to continue her work within the *colonias*, or settlements, of the Puerto Rican diaspora. Like Lola Rodríguez de Tío, who traveled to New York City in 1903 despairing over the situation in Puerto Rico,[32] Capetillo arrived in New York despondent but hopeful of gathering new strength and support in the Puerto Rican communities stateside. But it seems Capetillo was confronted with a whole new set of challenges to her radical beliefs and agenda among her peers in the United States. And as the situation became more hostile, Capetillo's anarcho-feminism became more adamant.

As all her work insists, the status quo in *Influencias* is represented as an intolerably backward affair. The appearance of things almost always masks an ugly truth, and unequal relations of power are both source and symptom of this masquerade. A decade before Gramsci would compose his prison notebooks, Capetillo is already writing of the inversion of reality via discourses that continually reproduce themselves in everyday life. In *Influencias* she applies this analysis of language and hegemony to the issue of political opportunism; crucially, the budding socialist organizations of her time were not immune to this critique.

Moreover, Capetillo's reading of power relations is vehemently positivist, which, in the best of the humanist tradition, often appears as the most natural expression of common sense. Words and concepts have essential meanings, according to Capetillo, and human usage of language—not language itself—is imprecise. We see this taken to near Neoplatonic proportions in *Influencias*. For example, Capetillo avers that a corrupt politician is an oxymoron, because politicians by definition should be naturally disinclined to corruption (54–55). The established codes of licit and illicit behavior in this text are also suspect. In Capetillo's reading, the only differences between an entrepreneur and a petty thief are the scenes of their crimes and the clothes they wear; the petty thief being, by all rights, the more socially acceptable of the two (54). In a similar semantic twist, the term "civilization" is convoluted in popular usage; Capetillo argues that the adjective "civilized" in reality signifies the ways Westerners use fashion to mask their inattention to hygiene, while the so-called barbarian races do not need hats, breath mints, and fancy overclothes, for their hair is habitually clean, they consume healthy food, and they need not hide dirty underclothes beneath expensive suits (96). Finally, what passes as "humanitarianism" in North America, it turns out, is not really so humane: Capetillo calls our attention to the fact that, while there were organizations to protect the rights of animals, no one seemed to have an interest in the welfare of the most vulnerable constituencies of human society, such as children, the elderly, and the sick (60).

This method of essentializing concepts, which Capetillo grounds in poetic renditions of "Nature" as the originary and benevolent referent, is a common device in nineteenth-century Euro-American romantic realism and certain strains of modernism. But the crucial difference in Capetillo's narratives, which she perhaps shares with some Latin American and Iberian modernist tendencies, is the constant imperative of literally returning to some semblance of the "natural order" by explicitly calling for revolutionary practice. And it is here precisely, as she narrates an anarcho-feminist outline for the practice of everyday life, that her writing undoes the binary logic that her essentialist method implies, because she derives her theory from the scene of practice, despite her positivist impulses. She cannot help but de-essentialize and de-romanticize social constructs, because her feminist and anarchist convictions require that she dwell on the very seams of the binary split between theory and practice; as she dwells on these overlapping edges, the contradictions, ambiguities, and other complications become apparent, even glaring. In fact, in Capetillo's daily life, every choice—from what she ate to what she wore—was loaded with political significance. Like her suits, the trappings Capetillo borrows from the Occidental tradition do not quite fit; the gendered politics of Capetillo's cross-dressing strategy—wearing clothes cut for men over a woman's body—might also be a useful metaphor for describing her scandalously inappropriate appropriation of patriarchal structures of thought and modes of writing. What may seem awkward at first glance may instead suggest a specifically feminine *escritura*, a highly complex articulation of gendered ambivalence that questions the very concept of male/female polarities and, with it, the binary logic endemic to the positivist tradition.

This cross-dressing effect is most clearly marked in her discussion of feminist practice in *Influencias*. Here, Capetillo clearly wants to base her ideas about gender in biology, or the most natural of the natural sciences, but her analyses ultimately overflow the biological concepts she borrows or invents. For example, in a fascinating section entitled "Cartas interesantes de un ácrata de Panama" (Interesting Letters from a Panamanian Anarchist), Capetillo includes a series of letters written to her from a Panamanian admirer, omitting her side of the correspondence. The anarchist's letters are reprinted in chronological order, and it is clear that Capetillo's side of the correspondence was friendly but argumentative. Yet since her letters are absent, the reader must guess what Capetillo's responses entailed. The Panamanian's letters subtly suggest Capetillo's critique of his positions, particularly his cynicism and his varied but problematic takes on feminism. One of his letters, for example, states that women should always be treated gently because tension causes their chest muscles to contract, which can damage their ability to lactate properly (149). Judging by his next letter, Capetillo had written him to say how bitter she had become because no one seemed to understand what she really meant to say; presumably, as his opinions in the previous letter insinuate, her Panamanian comrade was not much of an exception (149–150).

Capetillo's positions on feminism likewise begin to unfix themselves from their essentialist underpinnings in her final text. Sexuality in *Influencias* is no longer represented as a specifically male/female concern; she now characterizes love with terms that are not gender specific, such as the union of "beings" (*seres*), "souls" (*almas*), and "bodies" (*cuerpos*) (65–67). Likewise, the almost-constant conflation of womanhood with motherhood in her earlier work begins to subside in *Influencias*. Capetillo argues at one point that to be "complete" (*mujer completa*) a woman must have children, but then undercuts this claim by stating that all women are mothers, regardless of whether they literally bear children (65, 86).

Overall, *Influencias* tests the limits of romantic and modernist discourses of nature, finding them inadequate to the task of revolutionary feminist theory, fiction, and practice. When Capetillo returns to the issue of feminism, she does so by rejecting any and all formulas for behavior, dress, sexual practice, and love. Midway through the text, for example, she includes a dialogue on the *qué dirán* syndrome[33], exploring what others say about Elena, a woman they see getting into a car with a man named Andrés.[43] Elena and Andrés are attracted to each other and rather rationally decide to spend an afternoon together exploring the options of carnal desire and romance. A pair of *curiosos* (busybodies) are watching the action and discuss the implications of Elena's behavior. One of these voices keeps complaining that a woman should "belong" to one man only, while men have the right—indeed, the natural instinct—to pursue as many women as possible. The other busybody critiques this double standard, and they engage in a long, somewhat pedantic but amusing stichomythia. In the end, the *machista* (male supremacist) refuses to concede any ground in the argument, so he is dismissed by his friend with the words: "You are the representation of tyranny against women. See you later, liberator" (Ud. es la representación de la tiranía contra la mujer. Hasta otro día—Adiós libertador) (93). Meanwhile, Elena and Andrés drive off and make love in the open air, forging a lasting relationship free of coercion and matrimony, creating a happy ending to the story of Elena, who did what she thoughtfully pleased with her own body (94).

This freedom of form and movement, in terms of plot, generic experimentation, and political subtext, mirrors the significance of fiction itself in Capetillo's final work. *Influencias'* textual logic suggests that fiction became her last resort for exploring the revolutionary ideal, an ideal that her nonfictional writing and other projects had not apparently managed to articulate to her own satisfaction.

A certain innocent, sensuous desire is Capetillo's key vehicle for depicting this ideal in action. In *Influencias,* all of her stories' protagonists contest and transgress the social norms and mores that inhibit their most pristine filial, romantic, and erotic yearnings. Her first story, entitled "The Cashier," revises the usual nineteenth-century romantic realism of authors such as Charles Dickens, Charlotte Brontë, and Émile Zola by appropriating and critically reinventing the trope of the orphaned youth (105–113). This character, Ricardo, receives the disinterested help of a kind benefactor, who, pitying his plight, arranges and pays for his education. But unlike Jane Eyre, for example, who uses her mysteriously granted fortune to establish a bourgeois paradise, Ricardo is disgusted with his middle-class lifestyle and, successfully robbing a huge sum of money from his employers, runs off with the cash—and his beloved—to St. Petersburg. Another piece, a play aptly titled *The Corruption of the Rich and the Poor, or How to Prostitute a Rich and a Poor Woman*, opens with a young noblewoman engaged to a rich suitor against her emotional inclinations (167–196). On the eve of her marriage, she decides to elope with her true love and, in a very crafty way, sneaks off with the title to the land her mother left her as a dowry. In yet another play, *A Marriage without Love: Consequence—Adultery*, the heroine, Esmeralda, like Elena in the piece mentioned above, meets a handsome youth on the street while out shopping (171–178). Esmeralda's husband is a boring businessman who takes his young wife for granted. Rather than tolerate her loveless marriage, Esmeralda runs off with her lover. The adulterous consequence here is perfect happiness. In Esmeralda's terms, she needed "to feel that natural and spontaneous feeling that makes you feel delirious, that makes you commit the grandest insanities" (sentir ese natural y expontáneo sentimiento que hace sentir el delirio, cometer las mayores locuras), all of which her husband cannot inspire (173). Unlike Tolstoy's hapless Anna Karenina, as well as many other tragic heroines in nineteenth- and even twentieth-century literature, Capetillo's adulteresses live happily ever after.

In all of these stories, Capetillo devises ways for the revolutionary desires of women and men to break free from socially enforced psychological constraints and the miserable entailments of capital accumulation. In the pursuit of love and the fulfillment of sexual desire, Capetillo's characters literally run off from the scenes of their oppression, and her stories close with the blurring trails of their escape.

Unfortunately, Capetillo's literary career came to an end soon after she published her first collection of fiction in 1916. Just six years later, Capetillo died of tuberculosis. Unlike her characters, whose self-imposed exiles seem destined to end in bliss, Capetillo's new life in the United States caused her more trials, alienation, and disillusionment and ultimately exposed her to an incurable disease. She never ceased to struggle within the anarchist and socialist organizations of her time, but the tragic end to her own story forms a telling contrast to her literary characters'. She was buried in Río Piedras's municipal cemetery, after a humble service attended by a small group of her family and friends from the FLT, just a few miles away from the Ateneo Puertorriqueño, where eight years later the body of Manuel Zeno Gandía would lie in state, amid the glory of honor guards and an extravagant public funeral.[34] In critical response to her experiences in and between two national contexts, Capetillo wrote a wide spectrum of analyses of Puerto Rican women's oppressions, which ultimately called for them to win, protect, and enjoy, for themselves, in public and in private, what she considered their natural civil and sexual rights. Her legacy thus offers both testimony to the Boricua predicament at the initial moment of this community's formation in the wake of 1898 and a serious corpus of Boricua feminist public intellectual work extant among a tiny group of predominantly male peers. Like the work of Zora Neale Hurston and Phillis Wheatley, whose contributions to African American cultural intellectual history have been recuperated and duly appreciated, Luisa Capetillo's work is a major legacy, ripe for further study. Yet none of the four books Capetillo published has ever been reissued in its original Spanish or translated into English, few scholars have seriously broached her work in either Puerto Rican or American studies, and as a result her intellectual and literary legacies have languished in near-total obscurity.[35]

A radical anarcho-feminist may be the most apt foundational figure for a colonial diaspora's literary history. Indeed, Capetillo's intransigent rejection of geopolitical, gendered, erotic, philosophical, and generic borders as obsolete concepts suggests the kind of socially, ethically, sensually, and aesthetically engaged hermeneutics relevant to a community barred wealth and sociosymbolic status, in transit from one stifling national context to another. In this project, Capetillo was not alone. The entire first generation of Boricua writers were actively and consciously writing against the grain of what national literary canons conventionally imply as a concerted, celebratory expression of bourgeois sensibilities. These men and women were transnationalist agitators who labored in print and public to incite what they audaciously imagined as an impending social revolution, and in this, the very least of their concerns was writing the "Great American Novel." Recuperating Capetillo's

Influencias de las ideas modernas as the first major Boricua literary text thus points toward a politically contiguous recovery and analysis of Boricua cultural intellectual history.

NOTES

This essay is a chapter from Lisa Sánchez González's book *Boricua Literature: A Literary History of the Puerto Rican Diaspora* (New York: New York University Press, 2001). An earlier version, "Luisa Capetilla: An Anarcho-Feminist Pionera in the Mainland/Puerto Rican Narrative/Political Transition," was published in *Recovering the U.S. Hispanic Literary Heritage, Volume II* (1996), by Arte Público, which granted permission to reprint it here.

1. "Boricua" refers to the mainland Puerto Rican community.

2. Houston A. Baker Jr., "Critical Memory and the Black Public Sphere," in *The Black Public Sphere: A Public Culture Book*, ed. Black Public Sphere Collective (Chicago: University of Chicago Press, 1995), 35.

3. Mireya Navarro, "Puerto Rican Presence Wanes in New York: Falling Back; A Special Report," *New York Times*, 28 Feb. 2000, sec. A, 1 and 20.

4. Yanis Gordils, "Island and Continental Puerto Rican Literature: Cross-Cultural and Intertextual Considerations," *ADE Bulletin* 91 (Winter 1988): 52. Hereafter cited in text.

5. Tato Laviera, *La Carreta Made a U-Turn* (Gary, IN: Arte Público Press, 1979); Sandra María Esteves, "A Julia de Burgos," in *Yerba Buena: Dibujos y poemas*, Greenfield Review Chapbook 47 (Greenfield Center, NY: Greenfield Review Press, 1980).

6. Juan Flores, "Puerto Rican Literature in the United States: Stages and Perspectives," *ADE Bulletin* 91 (Winter 1988): 39–44. Hereafter cited in text.

7. Bernardo Vega, *Memorias de Bernardo Vega*, 4th ed., ed. César Andreu Iglesias (Río Piedras, PR: Ediciones Huracán, 1988); Jesús Colón, *A Puerto Rican in New York and Other Sketches*, 2d ed. (New York: International Publishers, 1982). Hereafter cited in text.

8. The most notable exceptions are Piñeiro de Rivera's anthology of Schomburg's essays and Ramos's anthology of selections from Capetillo's major work: Flor Piñero de Rivera, ed., *Arthur Alfonso Schomburg: A Puerto Rican's Quest for His Black Heritage* (San Juan: Centro de Estudios Avanzados de Puerto Rico y el Caribe, 1989); Julio Ramos, ed., *Amor y anarquía: Los escritos de Luisa Capetillo* (Río Piedras, PR: Ediciones Huracán, 1992).

9. Schomburg and Capetillo are fleetingly mentioned in Vega's *Memorias*, 88–89, 111–112, 120, 134–135.

10. Schomburg's legacy has been gathering more scholarly interest of late. For a take on his significance in Latino and African American studies, see Lisa Sánchez González, "Arturo Schomburg: A Transamerican Intellectual," in *African Roots/American Cultures:*

Africa in the Creation of the Americas, ed. Sheila Walker (Lanham, MD: Rowman and Littlefield, 2001), 139–152.

11. See, for example, Eugene Mohr's reading of Vega's *Memorias* as a heroic epic, in *The Nuyorican Experience: Literature of the Puerto Rican Minority* (Westport, CT: Greenwood Press, 1982), 3–23.

12. Ramos, *Amor y anarquía,* 15–16.

13. Unless otherwise noted, all translations are mine.

14. Ibid.

15. Capetillo's only biography is Norma Valle Ferrer, *Luisa Capetillo: Historia de una mujer proscrita* (San Juan: Editorial Cultural, 1990). Most of the biographical information here relies on this text and Ramos's chronology (*Amor y anarquía,* 65–66).

16. Valle Ferrer, *Luisa Capetillo,* 54.

17. Ramos, *Amor y anarquía,* 65.

18. For a detailed discussion of the practice of *lectores* in workshops, see ibid., 11–58.

19. Valle Ferrer, *Luisa Capetillo,* 131.

20. Yamila Azize Vargas, *La mujer en Puerto Rico: Ensayos de investigación* (Río Piedras, PR: Ediciones Huracán, 1987); Margarita Ostolazo Bey, *Política sexual en Puerto Rico* (Río Piedras, PR: Ediciones Huracán, 1989); Ivette Romero-Cesareo, "Whose Legacy? Voicing Women's Rights from the 1870's to the 1930's," *Callaloo* 17, no. 3 (1994): 770–789.

21. Luisa Capetillo Perón, *Ensayos libertarios* (Arecibo, PR: Imprenta Unión Obrera, 1907).

22. Louis Althusser, *Lenin and Philosophy and Other Essays,* trans. Ben Brewster (New York: Monthly Review Press, 1971), 127–186.

23. Capetillo, *Ensayos libertarios,* 6–7. Here and throughout my citations of Capetillo's work, I have corrected a few minor typographical errors, but I have deliberately refrained from standardizing her grammar.

24. Luisa Capetillo Perón, *Mi opinión: Sobre las libertades, derechos y deberes de la mujer como compañera, madre y ser independiente* (San Juan: Biblioteca Roja/The Times Publ., 1911). Hereafter cited in text.

25. For a full discussion, see Gervasio L. García and A. G. Quintero Rivera, *Desafío y solidaridad: Breve historia del movimiento obrero puertorriqueño* (Río Piedras, PR: Ediciones Huracán/CEREP, 1982), 33–41.

26. Igualdad Iglesias de Pagán suggests that the FLT leadership and its membership had been critical of the Autonomist movement as early as 1897; see her *El Obrerismo en Puerto Rico: Época de Santiago Iglesias (1896–1905)* (Palencia de Castilla, Spain: Ediciones Juan Ponce de León, 1973), 28.

27. Anarchist organizations in New York's Spanish-speaking community were an integral part of the city's political scene during the final decades of the nineteenth century. However, Bernardo Vega recollects that a group called La Resistencia was one of only a few of these organizations still intact after 1899, when the end of the Spanish-American War resulted in confusion and political disintegration among expatriate groups (107–109). Vega also mentions that a major controversy of the period was provoked by a speech

given by FLT leader Santiago Iglesias in Rochester, New York, which Arturo Schomburg and others attacked for its explicitly racist comparison of Puerto Rican and African American workers (111–112).

28. Garcia and Quintero Rivera, *Desafío y solidaridad*, 59.

29. Peter Kropotkin, *Fields, Factories, and Workshops* (1912; repr., New Brunswick, NJ: Transaction, 1993), 23.

30. Luisa Capetillo Perón, *Influencias de las ideas modernas* (San Juan: Tipografía Negrón Flores, 1916). Hereafter cited in text.

31. Fredric Jameson, *Postmodernism, or The Cultural Logic of Late Capitalism* (Durham, NC: Duke University Press, 1992), 17.

32. Vega, *Memorias*, 119–120.

33. *¿Qué dirán?* literally means "what will people say?"

34. Detailed in "Apuntes biográficos" of the 1992 reissue of Manuel Zeno Gandía's *La charca* (San Juan: Instituto de Cultura Puertorriqueña, 1894; repr., 1992), v. This edition is part of an Instituto de Cultura Puertorriqueña popular library series.

35. Happily, a translation of one of Luisa Capetillo's books, *Mi opinión,* into English has been launched since the original publication of this essay: Félix Matos-Rodríguez, ed., *A Nation of Women: An Early Feminist Speaks Out/Mi Opinión: Sobre las libertades, derechos, y deberes de la mujer*, trans. Alan West-Durán (Houston: Arte Público Press, 2005). Norma Valle Ferrer's Spanish monograph on Capetillo, which is the definitive biography to date, is now also available in English: *Luisa Capetillo: Pioneer Puerto Rican Feminist*, trans. Gloria Feiman Waldman-Schartz (New York: Peter Lang, 2006).

BIBLIOGRAPHY

Althusser, Louis. *Lenin and Philosophy and Other Essays*. Trans. Ben Brewster. New York: Monthly Review Press, 1971.

Azize Vargas, Yamila, ed. *La mujer en Puerto Rico: Ensayos de investigación*. Río Piedras, PR: Ediciones Huracán, 1987.

Baker, Houston A., Jr. "Critical Memory and the Black Public Sphere." In *The Black Public Sphere: A Public Culture Book*, ed. Black Public Sphere Collective, 5–37. Chicago: University of Chicago Press, 1995.

Capetillo Perón, Luisa. *Ensayos libertarios*. Arecibo, PR: Imprenta Unión Obrera, 1907.

———. *La humanidad en el futuro*. San Juan: Tipografía Real Hermanos, 1910.

———. *Influencias de las ideas modernas*. San Juan: Tipografía Negrón Flores, 1916.

———. *Mi opinión: Sobre las libertades, derechos y deberes de la mujer como compañera, madre y ser independiente*. San Juan: Biblioteca Roja/The Times Publ., 1911.

Colón, Jesús. *A Puerto Rican in New York and Other Sketches*. 2d ed. New York: International Publishers, 1982.

Esteves, Sandra María. *Yerba Buena: Dibujos y poemas*. Greenfield Review Chapbook 47. Greenfield Center, NY: Greenfield Review Press, 1980.

Flores, Juan. "Puerto Rican Literature in the United States: Stages and Perspectives." *ADE Bulletin* 91 (Winter 1988): 39–44.

García, Gervasio L., and A. G. Quintero Rivera. *Desafío y solidaridad: Breve historia del movimiento obrero puertorriqueño*. Río Piedras, PR: Ediciones Huracán/CEREP, 1982.

Gordils, Yanis. "Island and Continental Puerto Rican Literature: Cross-Cultural and Intertextual Considerations." *ADE Bulletin* 91 (Winter 1988): 52–55.

Iglesias de Pagán, Igualdad. *El Obrerismo en Puerto Rico: Época de Santiago Iglesias (1896–1905)*. Palencia de Castilla, Spain: Ediciones Juan Ponce de León, 1973.

Jameson, Fredric. *Postmodernism, or the Cultural Logic of Late Capitalism*. Durham, NC: Duke University Press, 1992.

Kropotkin, Peter. *Fields, Factories, and Workshops*. 1912; repr., New Brunswick, NJ: Transaction, 1993.

Laviera, Tato. *La Carreta Made a U-Turn*. Gary, IN: Arte Público Press, 1979.

Matos-Rodríguez, Félix, ed. *A Nation of Women: An Early Feminist Speaks Out/Mi opinion: Sobre las libertades, derechos, y deberes de la mujer.* Trans. Alan West-Durán. Houston: Arte Público Press, 2005.

Mohr, Eugene. *The Nuyorican Experience: Literature of the Puerto Rican Minority*. Westport, CT: Greenwood Press, 1982.

Navarro, Mireya. "Puerto Rican Presence Wanes in New York: Falling Back; A Special Report." *New York Times*, 28 Feb. 2000, sec. A, 1 and 20.

Ostolazo Bey, Margarita. *Política sexual en Puerto Rico*. Río Piedras, PR: Ediciones Huracán, 1989.

Piñero de Rivera, Flor, ed. *Arthur Alfonso Schomburg: A Puerto Rican's Quest for His Black Heritage*. San Juan: Centro de Estudios Avanzados de Puerto Rico y el Caribe, 1989.

Ramos, Julio, ed. *Amor y anarquía: Los escritos de Luisa Capetillo*. Río Piedras, PR: Ediciones Huracán, 1992.

Romero-Cesareo, Ivette. "Whose Legacy? Voicing Women's Rights from the 1870's to the 1930's." *Callaloo* 17, no. 3 (1994): 770–789.

Sánchez González, Lisa. "Arturo Schomburg: A Transamerican Intellectual." In *African Roots/American Cultures: Africa in the Creation of the Americas,* ed. Sheila Walker, 139–152. Lanham, MD: Rowman and Littlefield, 2001.

Valle Ferrer, Norma. *Luisa Capetillo: Historia de una mujer proscrita*. San Juan: Editorial Cultural, 1990.

———. *Luisa Capetillo: Pioneer Puerto Rican Feminist.* Trans. Gloria Feiman Waldman-Schartz. New York: Peter Lang, 2006.

Vega, Bernardo. *Memorias de Bernardo Vega*. 4th ed. Ed. César Andreu Iglesias. Río Piedras, PR: Ediciones Huracán, 1988.

Zeno Gandía, Manuel. *La charca*. San Juan: Instituto de Cultura Puertorriqueña, 1894. Repr., 1992.

3 WHEN "I" BECAME ETHNIC

Ethnogenesis and Three Early Puerto Rican Diaspora Writers

JOSÉ L. TORRES-PADILLA

In 1993 Addison-Wesley published Esmeralda Santiago's autobiographical work, *When I Was Puerto Rican*, to favorable reviews and healthy sales.[1] The response by Puerto Ricans, however, was not completely positive. Geoffrey Fox, author of *Hispanic Nation: Culture, Politics, and the Constructing of Identity*, writes that the title of Santiago's memoir "disturbed some American-reared descendents of migrants from the island, for it seems to imply that one can cease being Puerto Rican."[2] If "mainland" Puerto Ricans responded in this manner, Esmeralda Santiago's work received even more hostility from "islanders." In an article on *caribeña* writers in the United States, island-based critic Michele Dávila Gonçalves notes that the book, especially its title, "clashed with the patriotic-nationalist sensibility of Puerto Ricans from the island" (chocó mucho con la sensibilidad patriótica-nacionalista de los puertorriqueños de la isla).[3]

According to Lisa Sánchez González, island feminists in particular took Santiago to task for what they perceived as the work's effacement of the collective. This feminist perspective holds that the text contains "feminist trappings" that appear compelling and positive but in reality "feminize poverty" and embrace "assimilationist tenets of the 'American Dream,'" all of which "tends to satisfy a certain hegemonic thirst (and market demand) for the subaltern woman's acceptance—even celebration—of colonial paternalism."[4] Sánchez González's comments indicate that for once in recent memory island feminists have waived their traditional agenda and have actually come out to denounce the *machista*-bashing in Santiago's work in a concerted defense of the *patria*. This intriguing reaction apparently situates the feminist position within a seemingly larger, more imperative "national" one. Sánchez González claims that Santiago's memoir and the two other narratives analyzed in this particular chapter of her book—Carmen de Monteflores's *Cantando Bajito* and Judith Ortiz Cofer's *The Line of the Sun*—represent texts that "speak from the margin" only to validate the North American center.[5] These texts are thus deemed politically "insufficient," especially in comparison to the earlier feminist works (of Luisa Capetillo, for example) in Sánchez González's literary history of the Puerto Rican diaspora. Planting Santiago's memoir within a politicized context (and, given Puerto Rico's ambiguous and highly politicized condition, this seems inevitable), Sánchez González derisively dismisses it along with other "novels of assimilation" where the "uppity white female 'I' . . . might like to be in America without qualification" but "the brown and down female 'we' outside has many valid reasons *not* to."[6] That critical stance and the reaction the book has received from some Puerto Ricans contrast sharply with how Santiago views her own work.

In responding to the criticism of her book, it is revealing that Santiago refers to "immigrants who have returned to their countries" and who, she argues, accept and understand the irony of the past tense in the title and the "feeling that, while at one time they could not identify themselves as anything but the nationality to which they were born, once they've lived in the U.S. their 'cultural purity' has been compromised, and they no longer fit as well in their native countries, nor do they feel one hundred percent comfortable as Americans."[7] Here, Santiago refers primarily to questions of ethnicity rather than nationalism. She, like her book, articulates that odd Puerto Rican experience of transforming oneself from a "national" to an "ethnic" subject with the act of boarding a plane. In an interview with Carmen Dolores Hernández, Santiago recounts the strangeness of being renamed and refigured from "Puerto Rican" to "*hispano*." "It was the sense," she says, "the minute you arrive—that you lose your culture because *you're no longer from a specific place*, you're now lumped into this morass of Spanish-speaking people."[8] For Puerto Ricans who have constituted the diaspora in the flesh, what Santiago observes here is only the beginning. Like so many of her *compatriotas*, Santiago could not help but assimilate some "American" ways while still feeling a deep sense of *puertorriqueñidad.* "I don't know of any Puerto Rican who wants to be American," she asserts. "Every Puerto Rican I know wants to be Puerto Rican" (166). Moreover, like many mainland Puerto Ricans, she has experienced the bittersweet return to the "homeland" that only reinforces the adage that you can never return home. For Santiago, that *retorno* marked a significant revelation for her, that "home was no longer home" and that she had changed dramatically enough for Puerto Ricans on the island to see her as different: "*los puertorriqueños mismos me negaron* [Puerto Ricans themselves disowned me] because I was so Americanized" (165). And this rejection becomes ironically bitter when the prodigal son or daughter realizes how assimilated the island has become: "Puerto Rico was so Americanized. . . . I thought, how can *puertorriqueños* who have never left the island accuse us when they allow the American contamination I was seeing all around? There were McDonald's, Pizza Huts, and so on. I used to think this was not our culture. Big Macs are not our cultural legacy. We in the States at least have an excuse for being Americanized. This ambivalence was part of what drove me away" (163).

For many Puerto Ricans who have spent a good portion of their lives in the United States, Santiago's words resonate as validated truth. The title of her memoir attempts to describe the many complex nuances of that experience. Unfortunately, it is that title, with its suggestion of national and cultural abandonment, which irks some Puerto Ricans, especially those who cannot fully comprehend and accept a hybrid form of ethnicity that retains only traces of some perceived original, "purer" form. It was precisely the Nuyorican poets who began to articulate this uneasy disjunction with their island brethren. Miguel Piñero's poem "This Is Not the Place Where I Was Born" is an angry diatribe centered on the *retorno* theme. In that poem, Piñero portrays Puerto Rico as "this slave blessed land / where nuyoricans come in search of spiritual identity" and "are greeted with profanity." Like Santiago, he too points to the irony of being considered an outsider by his own people, who are colonized and, from his perspective, do not have a genuine respect or pride in their own culture:

puertorriqueños cannot assemble displaying the emblem
nuyoricans are fighting & dying for in newark, lower east side
south bronx where the fervor of being
puertorriqueños is not just rafael hernandez[9]

Similarly, Miguel Algarín's "A Mongo Affair" attacks the misconceptions and American Dream–inspired delusions that some islanders may have of life, and of Puerto Ricans, in the United States. Significantly, the poem also exhibits anger at recognizing and accepting the loss of "home," an anger that eventually finds a target in what the author perceives to be Puerto Rican dependency. In response to an old man's claims that Puerto Ricans in the States are doing better than their island compatriots, the speaker in the poem lashes out that this dependency has actually sucked the virility and spirit out of the Puerto Rican man, as represented by the extended metaphor of the flaccid penis that informs the poem's title:

mongo means *flojo*
mongo means bloodless
mongo means soft
mongo can not penetrate
mongo can only tease[10]

Like Algarín's poem, Tato Laviera's well-known poem "Brava" contains frustration and anger that explode when the Nuyorican female speaker defiantly confronts those who would dare question her Puerto Ricanness:

go ahead, ask me, on any street-
corner that I am not *puertorriqueña,*
come *dimelo aqui en mi cara*
offend me, *atrevete, a menos*
que tu no quieras que yo te meta
un tremendo bochinche de soplamoco
pezcoza that's gonna hurt you
in either language[11]

These poems, written more than two decades ago by three prominent Nuyorican poets, represent a strong, harsh response to an island identity that in these poets' minds eludes and alienates them. In certain ways, Santiago's memoir follows this Nuyorican tradition in narrative form. In an original and insightful approach to Santiago's autobiography, Hugo Rodríguez Vecchini argues that Santiago's "ethnographic autobiography" contains picaresque qualities with the significant difference that the generically expected conversion in her work is a partial one. Rodríguez Vecchini sees in the title the complexities of Santiago's attempt to narrate an incomplete past ("*un pasado inconcluso*") that defines "a chronological and cultural limit" at the heart of the author's perception of her hybrid identity and the narrative's "halfway conversion."[12] The book thus illustrates the contemporary Puerto Rican identity conundrum, what Rodríguez Vecchini calls the "cultural constant" of "the life destined to live simultaneously between two languages and two cultures" (156).

Rodríguez Vecchini claims that Santiago creates in her book a history of survival, a counterhistory of the American Dream (154). If this is the case, then it is intriguing to note the response to Santiago's attempt at narrating this "halfway conversion" and describing her "hybrid" experience. That her memoir, and its provocative title, aroused a "nationalistic" resistance against this construction of hybrid Puerto Ricanness in a 1990s narrative suggests that the anxiety over identity so prevalent in Puerto Rican culture resurfaced yet again to spill onto mainstream consciousness. More importantly, however, the critical murmurings over this text uncovered the fixated, essentialist perception of identity still alive within a section of the Puerto Rican community. According to Agustín Laó, the present schemata conceptualizing Puerto Rican national formation tend to value this very essentialized cultural identity that almost always has an "inner" authenticity in danger of being annihilated by cultural imperialism, or they construct this "purity" as a "privileged space of resistance from an indigenous 'high culture.'"[13] It can be argued, as most of the essayists in *Puerto Rican Jam: Essays in Culture and Politics* do, that the island's elite, the so-called *blanquitos* (white elite), continue to support and promote these essentialized schemata as a diluted nationalist project that demonstrates, more than anything, their failure to accomplish their historically assigned task of building the nation-state. Indeed, this seems an established critical position, one that José Luis González expounds in his seminal essay "Literatura e identidad nacional en Puerto Rico" while linking this nationalist agenda, and its attendant literary production, to racism.[14]

In the absence of a nation-state, and with the masses wary of and resistant to the traditionally conservative tendencies of nationalism in Puerto Rico, what has developed in the island, through its various ideological apparatuses, is a national identity based on an illusory "nation."[15] The present Estado Libre Asociado facilitates and promotes that illusion because it gives the sensation that the Puerto Rican people are controlling an "internal space" outside hegemonic capitalist control[16] when ultimate power remains in the hands of the U.S. Congress and president. In turn, the Puerto Rican diaspora has complicated matters, because now more than half of the Puerto Rican population resides outside the homeland. The distancing of Puerto Ricans from this illusory "nation" (which nonetheless affords a concrete geographical site) has led to the "imagining" of community based on "ethnicity" and national identity:

> The Puerto Rican people share a feeling of nationhood that has not translated into traditional nationalist claims to form a nation-state. Puerto Ricans have formed an "imaginary community" with an imaginary belonging to a territory that spans the island as well as certain areas on the mainland (e.g. South Bronx, Spanish Harlem, North Philadelphia). This imaginary community oscillates between feelings of nationhood and ethnicity; that is, Puerto Ricans simultaneously imagine themselves as a nation and as an ethnic group. Puerto Ricans' self-perception does not fit either the concept of a "nation" or that of an "ethnic group." I believe the concept of "ethno-nation" accommodates the Puerto Ricans' diverse and peculiar subject positions better than that of "nation."[17]

However, Puerto Ricans imagine themselves as an "ethno-nation" with different emphasis on both sides of the hyphen: self-representation is thus possible as a deterritorialized ethno-nation in the United States and as a territorialized ethno-nation in Puerto Rico.[18] The significance of this point cannot be overstated; the flexibility available to Puerto Ricans for their own self-representation gives us a clue to comprehending the fundamental differences between the literary production of Boricuas on the island and in the United States. It is important to consider Ramón Grosfoguel's comment that "the historical context of the Puerto Rican communities in question and what objectives are sought at any particular juncture" influence "the hegemony of ethnicity over nation or nation over ethnicity."[19] Most assessments of "ethnicity" support this assertion. Social anthropologists tend to view the construction of ethnicity as a response to a collective need. In fact, the term "ethnic" is rooted in the "othering" process.[20] A group will often define and represent itself to distinguish itself from others and, therefore, as a way to protect the collective and ensure its survival. There is, then, a political basis for ethnicity,[21] and as Werner Sollors argues, it is this political drive, fueled by the competition for power, that moves an ethnic collective to re-create their distinctiveness.[22] To achieve this distinctiveness, groups establish boundaries and mechanisms, which Manning Nash calls "cultural markers of difference," that maintain those boundaries; and where the usual ones of kinship, commensality, and common cult are not immediately present or visible, the collective will resort to secondary symbols that "make recognition at a distance."[23] Sometimes it is the preservation of that key cultural construct "tradition" that motivates and unites an ethnic group, although one cannot completely disassociate this concept from political concerns.

Returning to Grosfoguel's remark about the emphasis placed on either "ethno" or "nation," we can readily see that for Puerto Ricans in the United States there are obvious reasons behind the emphasizing of their ethnicity as opposed to nationality. Separated from their geographic base, "their homeland," and "othered" by North Americans, it is not surprising that Puerto Ricans in the States will seek ways of re-creating *puertorriqueñidad* for reasons of survival and political necessity. The ethnic signs produced in this process will not always jibe with the cultural production of the island, and they probably represent hybrid forms, but they do demonstrate a desire to keep a cultural connection alive. The murals in El Barrio are a wonderful example of the process and are a symbolic manifestation of "Puerto Rican" ethnicity.[24] With respect to these murals, and the "ethnic" literary texts produced by writers of Puerto Rican ancestry residing in the United States, it is crucial to note that what makes ethnicity a very real, living, and human process is not the content but rather the importance that individuals within the group ascribe to it.[25] More importantly, the cultural production of these two sets of United States–based Puerto Rican artists demonstrates Stuart Hall's idea, one that we should not ignore, that ethnicity and its signs acknowledge the place of history, language, and culture.[26]

The idea that Puerto Ricans constitute a "floating nation" has emerged as a viable metaphor for the Puerto Rican diasporic condition.[27] However, it is evident that, with every passing generation firmly rooted in the United States, the metaphor loses relevance and currency. The present and future generations of Puerto Rican ancestry in the United States do not and will not necessarily adhere or subscribe to this idea of "floating" nationhood. Writers representing these generations, such as Abraham Rodríguez, create literature grounded in a Puerto Rican ethnicity (if at all) that follows the beat of a different *timbalero*. It is quite possible that these writers view Puerto Rico from a widening distance that foments weary recognition of—if not disinterest in—island culture, politics, and current events. In an interview, Rodríguez declares that "the island is a myth. . . . It doesn't exist for me at all."[28] Rodríguez, and writers like him, may not feel any profound responsibility toward the Puerto Rican "nation," and they might even see their literary work, not as part of a Puerto Rican national literature, but instead as following the ethnic and immigrant traditions of U.S. literature—even as they consider themselves Boricuas. Despite these significant developments, the persistence to essentialize Puerto Rican national identity continues, and apparently so does the desire to nationalize all literature written by people of Puerto Rican ancestry.[29] The stubborn adherence to this essentialization on the part of some Puerto Rican critics and writers (even as postmodernist ideas inform literary and cultural studies) belies the actual emergence of a diasporic Puerto Rican literature that has always operated within a framework of hybridity[30] and that has primarily followed the dictates of ethnicity and ethnogenesis—or the semiotic process of producing signs that create or re-create ethnicity.[31] This misunderstanding and mishandling of the literature written from the diasporic subject's perspective underline a deeper cultural chasm that can only continue to widen. The nationalistic project and rhetoric lingering in the cultural space inhabited by Puerto Ricans "*de aqui y de alla*" (from here and there) hold some power in the Puerto Rican imaginary. However, our questions over this false totalization of Puerto Rican identity become more pressing and crucial when we realize that early writers of the diaspora were also compelled to create texts from an ethnic, rather than nationalistic, position, as they engaged with their new surroundings and met the demands that their new environment placed on them. From these earlier writers, and their texts, we begin to appreciate how the stark differences between the populations residing here and on the island grow more glaringly apparent with the consequent creative production of each generation. These are differences that will eventually necessitate resisting the nationalistic impulse to unite all writings created by all authors of Puerto Rican descent and establishing a space for literature written by Puerto Ricans born and residing in the United States.

In actuality, then, Santiago's contribution to the diasporic canon—or perhaps we should call it "Diasporican," following María "Mariposa" Fernández's lead—represents the latest in a series of literary texts written by authors more comfortable embracing a different brand of *puertorriqueñidad,* one that typically represents a stronger identification with ethnicity than nationality. As we have seen, the textual formation and expression of that identity are most recognizable in the Nuyorican writers, but there were precursors—Bernardo Vega and Guillermo Cotto-Thorner quickly come to mind—and others who, for the most part, have remained in obscurity. Jesús Colón, known but undertheorized, Pura Belpré, a children's book writer, and Graciany Miranda Archilla, an estranged island poet, are three such writers whose lives overlapped while they resided and wrote in New York City during a period that covered most of the twentieth century.[32] These three writers are among the few whose work we have available from the first wave of migration. In truth, selecting these three writers does not represent a question of choice as much as it follows the logic of dealing with what Sánchez González calls the Puerto Rican diaspora's "paperlessness."[33] These writers also produced narrative, a literary mode recognized for allowing members of a collective to represent their rhetorical exigencies and to draw possible resolutions for the social dramas concerning their group. Their work, although only a limited and partial representation of the possible literary production of all Puerto Ricans living in the United States at the time, nonetheless illustrates how three Puerto Ricans recreated ethnic identity through narrative in this new land, not only as a way to make sense of their respective and collective experience, but to fulfill that political collective need discussed earlier.

One of the earliest and most prolific Puerto Rican voices in the United States was Jesús Colón, who arrived in New York City as a stowaway in 1918 and five years later was contributing to several of the Spanish newspapers in the city. Colón was a lifelong communist and defender of Puerto Rican independence who held various unskilled jobs while he wrote. Eventually, he became a journalist and columnist for the *Daily Worker*, where he produced most of the material found in the two important volumes bearing his name: *A Puerto Rican in New York and Other Sketches*, originally published in 1961, and *The Way It Was, and Other Writings*, a posthumous collection published in 1993 under the auspices of the Recovering the United States Hispanic Literary Heritage Project and the Center for Puerto Rican Studies. In total, Colón wrote more than four hundred pieces throughout his life, according to Edna Acosta-Belén and Virginia Sánchez Korrol.[34] His sketches, the focus in this essay, are often narrative pieces that are written in a *costumbrista* style and sometimes contain fictional techniques such as dialogue and characterization.

Being a communist and internationalist, Colón reflects in his writing an intense concern for issues related to global capitalism and the working class. Despite his unyielding support of Puerto Rican independence, his writing rarely focuses on nationalist themes. We hardly ever witness a running display of signs appropriated from the Puerto Rican cultural encyclopedia to prop up a sense of national identity. "Cultural encyclopedia" refers to signs established within a group and available to the ethnic subject through "the processing system of Memory and Project."[35] The system is rhetorical in nature, since it involves a strategic method of recalling these ethnic signs from memory and imposing them within the ethnic sign's new terrain. Although Colón brings up some of these signs, it is rarely ever done nostalgically to praise the homeland. In fact, some sketches actually criticize the island, such as "The Fanguito Is Still There," which describes the famous San Juan slum, and "Angels in My Hometown Church," which criticizes the racism on the island.

Indeed, most of the sketches in *A Puerto Rican in New York* contain an undercurrent of loss—whatever signs represent ethnicity, or Puerto Ricanness, often are lost, stolen, or appropriated. Colón thus constructs a representation of Puerto Rican ethnicity based on the minority status of his group, one that takes into consideration its victimization and oppression. Notably, though, it is a construction of ethnicity that openly opposes U.S. hegemonic power. In "How to Know the Puerto Ricans," for example, he writes about the bells of the cathedral in San Juan, which were stolen by pirates and sold to the town of New Amsterdam, New York. This incident moves him to quip that when Puerto Ricans are asked why they come to the US, they should reply: "We came to take back our bells."[36] In another sketch titled "José," Colón narrates how a friend and fellow Puerto Rican has his idea for a Spanish tune stolen and it becomes a hit.

Even language, a distinct identity marker, functions textually to show victimization, alienation, and loss. The sketch "Because He Spoke in Spanish" relates the real incident of how Bernabé Nuñez, a soldier returning from Korea, is killed in a bar for speaking his native language. The sketch does not focus on the nationalistic pride involved in speaking Spanish, "the language of the Puerto Rican nation" (126), but uses linguistic difference to highlight the discrimination faced by Puerto Ricans at the hands of North Americans and the need to unite against their violence: "What we are saying now is that in order to avoid future murders and violations of rights, we have to organize the broad forces of decency in the neighborhoods for simple democratic rights" (128).

Colón often inverts signs to achieve rhetorical purpose. In "Carmencita," for instance, his mother-in-law's devout religiosity, including her rosary reading, become Puerto Rican signs appropriated for the defense of communism and Stalin. In the sketch, Carmencita slowly draws away from the tainted, commercialized forms of Catholic ritual found in the United States (accepting money for reading a rosary and playing bingo in the church, for example), and by the end of the narrative, she is reciting the Prayer of the Eleven Thousand Virgins as a way to ask "the Lord that nothing will ever happen to Stalin" (110). When a sign has a clear association with the island, as in "Castor Oil: Simple or Compound," it tends to illustrate the hybrid novelty of the diasporic condition. For example, when Colón writes about castor oil ("the purgative given to us by our grandmothers when I was a kid at Cayey, my home town in Puerto Rico"),[37] he does not attempt to evoke nostalgia but rather uses it to stress the cultural difference between the two geographic sites. Asked by the pharmacist if he wants the "simple" or "compound" version of the purgative, Colón chooses the worse tasting one out of ignorance and mistrust: "I drew a note of consolation when I congratulated myself for having chosen the castor oil simple, instead of the castor oil compound. Only my dead grandmother and the devil himself would have known all the fiendish oils and ashes that this yankee chemist would have mixed into the simple innocently crystal clear castor oil!"[38]

William Boelhower writes that "who you are" is a function of "where you are" and "where you have been," or what he calls "habitare," "the spatial unfolding of the proposition, 'I Am.'"[39] This is what gives uniqueness to the diasporic expression: the forging together of past and present spatial-temporal ontologies into one new one. In the ethnic text, awareness of geographic surroundings marks a high point, a moment of belonging, if not owning. It certainly demonstrates an assertive superimposing of identity or self onto the cultural terrain. We see these ideas clearly operating in the sketch "Wanted—a Statue," in which Colón argues for the dedication of a statue honoring a Puerto Rican figure and placing it "in the very heart of the city" (136). Even here, though, we must note that Colón has opted, not for recalling an existing sign that celebrates Puerto Ricanness, but for dwelling on what is absent. Yet it is equally evident, especially from this sketch, that Colón's sense of ethnicity, and the semiotic production or re-creation of it, are quite centered on his coming to grips with his immediate geographic location.

The sketch that contains the most revealing insight into Colón's position on ethnicity is "Nice to Have Friends in All Walks of Life." In it, Colón narrates how the club Vanguardia Puertorriqueña, for which he served on the executive board, decided to rent a larger-than-usual boat to get to its annual picnic at Bear Mountain. This sketch contains the most dominant Puerto Rican "national" signs of all those written, and the Puerto Rican enclave projecting so much nationalism is aboard a ship, floating, moving along a river, temporarily isolated from borders. Within this contained atmosphere, people eat the Puerto Rican delicacies that they have brought (while using the American hot dogs served onboard as baseballs), they sing songs reminiscent of the island, dance *danzas* and rumbas, listen to guitar playing, sprinkle their conversations with Spanish, and chant Puerto Rican children's songs. In this text we have signs that come very close to those primary "markers of difference" described by Nash, particularly those related to kinship and commensality that are most often associated with national culture. This scene recalls Boelhower's idea of the "typescene": "a hypercodified, pre-fabricated script" describing and defining ethnicity that illustrates ethnic cultural practice, usually for instructional purposes.[40] The "Feast" is a typescene found in many ethnic texts and emphasizes kinship and commensality. Most interesting, however, is Colón's humorous but sobering criticism of the club members' false ambition and foolish pride. The final message of this sketch alerts us to the values of pragmatism and com mon sense over the false allure of ethnic pride. The subtext in this narrative exemplifies Colón's restrained approach to shallow nationalistic fervor and his preference for an ethnicity that represents political opposition and struggle, especially from a Marxist perspective.

If Colón's narrative contains ethnicity, Pura Belpré's ethnic project served a more mediating political and social role. Belpré migrated to New York City in 1920 and shortly afterward began working at the public library. In 1926, she began formal studies in the Library School of the New York Public Library, where she found her talent and desire to write children's books. Her main concern was always to write multicultural books and, specifically, to reach the young Puerto Rican audience. Her first objective was to translate Puerto Rican folktales into English so that children could enjoy them and, through them, learn about their heritage. Belpré's first book, published in 1932, was a translation of the popular Puerto Rican folktale *Pérez y martina*. In 1946 she published *The Tiger and the Rabbit and Other Tales*, the first collection of Puerto Rican folktales written in English. Among her other numerous books are a collection of Juan Bobo stories and both English translations and Spanish-language editions of Latin American folktales and children's stories. Her work is now beginning to attain the recognition it justly deserves. Arte Público Press recently published a manuscript of her novel for adolescents written in the forties and titled *Firefly Summer*; and in 1996 the American Library Association honored her by naming an award for multicultural literature after her.[41]

Children's literature is not usually included among the more traditional literary canon and rarely, if ever, within ethnic literary studies. However, Belpré's work should interest scholars of Puerto Rican diasporic literature. Her translations of Puerto Rican folktales by themselves serve as a fascinating study of how a transplanted Puerto Rican views cultural material from her homeland and how it is reinstated in the translated, "Diasporican" text. The one text, though, pertinent to what has been proposed in this essay is her book *Santiago*.

Written in English and published in 1969, the story narrates how a little Puerto Rican boy, the Santiago of the title, tries to make everyone believe in the existence of Selina, a pet hen that he left behind on the island. This situation is complicated when he tells everyone that he saw another hen on his way to school. Santiago's desire to prove this hen's existence, as well as Selina's, becomes a desire tantamount to self-affirmation. Miss Taylor believes that "there was something else besides Selina, important as she was, that really mattered now."[42] The teacher realizes that the boy was living in "two places at once,"[43] but instead of criticizing him she accepts that his imagination is the bridge between those two worlds. Eventually, the boy, with the teacher's support, proves the existence of both hens.

Unlike Colón, Belpré utilizes the ethnic sign to advance a more hybrid and certainly less leftist ethnic project. The imposition of this particular "fowl" ethnic sign into the New York cityscape perhaps represents the "working out" of Belpré's own fantasm—Fredric Jameson's concept of a familial text cum master fantasy narrative—as she herself ventured from *campo* to metropolis.[44] This rather-fossilized view of the island inserts itself, textually speaking, into the new terrain and serves as a form of resistance that recalls Homi Bhabha's theorization of hybridity and its power to "destabilize the colonizer's disavowal of difference."[45] The ethnic sign in this story also materializes the absent presence of Puerto Rico, which certainly affirms Boelhower's idea that the ethnic project needs memory for validation. To understand the concept of "absent presence," one needs only to recall Piñero's line, "I tasted mango many years before the skin of the fruit / ever reached my teeth."[46] In *Santiago*, the act of remembering is heightened by two other ethnic signs: a gourd carved with the important events in Puerto Rican history and, to a lesser extent, the Hispanic Museum, which the children pass on their way to school. The textual re-creation of this absent presence conjures up a possible world that is rife with ideological content because it promotes a hybrid world where the Diasporican subject's past and present, his "here" and "there," come together to coexist. Surely, this possible world represents Jameson's "complex term," that part of Jameson's hermeneutic instrument, the "semiotic rectangle," appropriated from A. J. Greimas's work.

Jameson utilizes the semiotic rectangle "for exploring the semantic and ideological intricacies of the text" (47). The semiotic rectangle represents the binary oppositions and their contradictions within a text, and by analyzing the "mapping out" of these semes, the critic can better "read" the ideological content of the text. The complex term represents the "ideal synthesis of the two contraries," and in Santiago, these would be the United States and Puerto Rico, with the subcontraries being *campo* and metropolis (or city). The complex term in this text, then, would consider the "ideal synthesis" of both the United States and Puerto Rico; textually, it is a hybrid world where a hen can inhabit an urban space, but at a deeper level it is the representational solution for the political, cultural, and ideological conflict represented by the two contraries (166). Following Jameson's ideas, we can see how Belpré has transformed her fantasm into a narrative that constructs a "wish-fulfilling text" that in turn contains ideological content significant for her collective. And even as this text hints at resistance from a hybrid subject position, one can propose that a subtext tacitly supports the ideological underpinnings of the status quo, the Estado Libre Asociado, suggesting that hybridity does not always resist politically even as it does culturally. Despite vestiges of linkage to the island, Belpré's "ethnicity" demonstrates a strong desire to engage the realities that constitute her new environment, unlike Graciany Miranda Archilla.

Miranda migrated to the United States in 1951, at the height of political repression of *independentistas* on the island. Miranda is known as one of the founders of a poetic movement in the island called Atalaya de los Dioses that attempted to break away from romanticism and revolutionize Puerto Rican poetry in form and content. The poets also supported socially conscious poetry and easily gravitated to the growing independence movement. The repressive political climate of the fifties, plus the desire for better job opportunities, prompted Miranda to leave the island for New York City. While there, he worked for magazines and newspapers and actively participated in many Puerto Rican cultural and political clubs and organizations. His many works include essays and several books of poetry written in either Spanish or English.

Among his lesser-known works are three fictional pieces found in his papers at the Center for Puerto Rican Studies Archives. These three short stories are written in English under the pseudonym Mars Hillmar. Two of them, "The Shadow" and "When Lightning Strikes," are in manuscript form; the third, "Brambles," is a handwritten, at times unintelligible, rough draft.[47] It is beyond the scope of this essay to discuss these three narrative works in depth, but it should be noted that collectively they presented the most puzzling and challenging texts in this analysis of Puerto Rican ethnogenesis. One of the stories does not include any Puerto Rican sign or subject, and the other two include ethnicity that is not Puerto Rican. The glaring absence of the Puerto Rican sign and subject in these narratives actually makes them necessary additions to our study of Puerto Rican ethnic semiosis. Miranda's work naturally compels one to wonder why a nationalist *independentista* such as he would so blatantly efface any sense of Puerto Ricanness in these texts.

At first glance, one might imagine that Miranda's stories would share some similarities with those written by Pedro Juan Soto and José Luis González during the same period.[48] Both Soto and González wrote from the perspective of island Puerto Ricans looking at the diasporic subject. Theirs is a sympathetic gaze that views the Puerto Rican in the States as victim, but the reader senses a certain authorial distance. González, an early defender of Diasporican literature, writes that it is those Puerto Ricans living in the States who will produce the "most authentic" literature of the diasporic experience and adds that it will be necessarily written in English.[49] The work of Nuyorican writers, who are often cited as writing about the Puerto Rican from the standpoint of those who are in the United States to stay, confirms González's comment. Soto and González lived for a relatively short time in the States. Soto returned to the island and González lived a good portion of his life in Mexico. Miranda lived close to forty years in New York City and finally returned to live out his last years in Puerto Rico. In all of that time he seems to have retained, and even cultivated, the persona of an exile, and these narratives reflect that to an extreme. Though he lived considerably longer in the United States than Soto and González, his literary production in English does not integrate a Puerto Rican subject, not even one from a sympathetic distance.

There may be practical reasons why Miranda wrote short fiction in English under a pseudonym. He might have wanted to try his hand at making money in the genre and used a pen name to protect his reputation as a poet. Alternatively, he may have done it for pleasure or as a challenge for his English-language skills, which were considerable. Whatever the reasons, we learn from Miranda's exercise in popular fiction that the ethnic project is possible only to the extent that there is a felt rhetorical need for constructing it. And such a need must necessarily emerge from the author's direct engagement with the new geographical site. The author must have a purpose to play the ethnic game and how can this happen if he takes himself off the playing field? Ethnogenesis can occur only if the ethnic subject willingly enters what Boelhower calls the "frame," a concept similar to "border"—that place where the ethnic subject experiences the new world and recalls the cultural encyclopedia of his or her group to reinvent that ethnicity within that new cultural context or space.[50] Denial of the frame or border necessarily preempts the possibility of any ethnic project for any potential text written by a writer within the ethnic group who stubbornly clings to a descent perspective of ethnicity.[51] Miranda's null Puerto Ricanness in these narratives must lead us to conclude that he held on tenaciously to a nationalistic sense of identity that clashed with the hybrid identity embraced by his contemporaries. In other words, Miranda believed in an "essentialized" Puerto Ricanness that was constructed along nationalist lines and thus would not allow him to "re-create" in narrative form a subject he could only see as false.

Even as Miranda fights to retain an essentialist image of homeland alive in his heart, spirit, and mind, the overpowering force of *habitare* drives him toward an imaginary text that still attempts to mediate, however obliquely and tentatively, the conflict of here and there. In the story "The Shadow," for example, the character Pete Kultzke, a Polish immigrant, is used to subvert and resist the attraction of what Sollors calls "consent," which seems like a euphemism for "assimilation." Kultzke is drawn as a typical immigrant, a stowaway whose "hardships at home led him to hit the road" and who eventually arrives in America, "mother of exiles," to lead "a life of hopeful horizons and helpless toils."[52] Kultzke's story follows the pattern of a traditional immigrant story: he takes on odd jobs and, through hard work and saving, opens up a meat market. His downfall is an American woman, Mabel Jones, with whom he falls in love and marries. Miranda shapes Mabel into an unflattering character, a negative anthropomorphic representation of the United States. Miranda describes her as some sort of Medusa: "serpent-like" with "witchery black eyes, as though created to petrify man" (3–4). Mabel is also "narcissistic" and "debauched," a "succubus" who "behaved like a bird of prey" (4). Miranda intimates that Mabel's beauty and attractiveness, like Kultzke's new home, is deceptive and perverse and will never belong to someone like him. Two signs in the text support this reading: Kultzke's knife and apron. Both of these signs are "ethnicized" by their association with Kultzke's station and immigrant status. They represent working accoutrements, strongly linked to the type of unskilled labor that most immigrants traditionally perform. Miranda describes the apron as "white, with red dots and stains, like a banner" (3). The apron, tainted as it is with blood, recalls the emphasis placed on blood as the inexorable connection to one's ethnicity. Thus, it is quite revealing when Mabel yells out, "I hate his apron" (5). Similarly, the knife at times personifies Kultzke, as when short-lived happiness is described as "happy days for the butcher's knife" (7). In the text the knife often works as a synecdoche for Kultzke's class and ethnic status, and it is significant that the butcher hesitates to part with it. The knife "is a friend, silent, reliable, penetrating" (6). When he runs after his adulterous wife, Kultzke takes the knife with him. With that knife, he also "dismembers," "dissects," and "rends" the apartment in a jealous rage until he finds the "batch of fotographs" [*sic*] depicting "abnormality and monstrosity" and "Perversion. The sort of thing Nature shudders at" (9).

At the end, Mabel has apparently run off with the woman in the photographs, and Kultzke torches himself in the process of burning the eye-opening evidence. It is unfortunate that Miranda utilizes this heterosexist strategy even though it is situated within an ideologically oppositional agenda. However, it is clear that, although the Puerto Rican subject is absent, the text channels the author's ideological and political stance through another ethnicity. Unable to imagine an ethnic Puerto Rican separated from his geographical space, Miranda resorts to a circuitous method for creating an ethnic subject victimized and deceived by the false promises of the American Dream. In a passage from the story, Miranda writes: "A man often goes astray when fate plunges him into the realm of no return or when a blindfold runs down to naught in a fool's paradise" (8). Perhaps these words afford a glimpse into how Miranda saw his own exiled life in the United States. They may also offer some insight into the reasons behind the absence of the Puerto Rican subject in his short fiction.

The writings of these earlier Diasporican writers enhance our current understanding of how they faced the very same issues of identity that continue to vex our contemporary writers. Since they represent the first wave of migration, their narrative sheds new light on the issue of Puerto Rican identity and its textual representation. Whether the identity is actually represented in the text or, as in the case of Miranda's work, is absent, it is clear that each writer has a different view of and rhetorical purpose and use for Puerto Rican ethnicity. It is also evident that whenever ethnicity is emphasized, such as with Colón and Belpré, nationalistic concerns are displaced or minimized in the process. Conversely,

Miranda's insistence on a nationalist sense of identity perhaps inhibited his ability to perceive and conceive of a Puerto Rican subject functioning within a hybrid textual world. That the ethnic project differs in the case of each writer affirms the idea that ethnic identity, as social and textual construct, is perceived and valued differently. Even as we understand this, the lives and work of these writers also illustrate that the struggle for the ethnic subject to reconcile group and personal identity is fundamentally historical. These ideas suggest that we can view ethnogenesis as both a diachronic and a synchronic process. Taking such an approach would almost require reading Puerto Rican diasporic literature from a dialogic perspective that emphasizes listening to the many voices that speak of the many "*puertorriqueñidades*" across the continuum. If we listen carefully, we will come to understand that the point is not when we are, were, or became Puerto Rican, as suggested by the controversy over Esmeralda Santiago's book, but that we are always becoming Puerto Rican differently yet together. With this understanding should also come the acceptance of the cultural differences between Puerto Ricans "here" and "there" and respect for the future literature that those inherent differences may create.

NOTES

This essay was originally published in *Centro* 14, no. 2 (Fall 2002).

1. In 1994, Vintage picked up the book and published an English and Spanish version. Under Vintage the English version sold 16,000 hardcover copies, a good showing for a first book.

2. Geoffrey Fox, *Hispanic Nation: Culture, Politics, and the Constructing of Identity* (Tucson: University of Arizona Press, 1997), 201.

3. Michele Dávila Gonçalves, "La voz caribeña femenina en la literatura de los Estados Unidos," *Exegesis* 37/38 (2001): 44.

4. Lisa Sánchez González, *Boricua Literature: A Literary History of the Puerto Rican Diaspora* (New York: New York University Press, 2001), 159.

5. Ibid., 160.

6. Ibid.

7. Reading Group Center, "Esmeralda Santiago, a Note to the Reader," http://www.randomhouse.com/catalog/display.pperl?isbn=9780679756774&view=rg, accessed 13 Sept. 2006.

8. Carmen Dolores Hernández, *Puerto Rican Voices in English: Interviews with Writers* (Westport, CT: Praeger, 1997), 165. Hereafter cited in text.

9. Miguel Piñero, *La Bodega Sold Dreams* (Houston: Arte Público Press, 1985), 14.

10. Miguel Algarín, "A Mongo Affair," in *Boricuas: Influential Puerto Rican Writings—an Anthology,* ed. Roberto Santiago (New York: Ballantine, 1995), 109.

11. Tato Laviera, *AmeRícan* (Houston: Arte Público Press, 1986), 63 ("go ahead, ask me, on any street- / corner that I am not Puerto Rican / come say it here to my face / offend me, I dare you, unless / you don't want that I give you / a tremendous scandalous snot-clearing / slap that's gonna hurt you / in either language").

12. Hugo Rodríguez Vecchini, "Cuando Esmeralda 'era' puertorriqueña: Autobiografia etnográfica y autobiografia neopicaresca," *Nómada* 1 (1995): 145–160. Hereafter cited in text.

13. Agustín Laó, "Islands at the Crossroads: Puerto Ricanness Traveling between the Translocal Nation and the Global City," in *Puerto Rican Jam: Rethinking Colonialism and Nationalism,* ed. Frances Negrón-Muntaner and Ramón Grosfoguel (Minneapolis: University of Minnesota Press, 1997), 172.

14. José Luis González, *El pais de cuatro pisos y otros ensayos* (Río Piedras, PR: Ediciones Huracán, 1980), 43–84.

15. For illuminating discussions of nationalism in Puerto Rico, see the introduction to *Puerto Rican Jam,* "Beyond Nationalist and Colonialist Discourses: The *Jaiba* Politics of the Puerto Rican Ethno-nation," by Ramón Grosfoguel, Frances Negrón-Muntaner, and Chloe S. Georas; as well as Mariano Negrón-Portillo's "Puerto Rico: Surviving Colonialism and Nationalism" and Ramón Grosfoguel's "The Divorce of Nationalist Discourses from the Puerto Rican People: A Sociohistorical Perspective," both in the same collection.

16. Ramón Grosfoguel, Frances Negrón-Muntaner, and Chloe S. Georas, introduction to *Puerto Rican Jam,* 12.

17. Grosfoguel, "Divorce of Nationalist Discourses," 74–75.

18. Grosfoguel, Negrón-Muntaner, and Georas, introduction to *Puerto Rican Jam,* 17–19.

19. Ibid., 18.

20. See the foreword in Werner Sollors, ed., *Theories of Ethnicity: A Classical Reader* (New York: New York University Press, 1996), especially x–xii and the section on the etymology of the words "ethnic," "ethnical," "ethnicity," etc. (1–12). Also helpful in understanding the development of the term "ethnic" is the introduction to John Hutchinson and Anthony D. Smith, eds., *Ethnicity* (Oxford: Oxford University Press, 1996), especially 4–5.

21. See Paul R. Brass, "Ethnic Groups and Ethnic Identity Formation," in Hutchinson and Smith, *Ethnicity,* 85–90.

22. Sollors, *Theories of Ethnicity*, xv.

23. Manning Nash, "The Core Elements of Ethnicity," in Hutchinson and Smith, *Ethnicity*, 24–28. Nash states that the secondary features, or "surface pointers," include dress, language, and culturally denoted physical features. Beyond these secondary features there are also "subsidiary indices of separateness."

24. See Elsa B. Cardalda Sánchez and Amilcar Tirado Avilés, "Ambiguous Identities! The Affirmation of *Puertorriqueñidad* in the Community Murals of New York City," in *Mambo Montage: The Latinization of New York,* ed. Agustín Laó-Montes and Arlene M.

Dávila (New York: Columbia University Press, 2001), 263–289. Most of the murals in this study were political in nature.

25. Sollors, *Theories of Ethnicity*, xviii.

26. Stuart Hall, "The New Ethnicities," in Hutchinson and Smith, *Ethnicity,* 162.

27. In "Puerto Rican Identity Up in the Air: Air Migration, Its Cultural Representations, and Me 'Cruzando el Charco,'" Alberto Sandoval Sánchez explores the "floating nation" metaphor in this very personal essay in *Puerto Rican Jam*, 189–208.

28. Hernández, *Puerto Rican Voices in English*, 141.

29. In *Boricua Literature*, 18–21, Lisa Sánchez González analyzes the "nationalizing" moves of critics Yanis Gordils and Juan Flores, who both try to argue for the incorporation of "mainland" Puerto Rican literature into a wider national canon. Sánchez González criticizes this strategy because it ignores the "obvious and profound differences between these two literary histories," yet in further discussion of various mainland writers her own arguments evince a nationalizing undercurrent.

30. In his seminal essay "Puerto Rican Literature in the United States: Stages and Perspectives," Juan Flores writes that the literature's most "distinguishing" feature is precisely its "straddling" of "two national literatures and hemispheric perspectives." See Juan Flores, *Divided Borders: Essays on Puerto Rican Identity* (Houston: Arte Público Press, 1993), 145. Despite Flores's clear understanding of the hybrid nature of this literature, he argues for including it within a national Puerto Rican literature. See also n. 29 above.

31. The term "ethnogenesis" comes from the work of Werner Sollors and William Boelhower. In *Beyond Ethnicity: Consent and Descent in American Culture* (New York: Oxford University Press, 1986), Sollors introduces the term and credits it to Andrew M. Greeley, who used it to describe "the phenomenon of emerging ethnicity" (*Ethnicity in the United States: A Preliminary Reconnaissance* [New York: Wiley, 1974], 56–59). In his book *Through a Glass Darkly: Ethnic Semiosis in American Literature* (New York: Oxford University Press, 1987), Boelhower expands the concept through a semiotics approach to mean how ethnic signs are produced and how they operate rhetorically within a text.

32. Jesús Colón migrated to New York City in 1918, Belpré in 1920, and Miranda in 1951. The three writers lived and worked contemporaneously in New York City from 1951 up to 1974, the year Colón died.

33. Sánchez González, *Boricua Literature*, 68–70.

34. For information about Colón and his times, see Edna Acosta-Belén and Virginia Sánchez-Korrol's introduction to Jesús Colón, *The Way It Was, and Other Writings* (New York: Center for Puerto Rican Studies, 1993), 13–30.

35. Boelhower, *Through a Glass Darkly*, 87.

36. Jesús Colón, *A Puerto Rican in New York and Other Sketches,* 2d ed. (New York: International Publishers, 1982), 148. Hereafter cited in text.

37. Colón, *The Way It Was, and Other Writings,* 34.

38. Ibid.

39. Boelhower, *Through a Glass Darkly*, 43.

40. Ibid., 99.

41. For more biographical information on Pura Belpré and a critical analysis of her

work, see Lisa Sánchez González's chapter 3, "A Boricua in the Stacks: Pura Belpré," in *Boricua Literature*, 71–101.

42. Pura Belpré, *Santiago*, 6. Pagination refers to a manuscript of the book in the Center for Puerto Rican Studies Archives, reel 12, Hunter College, City University of New York. The book was published in New York in 1969 by the publisher Frederick Warne. It is available in the center's library. There is also a Spanish version published in 1971 by the same publisher.

43. Ibid., 3.

44. Fredric Jameson, *The Political Unconscious* (Ithaca, NY: Cornell University Press, 1981), 180–181. Hereafter cited in text.

45. Homi Bhabha, *The Location of Culture* (New York: Routledge, 1994).

46. Piñero, *La Bodega Sold Dreams*, 13.

47. Graciany Miranda Archilla Papers, reel 4, box 5, Center for Puerto Rican Studies Archives, Hunter College, City University of New York.

48. In particular, I refer to Pedro Juan Soto's collection of short stories *Spiks* (Mexico: Presentes, 1956), which was translated by Victoria Ortiz (New York: Monthly Review Press, 1973); and José Luis González's stories in *En Nueva York y otras desgracias* (Mexico: Siglo XXI, 1973; repr., Río Piedras, PR: Ediciones Huracán, 1981) and *Veinte cuentos y paisa* (Rio Piedras, PR: Editorial Cultural, 1973).

49. See José Luis González, "El escritor puertorriqueño en exilio," in *El pais de cuatro pisos*, 99–106.

50. Boelhower, *Through a Glass Darkly*, 110.

51. As defined by Werner Sollors, "descent" here means the perceived notion of ethnicity having "blood," "natural," or inherited traits or characteristics. Sollors opposes this concept to "consent," which refers to relations based on marriage or law. See his *Beyond Ethnicity*, 5–6.

52. Miranda Archllla, "The Shadow," 2, 7, manuscript from archives; see n. 47. Hereafter cited in text.

BIBLIOGRAPHY

Acosta-Belén, Edna, and Virginia Sánchez Korrol. Introduction to *The Way It Was, and Other Writings*, by Jesús Colón, 13–30. New York: Center for Puerto Rican Studies, 1993.

Algarín, Miguel. "A Mongo Affair." In *Boricuas: Influential Puerto Rican Writings—an Anthology*, ed. Roberto Santiago, 108–113. New York: Ballantine, 1995.

Belpré, Pura. *Firefly Summer*. Houston: Piñata Books, 1996.

———. Manuscript for *Santiago*. Reel 12. Center for Puerto Rican Studies Archives, Hunter College, City University of New York. 1969.

———. *Santiago*. New York: Frederick Warne, 1969.

Bhabha, Homi. *The Location of Culture*. New York: Routledge, 1994.

Boelhower, William. *Through a Glass Darkly: Ethnic Semiosis in American Literature*. New York: Oxford University Press, 1987.

Brass, Paul R. "Ethnic Groups and Ethnic Identity Formation." In *Ethnicity,* ed. John Hutchinson and Anthony D. Smith, 85–90. Oxford: Oxford University Press, 1996.

Cardalda Sánchez, Elsa B., and Amilcar Tirado Avilés. "Ambiguous Identities! The Affirmation of *Puertorriqueñidad* in the Community Murals of New York City." In *Mambo Montage: The Latinization of New York,* ed. Agustín Laó-Montes and Arlene M. Dávila, 263–289. New York: Columbia University Press, 2001.

Colón, Jesús. *A Puerto Rican in New York and Other Sketches.* 2d ed. New York: International Publishers, 1982.

———. *The Way It Was, and Other Writings.* New York: Center for Puerto Rican Studies, 1993.

Darder, Antonia, and Rodolfo D. Torres, eds. *The Latino Studies Reader: Culture, Economy and Society.* Oxford: Blackwell Publishers, 1998.

Dávila Gonçalves, Michele. "La voz caribeña en la literatura de los Estados Unidos." *Exegesis* 37/38 (2001): 42–46.

Flores, Juan. *Divided Borders: Essays on Puerto Rican Identity.* Houston: Arte Público Press, 1993.

Fox, Geoffrey. *Hispanic Nation: Culture, Politics, and the Constructing of Identity.* Tucson: University of Arizona Press, 1997.

González, José Luis. *En Nueva York y otras desgracias.* Mexico: Siglo XXI, 1973. Repr., Río Piedras, PR: Ediciones Huracán, 1981.

———. *El pais de cuatro pisos y otros ensayos.* Río Piedras, PR: Ediciones Huracán, 1980.

———. *Veinte cuentos y paisa.* Río Piedras, PR: Editorial Cultural, 1973.

Greeley, Andrew M. *Ethnicity in the United States: A Preliminary Reconnaissance.* New York: Wiley, 1974.

Grosfoguel, Ramón. "The Divorce of Nationalist Discourses from the Puerto Rican People: A Sociohistorical Perspective." In *Puerto Rican Jam: Rethinking Colonialism and Nationalism,* ed. Frances Negrón-Muntaner and Ramón Grosfoguel, 57–76. Minneapolis: University of Minnesota Press, 1997.

Grosfoguel, Ramón, Frances Negrón-Muntaner, and Chloe S. Georas. "Beyond Nationalist and Colonialist Discourses: The *Jaiba* Politics of the Puerto Rican Ethno-nation." Introduction to *Puerto Rican Jam: Rethinking Colonialism and Nationalism,* ed. Frances Negrón-Muntaner and Ramón Grosfoguel, 1–38. Minneapolis: University of Minnesota Press, 1997.

Hall, Stuart. "The New Ethnicities." In *Ethnicity,* ed. John Hutchinson and Anthony D. Smith, 161–163. Oxford: Oxford University Press, 1996.

Hernández, Carmen Dolores. *Puerto Rican Voices in English: Interviews with Writers.* Westport, CT: Praeger, 1997.

Hutchinson, John, and Anthony D. Smith, eds. *Ethnicity.* Oxford: Oxford University Press, 1996.

Jameson, Fredric. *The Political Unconscious.* Ithaca, NY: Cornell University Press, 1981.

Laó, Agustín. "Islands at the Crossroads: Puerto Ricanness Traveling between the Translocal Nation and the Global City." In *Puerto Rican Jam: Rethinking Colonial-

ism and Nationalism, ed. Frances Negrón-Muntaner and Ramón Grosfoguel. Minneapolis: University of Minnesota Press, 1997.

Laó-Montes, Agustín, and Arlene M. Dávila, eds. *Mambo Montage: The Latinization of New York*. New York: Columbia University Press, 2001.

Laviera, Tato. *AmeRícan*. Houston: Arte Público Press, 1985.

Miranda Archilla, Graciany. "The Shadow." Center for Puerto Rican Studies Archives, Hunter College, City University of New York. N.d.

Nash, Manning. "The Core Elements of Ethnicity." In *Ethnicity*, ed. John Hutchinson and Anthony D. Smith, 24–28. Oxford: Oxford University Press, 1996.

Negrón-Muntaner, Frances, and Ramón Grosfoguel, eds. *Puerto Rican Jam: Rethinking Colonialism and Nationalism*. Minneapolis: University of Minnesota Press, 1997.

Negrón-Portillo, Mariano. "Puerto Rico: Surviving Colonialism and Nationalism." In *Puerto Rican Jam: Rethinking Colonialism and Nationalism*, ed. Frances Negrón-Muntaner and Ramón Grosfoguel, 39–56. Minneapolis: University of Minnesota Press, 1997.

Piñero, Miguel. *La Bodega Sold Dreams*. Houston: Arte Público Press, 1985.

Reading Group Center. "Esmeralda Santiago, a Note to the Reader." http://www.randomhouse.com/catalog/display.pperl?isbn=9780679756774&view=rg (accessed 13 Sept. 2006).

Rodríguez Vecchini, Hugo. "Cuando Esmeralda 'era' puertorriqueña: Autobiografia etnográfica y autobiografia neopicaresca." *Nómada* 1 (1995): 145–160.

Sánchez González, Lisa. *Boricua Literature: A Literary History of the Puerto Rican Diaspora*. New York: New York University Press, 2001.

Sandoval Sánchez, Alberto. "Puerto Rican Identity Up in the Air: Air Migration, Its Cultural Representations, and Me 'Cruzando el Charco.'" In *Puerto Rican Jam: Rethinking Colonialism and Nationalism*, ed. Frances Negrón-Muntaner and Ramón Grosfoguel, 189–208. Minneapolis: University of Minnesota Press, 1997.

Santiago, Esmeralda. *When I Was Puerto Rican*. New York: Vintage, 1994.

Sollors, Werner. *Beyond Ethnicity: Consent and Descent in American Culture*. New York: Oxford University Press, 1986.

———, ed. *Theories of Ethnicity: A Classical Reader*. New York: New York University Press, 1996.

Soto, Pedro Juan. *Spiks*. Mexico: Presentes, 1956. Trans. Victoria Ortiz as *Spiks* (New York: Monthly Review Press, 1973).

PART II *Political and Historical*

4 ANARCHISM IN THE WORK OF AURORA LEVINS MORALES

FERDÂ ASYA

Critics are increasingly examining the work of Aurora Levins Morales for the themes of minority, multiple, or self-defined identity and instances of immigration, exile, or displacement. While some readers find the nonconformity of her work to a tradition or nation unique, others praise it for its equal affinity with Puerto Rican, Jewish, and American cultures. Most scholars indicate that these characteristics render the writer's work undefinable with respect to not only traditional theories of nation and culture but also more recent concepts such as the transnational or the multicultural. For example, examining the theme of home in the works of Aurora Levins Morales, Rosario Morales, and Esmeralda Santiago, Jamil Khader detects these writers' belonging to and reminiscence of home in their expression of their connection to transnational and transethnic communities of struggle rather than solely to the United States or the Puerto Rican diaspora, and he terms this condition as "subaltern cosmopolitanism." Monika Wadman, on the other hand, rejects the notion of allegiance to any community for the multicultural individual and discerns the emergence of a self whose identity is boundless and unlimited by ethnicity in Rosario Morales and Aurora Levins Morales's *Getting Home Alive*, and she marks this quality of the self as "multiculturality." Lourdes Rojas delineates various themes in *Getting Home Alive* and emphasizes its political and ideological purport. William Luis examines the two writers' book in the context of Puerto Rican American poetry and comments on their use of unconventional forms in portraying the complexity of the ethnic and cultural roots of Puerto Ricans. Rina Benmayor discusses the two writers' achievement of creating a multiplicity of innovative identities out of their common and different experiences as women, immigrants, and activists.

This body of criticism is especially useful in establishing Aurora Levins Morales's place in the literature of the Puerto Rican diaspora, identifying her themes, discovering her reasons for writing, and underscoring the social and political significance of her work. None of these criticisms, however, implies that Levins Morales's work discloses her close affinity with anarchism. Growing up in the rain forest of Indiera Baja in Maricao, Puerto Rico, raised on the liberal ideas of her parents, who were communist intellectuals and activists, and exposed to rebellion and communal resistance with the stories of her immigrant Puerto Rican and Jewish grandparents, Levins Morales inevitably became a progressive thinker. While her physical background planted in her the seeds of ecological anarchism, the radical intellectual ambiance created by her parents at home awakened in her the awareness of individualist anarchism. The heritage of the uncertain existence of her immigrant ancestors in the countries they had to leave and her own equivocal social and political ties to Puerto Rico and the United States incessantly taught her commitment to communist anarchism as a way of sustaining her radical personality, multiethnic existence, and revolutionary art. Reading the work of Levins Morales as a threefold theory of individualist, communist, and ecological anarchism reveals that one of the most important incentives for her to write was her desire to express her strong conviction in the ideology of anarchism.

At the end of the nineteenth century, anarchism was the most prominent force stirring societies, and it emerged split between the individualist regression of the romantic vision and the collectivist progress of Enlightenment thought. The representatives of the romantic vein of anarchism were the revolutionary Mikhail Bakunin and the individualist Max Stirner. The rationalistic William Godwin and the Darwinian Peter Kropotkin conformed to Enlightenment thought. The egoistic nihilism of Stirner associated him with Nietzsche and urged the separation of the self from society. Kropotkin based his communist anarchism on Darwin's theory of evolution; he posited that it was the smartest, not the strongest, who survived through evolution toward mutualism by cooperating with members of society rather than competing with them. Basing his theory of ecological anarchism on Kropotkin's concept of complementarity, Murray Bookchin demonstrates a continuity between nature and society until humans disrupt it by creating institutionalized hierarchies and power relationships in society.[1]

In *Remedios*, Aurora Levins Morales refers to the controversial paper about the origin of species that Charles Darwin presented to the scientific societies in England in 1833 and mentions Karl Marx's *Communist Manifesto*.[2] With the exception of her familiarity with the works of Darwin and Marx, on whose ideas Kropotkin and Bookchin based their anarchist theories, biographical information on Levins Morales yields no direct evidence that she had an affinity with anarchist ideology. However, her definition of herself as a descendant of anarchist, communist, rebellious, and revolutionary ancestors, as well as the textual evidence of her work, clearly shows a remarkable correspondence between her outlook on personal and social issues and the theories of anarchist thinkers such as Stirner, Kropotkin, and Bookchin. It is impossible to describe the defining features of anarchism as a political theory and summarize all the characteristics of the individualist anarchism of Stirner, the communist anarchism of Kropotkin, and the ecological anarchism of Bookchin in the scope of this essay. I will attempt, however, to illustrate some points of congruity between the social and political ideology of Levins Morales and Stirner's notion of individualist anarchism, Kropotkin's idea of mutualism, and Bookchin's conception of continuity between nature and human nature, which formed their theoretical perspectives on anarcho-communism.[3] The unique voice emerging from Levins Morales's work is familiar and innovative, provocative and serene, unified and diversified, public and personal. This voice carries on the Puerto Rican tradition of protest articulated by rebellious writers such as Jesús Colón, Piri Thomas, Felipe Luciano, Miguel Algarín, and Pedro Pietri, and by radical feminists such as Luisa Capetillo, Sandra María Esteves, Luz María Umpierre, and Levins Morales's mother, Rosario Morales. Another strain of this voice recounts, as writers such as Nicholasa Mohr and Esmeralda Santiago do, the personal vicissitudes and social and economic hardships of multiethnic women commuting between two cultures. Still another tone of this voice claims, together with such writers as Tato Laviera and Víctor Hernández Cruz, a nondiscriminatory wholeness of being inclusive of all marginal and oppressed people. The incomparable quality of this voice, however, is its expression of the voice of each one of its predecessors and contemporaries while being a multivocal summons of peace from an internationalist anarchist intellect.

Descending from Puerto Rican and Jewish ancestors, Aurora Levins Morales inherits anarchism as a historical tradition and familial legacy. The anarchist spirit of the Puerto Rican people can be traced back to the revolutionary image of *jíbara*, which, Levins Morales explains, "in the language of the Arawak people, [means] 'she who runs away to be free,' referring to the mixed-blood settlements of escaped slaves, fugitive Indians and European peasants who took to the mountains to escape state control."[4] Significantly, the writer describes herself as "a mountain-born, country-bred, homegrown jíbara child"[5] and derives her roots from revolutionary people close to nature: "Over the years I found peasants, small farmers, revolutionaries in my family tree."[6] George Woodcock states that, unlike Marxists, anarchists consider peasants important for revolution because of their closeness to nature and spontaneous receptivity to anarchic ideas.[7] In *Remedios*, Levins Morales also discovers her connection to people of rebellion through Indiera, her land of common inheritance with them: "In writing about what happened to me, I have found myself identifying with the original inhabitants of the land on which I was born and raised, and with all the runaways and rebels that found their way there over the centuries. As a child, I was proud of the heritage of resistance that seemed to linger."[8] Levins Morales readily discovers a disregard for authority, similar to her own, in the stories of her grandparents and in the lives of her parents. She imagines that her maternal great-great-grandmother Mercedes Gómez must have been "an independent spirit," because she visited her cousin Evaristo Izcoa Díaz in prison in 1895, defying the authorities.[9]

Apparently, in the formation of Levins Morales's anarchist perspective, her rebellious Jewish ancestors were just as influential as her Puerto Rican progenitors. Anarchism, in both its individualist form, with its strong contempt for obedience to authority, and in its communist form, with its rejection of central government, state, and individual leadership, was often attractive to the Jewish people. On her father's side, Levins Morales descends from Jewish immigrants who escaped from Ukraine. In the United States they joined a group of Jews who were, "[d]uring the first three decades of the 20th century, . . . strongly active in a multi-ethnic labor movement and in anarchist, socialist and communist organizing that prioritized identification with the poor and working classes across cultural lines."[10] She mentions that her paternal great-grandmother Leah took part in the garment strike uprising in 1933 and led "a circle of unemployed women, talking, writing, organizing."[11] Undeniably, her Jewish and Puerto Rican parents' thinking and lifestyle had a consequential impact not only on her progressive thinking but also on her radical perspective of life: "My parents, communists who were frequently under surveillance and harassment from the authorities, were obvious inheritors of this tradition [of runaways and rebels]; it was fitting that we lived within a mile of where Matias Brugman, a leader of the uprising against Spain in 1868 and a probable descendant of Jews, was killed by Spanish soldiers."[12] She attests to the significance of her origin for the shaping of her intellectual life: "How I think and what I think about grows from my identity as a jíbara shtetl intellectual and organizer."[13]

According to the individualist anarchist Max Stirner, one achieves the status of individualist anarchist only when one is completely severed from the notions of humanity and society and attains the state of "un-man," described by this thinker as "man who does not correspond to the *concept* man, as the inhuman is something human which is not conformed to the *concept* of the human." The un-man cannot abide society because its pharisaical language misnames his virtue as vice, deeming him the "devil" instead of the "un-man" or "egoistic man." Having no hope in the reformation of social institutions, the unique egoist completely "annihilate[s]" them and "work[s] himself forth out of society." He creates a value system antithetical to that of civilized society and posits: "I . . . put forth my *creations* from myself." He declares his omnipotence: "I am creator and creature." Having faith in nothing besides his own creation, the egoist "returns into his creative nothing, of which he is born."[14] The social universe has no importance for the egoist. Neither does the anarchism of the egoist have any bearing on society.

Aurora Levins Morales's social, altruistic, and philanthropic spirit prompts her to shift her anarchist consciousness from the individual to the social realm. Unlike the individualist anarchist, she has a profound conviction in the individual's power to change society. She strengthens her self-righteousness, as she knows that it is essential for social struggle, and does not allow mourning for the poor and the dead to weaken her sense of social mission. In *Getting Home Alive* she writes "Class Poem" to prove the uselessness of the "guilt" she is supposed to feel for her favorable circumstances among the less fortunate. She remembers her friend Tita, who had to curtail her desire of becoming a scientist to work in a factory,[15] "Norma / who died of parasites in her stomach when she was four," and "Angélica / who caught on fire while stealing kerosene for her family / and died in pain."[16] Instead of lamenting them, however, she celebrates her family members' and her own "privilege."[17] She believes that only self-confidence can promote the struggles for freedom from poverty, abuse, and death, personally and socially:

> I am going to strip apology from my voice
> my posture
> my apartment
> my clothing
> my dreams
> because the voice that says the only true puertorican
> is a dead or dying puertorican
> *is* the enemy's voice—
> . . . .
> I refuse to join them there.
> I will not suffocate.
> I will not hold back.
> Yes, I had books and food and shelter and medicine
> and I intend to survive.[18]

Although one can hear the egoistic Stirner's assertions such as "I am the unique" or "it is I alone who have everything"[19] reverberating in these lines, Levins Morales's purpose, unlike Stirner's, is not merely egoistic. She aims at delineating a milieu in which the individual is mentally transformed from a passive recipient of wounds and abuses into a fighter for personal and social justice and freedom. Levins Morales has "learned that suffering does not improve people, that slavery does not ennoble us for freedom, that oppression springs from oppression, echoing the twisted lessons we learn from our pain."[20] Stirneresque anarchist Margaret Anderson confirms the usefulness of Stirner's egoistic ideology for the social interest: "[S]elf-dependence is merely the first of one's intricate obligations to his universe, and self-completion the first step toward that wider consciousness which makes the giving-out of self valuable. . . . [T]hat human being is of most use to other people who has first become of most use to himself."[21] The individualist anarchist sensibility provides Levins Morales with an opportunity to reexamine her personal history and interpret it in the context of a larger history from an anarchist perspective. She mentions in both *Remedios* and *Medicine Stories* the ritual sexual abuse that she endured as a child.[22] She explains that her recovery was possible only by "[p]oliticizing the abuse, coming to understand its social context and meaning."[23] Noticeably, her individual injuries create in Levins Morales the need to search history for reasons for social evils and make her aware of the sources of personal and social violations; she knows that the personal is not far from the social: "In the violated places of my body I find the voices of the conquered of my island."[24] She realizes that her personal hurts empower her socially and discovers in her "[m]emory, individual and collective, . . . a significant site of social struggle."[25] In turn, the *remedios* (remedies) she writes to correct social wrongdoing restore her personal integrity: "There is no distance between conquest and abuse, battering and war. The journey of healing is the same."[26]

Levins Morales postulates her reason for writing her book *Remedios* as a desire "to frame historic events in ways that would contribute to decolonizing the historical identities and imaginations of Puerto Rican women and to the creation of a culture of resistance."[27] Indeed, in her book she advocates an international intellectual resistance to social transgressions by recovering the stories of the lives of women around the world—mothers, maidens, spinsters, writers, artists, slaves, queens, warriors, rebels, revolutionaries—beginning with the sub-Saharan African First Mother, who, she says, "was never the golden-haired Eve in Renaissance paintings. . . . She was walnut-skinned with hair like a thundercloud."[28] Levins Morales's individualist anarchism stimulates a mental "transformation" from passive personal to active social resistance rather than simply prompting an egoistic enterprise: "Cultural activism is not separate from the work of organizing people to do specific things. In fact, successful organizing depends on this *transformation* of vision; the most significant outcome of most organizing campaigns is the *transformation* that takes place in people who participate. . . . Cultural work, the work of infusing people's imaginations with possibility, with the belief in a bigger future, is the essential fuel of revolutionary fire."[29]

Peter Kropotkin's notion of anarcho-communism is based on a decentralized, stateless society whose members live and work in cooperation with each other in producing their commodities without depending on the wage system.[30] According to Kropotkin, the most essential condition of a stateless community is the absence of a government. He finds the parliamentary system of government not only inherently defective but also ineffective for the needs of people and asserts that, by overthrowing the state and transferring the power from government to community, people can obtain freedom and also make greater intellectual and economic progress: "By taking for our watchword anarchy in its sense of no-government, we intend to express a pronounced tendency of human society. In history we see that precisely those epochs when small parts of humanity broke down the power of their rulers and reassumed their freedom were epochs of the greatest progress, economic and intellectual."[31]

Throughout her entire oeuvre, Levins Morales establishes her social and political status outside the boundaries of state, ethnic group, and nation. Instead, she declares a sense of belonging to people or communities without borders. She devises a linkage with people around the world, as she is convinced that "our liberation is bound up with that of every other being on the planet."[32] In "Child of The Americas" and elsewhere in her work, she traces her lineage back to the people of Africa, Europe, the Americas, the Caribbean, and the Jewish diaspora.[33] Each one of her progenitors contributes an equal share in forming her heterogeneous being and obscures the borderlines of her existence, rendering her ineligible for the "ethno-racial pentagon" of American society, in which she presently lives.[34] The writer finds herself a misfit in the States, where ethnicity is depicted with cursory boundaries. As no official term is assigned to define her identity, she names it "new," and unable to develop a sense of belonging to a single country, she marks her birthplace "at the crossroads."[35] Like most Boricua writers, she seems to consider "Boricuas as a nationless nation coping with nationalist constructions of racial identity."[36] At the same time, however, like Kropotkin, who observes a greater intellectual progress in a society without state and government, Levins Morales perceives in Puerto Rican people, with limited rights of citizenship, a great capacity to create a unique literature:

> The literature of the diaspora is a literature of multiple vision, born of the intersections of oppression and resistance. This multiplicity has given us the tools to challenge inherited identities of gender, class and "race," and through it we have found a way to affirm our complex realities. It is this complexity, this many-sided seeing, this daring to name the uses and practices of power wherever they are found, that is our greatest gift—to the emerging cultures of the diaspora and to the changing island culture of Puerto Rico.[37]

Thus, Levins Morales regards the absence of state and government not only as freedom from oppression and limitation but also as progress toward a rich and powerful intellect capable of creating new forms of being and living.

Noticeably, no other theory has a more powerful impact on Levins Morales's work than the theories of Kropotkin and Bookchin on natural and social evolution. Both thinkers draw a parallel between mutual aid in natural evolution and cooperation in social life. In his work *Mutual Aid: A Factor of Evolution*, which disputes the principle of competition in Darwin's theory of evolution, Kropotkin stresses that the notions of cooperation, sociability, and mutual aid are effective in the lives and evolution of primal peoples, bands, tribes, and communities.[38] Notably, Kropotkin points out that the medieval era was a thriving period for community and mutual-aid practices and posits that the emergence of city-states caused these practices to diminish. He discovers the reappearance of the cooperative spirit of mutual-aid communities in present-day labor unions and strikes.[39] Basing his notion of mutualism on Kropotkin's concept of cooperation, Bookchin posits that "from an ecological standpoint, life-forms are related in an ecosystem not by the 'rivalries' and 'competitive' attributes imputed to them by Darwinian orthodoxy, but by the mutualistic attributes emphasized by a growing number of contemporary ecologists."[40] Both Kropotkin and Bookchin contrast human communities, which are natural, with the state, which is man-made and destructive of human communities, bands, and tribal groups.[41]

Levins Morales demonstrates that, as well as the development of city-states, the rise of capitalism and growth of modern civilization and culture weaken people's obligations toward each other and remove the communal spirit from society. Her regret for the loss of communal life becomes evident in *Remedios* in her study of Puerto Rican history before the era of the *caciques* (Arawak leaders). She explains that decentralized "clan" life was destroyed by the individual's accumulation of wealth: "In the long ago of our people, family was family and clans lived side by side without trying to boss each other. . . . The more naborías [the laboring class in Arawak society] generated wealth, the more wealth had to be defended."[42] In the next step of the so-called "progress,"[43] the wealthy individual's desire to dominate obliterated the communal spirit and the clan lost power. It was the end of mutually hospitable clan life. The contrast between the conviviality of the tribal people of Nigeria in 700 AD and the loneliness of the entrepreneurs of city-states in their ambitious moneymaking exemplifies Levins Morales's preference for communal life: "Here in the villages, African democracy is being woven with local ingredients: a weft of self-confidence and kinship, a warp of many places to enter and many ways to live. While the heads of merchant city-states reach for the sky, building higher and higher walls, the people of the villages make widening circles with their arms and notice who stands on either side."[44] Her anarchist spirit compels the writer to resist modern civilization, which separates communities and individuals from each other. Like many anarchists, she observes that the individual's endeavor to obtain the tools of modern civilization provides the individual with the privileges of middle-class life, but this effort breaks down the human contact engendered by mutual-aid practices: "Every one of these products [in airline catalogs] is designed to make it unnecessary to have human contact, to ask anyone for help, to have relationships of *mutual support*."[45] She also indicates that the denial of multicultural education is part of a policy of cultural imperialism and condemns those in political power for their antidemocratic inclination in education. They kill the social spirit of people by eliminating cultural interaction between communities of different cultural backgrounds: "The denial of our interrelatedness is killing this planet and too many of its people."[46]

Over the years, the ambiguous social and political status of the Puerto Rican people in the United States has weakened their allegiance to state organizations in both Puerto Rico and the United States and encouraged them to form independent mutual-aid communities.[47] Having no full state or government support, Puerto Ricans have turned to networks of their own people, who, having endured hardships themselves, are willing to provide support to others in need. Although the raison d'être of these communities is not to re-create the medieval era, their principle of mutual aid imitates the social structure of medieval communities. Their cooperative spirit is based on mutual need and support rather than dependence on the government. Levins Morales mentions the involvement of her family members in this particular variety of independent mutual aid in both *Remedios* and *Getting Home Alive*.[48] Her maternal grandmother tells her the way in which her grandfather Manolin found his job as janitor: "There was a group of Puerto Ricans, tú sabes [you know], people who all knew each other and looked out for each other, not familia, but parecido [similar], because, you know, there weren't so many of us in New York then."[49] In *Remedios*, the writer depicts an anarchist variation of this mutual-aid effort also in the work of her grandmothers and mother as organizers and members of unions and strikes: "My mothers stitch through the decades, through strikes and disasters, the changing fabrics passing through their hands."[50]

A striking similarity exists between the ecological perspective of Levins Morales and the ecological anarchism of Bookchin, who bases his theory of ecological anarchism on Kropotkin's principle of natural and social evolution.[51] Bookchin contends that the continuity between nature and society has been obstructed by man's competitive temperament to dominate not only each other but also nature, turning the relations of "organic community" into those of "consumer society" in a bourgeois industrial setting.[52] Levins Morales's anarchist social and political perspective discloses her familiarity with the individualist and communist anarchist theory. Her ecological anarchist philosophy, however, apart from revealing her formal training and historical heritage, originates primarily from her own lifestyle close to nature. She admits her intellectual affinity with ecology: "I am an ecologist's daughter."[53] She also notes the close attachment the people of Indiera form with the land: "They tend the forest like a mother and plant memory in the red soil."[54] She compares her ties with the land to the bloodline she shares with her ancestors: "I have inherited all the cities through which my people passed, and their dust has sifted and settled onto the black soil of my heart."[55] Yet, she attains her true ecological sensibility from her direct experience of living close to nature. She admits no discontinuity between the earth and herself: "I feel the earth under my feet. From the soles of my feet, roots grow down into the earth, deeper and deeper."[56] Her love of the earth is not limited to the boundaries of a nation. She explains: "Nationalism is about gaining control, not about loving land."[57] She holds modernization and urbanization responsible for interrupting the continuity between humans and nature and blames industrialism for destroying the ecosystem by turning land into commodity with "more housing developments, shopping malls, factories"[58] and also for depriving people of their land in Puerto Rico.[59] Her devotion to the land, free of national borders, renders her authentic to wherever she lives; hence, she inherits and inhabits the world.

Bookchin posits that the stability of an ecosystem is firmly dependent on the complexity, intricacy, and diversity of the interrelationships of an ecological community: "[B]y replacing a highly complex, organic environment with a simplified, inorganic one—man is disassembling the biotic pyramid that supported humanity for countless millennia."[60] He claims that the similarity between nature and society is in their ability to form a unity, a whole, in diversity. He explains that diversity is a vital factor in ensuring the survival of an ecosystem:

> In contrast to biotically complex temperate zones, relatively simple desert and arctic ecosystems are very fragile and break down easily with the loss or numerical decline of only a few species. The thrust of biotic evolution over great eras of organic evolution has been toward the increasing diversification of species and their interlocking into highly complex, basically mutualistic relationships, without which the widespread colonization of the planet by life would have been impossible.[61]

In both "Ending Poem" (which she wrote with her mother, Rosario Morales) and her poem "Child of The Americas," Levins Morales declares the "complexity" of her existence,[62] and in *Remedios*, she asserts that she owes her "whole[ness]" to her mixed origins: "I *am* the mix."[63] She claims to have inherited a diversity of cultures from Africa, the Americas, the Caribbean, Europe, and the Jewish people,[64] and includes in her family hummingbirds, lizards, frogs, and rats living in her house in the rain forest of Indiera: "I grew up in a house where the permeable boundaries of other worlds criss-crossed our own."[65] A variety of cultures and various elements of nature complement each other and culminate in the heterogeneous wholeness of personality she achieves.

Levins Morales demonstrates that both land and humans have mobility and neither can be confined to national boundaries. Using the examples of the Grand Canyon, which "shift[s] and collapse[s] and move[s] continually," and the soil erosion caused by heavy rainfall in Puerto Rico, she proves that "the real land, the soil and rocks and vegetation, is never still." She renders the term "homeland" unusable by claiming that "soil does not have nationality."[66] Bestowing to humans the same quality of mobility as that of land, she proclaims that nationality, as a concept, is meaningless. Instead, she believes in a global society and homeland: "[P]eople circulate like dust, intermingling and reforming, all of us equally ancient on this earth, all equally made of the fragments of long-exploded stars, and if, by some unlikely miracle, a branch of our ancestors has lived in the same place for a thousand years, this does not make them more real than the ones who have continued circulating for that same millennium. All of us have been here since people were people. All of us belong on earth."[67] As an alternative to owning land, Levins Morales discovers a tradition of sharing land practiced on the mountains of Puerto Rico from the 1570s to the 1860s by the indigenous people, who "didn't own the land. They moved across it and lived from it."[68] She is convinced that humans should not try to dominate nature, for "[e]cology undermines ownership,"[69] and thus she follows her communist father's advice and offers the family land in the highest point of Cordillera Central of western Puerto Rico to her neighbors for communal use.[70]

In her first piece in *Getting Home Alive*, Levins Morales writes about a wolf. The wolf comes to her dark, bare, and still surroundings out of the torrents of a formidable storm. The writer greets the wolf with extreme gladness and recognizes it as her "true self" in all its changing shapes "to protect itself from extinction," though they are all near-extinct species. Levins Morales is the only one who sees the "wildness and beauty of a wolf." Even so, she is unable to explain the wolf to the "younger, more unaware" people sharing the campfire with her. They have no notion of it; "they don't know what a wolf is. They have never seen one." Neither are they interested in her description of this animal, nor do they understand how "urgently, desperately important" the wolf is for the "survival" of the world. Levins Morales claims the wolf is her "totem."[71] Unlike the writer, younger people do not recognize the wolf as a symbol of the communal way of living in a clan; they are unable to understand the power and perfection attained by a libertarian, anarchic way of living. Illuminating as lightning and productive as rain, anarchism is the "true" nature of Aurora Levins Morales's art. Clearly, the writer is convinced that it is her responsibility to rekindle the principles of anarchism in society through her art to save not only the young people around the campfire but the whole world.

NOTES

1. See Murray Bookchin, *Post-Scarcity Anarchism* (Berkeley, CA: Ramparts Press, 1971). For a definition and leading figures of anarchism, see David Weir, *Anarchy & Culture: The Aesthetic Politics of Modernism* (Amherst: University of Massachusetts Press, 1997); Richard D. Sonn, *Anarchism* (New York: Twayne Publishers, 1992); John Clark, *The Anarchist Moment: Reflections on Culture, Nature and Power* (Montreal: Black Rose Books, 1984).

2. Aurora Levins Morales, *Remedios: Stories of Earth and Iron from the History of Puertorriqueñas* (Boston: Beacon Press, 1998), 150–151.

3. For basic principles of these thinkers and their theories, see Max Stirner, *The Ego and Its Own*, ed. David Leopold (Cambridge: Cambridge University Press, 1995); Peter Kropotkin, *Kropotkin's Revolutionary Pamphlets: A Collection of Writings by Peter Kropotkin*, ed. Roger N. Baldwin (New York: Benjamin Blom, 1968); Murray Bookchin, *The Ecology of Freedom: The Emergence and Dissolution of Hierarchy* (Palo Alto, CA: Cheshire, 1982).

4. Aurora Levins Morales, *Medicine Stories: History, Culture and the Politics of Integrity* (Cambridge, MA: South End Press, 1998), 68. See also Aurora Levins Morales and Rosario Morales, *Getting Home Alive* (Ithaca, NY: Firebrand Books, 1986), 54.

5. Levins Morales and Morales, *Getting Home Alive*, 90.

6. Levins Morales, *Medicine Stories*, 76.

7. George Woodcock, *Anarchism: A History of Libertarian Ideas and Movements* (New York: Meridian, 1962), 26–28.

8. Levins Morales, *Remedios*, xxviii.

9. Ibid., 160.

10. Levins Morales, *Medicine Stories*, 87–88; see also Levins Morales, *Remedios*, 184.

11. Levins Morales, *Remedios*, 185.

12. Ibid., xxviii–xxix.

13. Levins Morales, *Medicine Stories*, 68.

14. Stirner, *The Ego and Its Own*, 159, 296, 209, 238, 209, 135, 324.

15. Levins Morales and Morales, *Getting Home Alive*, 45, lines 6–13.

16. Ibid., 46, lines 47–48 and 52–54.

17. Ibid., 47, lines 66 and 76.

18. Ibid., 47, lines 79–86 and 90–94.

19. Stirner, *The Ego and Its Own*, 135, 162.

20. Levins Morales and Morales, *Getting Home Alive*, 201.

21. Margaret C. Anderson, "To the Innermost," *Little Review* 1, no. 7 (Oct. 1914):

2–3. Margaret Anderson uses this term to indicate an inner transformation in the individual from altruism to egoism. Although the speaker of "Class Poem" seems to display a similar transformation, Levins Morales's anarchism transcends the individual realm and takes the form of a self-defense mechanism of an oppressed community.

22. Levins Morales, *Remedios*, 19–20, 55–63; Levins Morales, *Medicine Stories*, 117–119.

23. Levins Morales, *Medicine Stories*, 3.

24. Levins Morales, *Remedios*, 55.

25. Levins Morales, *Medicine Stories*, 13.

26. Ibid., 55.

27. Levins Morales, *Remedios*, 25.

28. Ibid., 2.

29. Levins Morales, *Medicine Stories*, 4 (italics added).

30. Kropotkin's ideas on anarcho-communism can be found in *The Conquest of Bread and Other Writings,* ed. Marshall Shatz (Cambridge: Cambridge University Press, 1995); and *Kropotkin's Revolutionary Pamphlets*. For Bookchin's theoretical perspectives on anarcho-communism, see his *Toward an Ecological Society* (Montreal: Black Rose Books, 1980), especially 223–225.

31. Kropotkin, "Anarchist Communism: Its Basis and Principles," in *Kropotkin's Revolutionary Pamphlets*, 49, 62. For Kropotkin's ideas against the state, see also *Mutual Aid: A Factor of Evolution* (London: Freedom Press, 1987), especially 180–229; and *The State: Its Historic Role* (London: Freedom Press, 1903).

32. Levins Morales, *Medicine Stories*, 125.

33. Levins Morales and Morales, *Getting Home Alive*, 50.

34. Monika Wadman, in "Multiculturalism and Nonbelonging: Construction and Collapse of the Multicultural Self in Rosario and Aurora Levins Morales's *Getting Home Alive*," *Lit: Literature Interpretation Theory* 11, no. 2 (2000): 219–237, defines the term "ethno-racial pentagon," which she borrows from David Hollinger (*Postethnic America: Beyond Multiculturalism* [New York: Basic Books, 1995]), as "a grid of identities governing the ways of accounting for citizens in the United States" (221). Wadman explains: "By requiring its citizens to identify singly (by checking only one box on the census), the multiculturalist model also obscures the actual cultural crossovers and mixed subjectivities resulting from the American experience" (221).

35. Levins Morales and Morales, *Getting Home Alive*, 50, lines 18 and 19.

36. The term "Boricua," referring to the Puerto Rican diaspora community, comes from Lisa Sánchez González, *Boricua Literature: A Literary History of the Puerto Rican Diaspora* (New York: New York University Press, 2001), 8. In the chapter "Boricua Modernism: Arturo Schomburg and William Carlos Williams," 42–70, she posits that reading the works of Schomburg and Williams as black immigrant and white American texts respectively confutes the complexities of their work as Boricua literature. She reads their poetry in the colonial and African diasporic contexts.

37. Levins Morales, *Medicine Stories*, 65.

38. Kropotkin explains his ideas on evolution and mutual aid in *Mutual Aid*, as well as in "Anarchist Communism": "It has shown us that, in the long run of the struggle for

existence, 'the fittest' will prove to be those who combine intellectual knowledge with the knowledge necessary for the production of wealth, and not those who are now the richest because they, or their ancestors, have been momentarily the strongest" (53).

39. In his work *Ethics: Origin and Development*, trans. Louis S. Friedland and Joseph R. Piroshnikoff (Bristol, UK: Thoemmes Press, 1993), Kropotkin places his inquiry of evolution in the context of morality and argues that the basic principles of morality, solidarity, sociality, sympathy, and instinct are found in nature and people close to nature (73). See also "Anarchist Morality," in *Kropotkin's Revolutionary Pamphlets*, in which he bases the morality of anarchism on the principles of equality and uses the phrase "morality of equality" interchangeably with "morality of anarchism" (105).

40. Murray Bookchin, *The Modern Crisis* (Philadelphia: New Society Publishers, 1986), 56. Bookchin explores the concept of mutual aid in his work *The Ecology of Freedom* and states that mutualism is especially beneficial to the development of a large variety of species in nature. In *The Rise of Urbanization and the Decline of Citizenship* (San Francisco: Sierra Club Books, 1987), he describes the evolution of cities as ecocommunities and presents civic participation as a social counterpart to biological mutualism.

41. It is the rebellion against the state that causes these thinkers' theories of mutual aid to be anarchist. See Kropotkin, *Mutual Aid* and "Anarchist Morality"; and Bookchin, *The Ecology of Freedom*.

42. Levins Morales, *Remedios*, 34.

43. Ibid., 35.

44. Ibid., 28–29.

45. Levins Morales, *Medicine Stories*, 94 (italics added).

46. Ibid., 14.

47. See Denis Lynn Daly Heyck, *Barrios and Borderlands: Cultures of Latinos and Latinas in the United States* (New York: Routledge, 1994), for a brief overview of the social, cultural, and political status of the Puerto Rican people in the United States and the community organizations they have formed as a social support system since the 1950s.

48. See, e.g., Levins Morales, *Remedios*, 181–182.

49. Levins Morales and Morales, *Getting Home Alive*, 42.

50. Levins Morales, *Remedios*, 184.

51. In the acknowledgments of his book *Ecology of Freedom*, Bookchin expresses his indebtedness to Kropotkin's natural and social mutualism: "Kropotkin is unique in his emphasis on the need for a reconciliation of humanity with nature, the role of mutual aid in natural and social evolution, his hatred of hierarchy, and his vision of a new technics based on decentralization and human scale" (no page number in text).

52. Bookchin, *Post-Scarcity Anarchism*, 63.

53. Levins Morales, *Medicine Stories*, 99.

54. Levins Morales, *Remedios*, 96.

55. Levins Morales and Morales, *Getting Home Alive*, 90.

56. Ibid., 133.

57. Levins Morales, *Medicine Stories*, 108.

58. Ibid., 107.

59. Operation Bootstrap was an experimental program initiated by the U.S. govern-

ment in the 1950s to industrialize Puerto Rico. It caused many people to lose their land on the island and migrate to the United States. For Kropotkin's ideas on the integration of industry and manufacturing with agriculture and his criticism of global market economy in favor of regionalist economy, which discourages competition, see *Fields, Factories and Workshops Tomorrow,* ed. Colin Ward (London: George Allen & Unwin, 1974), especially the chapter "Small Industries and Industrial Villages," 121–168.

60. Bookchin, *Post-Scarcity Anarchism*, 67. For Bookchin's views on organic society and hierarchy, see *The Ecology of Freedom*, especially the chapters "The Outlook of Organic Society," 43–61, and "The Emergence of Hierarchy," 62–88.

61. Bookchin, *The Modern Crisis*, 58. Also in *The Modern Crisis* Bookchin notes: "The evolution of society out of nature and the ongoing interaction between the two tend to be lost in words that do not tell us enough about the vital association between nature and society and about the importance of defining such disciplines as economics, psychology, and sociology in natural as well as social terms" (59).

62. Levins Morales and Morales, *Getting Home Alive*, 212–213, 50.

63. Levins Morales, *Remedios*, 196.

64. Levins Morales and Morales, *Getting Home Alive*, 50.

65. Levins Morales, *Medicine Stories*, 99.

66. Ibid., 103.

67. Ibid., 104.

68. Ibid., 106.

69. Ibid., 100.

70. Ibid., 98, 106.

71. Levins Morales and Morales, *Getting Home Alive*, 16.

BIBLIOGRAPHY

Anderson, Margaret C. "To the Innermost." *Little Review* 1, no. 7 (Oct. 1914): 2–5.

Benmayor, Rina. "Crossing Borders: The Politics of Multiple Identity." *Centro de Estudios Puertorriqueños Bulletin* 2, no. 3 (Spring 1988): 71–77.

Bookchin, Murray. *The Ecology of Freedom: The Emergence and Dissolution of Hierarchy*. Palo Alto, CA: Cheshire, 1982.

———. *The Modern Crisis*. Philadelphia: New Society Publishers, 1986.

———. *Post-Scarcity Anarchism*. Berkeley, CA: Ramparts Press, 1971.

———. *The Rise of Urbanization and the Decline of Citizenship*. San Francisco: Sierra Club Books, 1987.

———. *Toward an Ecological Society*. Montreal: Black Rose Books, 1980.

Clark, John. *The Anarchist Moment: Reflections on Culture, Nature and Power*. Montreal: Black Rose Books, 1984.

Heyck, Denis Lynn Daly. *Barrios and Borderlands: Cultures of Latinos and Latinas in the United States*. New York: Routledge, 1994.

Hollinger, David. *Postethnic America: Beyond Multiculturalism*. New York: Basic Books, 1995.

Khader, Jamil. "Subaltern Cosmopolitanism: Community and Transnational Mobility in Caribbean Postcolonial Feminist Writings." *Feminist Studies* 29, no. 1 (Spring 2003): 63–81.

Kropotkin, Peter. "Anarchist Communism: Its Basis and Principles." In *Kropotkin's Revolutionary Pamphlets: A Collection of Writings by Peter Kropotkin*, ed. Roger N. Baldwin, 44–78. New York: Benjamin Blom, 1968.

———. "Anarchist Morality." In *Kropotkin's Revolutionary Pamphlets: A Collection of Writings by Peter Kropotkin*, ed. Roger N. Baldwin, 79–113. New York: Benjamin Blom, 1968.

———. *The Conquest of Bread and Other Writings*. Ed. Marshall Shatz. Cambridge: Cambridge University Press, 1995.

———. *Ethics: Origin and Development*. Trans. Louis S. Friedland and Joseph R. Piroshnikoff. Bristol, UK: Thoemmes Press, 1993.

———. *Fields, Factories and Workshops Tomorrow*. Ed. Colin Ward. London: George Allen & Unwin, 1974.

———. *Kropotkin's Revolutionary Pamphlets: A Collection of Writings by Peter Kropotkin*. Ed. Roger N. Baldwin. New York: Benjamin Blom, 1968.

———. *Mutual Aid: A Factor of Evolution*. London: Freedom Press, 1987.

———. *The State: Its Historic Role*. London: Freedom Press, 1903.

Levins Morales, Aurora. *Medicine Stories: History, Culture and the Politics of Integrity*. Cambridge, MA: South End Press, 1998.

———. *Remedios: Stories of Earth and Iron from the History of Puertorriqueñas*. Boston: Beacon Press, 1998.

Levins Morales, Aurora, and Rosario Morales. *Getting Home Alive*. Ithaca, NY: Firebrand Books, 1986.

Luis, William. *Dance between Two Cultures: Latino Caribbean Literature Written in the United States*. Nashville, TN: Vanderbilt University Press, 1997.

Rojas, Lourdes. "Latinas at the Crossroads: An Affirmation of Life in Rosario Morales and Aurora Levins Morales' *Getting Home Alive*." In *Breaking Boundaries: Latina Writing and Critical Readings*, ed. Asunción Horno-Delgado et al., 166–177. Amherst: University of Massachusetts Press, 1989.

Sánchez González, Lisa. *Boricua Literature: A Literary History of the Puerto Rican Diaspora*. New York: New York University Press, 2001.

Sonn, Richard D. *Anarchism*. New York: Twayne Publishers, 1992.

Stirner, Max. *The Ego and Its Own*. Ed. David Leopold. Cambridge: Cambridge University Press, 1995.

Wadman, Monika. "Multiculturalism and Nonbelonging: Construction and Collapse of the Multicultural Self in Rosario and Aurora Levins Morales's *Getting Home Alive*." *Lit: Literature Interpretation Theory* 11, no. 2 (2000): 219–237.

Weir, David. *Anarchy & Culture: The Aesthetic Politics of Modernism*. Amherst: University of Massachusetts Press, 1997.

Woodcock, George. *Anarchism: A History of Libertarian Ideas and Movements*. New York: Meridian, 1962.

5 PUERTO RICAN LITERATURE IN A NEW CLAVE

Notes on the Emergence of DiaspoRican

WILLIAM BURGOS

That the study of Puerto Rican literature written outside Puerto Rico has reached a new formal stage is indicated by the publication in 2001 of Lisa Sánchez González's *Boricua Literature: A Literary History of the Puerto Rican Diaspora.* Sánchez González herself comments on this in her introduction, where she points out, correctly, that "despite our numbers and over a century of community building in our colonial metropole, no complete study of our literature has ever been published."[1] This fact places Sánchez González in the unique position of defining that hundred-year arc of Boricua literature, its origins, its salient characteristics, and its milestones. Like all good literary historians, Sánchez González is helping to give form and meaning to a complex corpus of texts by providing a set of terms and a model for their interrelatedness, a model that, in turn, others will respond to, build on, react against, or reconstruct. Sánchez González's study not only is a literary history, in other words, but is now part of the history she writes about. In this respect, two key words in her title—"Boricua" and "diaspora"—merit commentary because they reflect something about the contemporary moment in which the study and the literature are written.

Sánchez González provides us with a context for her choice of terms. She identifies both "Boricua" and "Nuyorican" as important signifiers of cultural affiliation, especially for Puerto Ricans in the United States.

Though she uses both in her study, she is careful to point out that "Boricua" is obviously the more inclusive of the two, in part because it is linguistically rooted in the indigenous, though now mostly vestigial, Taíno culture of Puerto Rico. Straightforward as Sánchez González's positioning of these terms in relation to each other is, it reflects an interesting shift in historical perspective. New York, certainly since the end of World War II, was arguably the center of the Puerto Rican *colonia*, as Sánchez Korrol termed it,[2] and people's perceptions of Puerto Ricans in the United States came to be dominated by the images and issues associated with it. As other Latino groups are now displacing Puerto Ricans in New York neighborhoods they once dominated, and as Nuyoricans are increasingly moving to other places in the United States or moving back to Puerto Rico, the centrality, indeed the hegemony, of that New York–based culture may now be ending or entering a new phase. Sánchez González's subordination of "Nuyorican" to "Boricua" encapsulates this trend.

Her choice of "diaspora" as a key term in her study clearly indicates that Sánchez González is drawing on the relatively new field of diaspora studies to provide a theoretical framework for her analysis of the literature. One of the problems with framing Puerto Rican experience vis-à-vis the United States derives, as so many have discussed, from Puerto Rico's unique, one could even say anomalous, political and social contract with the United States: the Commonwealth, or Estado Libre Asociado. By the congressional fiat of 1917, Puerto Ricans born in Puerto Rico—which is not a state of the United States—are U.S. citizens. This simple fact, and all its complex consequences, stymied sociologists' attempts to analyze Puerto Rican migration to the United States according to the paradigms used for other immigrant groups (the Irish, Italians, Eastern European Jews, etc.). "Immigrant" Puerto Ricans just did not "behave" like these others. Marxist discourse, to take another example, has also met with Puerto Rico's recalcitrance to fit in. Despite perceptive and persuasive Marxist critiques of U.S. imperialist exploitation of Puerto Rico, Puerto Ricans have consistently voted to maintain the status quo, somehow preferring to work outside the box of more orthodox political arrangements, whether they be statehood or independence. These are just two examples of what could be a long list of instances of the ways Puerto Ricans, for whatever reasons, defy or unsettle categorization.

The diaspora model Sánchez González favors for her work is promising precisely because it is premised on the postmodernist awareness that the conceptual boundaries between categories are permeable and elastic, and so are peoples' behaviors. To frame Puerto Rican literature written outside the island as the result and expression of the experience of "scattering" and "forced dislocation" (as Sánchez González does) provides a means of at least getting at the oddity of Puerto Rican experience. But it is also true that that experience no longer seems so "odd" now that we have a theoretical model that privileges examining the complex ways in which displaced peoples create, renew, and improvise their cultures. Bricolage, it seems, is endemic in the global village, and Puerto Ricans have been bricoleurs for quite a while.

My own project in the remainder of this essay will be to complement Lisa Sánchez González's pioneering work by looking a little more closely at the twenty-five-year period from 1975 to 2000, which began with the prevalence of the Nuyorican and ends with the reconception of Puerto Rican identity as "diasporan" or (to echo Tato Laviera's coinage "AmeRícan")[3] as DiaspoRican. The following "Notes on the Emergence of DiaspoRican," based on some close readings, gathers observations and thoughts for what clearly needs to be a larger undertaking.

Hybridity and Fusion: Porto Rican (1898) → Nuyorican (1975)

Surely the prehistory of Nuyorican begins with "Porto Rican." Here are some notes for that prehistory.

Porto Rico: In the early documents of the U.S. occupation of Puerto Rico, the island's name appears thus.[4]

There is no word *porto* in either the Spanish dictionary or the English.

Porto: An Anglo-Spanish fusion resulting from the difficulty English-speaking North Americans have in trilling the Spanish *r*. "Porto" also assimilates Spanish *puerto* to its English cognate "port." The "port" in "Porto" Anglicizes the Spanish *puerto*, and the terminal *o* in "Porto" Hispanicizes the English "port."

Porto as linguistic emblem of the contact zone in which cultures [Anglo–North American/Puerto Rican] meet, clash, and grapple with each other, often in contexts of highly asymmetrical relations of power, such as colonialism, slavery, or their aftermaths as they are lived out in many parts of the world today.[5]

In "Porto" there is certainly evidence of grappling: English has Spanish in a headlock.

"Porto" is an American coinage denoting the first phase of U.S.–Puerto Rican cultural relations: imposition. Germinating in "Porto" is the attempt to designate English as one of the official, if not the official, insular languages. (Years of compulsory English-language education on the island failed.) Perhaps the Jones Act too is latent in "Porto." Certainly the assumption of assimilation is that, as "Porto" draws "Puerto" toward English, so the United States assumed it could "Americanize" Puerto Rico and make it "a showcase for democracy."

Has there ever been such a thing as a *Porto* Rican? Maybe "Porto Ricans" is just the failed abracadabra of the United States for commanding assimilated islanders into existence. (It proved easier to just give them citizenship.) The Porto Rican is a projected hybrid, the colonizer's desideratum: the Anglicized Puerto Rican. This project remained unachieved: hybrids can be achieved by grafting, but sometimes the graft does not take.

Porto Rican did not take.

The botanical metaphor of grafting suggests one model for achieving hybridity: imposition. In science, this may often be a good thing, but in human relations, as we all know, it often causes problems. "Porto Rican" as a metaphor for U.S–Puerto Rican cultural relations marks a path not taken, a certain type of failed hybridization. But there is an alimentary metaphor that offers another working model for hybridity: eating. The Latino critic who currently wields this metaphor to great rhetorical effect is Richard Rodriguez. Here's Rodriguez in an interview talking about the mixing of cultures (*mestizaje*): "There may be a feminine impulse within colonial history that we do not understand. It's not as simple as two males butting heads—one wins, the other loses. Perhaps there is such a thing as seduction. Conversion. Perhaps cultures absorb one another. If it is true that the Franciscan padre forced the Eucharist down the Indian's throat, maybe she forgot to close her mouth. Maybe she swallowed the Franciscan priest."[6] Remarkable here is the way Rodriguez takes a familiar scene of colonial oppression (the Franciscan padre and his wafer) and suddenly allows us to see it from the perspective of the oppressed, suggesting that what appears to be an act of submission may also be an act of consumption. The *india* eats more than the emblem of European hegemony. She eats the European.

If one applies this metaphor to the U.S–Puerto Rican dynamic, then "Porto Rican" is the Anglo–North American speaking through gritted teeth, a safeguard against ingesting foreign substances. "Porto" resists Spanish. But from the Puerto Rican side of the contact zone, "Nuyorican" means that we "forgot" to close our mouths. Nuyoricans swallowed English and along with it New York. Hybridity in this case is marked by linguistic incorporation, resulting in a new patois, intermingling vocabularies, syntaxes, and grammars.

Like many groups nicknamed pejoratively because of their "deviance," Nuyoricans embraced or, to use Rodriguez's metaphor, swallowed the name island Puerto Ricans used to designate their culturally mongrel compatriots. When did this happen? If we go by the literary record, the Nuyorican is a result of the post–World War II Great Migration. Piri Thomas's *Down These Mean Streets* documents the cultural milieu for Puerto Ricans in New York prior to the full cultural consequences of that migration. Thomas's family belonged to the Pionero Migration (1898–1945). Born in 1928, when there was a growing but still small Puerto Rican presence in New York, Thomas lived in a city where the discourse on Puerto Rican identity was scarcely available, and Thomas found his thinking about his identity dominated by the Anglo-American/African American discourse on race, which polarized identity literally in terms of white and black.[7] By the time Thomas's autobiography appeared in 1967, the Puerto Rican population in New York had exploded, and the discourse on Puerto Rican identity entered a new phase.

If there is a Nuyorican Manifesto, it is arguably Miguel Algarín's introduction to the groundbreaking anthology he edited with Miguel Piñero in 1975, *Nuyorican Poetry: An Anthology of Puerto Rican Words and Feelings*. A political activist, poet, and educator, Algarín was in a unique position to articulate what Nuyorican meant, both to the Nuyorican community itself and those outside it. Born in Puerto Rico in 1941 but raised in New York City, Algarín belongs to the generation of the Great Migration and came of age in the sixties, when the civil rights movement gave rise to the Black Power movement, which in turn provided a model for the Chicano movement and the Nuyorican movement. In his introduction, Algarín writes as a participant in the great changes taking place in the United States and his barrio, but he is also distinguished from other Nuyorican writers because he is academically trained. (At the time he edited the anthology, he was already a professor of English literature at Livingstone College, Rutgers University.) The combined perspectives of objective literary critic and impassioned Nuyorican are evident throughout Algarín's introduction, as in the following passage, where he theorizes about the emergence of Nuyorican language:

> Language and action are simultaneous realities. Actions create the need for verbal expression. If the action is new so must the words that express it come through as new. Newness in language grows as people do and learn things never done or learned before. The experience of Puerto Ricans on the streets of New York has caused a new language to grow: Nuyorican. Nuyoricans are a special experience in the immigration history of the city of New York. We come to the city as citizens and can retain the use of Spanish and include English. . . . Everything is in English in the U.S.A., yet there is also a lot of Spanish, and Spanish is now gaining. The mixture of both yields new verbal possibilities, new images to deal with the stresses of living on tar and cement.[8]

The key idea underpinning Algarín's discussion is "mixture," a linguistic mixture ("new verbal possibilities") that results from lived experience. "The experience of Puerto Ricans on the streets of New York has caused a new language to grow: Nuyorican." In this sentence Algarín encapsulates the progression from Puerto Rican to Nuyorican, with the catalyst for change being the streets of New York. Though Algarín goes on to point out that Nuyorican is the dialect of a "slave class" akin to all those that empire collects around its wealth and power (15), it is also inventive because "there are no boundaries around it," no "empires of rules" (19). As his choice of words suggest, Algarín is well aware of the social and political pressures that precipitated Nuyorican culture and language, and yet throughout his introduction, he envisions a dynamic interaction and creative fusion of cultures. Decades before what is now referred to as the "browning" of America (Latinos have surpassed African Americans as the largest "minority" in the United States), Algarín points out that despite the prevalence of English in the United States, "there is also a lot of Spanish, and Spanish is now gaining." The implication here is that Nuyoricans are not merely the by-products of empire but also part of a larger cultural process still in progress (the complex interaction among the Spanish, English, African, and indigenous peoples on the North American continent).[9]

Nuyorican, in Algarín's text, represents a positive model of "hybridity," a fusion of cultures that assimilate each other and, out of this mutual assimilation, produce something new. Much of Nuyorican literature celebrates this "newness" or explores (to borrow Algarín's terms) the "disruptions" or "tensions" concomitant with it. The poem that best captures both these aspects of Nuyorican newness is Tato Laviera's now-canonical "My Graduation Speech" (1979).[10] The poem's speaker addresses us by asserting,

> i think in Spanish
> i write in english

Note that these are paratactic assertions. The speaker does not say, "I think in Spanish, *but* I write in English" or vice versa. Neither English nor Spanish is subordinated to the other, but both are equally a part of the speaker. He does, however, mark a distinction between an inner and outer language (or a private and a public): Spanish is the language of thought (perhaps the language he is "born with"), and English is the language of public expression (what he learned at school). Yet as the poem proceeds, this neat division of languages does not hold. The speaker cannot keep English out of his thoughts or Spanish out of his writing. As the "graduate" ricochets between the two linguistic poles of his identity, a third term emerges: "spanglish" or "spanenglish." And it is broken (*matao*) "spanglish" that breaks forth in the "speech's" peroration:

> hablo lo inglés matao
> hablo lo español matao
> no sé leer ninguno bien
>
> so it is spanglish to matao
> what i digo
> !ay, virgen, yo no sé hablar!

The speaker concludes by lamenting that he does not speak any of his languages well. It is possible that the "graduate" is sincere, and if this is so, then Laviera is giving us a representation of a Nuyorican who feels marginal to both the cultures he inhabits and ashamed because of his marginality ("tonto in both languages"). But it is also possible that Laviera's graduate addresses his audience ironically. Though he pretends to be "jodío" (fucked up or fucked) because he is a graduate of two cultures, master of none (as some in the audience see him), his "speech" in fact displays a dazzling—and funny—verbal dexterity as he manipulates the three languages he knows, inflecting them with what Algarín identified as the "bomba rhythm" (15–16) of Nuyorican speech. Laviera's representation of the Nuyorican celebrates the new culture but also acknowledges, as the graduate says, that "estamos jodíos." This is how some outsiders to the community see Nuyoricans and also, as Laviera's poem suggests, how Nuyoricans who are unable to make sense of their "marginality" see themselves.

Whereas Laviera uses irony to show us that Nuyoricans have a cultural integrity that is not always recognized as such, Ana Lydia Vega, a writer and professor of French literature living in Puerto Rico, uses satire to expose what she sees as the fundamental confusions of Nuyorican identity in her 1977 short story "Pollito/Chicken."[11] The story's title is taken from a song known to all children in Puerto Rico's public school system. The song's lyrics are meant to teach children English: "Pollito, chicken/Gallina, hen/Lapiz, pencil/Y pluma, pen." Vega's allusion to the song serves two purposes. It evokes the history of the U.S. attempt to impose its culture on the island (in this instance, by mandating the teaching of English to Puerto Rican schoolchildren). Vega also uses the song to raise some profound questions about translation. The lyrics innocently seem to suggest that the words of the two languages are equivalent to each other: *pollito* = chicken. But Vega's story questions this equivalence, suggesting that though *pollito* and "chicken" share the same referent, they represent completely different cultural perspectives on the bird. In other words, what a *jíbaro* in the mountains of Puerto Rico understands by *pollito*—the images, associations, even taste and texture, conjured by the word—is different from what the farmer in Iowa understands by "chicken." The Latin root of "translation" means "brought or carried across," and when we translate, we bring meaning from one language into another. This etymology reveals a spatial metaphor of movement (carry across), and in her story, Vega works with the literal and figurative implications of this metaphor: what happens when

Puerto Ricans translate themselves from one place to another (Puerto Rico/New York) and from one culture to another? In the end, her story suggests that Puerto Rican identity is untranslatable.

Suzie Bermiúdez, the story's protagonist, is the titular "*pollito*/chicken." She has lived away from Puerto Rico for ten years and in the interim has "assimilated" to U.S. culture. Vega's representation of the "Nuyorican" emphasizes, not a fusion of cultures, but the suppression of one by the other. The story is written in a free indirect discourse, which gives us access to Suzie's "consciousness." As Vega represents it, it is a consciousness colonized by American capitalist culture. Here is an excerpt narrating what prompts Suzie to take an impromptu vacation in Puerto Rico: "Lo que la decidió fue el breathtaking poster de Fomento que vio en la travel agency del lobby de su building. El breathtaking poster mentado representaba una pareja de beautiful people holding hands en el funicular del Hotel Conquistador." For this story, Vega does not use the Nuyorican speech Algarín celebrates but creates a parody of it, in which English is inserted into the flow of the Spanish (the way "gringos" insert themselves into the tropical Caribbean landscape represented by the poster). All the phrases in English, throughout the story, are catchphrases and clichés, many derived from U.S. advertising. Suzie's consciousness—as Vega represents it—exhibits, not the vitality of a new dialect for a new environment (as Algarín describes "Nuyorican"), but one language colonized by another, producing, not enhanced speech, but empty, materialist discourse. So assimilated is Suzie to the rank commercialism of the United States (as the story has it) that she does not see the irony of her "nostalgia" for Puerto Rico being prompted by a travel agency poster. She desires a Puerto Rico that has been marketed to her as a commodity for her consumption.

The rest of the story goes on to show that "visiting" Puerto Rico is more complicated for Suzie than it is for the "beautiful people" of the travel poster. For one thing, Suzie is not just "visiting"; she is also returning, and in the Freudian framework that Vega uses, she is returning to what has been "repressed," which are the irrepressible and inerasable traces of her origins. To be sure, Suzie attempts to cover or suppress these traces: she decides not to visit her "Grandma" in Lares; she dyes her hair (the signifier of her native "kinkiness") with "Wild Auburn" and straightens it with "Curl-free"; and she speaks to everyone in "inglés legal." But despite her attempts to wear "white face," Suzie is finally "outed" as a "genuine" Puerto Rican by her sexual desire for a "native" bartender. He, unlike the Puerto Rico of the "breathtaking poster," is the real Puerto Rico, with which at the story's end Suzie is literally and figuratively united. She sleeps with the bartender, and her surrender to her libidinal urges coincides with the Puerto Rican nationalist that apparently has always been latent (though repressed) in her, as evidenced by her shouting "¡VIVA PUELTO RICO LIBREEEEEEEEEEEEEEEE!" at the precise moment of her orgasm.

Vega's "Pollito/Chicken" exemplifies an essentialist nationalist discourse similar to the kind underlying the coinage of "Porto Rican" by the United States. In this kind of nationalist discourse, cultures don't "fuse" or "interact," and if they do, then the result is something "inauthentic," "impure," or "illicit." This kind of nationalist discourse frames contact between cultures as combative. Vega wrote her story in response to the hoopla in the United States over the bicentennial (Suzie Bermiúdez applies "Bicentennial Red" lipstick before going to the swimming pool at the Hotel Conquistador). As the United States celebrated two hundred years of independence, Vega wrote to remind her readers that Puerto Ricans, a colonized people, were not free. In choosing a Nuyorican to represent a colonized society, however, Vega perpetuated a conservative model of Puerto Rican identity, which presumes that it is grounded in the island's culture and rejects hybridity as mere schizophrenia. (As the bartender says about Suzie to his "buddies," "La tipa . . . no se sabe si es gringa o pueltorra, bródel.") While Algarín in New York praised "Nuyorican" as "a new language, a new tradition of communication" (9), Ana Lydia Vega in Puerto Rico insisted that Puerto Rican identity does not translate. You are either a *pollito* or a chicken.[12]

Diffusion and Diaspora (1975–2003)

The different perspectives on "Nuyorican" reflected in Algarín's anthology introduction and Ana Lydia Vega's short story represent two opposed camps in the debate about Puerto Rican identity (which are of course specific instances of two generic models for defining "national identity," the essentializing and the relativizing). The fact that Algarín was raised in the United States and Vega predominantly in Puerto Rico seems to confirm the stereotype that in the *colonia* the definition of *puertorriquenidad* tends to be more "open" and inclusive, whereas among

Puerto Ricans on the island it is conservative and restrictive. But of course these kinds of polarities simplify what is in reality a more complex situation. In April 1983, at Rutgers University, Newark, an important conference took place on Puerto Rican identity, out of which emerged a more complex commentary on *puertorriqueñidad* in the form of a collection of essays, *Images and Identities: The Puerto Rican in Two World Contexts*.[13] The title of the collection is telling: the use of "identities" rather than "identity" acknowledges that Puerto Ricans, whatever they are, are not one thing nor ought to be. There is also the acknowledgment of "contexts," two "worlds"—cultural spaces, geographies—that affect the identities. The word "images" alludes to the issue of representation, and indeed many of the pieces in the collection focus on how Puerto Ricans have been represented in various media, particularly in literature.

One of these texts, "La guagua aérea,"[14] is unique because it both reflects on representations of Puerto Rican identity and now belongs to the canon of texts—stretching all the way back to the "origins" of the national literature, Manuel A. Alonso's *El jíbaro* (1849)—dedicated to "representing" or formulating that identity. Luis Rafael Sánchez, like Ana Lydia Vega, was born, lives, and works in Puerto Rico. But unlike his compatriot, Sánchez's vision of Puerto Rican identity avoids the polarities of "authentic" and "colonized" that inform Vega's. His text, of all the texts in the collection, offers a postmodernist perspective on Puerto Rican identity, drawing with versatile sophistication on the full arsenal of techniques that characterize postmodernist texts: nonhierarchized juxtapositions of high and low cultural references, dizzying shifts in narrative perspective, the absence of a "unifying" voice or perspective, and the pervasive use of parody to put all perspectives into "free play," to name just a few.

Sánchez's story begins with two nonverbal "events": a scream and laughter.[15] The scream issues from a stewardess, who, significantly, is North American, "rubia de helada intensidad" (23). The scream is in response to seeing two "jueyes" (mangrove crabs), illegally smuggled onto the plane by a Puerto Rican passenger (the setting is a night flight from San Juan to New York), which have escaped and are crawling around the cabin. The scream is answered by "una carcajada" (a burst of laughter) coming from the Puerto Rican passengers, who, initially terrified by the scream, now realize that its cause was nothing more than two harmless crabs. The crabs, however, are not merely harmless; they mark the cultural difference between the "tripulación, uniformemente gringa" (the uniformly gringo flight crew) and the "gentío mestizo" (mob of mestizos), the passengers. The gringo flight crew represents the idea of uniformity, the attempt to impose it on others, and, by implication, the resistance to "difference." The stewardess's scream inadvertently exposes this resistance as fear of otherness, which is usually masked by the decorum of the so-called rules and regulations of air travel (such as health regulations forbidding the transportation of produce and live animals). The scream also exposes how absurd this fear of otherness is. Its object, after all, is nothing more than two crabs, a familiar sight to Puerto Ricans and a savory part of the diet on the island.

The passengers' laughter signals their awareness that the power and sophistication of U.S. technology have been eluded by some cunning passenger determined to bring to New York a taste of Puerto Rico, and that the stewardess's overreaction reveals a fear underlying what seemed to be the calm assurance and authority of the gringos. The laughter pinpoints the inception of an ironic consciousness among the passengers: for the first time the mestizos "see" the "gringos" from a double perspective, how the "gringos" present themselves and what they hide. (Mestizo laughter is always ironic.) This insight, as the story exemplifies, is liberating. It initiates a stream of verbal discourse that ends only with the story's ending, and it is through this effusion of language that Sanchez represents two of the story's fundamental assertions about Puerto Rican identity: *mestizaje* and its link to the Puerto Rican diaspora.

Mestizaje and the diaspora are linked in numerous ways in Sanchez's baroque text, but the most significant instance also coincides with the story's conclusion. In the Spanish original, the third paragraph (in which the passengers' communal laughter breaks into a polyphony of voices) is an unbroken nonstop rush of exuberant prose. Near the end, however, there is a surprise: a narrative "I" emerges. The narrator proceeds to describe a conversation with a woman seated next to him, a conversation he describes as a "rito" (ritual) (29) that no member of the "comunidad tribal" can avoid. The shift here to language evoking anthropology and its study of "primitive cultures" already prepares us for an objectifying look at the Puerto Ricans, whose discourse we have been immersed in for most of the story with little commentary.

The ritual the narrator and the woman participate in is a Q and A, in which each, as fellow Puerto Ricans, is expected to ask the other, "Where are you from?" The narrator, however, deliberately answers this question obtusely ("de Puerto Rico"), knowing that the woman already assumes that he is Puerto Rican (they are on *la guagua aérea*, after all). His point, though, is to tease the woman, to make her aware that she's making assumptions about him based on appearance. When the woman presses him for specific information ("¿De qué pueblo?"), he answers Humacao, a town with an indigenous name, evoking with it the history of Spanish conquest and mixture with the peoples of the New World.

The narrator knows he must complete his part of the ritual dialogue by asking the woman in turn where she is from. At this point the woman takes the narrator's initial ironic response to her a step further. She too answers "de Puerto Rico." The narrator then tells us that he had assumed that that would be her answer ("me requetesé la respuesta"), but when he presses her to name the specific town, she surprises him with "de Nueva York." That the answer comes as a surprise is indicated by the narrator's concluding meditation on all the possible meanings of the unexpected answer. The irony of the woman's final answer trumps the narrator's previous answer to her question about his origins. He had sought to make her aware that his presence on the airplane did not necessarily mean he was Puerto Rican. But her answer turns the tables and teaches him—and by extension the reader—that Puerto Rican "pueblos" are not all in Puerto Rico. The island is dispersed. The diaspora as an essential catalyst of Puerto Rican identity is invoked in the story's final line: "una nación flotante entre dos puertos de contrabandear esperanzas" (30).

In 1983, when Sánchez wrote "La guagua aérea," he achieved one of the first (if not the first) complex, multivalent representations of Puerto Rican identity in the literature. The previous era of the "Nuyorican" tended to polarize Puerto Rican identity in terms of the fusion of Puerto Rico and New York (or negatively, as Vega does, as "schizophrenia"). Sánchez's story brings to the foreground the dynamism of the diaspora itself and its impact on Puerto Ricans' sense of themselves. In the twenty-year period since Sánchez wrote his short story, the field of diaspora studies has emerged, which examines the impact of geographical dispersal on different peoples. To examine Puerto Rican identity from a diasporan perspective is to take into account the full range of geographies and the rich complex of racial and cultural mixtures that define *puertorriqueñidad.* In other words, a diasporan perspective leads to an emphasis on *mestizaje.* The discourse of "Diasporicanization" that Sánchez opened up finds expression in the work of contemporary Puerto Rican poets and writers, who are exploring the implications of *mestizaje* in our culture. The performance artist Mariposa (born Maria Teresa Fernandez) confronts these implications directly in "Ode to the DiaspoRican." The poem begins and ends with a physical geography, in which the speaker traces the markers of her mixed racial heritage:

Mira a mi cara Puertorriqueña
A mi pelo vivo
A mis manos trigueñas
Mira mi corazón que se llena de orgullo
y di me que no soy Boricua

The wheat-colored hands and the kinky hair mentioned in this stanza are well-known indicators in the Caribbean of racial mixture and are sometimes used by the (usually Eurocentric) elite to confer a lower status on those who bear them. In between these opening and closing confrontational stanzas, Mariposa traces another geography, this time an urban landscape:

Some people say that I'm not the real thing
Boricua, that is
cuz I wasn't born on the enchanted island
cuz I was born on the mainland
north of Spanish Harlem
cuz I was born in the Bronx . . .
some people think that I'm not bonafide
cuz my playground was a concrete jungle
cuz my Rio Grande de Loiza was the Bronx River
cuz my Fajardo was City Island
my Luquillo, Orchard Beach
and summer nights were filled with city noises
instead of coquis

and Puerto Rico
was just some paradise
that we only saw in pictures.

The switch from Spanish to English signals a shift from identity embedded in the body (the "cara Puertorriqueña")[16] and deriving from the island (and ultimately Africa and Europe) to identity resulting from the diaspora, the movement to the United States, to New York City (and, even within New York City, the minidiaspora of Puerto Ricans born "north of Spanish Harlem" in the Bronx). Through a series of juxtaposed place-names (Rio Grande de Loiza/Bronx River, Fajardo/City Island, Luquillo/Orchard Beach), the speaker makes the conventional contrast in Puerto Rican American literature between the Puerto Rican pastoral and the U.S. urban environments that represent the two termini of Puerto Rican migration. But Mariposa also suggests that the Bronx River is *translated* into the Rio Grande de Loiza: having moved across the Atlantic, the poem argues, not only are Puerto Ricans transformed or, to be more precise, transculturated, but they transform the place they inhabit. This process of translating the place of origin is beautifully captured in the couplet preceding the closing stanza:

No nací en Puerto Rico
Puerto Rico nació en mí

Implicit in these lines is Benedict Anderson's idea of "nationality" and "nationhood" as "imagined communities."[17] The Puerto Rico of the diaspora, as Luis Rafael Sánchez depicts it and as Mariposa lyricizes it, exists beyond mere geographical boundaries and is more than fusions of polarized cultures. This epistemological shift in how we think of cultural identity is now, to borrow from Wallace Stevens, the climate of our poetic imaginings of who we are.

NOTES

1. Lisa Sánchez González, *Boricua Literature: A Literary History of the Puerto Rican Diaspora* (New York: New York University Press, 2001), 1.

2. Virginia Sánchez Korrol, *From Colonia to Community: The History of Puerto*

Ricans in New York City*, 2d ed. (Berkeley and Los Angeles: University of California Press, 1994).

3. Tato Laviera, *AmeRícan* (Houston: Arte Público Press, 1985).

4. For some examples, see Kal Wagenheim and Olga Jiménez de Wagenheim, eds., *Puerto Ricans: A Documentary History* (New York: Doubleday, 1973), in particular part 5, "Citizens of Porto Rico."

5. Mary Louise Pratt, "Arts of the Contact Zone," in *Ways of Reading*, 5th ed., ed. David Bartholomae and Anthony Petrosky (Boston: Bedford/St. Martin's, 1999), 584. See also Pratt's *Imperial Eyes: Travel, Writing and Transculturation* (London: Routledge, 1992), 1–11.

6. Paul Cowley, "An Ancient Catholic: Interview with Richard Rodriguez," *America*, 23 Sept. 1995, 8. Juan E. de Castro cites this passage in his insightful analysis of Rodriguez's contributions to the discourse of *mestizaje*. See Juan E. de Castro, *Mestizo Nations: Culture, Race, and Conformity in Latin American Literature* (Tucson: University of Arizona Press, 2002), chap. 8, "Richard Rodriguez in 'Borderland': The Relocation of the Discourse of Mestizaje."

7. For an excellent discussion of Thomas's dilemma as a Puerto Rican writer trying to understand his identity, see Sánchez Gonzalez's *Boricua Literature*, chap. 4, "The Boricua Novel: Civil Rights and 'New School' Nuyorican Narratives." The issue of race in Puerto Rican identity has not disappeared, but the discourse that has evolved in the U.S. Puerto Rican community allows it to be addressed in ways that circumvent mere polarization. See, e.g., Willie Perdomo's "Nigger Reecan Blues" (a poem dedicated to Piri Thomas), in his *Where a Nickel Costs a Dime* (New York: W. W. Norton, 1996); and Martin Espada's "Niggerlips," in his *Rebellion Is the Circle of a Lover's Hands* (Willimantic, CT: Curbstone Press, 1990).

8. Miguel Algarín and Miguel Piñero, eds., *Nuyorican Poetry: An Anthology of Puerto Rican Words and Feelings* (New York: William Morrow, 1975), 15. Hereafter cited in text.

9. For two insightful short discussions of this process and the so-called Latinization of the United States, see Richard Rodriguez, *Brown: The Last Discovery of America* (New York: Viking Press, 2002); and Mike Davis, *Magical Urbanism: Latinos Reinvent the U.S. Big City* (New York: Verso Books, 2001).

10. Tato Laviera, *La Carreta Made a U-Turn* (Gary, IN: Arte Público Press, 1979), 7.

11. Ana Lydia Vega and Carmen Lugo Filippi, *Vírgenes y mártires* (Río Piedras, PR: Editorial Antillana, 1981), 73–80.

12. Another text to consider in relation to Vega's is Jaime Carrero's "Jet Neorriqueño/Neo-Rican Jetliner," first published in *San Juan Review* in Apr. 1965 and reprinted in Wagenheim and Wagenheim, *Puerto Ricans*.

13. Asela Rodríguez-Seda de Laguna, ed. and trans., *Images and Identities: The Puerto Rican in Two World Contexts* (New Brunswick, NJ: Transaction, 1987). I'm working with the English title of this collection. The essays gathered for the book, however, were first published by the same editor in a Spanish-language edition, *Imágenes e identidades: El puertorriqueño en la literatura* (Río Piedras, PR: Ediciones Huracán, 1985). Sanchez's short story "La guagua aérea" was written in Spanish, and I quote from that text. The

story is to be found in the English edition as "The Flying Bus" (17–25). Since 1987 there has been another translation, by Diana Vélez, first published in the *Village Voice* and then later in *Catalog: Exposición "La casa de todos nosotros/A House for Us All"* (New York: El Museo del Barrio, 1992), 24–39.

14. For an excellent discussion of "La guagua aérea," see Alberto Sandoval Sánchez's "Puerto Rican Identity Up in the Air: Air Migration, Its Cultural Representations, and Me 'Cruzando el Charco,'" in *Puerto Rican Jam: Rethinking Colonialism and Nationalism*, ed. Frances Negrón-Muntaner and Ramón Grosfoguel (Minneapolis: University of Minnesota Press, 1997), 189–208.

15. I stress the nonverbalness of the events Sánchez begins with because they are his way of indicating the primalness of the responses of all the parties involved.

16. For another poem that explores Puerto Rican identity in corporeal and geographical tropes, see Chloé S. Georos's "native of nowhere" in Negrón-Muntaner and Grosfoguel, *Puerto Rican Jam.*

17. Benedict Anderson, *Imagined Communities: Reflections on the Origin and Spread of Nationalism* (London: Verso, 1991).

BIBLIOGRAPHY

Algarín, Miguel, and Miguel Piñero, eds. *Nuyorican Poetry: An Anthology of Puerto Rican Words and Feelings*. New York: William Morrow, 1975.

Anderson, Benedict. *Imagined Communities: Reflections on the Origin and Spread of Nationalism*. London: Verso, 1991.

Castro, Juan E. de. *Mestizo Nations: Culture, Race, and Conformity in Latin American Literature*. Tucson: University of Arizona Press, 2002.

Cowley, Paul. "An Ancient Catholic: Interview with Richard Rodriguez." *America*, 23 Sept. 1995.

Davis, Mike. *Magical Urbanism: Latinos Reinvent the U.S. Big City*. New York: Verso Books, 2001.

Espada, Martin. *Rebellion Is the Circle of a Lover's Hands*. Willimantic, CT: Curbstone Press, 1990.

Laviera, Tato. *AmeRícan*. Houston: Arte Público Press, 1985.

———. *La Carreta Made a U-Turn*. Gary, IN: Arte Público Press, 1979.

Perdomo, Willie. *Where a Nickel Costs a Dime*. New York: W. W. Norton, 1996.

Pratt, Mary Louise. "Arts of the Contact Zone." In *Ways of Reading*, 5th ed., ed. David Bartholomae and Anthony Petrosky, 581–596. Boston: Bedford/St. Martin's, 1999.

———. *Imperial Eyes: Travel, Writing and Transculturation*. London: Routledge, 1992.

Rodriguez, Richard. *Brown: The Last Discovery of America*. New York: Viking Press, 2002.

Rodríguez-Seda de Laguna, Asela, ed. *Imágenes e identidades: El puertorriqueño en la literatura*. Río Piedras, PR: Ediciones Huracán, 1985.

———, ed. and trans. *Images and Identities: The Puerto Rican in Two World Contexts*. New Brunswick, NJ: Transaction, 1987.

Sánchez González, Lisa. *Boricua Literature: A Literary History of the Puerto Rican Diaspora*. New York: New York University Press, 2001.

Sánchez Korrol, Virginia. *From Colonia to Community: The History of Puerto Ricans in New York City*. 2d ed. Berkeley and Los Angeles: University of California Press, 1994.

Sandoval Sánchez, Alberto. "Puerto Rican Identity Up in the Air: Air Migration, Its Cultural Representations, and Me 'Cruzando el Charco.'" In *Puerto Rican Jam: Rethinking Colonialism and Nationalism*, ed. Frances Negrón-Muntaner and Ramón Grosfoguel, 189–208. Minneapolis: University of Minnesota Press, 1997.

Thomas, Piri. *Down These Mean Streets*. New York: Knopf, 1967.

Vega, Ana Lydia, and Carmen Lugo Filippi. *Vírgenes y mártires*. Río Piedras, PR: Editorial Antillana, 1981.

Wagenheim, Kal, and Olga Jiménez de Wagenheim, eds. *Puerto Ricans: A Documentary History*. New York: Doubleday, 1973.

6 THE POLITICAL LEFT AND THE DEVELOPMENT OF NUYORICAN POETRY

TRENTON HICKMAN

The subject of historical knowledge is the struggling, oppressed class itself. . . . What characterizes revolutionary classes at their moment of action is the awareness that they are about to make the continuum of history explode.

—WALTER BENJAMIN, "On the Concept of History" (1940)

The explosion of Nuyorican poetry, with its self-awareness as a new rupture in literary development, owes its foundational energy to its connection to the political Left and radical revolutionary politics. William Luis' *Dance between Two Cultures* (1997) provides an excellent study of Nuyorican poetry's indebtedness to at least one politically radical institution born of the Puerto Rican diaspora, the Young Lords. While I agree with Luis' assertion that the revolutionary politics of the Young Lords fired much of the Nuyorican poetry scene, I argue that Nuyorican poetry's ties to radical leftist politics can be traced to several other sources as well—to the social clubs and social gatherings of the early diasporic Puerto Rican *colonias* and their associated publications, to contact with U.S. prison culture in the 1960s and 1970s, and to the encouragement and sponsorship of various political and cultural organizations, from the Socialist and Communist parties to other avant-garde artistic movements in New York City that also evidenced a commitment to "alternative" politics. As the global spread of the Puerto

Rican diaspora increasingly moves Nuyorican poetry into contact with larger currents of the American political Left, it may be that Nuyorican poetry's prolonged interconnection with the political Left has forced the evolution of Nuyorican poetry into its next incarnation of artistic identity.[1]

Poetry and the Puerto Rican Social Clubs of New York City

In 1970, Federico Ribes Tovar published *El libro puertorriqueño de Nueva York*, a bilingual "handbook" to the New York Puerto Rican community. One of the aspects of New York Puerto Rican culture that Ribes Tovar highlights is its devotion to poetry:

> Hundreds of thousands of Puerto Ricans have arrived in this city of New York and established residence here. With them they have brought their music, their family traditions, and above all else, their poetry, for Puerto Rico is a land of poetry and poets. It seems incredible to the other ethnic groups which make up the population of New York that the Puerto Ricans assiduously attend the frequent poetry recitals given in this city by both amateur reciters and those of international reputation and the lectures on verse which are held at social and cultural clubs, as well as listening avidly to the poetry recitals broadcast over the radio.[2]

While it is easy to detect an apologist eagerness in the tone of his words, Ribes Tovar highlights a fact often overlooked in considering the genesis of Nuyorican poetry: the men and women of Puerto Rican heritage in New York who would become the Nuyorican poets grew up with poetry playing an integral role in private and public events in their communities. As such, these Puerto Rican New Yorkers did not need to embrace the public performance of poetry merely as an imitative reaction to the Beats, the St. Mark's Poetry project, or other poetry movements in New York City, though this predisposition and conditioning to public poetry in New York Puerto Rican communities would create natural affinities with these other artistic movements.[3] From the time when enclaves of Puerto Ricans—which Virginia Sánchez Korrol and others have dubbed "*colonias*"—formed in various sections of New York City, social clubs and organizations promoted poetry as part of their parties, festivals, and other social activities. Jesús Colón's personal archive of printed programs from these different gatherings demonstrates that the public performance of at least one poem, if not more, was extremely common.[4]

While not all these social clubs and their associated activities had direct ties to radical leftist politics, many of them allied themselves with the political stances of the Left, which they saw as friendly to Puerto Rican issues concerning the national status of the home island, sympathetic to the desire for many Puerto Rican workers to participate in labor unions, and helpful for generating resistance to the racism that many Puerto Ricans encountered as they lived and worked in New York City. Virginia Sánchez Korrol has shown how the first of these social groups derived from "tobacco workers' associations, mutual aid groups, and trade unions"—some of the most left-leaning, politically active Puerto Rican entities to be found in New York City.[5] Soon thereafter, the Communist Party of America, the International Workers Order, the Socialist Labor Party, and other leftist groups saw the opportunity for such gatherings to create enthusiasm for their own political goals.[6] These groups were encouraged by writers who were also members of the organizations, like Jesús Colón, Juan Antonio Corretjer, Bernardo Vega, Clemente Soto Vélez and others, to use neighborhood gatherings to nurture connections. The journal *Pueblos Hispanos*, which was edited by Bernardo Vega and provided significant sponsorship of many of these community gatherings during its publication run, is but one example of what was produced in these political outreach efforts.[7] These activist-writers were involved enough in the leftist political scene of New York City that Colón and his compatriots garnered the unwelcome interest of the House Un-American Activities Committee, which accused Colón and his friends of a "Communist penetration of the Puerto Rican nationality group" and the "disseminat[ion] and distribut[ion] among the Puerto Rican nationality group in New York City Communist propaganda emanating from behind the Iron Curtain and emanating from San Juan, Puerto Rico."[8]

Despite the committee's paranoia, it would appear that most of the poems delivered as part of club-sponsored social gatherings, even the Communist Party ones, appealed to leftist political sensibilities only in a general sense. The archival material preserved by Colón and others demonstrates that the poems at Puerto Rican social gatherings did not express unadulterated party rhetoric but instead spoke of Puerto Rican national and ethnic pride, the desire to remember and preserve Puerto Rican heritage, and the longing for Puerto Rican independence in the tradition of José Martí (one of the earliest Cuban poets to reside in New York City). At a fundamental level, these poems set the stage for the Nuyorican poetry that would come later and that was, as María Teresa Babín has argued, "a continuity of the island heritage."[9] Over time, however, overt support for the workers, for the Republican resistance in Spain, and other leftist political causes would be mentioned with relative frequency in the poetry, constituting what Michel de Certeau might identify as a "tactic" of resistance against dominant conservative politics, which "insinuates itself into the other's place, fragmentarily, without taking it over in its entirety, without being able to keep it at a distance."[10]

As the Puerto Rican diaspora diffused outward from the enclaves of the *colonias* and dispersed Puerto Ricans more extensively into New York City as a whole, the leftist politics of the New York underclass insinuated itself into the New York Puerto Rican consciousness. Its subtle tactics of resistance proved crucial in laying the groundwork for the confrontational, acerbic political overtones that would eventually find full fruition in the Nuyorican poetry of the rising generations.

Poverty, Leftist Politics in Puerto Rican New York, and Nuyorican Poetry

Much has been made about poverty being the prime mover of Nuyorican poetry.[11] Indeed, some of the sense of poverty's importance to Nuyorican aesthetics has been fostered by the Nuyorican poets themselves. For instance, Miguel Algarín depicts the following scene in the Lower East Side as he sets the stage of social conditions that give rise to what he calls "Nuyorican language" in the introduction to the seminal *Nuyorican Poetry* anthology he coedited with Miguel Piñero in 1975:

> A birthday party must be celebrated. Joey's mother spent her actual cash on the cake. She took the beer from la bodega on credit, potato chips provided by her sister, candles for the cake left from last year except for six that Muñeca brought with her. Joey's mother plans to sell "*frituras*" on Sundays to make up the money. She is nowadays a little afraid of the park because she was robbed last week. Nevertheless, she'll make up this debt. The party has to be paid for because she'll need to do it again next year. . . . Most people manage it. Joey's mother is risking it all.[12]

I do not think that Algarín wishes to create what Timothy Brennan has called "the sublimation of poverty," glorifying and aestheticizing the experience of the poor so as to make it an object of desire and beauty unto itself; after all, as Rosalyn Deutsche and Cara Ryan more pointedly put the matter, "once the poor become aestheticized [and, one might add, demonized], poverty itself moves out of our field of vision."[13] Instead, Algarín aims to contextualize the emergence of Nuyorican poetry in economically impoverished neighborhoods to explain its commitment to the radical politics of the Left. Immediately following his anecdote about the birthday party, Algarín shifts to a description of "a coalition government" called the "Renigade Dynamites," formed by two rival Nuyorican gangs to renovate the decaying infrastructure of Nuyorican neighborhoods in New York City.[14] Where the city was slow to address the basic living needs of New York Puerto Ricans, improvisational, radical politics takes control and solves the problem in Algarín's account.

For Algarín's anthology, this latter anecdote proves metonymous for Nuyorican poetry and for its frequent alliance with the activist sensibility. What becomes significant is not the poverty of Nuyorican space per se—after all, New York Puerto Ricans had lived in these conditions of poverty ever since the arrival of the first Puerto Ricans in the city in the early twentieth century—but the galvanizing effect of radical leftist politics to convert these sociocultural frustrations into poetry infused with social protest. Because of the leftist political response to what Juan Flores has called "adjustments in the city as postindustrial command center,"[15] even a poet like Jesús 'Papoleto' Meléndez, who grew up comparatively well-off by "El Barrio standards" in "an exotic apartment" could comfortably participate in Nuyorican poetic discourse by adopting the *politics* of poverty rather than the poverty itself.[16]

An example of this focus on political issues in the midst of poverty can be seen in Miguel Piñero's foundational Nuyorican poem "The Book of Genesis according to St. Miguelito," which offers a caustic rewriting of Genesis as a political critique of the systems that produced the poverty of Nuyorican Manhattan.[17] Included in both the seminal anthology *Nuyorican Poetry* and reprinted in the 1994 Nuyorican anthology *Aloud*, Piñero's poem frames the Lower East Side's (Loisaida's) sociohistorical marginality as an originary centrality, allowing Loisaida to burst its narrow borders and expand along new *fronteras* that resist the pressures of a more "normative" United States. Piñero's poem traces a bevy of social ills—"ghettos & slums," "lead-based paint," "garbage & filth," "hepatitis," "lockjaw," "malaria," "degradation," among others (lines 4–33)—to "capitalism," which in turn spawns "racism," "exploitation," "male chauvinism," and "machismo" and also fathers "imperialism," "colonialism," "wall street," and "foreign wars" (lines 45–55). Poverty is not the root evil in Piñero's poem but instead one symptom of oppression created by these historico-political institutions, fed by "wall street" and internationalized by "foreign wars," U.S. colonialism, imperialism, and foreign policy. As the God of Piñero's creation tells the poor "to be / COOL" (lines 96–97), what he asks for is not an acceptance of poverty and filth but a capitulation to the conservative politics that preserve stasis in the Nuyorican community; this is a god to be hewn down with radical leftist political agitation.

Just as early New York Puerto Ricans fused poetry and poetry performance with social activism and frequently with leftist politics, Nuyorican poets have also often produced their art in conjunction with similar groups. Because the Young Lords Party was so visible in the race politics of New York City and elsewhere during the late 1960s and early 1970s and because *Palante*, the publication produced by their Ministry of Information, was the first to publish Pedro Pietri's "Puerto Rican Obituary," they have been prominently linked to the development of Nuyorican poetry in the scholarship of William Luis and others.[18] But the Young Lords were only one of the leftist political groups with which the Nuyorican poets involved themselves or with which they had close association. Sandra María Esteves links her development as a poet to her time with El Grupo, a politico-artistic group that "had connections to the Puerto Rican Socialist party and to El Grupo Taoné" and that also included Nuyoricans Papoleto Meléndez and Américo Casiano. Esteves explains, "I hooked up with El Grupo, and they began politicizing me. These were all very conscious, political individuals. I was the baby, politically speaking. I began learning, I began to become aware of what it means socially and politically to be Puerto Rican."[19] Lucky Cienfuegos wrote poems dedicated to the cause of Lolita Lebrón and the Puerto Rican nationalists; Miguel Piñero preferred to address the issues of the *lumpen proletariat* as he had become acquainted with them while serving time in Sing Sing, which, like Attica (where prison riots would shut the facility down in 1971), was a hotbed of radical race politics. *Nuyo-*

rican Poetry: An Anthology of Puerto Rican Words and Feelings, which Algarín and Piñero published in 1975 and which for years was the most widely distributed anthology of Nuyorican poetry, dedicates the majority of its pages to political poems of the Left, though only some are labeled as such.

In the vast majority of cases, these Nuyorican poets felt their leftist politics to be inseparable from the immediacy of their poetry. Even in moments when this commitment to leftist politics was not worn on the sleeve, the very attire of these poets allied them with the political Left. Consider this description of Lucky Cienfuegos, written by a New York Times News Service correspondent in 1976: "Lucky CienFuegos [*sic*] is 25. His head is crowned with a huge Afro hairdo that makes him look taller than he actually is. His scarf dangles from his shoulders to his knees, but that is not as noticeable as the rainbow colors of the shirts that top his jeans."[20] Cienfuegos's hair connects him to images of black nationalism; his clothes remind *New York Times* readers of the hippie movement. That the reporter could not comment on the opening of the Nuyorican Poets Café (ostensibly the subject of the news article) without linking the café to the political statement of Cienfuegos's attire is indicative of the seemingly necessary blending of the two.

Other Nuyorican poets, like Bimbo Rivas, who along with Chino García famously rechristened the Lower East Side as "Loisaida" in his poetry, found different but allied forms of political outreach.[21] Until his untimely death in 1990 from a heart attack, Rivas engaged with Charas and other Loisaida social organizations to reclaim the broken-down buildings and other public and private spaces in the Lower East Side as part of an effort to reinvigorate that terrain for the Nuyoricans living there.[22] While not exclusively a "leftist" effort, Rivas's project evidences a continued link between poetry and the protection of Puerto Rican diasporic interests in New York City, if for no other reason than his desperate critique of establishment politics: "A man without a JOB / is lost in the labyrinth of / HELL," he writes.[23]

Nuyorican Poetry, the Diaspora, and the Challenge of Alterity

In 1993, Juan Flores suggested that "by its Nuyorican stage, Puerto Rican literature in the United States comes to share the features of 'minority' or noncanonical literatures of the United States. Like them, it is a literature of recovery and collective affirmation, and it is a literature of 'mingling and sharing,' of interaction and exchange with neighboring, complementary cultures."[24] He describes a vision of Nuyorican literature comfortably coexisting with other "minority" literatures while still retaining its own energies and characteristics. By the turn of the millennium, however, Flores's depiction of Nuyorican literature's symbiotic coexistence with other minority literatures had shifted into an argument that Nuyorican literature had all but dissolved into a "pan-Latino" aesthetic: "even the term *Nuyorican* has become an anachronism."[25] Flores favors instead labels like poet Tato Laviera's recently coined "AmeRícan" or another equally postmodern moniker, "DiaspoRican," which for Flores more accurately signifies the new "diasporic" mode of Puerto Rican existence.[26] He contends that the notion of "Nuyorican" is outmoded because the Puerto Rican in New York never had the same "cultural capital" as Latino groups originating in Latin American countries with autonomous political identities. The "newly arrived 'Latino' writers" all come from countries that are independent, have embassies, and have well-defined cultural identities, says Flores, and therefore function as "overseas representatives" of their countries of origin; Nuyoricans, if they still exist, have no cultural homeland except for the makeshift ones that they have tried to carve out of neighborhoods in New York City.[27]

While I agree with Flores that the situation of the Nuyoricans differs from that of other Latino groups in New York and elsewhere and that the spread of Puerto Ricans throughout the major metropoles of the United States makes the DiaspoRican a reality, one could also argue that the main threat to a sense of "Nuyoricanness" is not the lack of a "homeland," or pan-Latinidad, but the desire of its allies on the political Left to subsume it in a larger program of cultural and political alterity. Because New York City has emerged over the last half century as the media capital of the world, New York's Left finds itself with a bully pulpit unlike any other. If this historical situation becomes linked to the attractiveness of the Nuyorican as a provocative voice from the margins in an age when "multiculturalism" is the ultimate source of cultural capital, Nuyoricanness will find itself threatened. More specifically, if Nuyorican poetry allows its commitment to the political Left and involvement in progressive identity politics to eclipse its ties to its historical communities and causes in New York City, then the DiaspoRican will be the next aesthetic mode to be subsumed by larger "alternative" artistic movements, displacing it from its cultural origins.

The story of the Nuyorican Poets Café provides one of the most provocative case studies in tracking Nuyorican poetry's flirtation with the aspects of multiculturalism that privilege exoticized essentialisms and marks Nuyorican poetry's potential dissolution into larger cultural configurations of the political Left. Miguel Algarín, now well known as one of the cofounders of the café, figured "Nuyoricanness" in the earliest days of the café as foregrounding what he saw as a necessary connection between Nuyorican literature, Nuyorican ethnicity, and Nuyorican literature's oppositional nature to "white American writers," "English," "Uncle Sam," and so on.[28] But in an essay written in 1994, Algarín revises his earlier stance dramatically. In "The Sidewalk of High Art," Algarín's introduction to *Aloud*, the anthology of poems from the Nuyorican Poets Café that won the 1994 American Book Award, he contends that the "philosophy and purpose of the Nuyorican Poets Café has *always* been to reveal poetry as a living art" and that the café "seeks to promote a tolerance and understanding between people" as one organization that has "gone a long way toward changing the so-called black/white dialogue that has been the breeding ground for social, cultural, and political conflict in the United States."[29] Quickly, Algarín's argument spins into a discussion of Janet Jackson, Maya Angelou, and Alexander Hamilton (yes, of the Federalist Papers!). Where Algarín's earlier essay emphasized the Nuyorican indebtedness to a distinctly Puerto Rican ancestry of *salsa*, Catholicism, African religions, and a shared hatred of the Jones Act, which forced U.S. citizenry upon Puerto Rican nationals, this later essay argues that the Nuyorican Poets Café's slam is but a version of the slam held at Chicago's Green Mill, and that both slams owe their heritage to cultural sources in Greece, Africa, and Japan.[30]

Even the "example" poets discussed in Algarín's later essay seem handpicked to rewrite Nuyorican literary history. Algarín lists Regie Cabico, whom Algarín identifies as "a young gay Filipino"; Shirley LaFlore, "a poet in her fifties [who] evokes the great poetic jazz tradition of Baraka at his most musical," as well as the "almost magical world of Coltrane strains, . . . of Miles, of Armstrong, of Changó"; Julie Patton, a woman "from the state of Washington" whose "references to Shakespeare and Faulkner and everyday life" mark her poetry with kudos to the canon; and Anne Elliott, whose "classic Northern European look" provides "an extraordinary contrast to the first three poets' presences" and who offers a poetry that is "the all-new Gregorian chant." Yes, Sekou Sundiata is mentioned later in Algarín's essay, but so are Adrienne Su (an "Asian-American woman"), Tracie Morris and Reg E. Gaines ("young African-American[s]"), and Hal Sirowitz (a "Jewish-American" poet), to name a few.[31] Clearly, Algarín's "Sidewalk of High Art" wants to reimagine the borders of the Nuyorican nation, almost to the point of making them "coterminous with [hu]mankind," to use Benedict Anderson's phrase.[32] Who are the great Nuyorican fathers and mothers? Find them here in the "Founding Poems" section. Who are the new Nuyoricans? The "Open Room" gives you a "representative" selection.

The appearance of *Aloud* marked Nuyoricanness as the next great product of the alternative culture machine, with the "new" Nuyorican poetry even being featured in a series of spoken-word poetry shows by what is arguably the most important huckster of ready-made "alternative living" in our time, MTV. Nuyoricans competed in poetry slams from Taos, New Mexico, to Seattle, Washington, and a traveling troupe of Nuyorican poets even appeared in theaters of sleepy towns across the United States in what one author called "a traveling freak show from the inner city." "'I remember landing in Portland, Oregon, and getting to our performance space, a renovated movie theater," reminisces Willie Perdomo, one of the well-known Nuyorican poets on the tour. "There's a huge marquee that says *Nuyorican Poets Café Live*, and there's a line around the corner for tickets. They sat there and ate popcorn through our whole show.'"[33]

Riding this crest of the large-scale dispersal of Nuyorican literature was the Nuyorican Poets Café, situated squarely in the territory now being gentrified by outsiders to the Nuyorican community. Tellingly, it was not Nuyorican Poets Café founder and poet Miguel Algarín spearheading the effort as much as his new partner, Chicago neo-Beat performance poet Bob Holman. Holman touted the café on the *Charlie Rose Show*, Ted Koppel's *Nightline*, *Good Morning America*, and *ABC News Magazine* and was interviewed by the *New York Times*, *Time* magazine, and the *Village Voice* as well as on National Public Radio.[34] As

Ed Morales has detailed, the small, renovated warehouse space of the café in Loisaida received a decreasing amount of attention as it found itself eclipsed by larger "multicultural" interests.[35] Eventually, these events forced a rift to grow between Algarín and Holman. Holman now acknowledges that in "having poetry find a place in the world" through his promotion of the café, he "was on Miguel's turf" and "ran afoul" of him, or as an anonymous Nuyorican poet suggests, "Bob came in and made Miguel's house popular. . . . Now Miguel wants it back."[36]

Where Ed Morales sees these changes as a positive development that shows "that a Spanglish-based institution served as a staging ground for one of New York's most viable multicultural happenings,"[37] I would argue that Algarín's and Holman's feud evidences at the very least a change in the relationship between Nuyorican poetry and leftist politics and perhaps signals the dissolution of an ethnically and geographically rooted Nuyoricanness into a polyglot coalition of postnational liberal interests. Where writers from the New York Puerto Rican *colonias* and the socialist organizations of New York City's political Left once saw New York Puerto Ricans as a separate group sympathetic to leftist politics who would bolster these movements with their support, the conflation of Nuyoricanness with a diffuse political and social liberalism means that the people producing the literature and their shared commitments to leftist politics become indistinguishable from each other. In this way, the label "Nuyorican" can be adopted by a poet with no ties to the ethnic heritage of the historical Nuyoricans of New York City, and Nuyoricanness becomes more of an avant-garde posture and a social and artistic position than a specific cultural signifier—a state of mind, finally, or perhaps a mental condition whose increasing ubiquity renders it intellectually and artistically useful only in the most dilute terms. In this sense, the problem is less one of a Nuyorican being reduced to a mere "spic," as Abraham Rodriguez's character worries in *Spidertown*,[38] than of leftist politics moving from a collaboration with Nuyorican poets to a co-optation of their identities as poets with a special multicultural cachet value. Finally, being "Nuyorican" might come to mean something as bland as "racially and politically progressive and friendly to multicultural interests."

In making these points, I do not advocate an alternative world where Nuyorican poetry becomes, in the words of Juan Flores, an "unassimilated ethnic cyst."[39] Indeed, all poetry movements change over time, and at one level it would seem naïve to gnash one's teeth over the natural metamorphosis of Nuyorican poetry in light of the diaspora's expanse. The very nature of the Puerto Rican diaspora likely signals the death of an older "Nuyorican" mode of poetry, as nationality itself becomes more of an individually felt sensibility than a territorial marker. As writers like Antonio Benitez-Rojo have repeatedly argued, the heritage of all Caribbean peoples—including those like the Nuyoricans, who find themselves more far-flung in the fluvial currents of the larger Caribbean diaspora—is to find themselves always-already mixed between the national identities of hemispheres old and new.

Still, it seems important for any student of Nuyorican poetry to note the degree to which the exoticized presentation of the political situation of the poetry might supersede the poetry itself, and if the "DiaspoRican" has indeed rendered the "Nuyorican" obsolete, then the literary history of the U.S. Puerto Rican experience should be marked and altered accordingly. If this obsolescence is indeed a reality, it places Nuyorican literature in a curious spot, for it forces us to acknowledge that Nuyorican literature—which marks itself in subject and tone as a defiant, nationalist literature—has moved into a postnational mode before it ever really secured a "nation" for itself. Because of the colonial experience, the Nuyorican homeland that never was has been sacrificed for a new DiaspoRican homelessness that would seem to "leapfrog" the DiaspoRican experience from a protomodern to a postmodern, postnational moment without the cultural and ideological struggles that marked the movement of more dominant national literatures into the present moment.

In the end, the relationship between the political Left of New York City and the creation, promulgation, and evolution of Nuyorican poetry is both prolonged and pronounced. While it is easy to point to the particular political entities during the late 1960s and early 1970s or to credit other New York poetry movements as the inspiration and source of a sense of political commitment in Nuyorican poetry, it would seem that the relationship between Nuyorican poetry and politics dates at least to the New York Puerto Rican *colonias* and the interest of New York leftists in these *colonias* as staging grounds for their respective revolutions, if not to earlier Puerto Rican impulses toward progressive political change and autonomy.

NOTES

I would like to thank the Center for Puerto Rican Studies at Hunter College, CUNY, for their permission to use unpublished material from their archives in this essay. I offer special thanks to Pedro Juan Hernández and Nélida Pérez for their dedicated help in scouring the archives for the more obscure information I needed.

1. For the purposes of this essay, I use the label "New York Puerto Rican" to indicate those Puerto Ricans who first settled the Puerto Rican *colonias* of New York City from the first decade of the twentieth century onward, eschewing Eugene Mohr's more awkward "Proto-Nuyorican" label. By "Nuyorican," I mean the children of these New York Puerto Ricans or the children of the Puerto Ricans who arrived as part of Operation Bootstrap in the post–World War II era and who came of age in New York City in the 1960s and later. Obviously, the line between "New York Puerto Rican" and "Nuyorican" is a blurred and difficult one, and the distinction between the two is sometimes less productive that I had hoped, especially given the fact that many New York Puerto Ricans and Nuyoricans returned to Puerto Rico for a portion of their lives, if not permanently. I make every effort to work with these terms as I have defined them here. Also, entire books have sought to detail the differences between the words "liberal," "leftist," "socialist," "revolutionary," and so forth. I have chosen the words "Left" and "leftist" in my essay to indicate those groups committed to radical social, economic, and political change, often through protest of established institutional policies and politics and sometimes through violent revolutionary conflict and exchange.

2. Federico Ribes Tovar, *El libro puertorriqueño de Nueva York: Handbook of the Puerto Rican Community* (New York: Plus Ultra Educational Publishers, 1970; repr., New York: Arno Press, 1980), 188–189.

3. Certainly, Nuyorican poetry was often aided by these contemporary movements, and when the Nuyorican Poets Café emerged as a special site for the production and promulgation of Nuyorican poetry in the early 1970s, patrons and supporters of these allied poetry movements lent valuable aid and enthusiasm, which should not be ignored; however, Julio Marzán's assertion that Nuyorican poetry has "evolved from the social consciousness of the sixties to experiment with more universal currents" might afford these sister movements too much credit for the emergent Nuyorican literary movement, which did not require outside help to innovate its art forms, since sufficient impetus already existed within its communities from the epoch of the *colonias* onward; see Julio Marzán, introduction to *Inventing a Word: An Anthology of Twentieth-Century Puerto Rican Poetry*, ed. Julio Marzán (New York: Columbia University Press, 1980), xxiv. In a *Chicano-Riqueña* article from 1978, Miguel Algarín was asked if the similarities in political issues addressed by Miguel Piñero and Lawrence Ferlinghetti pointed to a "connection" between the two poets. Algarín responded, "Prior to Ferlinghetti being at the Café and Mikey meeting Ferlinghetti there, I don't think they knew each other." See Miguel Algarín, "Volume and Value of the Breath in Poetry," *Revista Chicano-Riqueña* 6, no. 3 (1978): 61.

4. See the Jesús Colón Papers, ser. V, VI, and X, Center for Puerto Rican Studies Archives, Hunter College, City University of New York. Though most of Jesús Colón's

collection of cultural groups' programs and pamphlets in the center archives remains unpublished, some images of these documents have appeared in the recent collection by Félix V. Matos-Rodríguez and Pedro Juan Hernández, *Pioneros: Puerto Ricans in New York City, 1896–1948* (Charleston, SC: Arcadia Press, 2001). Though the pervasiveness of poetry during these social gatherings cannot be completely assessed from these images, they reproduce several examples of poetry and announcements of poetry readings. See Matos-Rodríguez and Hernández, *Pioneros*, 81–100.

5. Virginia E. Sánchez Korrol, *From Colonia to Community: The History of Puerto Ricans in New York City* (Berkeley and Los Angeles: University of California Press, 1994), 141. Jesús Colón's "A Voice through the Window," in his *A Puerto Rican in New York and Other Sketches* (1961; repr., New York: Arno Press, 1975), 11–13, and Bernardo Vega's "The Customs and Traditions of the *Tabaqueros* and What It Was Like to Work in a Cigar Factory in New York City," from *Memoirs of Bernardo Vega: A Contribution to the History of the Puerto Rican Community in New York*, ed. César Andreu Iglesias, trans. Juan Flores (New York: Monthly Review Press, 1984), 19–26, both highlight how the ideologies of Karl Marx and other leftist political thinkers were prominently featured by the *lectores*, who would read to the workers throughout the workday. Lisa Sánchez González's treatment of "boricua modernism" also highlights the role of Luisa Capetillo not only as a socialist and *lectora* in the tobacco workshops but as one of the first New York Puerto Ricans to meld poetics and politics. See Lisa Sánchez González, *Boricua Literature: A Literary History of the Puerto Rican Diaspora* (New York: New York University Press, 2001), 23–41.

6. Roberto P. Rodríguez-Morrazoni, "Political Cultures of the Puerto Rican Left in the United States, in *The Puerto Rican Movement: Voices from the Diaspora*, ed. Andrés Torres and José E. Velásquez (Philadelphia: Temple University Press, 1998), 30.

7. Ibid.

8. See the U.S. House Committee on Un-American Activities, "Communist Activities among Puerto Ricans in New York City and Puerto Rico (New York City—Part 1)," in *Hearings of the United States Congress*, 86th Cong., 1st sess., 16–17 Nov. 1959 (Washington, DC: Government Printing Office, 1960), 1544–1545. The evidence against Colón and others of their "conspiratorial" designs against the United States was gathered by Mildred Blauvelt, a detective for the New York Police Department who was assigned in 1943 to infiltrate the Communist Party in New York City. Blauvelt identified Colón as the leader of a social club with communist affiliations, the Pasionaria Club, as well as the writer of communist literature published in the *Daily Worker*. In truth, Colón was a member of many more clubs as well, including the Liga Puertorriqueña and the Círculo de Escritores y Poetas Iberamericanos de Nueva York, that might have given him more informal opportunities to stump for leftist political goals through social gatherings.

9. See María Teresa Babín, "Introduction: The Path and the Voice," in *Borinquen: An Anthology of Puerto Rican Literature*, ed. María Teresa Babín and Stan Steiner (New York: Knopf, 1974), xxv.

10. Michel de Certeau, *The Practice of Everyday Life*, trans. Steven Rendall (Berkeley and Los Angeles: University of California Press, 1984), xix. This process would also be accelerated along equally oblique but appreciable channels of Puerto Rican perception

as conservative political groups in New York City consistently (and, for the New York City "mainstream," successfully) portrayed Puerto Ricans in New York as hoodlums and delinquents and as a generalized drain on the city's social programs. It would be difficult to embrace the conservatives behind the roundups of Puerto Rican youth in the wake of the Salvador Agrón "Capeman" case, for instance, or those behind the preparation of the infamous New York Board of Education reports that saw Puerto Rican youth as intellectually inferior to their counterparts or as a "problem" for the educational system. In light of these negative depictions of New York Puerto Ricans, Jesús Colón's public agenda during the years following his publication of *A Puerto Rican in New York* might be seen as a public-relations effort of sorts, trying to correct the erroneous public perceptions of "average" New York Puerto Ricans.

11. Certainly, the neighborhoods from which Nuyorican poetry derives are impoverished. One of these neighborhoods, the Lower East Side of Manhattan, possesses a long and tumultuous history. Until the early 1800s, what is now the Lower East Side was "open land"—mostly swampy, marginal land that had not already been parceled out to the landowners who divided the Manhattan peninsula between themselves (Stuyvesant, DeLancey, and Rutgers among them). But by the middle of the nineteenth century, impoverished European immigrants (first Irish, then German Jews, and later Chinese, Italians, Russians, Poles, Ukrainians, Hungarians, and Romanians) scrambled to survive in tenements ravaged by cholera and typhus outbreaks in the massively overcrowded neighborhood. By 1910, over 540,000 people lived within these "slums." Atrocious living conditions and infrastructural decay—most significantly of buildings erected on unstable land to begin with—did not stop Puerto Ricans from entering the area. By 1970, as many as 174,532 Nuyoricans called the Lower East Side home, and by 1990, at least 161,617 still officially resided in these few blocks of Manhattan. Currently, Nuyoricans make up one-fourth of the area's inhabitants, up from only one-sixth of the Lower East Side's population in 1950; see Malve von Hassell, *Homesteading in New York City, 1978–1993: The Divided Heart of Loisaida* (Westport, CT: Bergin and Garvey, 1996), 38, 41–43, 45–47. In this manner, the Nuyoricans claim their stake in what Timothy Brennan labels an "area traditionally represented [as an] encampment of neglect, overcrowding, and minimal social services" and "an immigrant warehouse." See Brennan, *At Home in the World: Cosmopolitanism Now* (Cambridge, MA: Harvard University Press, 1997), 165–166.

12. Miguel Algarín, "Introduction: Nuyorican Language," in *Nuyorican Poetry: An Anthology of Puerto Rican Words and Feelings,* ed. Miguel Algarín and Miguel Piñero (New York: William Morrow, 1975), 12.

13. See Brennan, *At Home in the World*, 165–180; and Rosalyn Deutsch and Cara Gendel Ryan, "The Fine Art of Gentrification," *October* 31 (Winter 1984): 110–111.

14. Algarín, "Introduction," 14–18.

15. Juan Flores, *From Bomba to Hip-Hop: Puerto Rican Culture and Latino Identity* (New York: Columbia University Press, 2000), 146.

16. Raquel Velásquez, "Versed in the Streets," *San Juan Star (Venue),* 11 June 1995, 7.

17. Miguel Piñero, "The Book of Genesis according to St. Miguelito," in *Aloud: Voices from the Nuyorican Poets Café,* ed. Miguel Algarín and Bob Holman (New York: Henry Holt, 1994), 349–351.

18. See William Luis, *Dance between Two Cultures: Latino Caribbean Literature Written in the United States* (Nashville, TN: Vanderbilt University Press, 1997), 43–52. For information on the role of the Young Lords Party in the publication of Pedro Pietri's now widely anthologized poem "Puerto Rican Obituary," see the Young Lords Party and Michael Abramson, *Palante: Young Lords Party* (New York: McGraw Hill, 1971), 16–22; and Iris Morales, "¡Palante, Siempre Palante!" in Torres and Velásquez, *Puerto Rican Movement*, 214–215.

19. Carmen Dolores Hernández, *Puerto Rican Voices in English: Interviews with Writers* (Westport, CT: Praeger, 1997), 57.

20. David Vidal, "Nuyorican Poetry Flowers in New York Café," *San Juan Star*, 18 May 1976, portfolio section, 1.

21. García's and Rivas's texts named the area of the Lower East Side from Avenue A to Avenue D and from Fourteenth Street to Houston Street "Loisaida" in the early 1970s. In 1984, this Nuyorican "bilingual homonym" for the Lower East Side, which was first imagined, recited, and promulgated via channels of literary performance, was translated into actual legislation when the term "Loisaida" "was formalized and officially recognized in the public record" when the Community Board renamed Avenue C as "Avenida de Loisaida"; see von Hassell, *Homesteading*, 7. *Loisaida*, the "quality of life in Loisaida" publication of the neighborhood that Rivas loved, featured a lengthy elegy to Rivas, saying, "You were a cornerstone of our community, you have given us [the] name 'Loisaida,' a name that will never disappear." See Carmen Pabon, "A Bimbo Rivas," *Loisaida* 16, no. 2 (Summer 1993): 38.

22. Liz Ševčenko, "Making Loisaida: Placing Puertorriqueñidad in Lower Manhattan," in *Mambo Montage: The Latinization of New York*, ed. Agustín Laó-Montes and Arlene Dávila (New York: Columbia University Press, 2001), 296–300, 304–309.

23. Bimbo Rivas, "A Job," in Algarín and Piñero, *Nuyorican Poetry*, 94.

24. Juan Flores, *Divided Borders: Essays on Puerto Rican Identity* (Houston: Arte Público Press, 1993), 152.

25. Flores, *Bomba*, 186–187.

26. Ibid., 187–188.

27. Ibid., 177–179.

28. Miguel Algarín, "Nuyorican Aesthetics," in *Images and Identities: The Puerto Rican in Two World Contexts*, ed. and trans. Asela Rodríguez de Laguna (New Brunswick, NJ: Transaction, 1987), 161–163.

29. Miguel Algarín, "The Sidewalk of High Art," in Algarín and Holman, *Aloud*, 8–9 (italics added).

30. See Algarín, "Nuyorican Aesthetics," 161–162; and Algarín, "Sidewalk," 16.

31. See Algarín, "Sidewalk," 17–22, for these various references.

32. Benedict Anderson, *Imagined Communities: Reflections on the Origin and Spread of Nationalism* (London: Verso, 1983), 7.

33. Ed Morales, "Grand Slam: The Last Word at the Nuyorican Poets Café," *Village Voice*, 14 Oct. 1997, 62, 63.

34. See Edward Halsey Foster, "Bob Holman, Performance Poetry, and the Nuyori-

can Poets Café," *Multicultural Review* 2, no. 2 (1993): 46–47; and Ed Morales, "Grand Slam," 62–63.

35. Ed Morales, *Living in Spanglish: The Search for Latino Identity in America* (New York: St. Martin's Press, 2002), 110–111.

36. Ed Morales, "Grand Slam," 62.

37. Ed Morales, *Spanglish,* 114.

38. Flores, *Bomba,* 180.

39. Flores, *Divided Borders*, 141.

BIBLIOGRAPHY

Algarín, Miguel. "Introduction: Nuyorican Language." In *Nuyorican Poetry: An Anthology of Puerto Rican Words and Feelings,* ed. Miguel Algarín and Miguel Piñero, 9–20. New York: William Morrow, 1975.

———. "Nuyorican Aesthetics." In *Images and Identities: The Puerto Rican in Two World Contexts*, ed. and trans. Asela Rodríguez de Laguna, 161–163. New Brunswick, NJ: Transaction, 1987.

———. "The Sidewalk of High Art." In *Aloud: Voices from the Nuyorican Poets Café,* ed. Miguel Algarín and Bob Holman, 3–28. New York: Henry Holt, 1994.

———. "Volume and Value of the Breath in Poetry." *Revista Chicano-Riqueña* 6, no. 3 (1978): 52–69.

Algarín, Miguel, and Bob Holman, eds. *Aloud: Voices from the Nuyorican Poets Café.* New York: Henry Holt, 1994.

Anderson, Benedict. *Imagined Communities: Reflections on the Origin and Spread of Nationalism*. London: Verso, 1983.

Babín, María Teresa. "Introduction: The Path and the Voice." In *Borinquen: An Anthology of Puerto Rican Literature,* ed. María Teresa Babín and Stan Steiner. New York: Knopf, 1974.

Brennan, Timothy. *At Home in the World: Cosmopolitanism Now.* Cambridge, MA: Harvard University Press, 1997.

Colón, Jesús. Jesús Colón Papers. Center for Puerto Rican Studies Archives, Hunter College, City University of New York.

———. *A Puerto Rican in New York and Other Sketches*. 1961; repr., New York: Arno Press, 1975.

de Certeau, Michel. *The Practice of Everyday Life*. Trans. Steven Rendall. Berkeley and Los Angeles: University of California Press, 1984.

Deutsch, Rosalyn, and Cara Gendel Ryan. "The Fine Art of Gentrification." *October* 31 (Winter 1984): 91–111.

Flores, Juan. *Divided Borders: Essays on Puerto Rican Identity*. Houston: Arte Público Press, 1993.

———. *From Bomba to Hip-Hop: Puerto Rican Culture and Latino Identity*. New York: Columbia University Press, 2000.

Foster, Edward Halsey. "Bob Holman, Performance Poetry, and the Nuyorican Poets Café." *Multicultural Review* 2, no. 2 (1993): 46–48.

Hernández, Carmen Dolores. *Puerto Rican Voices in English: Interviews with Writers.* Westport, CT: Praeger, 1997.

Luis, William. *Dance between Two Cultures: Latino Caribbean Literature Written in the United States.* Nashville, TN: Vanderbilt University Press, 1997.

Marzán, Julio. Introduction to *Inventing a Word: An Anthology of Twentieth-Century Puerto Rican Poetry,* ed. Julio Marzán, xi–xxvii. New York: Columbia University Press, 1980.

Matos-Rodríguez, Félix V., and Pedro Juan Hernández. *Pioneros: Puerto Ricans in New York City, 1896–1948.* Charleston, SC: Arcadia Press, 2001.

Mohr, Eugene V. *The Nuyorican Experience: Literature of the Puerto Rican Minority.* Westport, CT: Greenwood Press, 1982.

Morales, Ed. "Grand Slam: The Last Word at the Nuyorican Poets Café." *Village Voice,* 14 Oct. 1997, 62–63.

———. *Living in Spanglish: The Search for Latino Identity in America.* New York: St. Martin's Press, 2002.

Morales, Iris. "¡Palante, Siempre Palante!" In *The Puerto Rican Movement: Voices from the Diaspora,* ed. Andrés Torres and José E. Velázquez, 210–227. Philadelphia: Temple University Press, 1998.

Pabon, Carmen. "A Bimbo Rivas." *Loisaida* 16, no. 2 (Summer 1993): 38.

Piñero, Miguel. "The Book of Genesis according to St. Miguelito." In *Aloud: Voices from the Nuyorican Poets Café,* ed. Miguel Algarín and Bob Holman, 349–351. New York: Henry Holt, 1994.

Ribes Tovar, Federico. *El libro puertorriqueño de Nueva York: Handbook of the Puerto Rican Community.* New York: Plus Ultra Educational Publishers, 1970. Repr., New York: Arno Press, 1980.

Rivas, Bimbo. "A Job." In *Nuyorican Poetry: An Anthology of Puerto Rican Words and Feelings*, ed. Miguel Algarín and Miguel Piñero, 93–94. New York: William Morrow, 1975.

Rodríguez-Morrazoni, Roberto P. "Political Cultures of the Puerto Rican Left in the United States." In *The Puerto Rican Movement: Voices from the Diaspora*, ed. Andrés Torres and José E. Velázquez, 25–47. Philadelphia: Temple University Press, 1998.

Sánchez González, Lisa. *Boricua Literature: A Literary History of the Puerto Rican Diaspora.* New York: New York University Press, 2001.

Sánchez Korrol, Virginia E. *From Colonia to Community: The History of Puerto Ricans in New York City.* Berkeley and Los Angeles: University of California Press, 1994.

Ševčenko, Liz. "Making Loisaida: Placing Puertorriqueñidad in Lower Manhattan." In *Mambo Montage: The Latinization of New York*, ed. Agustín Laó-Montes and Arlene Dávila, 293–318. New York: Columbia University Press, 2001.

U.S. Congress. House. Committee on Un-American Activities. "Communist Activities among Puerto Ricans in New York City and Puerto Rico (New York City—Part 1)." In *Hearings of the United States Congress.* 86th Cong., 1st sess. 16–17 Nov. 1959. Washington, DC: Government Printing Office, 1960.

Vega, Bernardo. *Memoirs of Bernardo Vega: A Contribution to the History of the Puerto Rican Community in New York*. Ed. César Andreu Iglesias. Trans. Juan Flores. New York: Monthly Review Press, 1984.

Velázquez, Raquel. "Versed in the Streets." *San Juan Star* (*Venue*), 11 June 1995, 7–9.

Vidal, David. "Nuyorican Poetry Flowers in New York Café." *San Juan Star*, 18 May 1976, portfolio section, 1.

von Hassell, Malve. *Homesteading in New York City, 1978–1993: The Divided Heart of Loisaida*. Westport, CT: Bergin and Garvey, 1996.

Young Lords Party and Michael Abramson. *Palante: Young Lords Party*. New York: McGraw Hill, 1971.

PART III *Identity and Place*

7 LITERARY TROPICALIZATIONS OF THE BARRIO

Ernesto Quiñonez's Bodega Dreams *and Ed Vega's* Mendoza's Dreams

ANTONIA DOMÍNGUEZ MIGUELA

From the first stages of Puerto Rican migration to the United States, the urban barrios, especially East Harlem in New York, represented the new existential space for the Puerto Rican diaspora. Early writings by and about Puerto Ricans in New York, like Jesús Colón's *A Puerto Rican in New York* and Bernardo Vega's *Memorias de Bernardo Vega*, already described the barrios as a space constantly transformed by the arrival of a growing number of Puerto Ricans.[1] The massive migration in the fifties established "the barrio" as the predominant space of arrival for Puerto Ricans. It was also in the forties and fifties when conditions in the barrio helped to develop a negative vision of this new ethnic ghetto. Island authors were aware of the situation and destiny of thousands of Puerto Rican migrants, as evidenced by the publication of works dealing with Puerto Rican lives in the northern barrios: Guillermo Cotto-Thorner's *Trópico en Manhattan*; René Marqués's *La carreta*, Pedro Juan Soto's *Ardiente suelo, fría estación* and *Spiks*.[2]

During the sixties and seventies, a group of Puerto Rican activists, poets, and playwrights living in the barrio began to describe that Puerto Rican experience from inside and from a critical perspective. They developed what would be called a *Nuyorican* aesthetics and literature deeply concerned with the community's living conditions and its daily fight for survival. With the Young Lords, a community-oriented organization which also denounced the poor living conditions of Puerto Ricans in the barrio, the Nuyorican group tried to uplift the community by redefining the term "Nuyorican" as a positive one that described a new experience and a language for the Puerto Rican diaspora in New York. Nuyorican writers were the poetic troubadours of a time when the barrio's social and political life gained much significance for the community. As an omnipresent geopolitical space for a community of people who were trying to establish a new home in the United States, the barrio was usually represented in ambivalent terms, being at the same time a refuge and a trap for its inhabitants.

Much of the literature written in the sixties and seventies about the barrio followed the tradition of African American works that depicted the ethnic ghettos as alienating spaces of social ostracism and discrimination. Well-known examples of this tradition are Richard Wright's *Native Son* and Ralph Ellison's *Invisible Man.*[3]

This literature gained much popularity in the sixties, especially after the publication of Claude Brown's *Manchild in the Promised Land*,[4] which soon became a classic. *Manchild* addressed important issues similar to those we find in Puerto Rican urban narratives, like the neighborhood's miserable living conditions and the disappointment with a trip north that had meant freedom and prosperity but that had led only to a dehumanizing space of poverty and segregation where the American Dream was only available for whites.

Though showing a negative vision of the city, the black writer's perspective also considered the urban ghetto as a village within the city. As Toni Morrison comments, although the city was depicted negatively, the characters' nostalgia for certain aspects of "urban-village" life provoked an identity crisis: urban life is lovable when the "ancestor," traditionally identified with the village, is there. Therefore, Harlem was also perceived as a positive place where joy and protection could be found within the clan.[5] Morrison's emphasis on the importance of community is a key issue in my analysis of the works by Ernesto Quiñonez and Ed Vega, who, though belonging to different generations, provide interesting representations of the barrio.

Piri Thomas's *Down These Mean Streets* recounts urban Puerto Rican experiences in the tradition of African American urban narratives.[6] Dealing with the experience of crime, poverty, and racial discrimination by a Puerto Rican black, Thomas's story has strong similarities with

Brown's *Manchild*. Harlem and the barrio were sites of constant struggles for survival and self-definition, and both works present a shocking culture of violence that was morbidly attractive to mainstream audiences. Besides the negative description of the physical neighborhoods, these works also represent these spaces as refuges and new homes for communities relocated in American cities. The dichotomy of good versus evil traditionally represented by urban narratives takes on new dimensions once issues like social class, race, and economics are raised in these works. *Down These Mean Streets* concentrates on the crisis of identity of a Puerto Rican black man trapped in the underworld of the barrio. He suffers discrimination because of his culture and skin color. The streets become for Thomas the refuge, the place where he belongs, but life in the streets also leads him to the world of drugs and crime until he realizes that those paths are not the right way to belong anywhere.

Chicano works have presented similar experiences, like J. L. Navarro's *Blue Day on Main Street*, a collection of short stories on drug abuse, prostitution, and promiscuity that suggest society's responsibility for the degradation of Latino youth, and Luis J. Rodríguez's *Always Running: La Vida Loca; Gang Days in L.A.*, which describes how city life and its racialized spaces lead Chicano young people to crime and violence as a response to their situation.[7] Most of these characters engage in a spiritual quest like those in the works of Piri Thomas and Richard Wright. However, as we move to the present, Latino writers are increasingly becoming aware of the necessity to instill a resistant positive attitude to prevent the internalization of stereotypes about Latinos.

The tradition of ghetto literature is still present in most of the works by Ernesto Quiñonez and Ed Vega. Ernesto Quiñonez was born in Ecuador of a Puerto Rican mother, whereas Ed Vega was born in Puerto Rico. Both of them grew up in Puerto Rican barrios in the United States, though they belong to different literary generations, representing the variety and complexity of the Puerto Rican diaspora in the United States. Once again these authors and their work consolidate the development of a U.S. Puerto Rican identity that defies obsolete identity definitions and geographical limits. Ernesto Quiñonez has published two books, *Bodega Dreams* and *Chango's Fire*.[8] Ed Vega is a much more prolific author, with works such as *The Comeback*; *Mendoza's Dreams*; *Casualty Report*; *No Matter How Much You Promise to Cook or Pay the Rent You Blew It Cauze Bill Bailey Ain't Never Coming Home Again*; *The*

Lamentable Journey of Omaha Bigelow into the Impenetrable Loisaida Jungle; and *Blood Fugues*.[9]

Ernesto Quiñonez's *Bodega Dreams* and Ed Vega's *Mendoza's Dreams* are clearly indebted to Piri Thomas's depiction of Puerto Rican life in the barrio even though they react to this ghetto tradition in different ways. The barrio may sometimes be described in negative terms, but the main plots are not necessarily related to surviving crime and violence as in the case of Piri Thomas's book and other African American works. This is especially true in *Mendoza's Dreams,* where the narrator—the author's alter ego—rejects writing autobiographical ghetto literature in the first chapter, "Back by Popular Demand." A writer who had written many such books, he now realizes that this literature had appeared "out of their morbid fear and their need to see the people in a certain light"[10] and that the community is asking for something else. The people want their dreams to come true in his stories, even though that is not what the mainstream audience wants to read. He states his point clearly to his friend Larry: "I said I was taking care of my social responsibility . . . I wanted to tell him about Mercado, the barber. He wants me to build him a dream about a thin wife who does not nag him. . . . And about Lydia Ramos, the checkout clerk at Met Foods, who wants a two-story dream with six boyfriends on the top story and a rich gringo husband at the bottom one."[11]

The mention of social responsibility is a key phrase in my analysis, because it is precisely that social responsibility that makes Ed Vega and Ernesto Quiñonez depart from the literary tradition of Piri Thomas and lead readers into a more critical and different depiction of the barrio, closer to Puerto Ricans' daily routines, problems, and dreams. In *Bodega Dreams,* the title reminds us that this is also a story about dreams. At this point we need to notice that, although there is a character named Bodega in the book, the dreams of the title are not a character's dreams, that is, "Bodega's Dreams." The author is consciously playing with the word "bodega," a Spanish word already adopted by the English language to designate a very peculiar place that is common to all Latino barrios and that therefore functions as a symbol of the larger space of Latino neighborhoods and the community of people who live in them. Even though *Bodega Dreams* has some elements from ghetto literature, such as drug dealing and violence, these elements are not central in the narrative. Instead, the narrator, Chino, serves as the thread that leads the reader to a more compromised reading of life in the barrios and the possibilities for community improvement. In both works the individual's quest for self-identity accompanies a more collective representation of Puerto Rican lives in the barrio.

The Barrio and the Puerto Rican Diaspora

Puerto Ricans in the United States have developed a diasporic identity that is a direct product of historical, social, and cultural transformations. This identity is characterized by a complex set of daily practices that describe a people's survival in a hostile environment. In the north, Puerto Ricans coming from the island in the early forties and fifties hoped to find a piece of the American Dream. However, the "promised land" was limited to the world of the barrio and its daily struggles and deception. The barrio represents a figurative borderland between the past and the future, a transitional space of complex internal transformations. It is definitely a socially constructed public space where ethnic difference is contained; but the barrio, as a space that is constantly renewed and refreshed by newcomers, also fulfills the needs and desires of Puerto Ricans in different ways.

In *Barrio-Logos: Space and Place in Urban Chicano Literature and Culture*, Raúl Romero Villa explores the significance of urban spaces in the development of Chicano communities. He juxtaposes *barriozation* of the Mexican population, which he defines as "the formation of residentially and socially segregated Chicano barrios and neighborhoods," with *barriology*, which is related to "a cumulative 'anti-discipline' that subverts the totalizing impulse of the dominant social space containing the barrios" and "a playful but serious promotion of the cultural knowledge and practices particular to the barrio."[12] In this way, Romero and other critics he mentions explain Chicanos' attachment to the barrio as their home as an attempt to maintain a social and cultural space that is threatened by urban renewal, gentrified redevelopment projects, and general urban-space restructuring. A similar situation can be found in East Harlem, and according to Romero, that may be the reason why authors like Quiñonez and Vega make an appeal for "positive articulations of community consciousness which contribute to a psychologically and materially sustaining sense of 'home' location."[13]

Chino, the narrator of *Bodega Dreams*, is the agent of these progressive, positive articulations of community consciousness throughout his own evolution from an individualist to being increasingly involved in community issues. At the beginning of the novel Chino and his girlfriend, Blanca, consider the barrio a dangerous place: "You lived in projects with pissed-up elevators, junkies on the stairs, posters of the rapist of the month. . . . Fires, junkies dying, holdups, babies falling out of windows were things you took as part of life."[14] Chino and Blanca represent many Puerto Ricans who have left or want to leave the barrio to live with dignity far from the problems always haunting them. For Chino, the barrio is an obstacle to getting a good education, attaining a comfortable financial situation, and being able to create his own future. When he is accepted at the High School of Art and Design, "a lot of things seemed different": "I no longer wanted the world to be just my neighborhood anymore. Blanca thought the same, and when we started going out we would talk about this all the time."[15]

However, when he meets Bodega and becomes fascinated by his ideals and dreams for the community, Chino starts to consider his own social responsibility in transforming the barrio to make it a better place. Bodega, another central character, pursues a dream of economic success and power by dealing drugs and spending the profits in repairing old buildings, which are then reinhabited by Puerto Ricans. This is what makes Bodega's dream different and what makes him a romantic and attractive figure for Chino. Bodega has a personal dream (to be popular and rich and to recover Vera's lost love), but it is also a dream with extraordinary consequences for the Puerto Rican community: he wants to literally own the barrio and give it back to his people, to take that space from whites and make it a better place for the Puerto Rican community. His project is obviously a counterinvasion, a reappropriation of a "home" that has been historically denied to Puerto Ricans.

Creating a Home in the Barrio

Building a physical and an emotional "home" in the United States is one of the most important issues addressed by the literature of the Puerto Rican diaspora and by other Latino literatures. The search for a home is not just the desire to have a house of their own but a desire to redefine their new home/identity as Latinos in the United States. I use the term "home" here in the sense of a physical, social, and psychic space where the individual feels at ease and "at home." The emphasis is on the unstable, relative, and fictional quality of home not only as an individual's "imagined location" but also as a communal construction related to the concept of "home country," which suggests "the particular intersection of private and public and of individual and communal that is manifest in imagining a space as home."[16]

Because of the complex nature of Puerto Rican national identity, the concept of home country is certainly affected by a history of colonization and the experience of migration. Puerto Rican national identity is even more complex for mainland Puerto Ricans, who frequently show strong political feelings about their Puerto Ricanness as a symbol of nonassimilationist practices. They have developed a new home/identity as U.S. Puerto Ricans that resides at the borders of cultures. Because of its spatial multiplicities, I prefer to describe this new identity as a *pendulous identity,* which implies a constant movement among the cultural, social, and emotional spaces the individual inhabits. This constant movement responds to the constant negotiations the individual is involved in every day and to the "world traveling" that applies to anyone living between cultures.[17]

Ernesto Quiñonez and Ed Vega are especially concerned about describing how Puerto Ricans develop a sense of place and identity during their search for a space in American society and subsequent creation of a "home" in the United States. Although barrio conditions are still described negatively, these works retain the importance of the barrio as a space of community where Puerto Ricans find a cultural refuge from the social and racial discrimination that occurs on the "outside." Thus, the barrio acquires a prominence that goes beyond geography to become a (relative) "home" for a transnational diasporic community.

Together with other Latino communities such as Chicanos, Puerto Ricans occupy a social and cultural space that Juan Flores perceptively characterizes as a "delocalized transnation."[18] But we need to understand "nation" in a flexible, unofficial way as "a group of people who feel themselves to be a community bound together by ties of history, culture, and common ancestry."[19] We should also bear in mind this nation's "imaginary" and communal qualities, which Benedict Anderson has described in *Imagined Communities*: "the nation . . . is imagined as a *community,* because . . . the nation is always conceived as a deep, horizontal comradeship."[20] Puerto Ricans in the United States create such an "imaginative project," a sense of community and home/identity deriving from a fluid concept of nation that is illustrated by definitions like "translocal nation." According to Agustín Laó, to imagine the Puerto Rican national community as a translocal nation "is to refer to the tailoring of a formation of peoplehood that, though hyperfragmented and dispersed, is netted by the web of coloniality (subordinate citizenship, racialization) and intertwined by multiple networks (political organizations, professional associations, town clubs) and flows (phone, faxes, salsanet) to constitute a deterritorialized-reterritorialized 'imagined community' and a 'social space.' . . . this social space is located beyond the immediacy of place and is intersected by other spaces."[21]

Puerto Ricans show an ambivalent political stance as they simultaneously maintain allegiance to the island and claim a space in the United States. They have become citizens of a global city which "transcends (and often competes with) the borders of the nation-state"; the city and the barrio are constantly transformed by their inhabitants as they become social border spaces, "a transnational enclave, a translocal crossroads whose location stands both below and beyond the U.S. nation state."[22]

As we can see, the barrio has a strong set of qualities that make it a perfect place for the creation of a new home/identity for Puerto Ricans in the United States. The barrio is justifiably subject to the reimagining and redefinition of American space by a displaced and colonized people. This transformation of social space and the construction of a sense of place and identity inform and become central elements of the narratives by Quiñonez and Vega. Their works also become discursive spaces where the nation and the home are represented through a fictionalized form that nevertheless stays faithful to the real dreams of Puerto Ricans. These literary representations of the barrio and of Puerto Ricans building community and "home" in the United States are based on a "rhetoric of displacement" which constantly alludes to "the struggle to assert identity out of place."[23] The barrio, as a border space where different cultures coexist, is the perfect setting to explore the complexities and problems of creating a sense of identity, of home, and of community in urban America. Quiñonez's and Vega's writing brings to center stage the postmodern quality of the city and its neighborhoods and their being inhabited by displaced people reimagining American urban space through the lens of their own cultural and community values.

Most of the time, the physical home is an extension of the individual and influences his or her state of mind. The barrio's apartments make their inhabitants feel confined and physically oppressed, and this explains Chino and Blanca's dream of a larger and better house. Having a comfortable physical home is a recurrent theme among diasporic and Latino writers whose most quoted example is in Sandra Cisneros's *The House on Mango Street*. The search for a better, stable home usually functions as a symbol for finding a place and a self in America. The physical space of the houses that Bodega gives back to the community becomes a more fundamental symbolic Puerto Rican space where a definite home/identity can be established on American soil. This owning "a house of their own" also represents the spatial *counterinvasion* and *tropicalization* of the American space. It is important to notice that this very issue is what makes Chino establish a relationship with Bodega when the latter provides a larger apartment for Chino and Blanca. Bodega sells dreams and transmits ideals from the past in order to organize a better future for the community.

Tropicalizing the Barrio

How transformations of the American space are represented in the literary works by Quiñonez and Vega can be best understood by exploring the process of *tropicalization*. Originally coined by Puerto Rican poet Víctor Hernández Cruz in his book *Tropicalization*,[24] the term is used by Frances Aparicio and Susana Chávez-Silverman in their excellent study *Tropicalizations: Transcultural Representations of Latinidad* to define a set of cultural and literary techniques that seek "to imbue a particular space, geography, group, or nation with a set of traits, images and values."[25] Quiñonez's and Vega's works show the tropicalization of the barrio as Puerto Ricans make it their own with their daily practices. The presence of Puerto Rican characters, places, music, smells, meals, and cultural traditions problematizes the qualities of a space located at the heart of the American nation.

In *Bodega Dreams* the reappropriation and tropicalization of the barrio are reflected in its characters' lives, recurrent themes, imagery, and literary language. Literal tropicalization of the barrio is represented by Bodega's project of owning the neighborhood, renovating buildings, and giving back those spaces to the Puerto Rican community. This would ensure the survival of their culture and the creation of a new home in America. In this way, the counterinvasion mentioned before is literally enforced through Bodega's project. A piece of American land is owned, transformed, and turned into a little Puerto Rican nation that takes control of its future. Even though at first Chino can hardly believe in the existence of a person with such ideals, he soon realizes that Bodega's dream has brought back hope to the community. Bodega represents "a time when all things seemed possible,"[26] and it is precisely his ideals of social change that provoke Chino's admiration for and fascination with Bodega.

For Chino, the barrio has a very ambiguous significance. The barrio's contradictions as a borderland where good and evil coexist pose a dilemma for Chino, who also feels the need to collaborate in the humanization of the barrio, in giving back dignity to a people living in a "paradox of crime and kindness."[27] He progressively leads the reader to discover that the "heart of darkness" in the barrio is an ambivalent space with negative and positive qualities and therefore needs to be improved by its inhabitants. Chino is certainly aware of Bodega's illegal means, but in the end he also considers the possible justification for Bodega's acts.

Bodega seems to fit the model posed by Jay Gatsby, but his dream differs from Gatsby's in that it responds to his community's social and economic needs. As Jay Gatsby was the hero and the epitome of the American Dream in the twenties, Bodega represents the possibility of achieving a different Puerto Rican dream in the barrio. The American Dream of social success and economic power clearly contrasts with the social ideals at the heart of Bodega's dream of transforming the barrio. The social commitment that Bodega exhibits is further explained by his past as a Young Lord during the sixties. Chino deeply admires the social initiatives, idealism, and aesthetics of the Young Lords, and this makes Bodega an even more attractive figure for Chino.

As the story concludes, Bodega's figure, his ideals, and his dream stay with Chino as a valuable heritage. The story of Bodega leaves a mark on Chino, who finally feels the need to continue Bodega's dream of providing a home for the community when in the end he takes into his home two newly arrived Puerto Ricans from the island. At the end of the novel, Chino is a transformed person who has learned a lesson, as suggested by his intention to stay in the barrio. The barrio will always stay with him, as Bodega told him: "Just remember one thing from an old *pana* who has been here longer than you, just remember, bro, that no matter how much you learn, no matter how many books you read, how many degrees you get, in the end, you are from East Harlem."[28] Bodega's words raise the issue of those who leave the barrio and their culture behind, get an education in pursuit of the American Dream of prosperity, and forget about the people who are still in the barrio. These words also make Chino reflect about the community as a whole and his responsibility for improving living conditions in the barrio. The final message is clear: the barrio "seemed like a good place to start";[29] the barrio provides that sense of home and identity necessary to start searching for a dream that has much more to do with creating a prosperous Puerto Rican community than with achieving the material American Dream. Using the language of the "masters," and in some ways disguised as ghetto literature, *Bodega Dreams* tropicalizes the American space of the barrio and builds a Puerto Rican sense of community as it transforms the American Dream into a Puerto Rican communal dream.

Through the subtlety that satire and irony give to literary discourse, Ed Vega similarly constructs a different representation of barrio life and Puerto Rican versions of the success story. Dreams are again a key theme in Vega's representation of the Puerto Rican experience in the United States. The dreams Mendoza writes are Puerto Rican dreams coming from the barrio and are about overcoming the barrio's negative reality through new hopes for a better future. *Mendoza's Dreams* presents a very ironic and biting vision of intercultural relations in the United States and of the failure of the American Dream for those at the margins of society.

In the story "Mercury Gómez" the American Dream has been tropicalized and transformed into a very peculiar Puerto Rican story of success. Mercury, a small Puerto Rican black man who had always been "invisible" to Anglo-Americans and who would never fit the image of the successful American, becomes a powerful rich man by building an empire of media companies from a messenger service. He organizes a group of small black men who carry the packages very quickly, making the customer believe that it was only one black man who did all the deliveries. The key to success is how these small black men are strategically located in different spaces from which they can easily control the traffic of packages. Merc's success emerges from his own marginality, and his story symbolizes the subversion of the system by benefiting from his own social invisibility. Mendoza, after hearing the story and still amazed by how Merc had beaten the system, finally comments: "Out in the street I couldn't stop smiling. Those Rough Riders had definitely made a mistake back in 1898 when they landed in Guanica and annexed the island. Boy, had they made a mistake."[30]

The collection's most outstanding example of tropicalization and transformation of the American space can be found in the story "The Barbosa Express." Jesús Barbosa, a motorman with the New York City Transit Authority, feels discriminated against when after seventeen years of service he is denied one of the new trains to drive. Enraged with the whole system, he decides to take an old train and, with the help of friends and relatives from the barrio, transforms the train to carry a traveling Latin Fourth of July party all along Manhattan. When he invites Mendoza to a "surprise party" without telling him about the details, his words are "We're celebrating our independence."[31] And rightly so, the event becomes a real act of transgression and assertion of Puerto Rican presence in Manhattan. All the cars had been renamed either "The Barbosa Express" or "El son de Barbosa" in huge letters and had been decorated and prepared by Puerto Rican people from the barrio: relatives, friends, an engineering student, an executive from AT&T, and a even a grandchild who works for the Pentagon made Barbosa's dream come true. Everything was arranged to deceive the officials and make them believe that graffiti artists had hijacked the train.

The Puerto Ricans' transformation of Independence Day into a Latin day for a few hours is an act of subversion and a clear example of tropicalization of the American space. The intrusion of this "Puerto Rican" train running through New York, on such a special day, dramatically changes New York's landscape and becomes a living symbol of Puerto Ricans' ability to make themselves visible. The readers and Mendoza himself are shocked by the fact that a group of Puerto Ricans have been able to boycott Independence Day celebrations, destabilizing the system and leaving signs of a long-ignored community. The train is not a reflection of nostalgia for a cultural past left behind but, quite the contrary, the reassertion of a community and identity there to stay. The message, as Mendoza explains, is clear because a constantly growing, unsatisfied Latino population can no longer be ignored: "By the time I reached my apartment I knew one thing for certain. I knew that the United States of

America would have to pay for passing the Jones Act in 1917, giving the people automatic U.S. citizenship and allowing so many of them to enter their country. As they say in the street: 'What goes around, comes around.'"[32]

This is another counterinvasion that brings to center stage the confrontational practices that can emerge from the Puerto Rican community. Puerto Ricans are part of American space, and in reclaiming their space they also demand that their presence be acknowledged and respected. Another story that uses humor and unusual situations to transform American space and create a Puerto Rican version of an incredible success story is "The Pursuit of Happiness," where Don Sinfo, a working-class Puerto Rican, decides to make a fortune by raising a goat in his home and selling its meat in the barrio. The intrusion of the animal into the neighborhood, which already destabilizes the urban landscape, has a greater effect when the animal escapes and causes a commotion in the neighborhood. The people run at the sight of the animal, forming an unruly mob that is mistaken for a revolution by police officials and the local government. The confusion and absurd situations that the escape of the animal brings about call attention to the existing tensions among ethnic groups, repressed political feelings, and cultural misunderstandings existing in New York City. The happy and surreal end of the story presents, after a series of chaotic and absurd episodes, Don Sinfo marrying a rich Anglo spinster who believes Don Sinfo has saved her from the goat and from an old suitor. Don Sinfo's success story makes his comment, "In the U.S. anything is possible," ironically true and turns inside out the national myth of the American Dream.

Tropicalization of the English Literary Language

The tropicalization of the English language in these literary works is especially interesting for its many creative possibilities and its subtle challenge to the dominant discourse. The inclusion of Spanish words, place-names, and concepts defamiliarizes the English language and implies a "deterritorialization" of the dominant language by a group whose language has been dismissed. Other tropicalization techniques consist in the manipulation of English so that it becomes impregnated by a cultural and linguistic Latino substratum: "a transformation and rewriting of Anglo signifiers from the Latino cultural vantage point."[33]

The tropicalization of the literary language found in Quiñonez's and Vega's works usually functions as a means to make the Anglo reader transcend the mere ethnographic and exotic narration in order to understand political, cultural, and historical implications in the development of the Latino/a identity. What these writers are trying to do is to claim their place in American society not only by stressing their difference but by challenging obsolete representations of the ethnic subject and encouraging true intercultural dialogue.

In *Mendoza's Dream,* Vega displays his mastery by introducing Puerto Rican names of foods, holidays, and concepts and Spanish signifiers that make the reader feel the distance of being foreign in his or her own language. An example is a passage where the narrator, talking about a Christmas celebration, alludes to an aroma using an array of words foreign to the Anglo reader: "Words went back and forth and in each one there was the aroma of *pernil, arroz con gandules, pastels, salmoreja de jueyes, empanadas, alcapurias, morcillas, mofongo, arroz con dulce, majarete, tembleque, almendras, nueces, turrón de alicante, turrón de jijona de mazapán* and to top it all off *coquito. Ay, madre santísima.* You couldn't believe how tongues were watering as men wished each other *Felicidades.*"[34] Obviously, these words have no effect on the Anglo reader's nose since they are completely strange, but for several lines Anglo readers have felt completely displaced from the text. In another instance, the narrator stresses this effect by devoting an explanation that takes more than a page and includes three entries from the *New Comprehensive International Dictionary of the English Language* to the implications of the word *batata* and of being called "Batatini." At the end of the passage the narrator ironically plays with Anglo readers, exposing their ignorance and creating further distance: "If you are a Spanish speaker and have used the word you may have by now taken the word for granted or mastered its inherently incongruent sound. If on the other hand you speak solely English, try pronouncing it as it sounds in Spanish. Now don't muff it and say things like baytayra or bat-tara, but say BAH-TAH-TAH with the accent on the second syllable."[35] In this example, bilingual readers are favored by the author, who deliberately places Anglo readers in an inferior position and obliges them to experience the anxiety of dealing with a strange language. The intention is clearly to make Anglo readers reflect upon cultural and linguistic difference as an erroneous basis for discriminatory practices. Linguistic puns on the characters' names and the intrusion of Spanish syntax and lexicon such as "It was absolutely the best of nights, this *Nochebuena*," impregnate the text with traits of the Spanish language and culture and defamiliarize English signifiers, adding to them new Latino signifieds.

In other instances, Spanish phrases are not translated, with the clear intent to leave Anglo readers ignorant about what is really going on and to make them feel "out of place" and alienated from the English text. This is what we find in the following passage about racial discrimination from "Mercury Gómez": "And then he said that after working for about a year for Silver Streak Services he realized he was pretty much anonymous. 'Just another black guy. And worse than that I was small. "The little black guy," I useta hear people say and I useta feel like saying, "*puñeta, váyanse pa'l carajo, coño! Yo soy boricua! Negro pero boricua y si no le cae bien, cáguense en su madre!*" Know what I mean?' 'Of course,' I said, 'I've suffered similar discrimination.'"[36] The effect of this passage gains further significance if we notice that the Spanish phrases disguise direct insults at Anglos. While an Anglo reader probably is at risk of not understanding a harsh critique of American society, a bilingual Latino reader is able to establish a sort of complicity with the writer, thereby making the message more powerful. In this way, Vega's narrative has multiple readings and messages, depending on the reader's ethnicity and culture.

The introduction of Spanglish in the narrative discourse is another powerful tropicalizing technique. In *Bodega Dreams,* the language of the streets and Spanglish permeate the whole novel, emerging in the dialogue and characterizing the inhabitants of the barrio. Puerto Ricans are reinventing themselves, and a new language comes to characterize this new identity. In the last chapter of the novel, "A New Language Being Born," this issue is directly addressed as a fundamental element in the barrio and a distinctive feature of Puerto Rican identity in the United States: "at a window next door to us, a woman yelled to her son down on the street: '*Mira*, Junito, go buy *un mapo, un contén de leche,* and tell *el bodeguero yo le pago* next Friday. And I don't want to see you in *el rufo!*'"[37] We can clearly appreciate how this new language not only shows syntactical influences from both Spanish and English but also includes new words such as *mapo* from "mop" and *rufo* from "roof." Spanglish is the linguistic symbol of the future of a community that still retains all its vitality and strength, as described by Bodega at the end of the novel: "A new language means a new race. *Spanglish* is the future. It's a new language being born out of the ashes of two cultures clashing with each other. You will use a new language. Words that they might not teach you in that college. Words that aren't English or Spanish but at the same time are both. . . . Our people are evolving into something completely new. . . . this new language is not completely correct; but then few things are."[38]

The Puerto Rican heritage stays alive in this language because Spanish words and structures impregnate the English that Puerto Ricans are compelled to use as the dominant language. Spanglish becomes a symbol of the home/identity that is created out of a multiple heritage. The complex geography of a new Puerto Rican identity is therefore exemplified by the interesting relationship that is established between the Puerto Rican community and the new American space it inhabits. Quiñonez's and Vega's tropicalized narratives actually turn the barrio into a "different" space that is more like "home" for the Puerto Rican community, but most of all, these narratives become aesthetic homes where the Puerto Rican experience justly finds its space in American literature.

NOTES

1. Jesús Colón, *A Puerto Rican in New York and Other Sketches* (New York: Masses and Mainstream Publishers, 1961); Bernardo Vega, *Memorias de Bernardo Vega,* ed. César Andreu Iglesias (Río Piedras, PR: Huracán, 1977).

2. Guillermo Cotto-Thorner, *Trópico en Manhattan* (New York: Las Americas, 1959); René Marqués, *La carreta* (Río Piedras, PR: Editorial Cultural, 1955); Pedro Juan Soto, *Ardiente suelo, fría estación* (Mexico: Editorial Veracruzana, 1961); and Pedro Juan Soto, *Spiks* (Río Piedras, PR: Editorial Cultural, 1973).

3. Richard Wright, *Native Son* (New York: Harper, 1940); Ralph Ellison, *Invisible Man* (New York: Random House, 1952).

4. Claude Brown, *Manchild in the Promised Land* (New York: Macmillan, 1965).

5. Toni Morrison, "City Limits, Village Values: Concepts of the Neighborhood in Black Fiction," in *Literature and Urban Experience*, ed. Michael Jaye and Ann Chalmers Watts (New Brunswick, NJ: Rutgers University Press, 1981), 39.

6. Piri Thomas, *Down These Mean Streets* (New York: Knopf, 1967).

7. J. L. Navarro, *Blue Day on Main Street* (Berkeley: Quinto Sol, 1973); Luis J. Rodríguez, *Always Running: La Vida Loca; Gang Days in L.A.* (New York: Touchstone, 1993).

8. Ernesto Quiñonez, *Bodega Dreams* (New York: Vintage, 2000); Ernesto Quiñonez, *Chango's Fire* (New York: HarperCollins, 2004).

9. Ed Vega, *The Comeback* (Houston: Arte Público Press, 1985); Ed Vega, *Mendoza's Dreams* (Houston: Arte Público Press, 1987); Ed Vega, *Casualty Report* (Houston: Arte Público Press, 1991); Ed Vega, *No Matter How Much You Promise to Cook or Pay the Rent You Blew It Cauze Bill Bailey Ain't Never Coming Home Again* (New York: Farrar, Straus and Giroux, 2003); Ed Vega, *The Lamentable Journey of Omaha Bigelow into the Impenetrable Loisaida Jungle* (Woodstock, NY: Overlook Press, 2004); Ed Vega, *Blood Fugues* (New York: Rayo/HarperCollins, 2005).

10. Ed Vega, *Mendoza's Dreams*, 11.

11. Ibid.,7.

12. Raúl Romero Villa, *Barrio-Logos: Space and Place in Urban Chicano Literature and Culture* (Austin: University of Texas Press, 2000), 4, 6.

13. Ibid., 5.

14. Quiñonez, *Bodega Dreams*, 5.

15. Ibid., 13.

16. Rosemary M. George, *The Politics of Home: Postcolonial Relocations and Twentieth-Century Fiction* (Cambridge: Cambridge University Press, 1996), 11.

17. María Lugones describes this world traveling as a significant quality of people living on the borders: "Those of us who are 'world'-travellers have the distinct experience of being different in different 'worlds' and ourselves in them. . . . The shift from being one person to being a different person is what I call 'travel.' . . . One can 'travel' between these 'worlds' and one can inhabit more than one of these 'worlds' at the very same time. I think that most of us who are outside the mainstream U.S. construction or organization of life are 'world-travellers' as a matter of necessity and of survival." María Lugones, "Playfulness, 'World'-Travelling, and Loving Perception," in *Making Face, Making Soul/Haciendo Caras: Creative and Critical Perspectives by Women of Color*, ed. Gloria Anzaldúa (San Francisco: Aunt Lute, 1990), 396.

18. Juan Flores, "The Latino Imaginary: Dimensions of Community and Identity," in *Tropicalizations: Transcultural Representations of Latinidad,* ed. Frances R. Aparicio and Susana Chávez-Silverman (Hanover, NH: University Press of New England, 1997), 190.

19. James G. Kellas, *The Politics of Nationalism and Ethnicity* (London: Macmillan, 1991), 2.

20. Benedict Anderson, *Imagined Communities: Reflections on the Origin and Spread of Nationalism* (London: Verso, 1983), 6.

21. Agustín Laó, "Islands at the Crossroads: Puerto Ricanness Traveling between the Translocal Nation and the Global City," in *Puerto Rican Jam: Rethinking Colonialism and Nationalism,* ed. Frances Negrón-Muntaner and Ramón Grosfoguel (Minneapolis: University of Minnesota Press, 1997), 176.

22. Ibid., 181.

23. Nico Israel, *Outlandish: Writing between Exile and Diaspora* (Stanford, CA: Stanford University Press, 2000), ix.

24. For Víctor Hernández Cruz the tropicalization process allows him to transform poetic language into something strange for the Anglo reader, as it is defamiliarized by the

images and signifieds from a Latin American culture. The linguistic pun and the intrusion of objects and images alien to the American landscape allow the creation of a defamiliarized world within the barrio and the urban space, which are therefore transformed and permeated by Puerto Rican rhythms, traces, and values. See his *Tropicalization* (New York: Reed, Cannon and Johnson, 1976).

25. Frances Aparicio and Susana Chávez-Silverman, introduction to Aparicio and Chávez-Silverman, *Tropicalizations*, 8.

26. Quiñonez, *Bodega Dreams*, 31.

27. Ibid., 161.

28. Ibid., 36.

29. Ibid., 213.

30. Quiñonez, *Mendoza's Dreams*, 148.

31. Ibid., 117.

32. Ibid., 124.

33. Frances Aparicio, "On Subversive Signifiers: U.S. Latina/o Writers Tropicalize English," *American Literature* 66 (Dec. 1994): 797.

34. Ed Vega, *Mendoza's Dreams*, 76.

35. Ibid., 175.

36. Ibid., 144.

37. Quiñonez, *Bodega Dreams*, 211.

38. Ibid., 212.

BIBLIOGRAPHY

Anderson, Benedict. *Imagined Communities: Reflections on the Origin and Spread of Nationalism*. London: Verso, 1983.

Aparicio, Frances R. "On Subversive Signifiers: U.S. Latina/o Writers Tropicalize English." *American Literature* 66 (Dec. 1994): 795–801.

Aparicio, Frances R., and Susana Chávez-Silverman, eds. *Tropicalizations: Transcultural Representations of Latinidad*. Hanover, NH: University Press of New England, 1997.

Brown, Claude. *Manchild in the Promised Land*. New York: Macmillan, 1965.

Cisneros, Sandra. *The House on Mango Street*. New York: Vintage, 1984.

Colón, Jesús. *A Puerto Rican in New York and Other Sketches*. New York: Masses and Mainstream Publishers, 1961.

Cotto-Thorner, Guillermo. *Trópico en Manhattan*. New York: Las Americas, 1959.

Ellison, Ralph. *Invisible Man*. New York: Random House, 1952.

Flores, Juan. "The Latino Imaginary: Dimensions of Community and Identity." In *Tropicalizations: Transcultural Representations of Latinidad,* ed. Frances R. Aparicio and Susana Chávez-Silverman, 183–193. Hanover, NH: University Press of New England, 1997.

George, Rosemary M. *The Politics of Home: Postcolonial Relocations and Twentieth-Century Fiction*. Cambridge: Cambridge University Press, 1996.

Hernández Cruz, Víctor. *Tropicalization.* New York: Reed, Cannon and Johnson, 1976.

Israel, Nico. *Outlandish: Writing between Exile and Diaspora.* Stanford, CA: Stanford University Press, 2000.

Kellas, James G. *The Politics of Nationalism and Ethnicity.* London: Macmillan, 1991.

Laó, Agustín. "Islands at the Crossroads: Puerto Ricanness Traveling between the Translocal Nation and the Global City." In *Puerto Rican Jam: Rethinking Colonialism and Nationalism,* ed. Frances Negrón-Muntaner and Ramón Grosfoguel, 169–188. Minneapolis: University of Minnesota Press, 1997.

Lugones, María. "Playfulness, 'World'-Travelling, and Loving Perception." In *Making Face, Making Soul/Haciendo Caras: Creative and Critical Perspectives by Women of Color,* ed. Gloria Anzaldúa, 390–402. San Francisco: Aunt Lute, 1990.

Marqués, René. *La carreta.* Río Piedras, PR: Editorial Cultural, 1955.

Morrison, Toni. "City Limits, Village Values: Concepts of the Neighborhood in Black Fiction." In *Literature and Urban Experience*, ed. Michael Jaye and Ann Chalmers Watts, 35–43. New Brunswick, NJ: Rutgers University Press, 1981.

Navarro, J. L. *Blue Day on Main Street.* Berkeley: Quinto Sol, 1973.

Quiñonez, Ernesto. *Bodega Dreams.* New York: Vintage, 2000.

———. *Chango's Fire.* New York: HarperCollins, 2004.

Rodríguez, Luis J. *Always Running: La Vida Loca; Gang Days in L.A.* New York: Touchstone, 1993.

Romero Villa, Raúl. *Barrio-Logos: Space and Place in Urban Chicano Literature and Culture.* Austin: University of Texas Press, 2000.

Soto, Pedro Juan. *Ardiente suelo, fría estación.* Mexico: Editorial Veracruzana, 1961.

———. *Spiks.* Río Piedras, PR: Editorial Cultural, 1973.

Thomas, Piri. *Down These Mean Streets.* New York: Knopf, 1967.

Vega, Bernardo. *Memorias de Bernardo Vega.* Ed. César Andreu Iglesias. Río Piedras, PR: Huracán, 1977.

Vega, Ed. *Blood Fugues.* New York: Rayo/HarperCollins, 2005.

———. *Casualty Report.* Houston: Arte Público Press, 1991.

———. *The Comeback.* Houston: Arte Público Press, 1985.

———. *The Lamentable Journey of Omaha Bigelow into the Impenetrable Loisaida Jungle.* Woodstock, NY: Overlook Press, 2004.

———. *Mendoza's Dreams.* Houston: Arte Público Press, 1987.

———. *No Matter How Much You Promise to Cook or Pay the Rent You Blew It Cauze Bill Bailey Ain't Never Coming Home Again.* New York: Farrar, Straus and Giroux, 2003.

Wright, Richard. *Native Son.* New York: Harper, 1940.

8 DISCORDANT DIFFERENCES

Strategic Puerto Ricanness in Pedro Pietri's Puerto Rican Obituary

VÍCTOR FIGUEROA

Commenting on what German immigrants should expect of their new life in America, John Quincy Adams wrote in 1819: "To one thing they must make up their minds, or they will be disappointed in every expectation of happiness as Americans. They must cast off the European skin, never to resume it. They must look forward to their posterity rather than backward to their ancestors; they must be sure that whatever their own feelings may be, those of their children will cling to the prejudices of this country."[1] What I find interesting about Adams's words, besides their avowal of the classic "melting pot" theory, is their somewhat-understated acknowledgment of the fact that "assimilation" is a two-sided coin. There is the side of the immigrant, who must be willing to "cast off" his or her old skin. But there is also the side of the "host country," with its particular prejudices (the word, which admittedly meant something different for Adams in the nineteenth century, sounds right to modern ears) and its willingness, or unwillingness, to accept the newcomers. Even if one were to accept the notion of an American melting pot, the question remains of whether it operated in the same way for the different immigrants that came to America. The answer, evidently, is no. Some groups were not able to participate, effectively and in equal terms at least, in the mainstream socioeconomic and political life of

America. It was only after the arduous struggles for civil rights that many of these groups were able to gain limited access to the public sphere, and most of them still struggle to maintain those achievements. And while Adams focuses on the immigrant's willingness to "cast off" his old skin, his own choice of words begs for an examination of at least some of those prejudices that confront the immigrant on his or her arrival.

In our own times, of course, the orthodoxy of Adams's position has been superseded by a seeming celebration of multiculturalism, where the pot's role is not to melt differences but to combine them in a soup that, while remaining one and unique, allows its diverse ingredients to shine in their own right. However, a paradox of the multiculturalist position is that, while celebrating what Adams would have condemned, it very often departs from Adams's assumption that the "nonassimilation" of certain immigrants is the result of their resistance (or, perhaps, their enthusiastic pride in their heritage).[2] Leaving aside for the moment the issue of the immigrants' celebration and preservation of their own culture, which of course is true to a certain extent of all immigrant groups, we should notice that this approach takes into account only one aspect of the immigrant's experience: his or her "willingness." But what about the equally important issue of the host society's "prejudices"? Would it be possible to argue that some of these immigrants were "willing" to integrate themselves but, for reasons that include race, language, and religion among others, were not allowed to? In the same way, it may be possible to argue, at least to a certain extent, that the celebration and affirmation of identity and "difference" in these groups (an activity whose value, by now accepted by all, I am not trying to deny) did not precede their marginalization but were actually a result of it.

I would like to examine some of these issues as they appear in the work of Nuyorican poet Pedro Pietri. Pietri was born in Ponce, Puerto Rico, in 1944, but his family moved to New York in 1947, and the poet lived in the city until his untimely death from cancer in 2004. He is one of the founding voices of Nuyorican literature, a term that refers to the work of writers of Puerto Rican descent established in New York. Consisting mostly of English, Spanglish, and bilingual texts, Nuyorican literature includes such names as Miguel Algarín, Tato Laviera, Sandra María Esteves, and Miguel Piñero, among others.[3] Although Pietri was a prolific writer of poetry, plays, and fiction (and a performer of his poetry and plays), he remains known mostly for his first collection of poems, the extraordinary *Puerto Rican Obituary*, from 1973.[4] It is on this work that I will focus.[5]

The book's title already gives an indication of its character. It works as a catalog of the different forms of spiritual or literal death that Puerto Ricans face in New York City. The tragic character of these experiences is enhanced by the fact that they are portrayed through the use of a vividly metaphorical, surreal style that gives to them a dramatic, nightmarish quality. For example, the dead Puerto Ricans in the poem "Puerto Rican Obituary"

> . . . are together
> in the main lobby of the void
> Addicted to silence
> Off limits to the wind
> Confine to worm supremacy. (9)

And note the horrific images in "A Prayer Backwards," which is a critique of U.S. militarism:

> Whose arms
> will we have for breakfast
> tomorrow morning?
> & whose legs
> will we have for lunch
> if the afternoon ever comes?
> & if we are not extinct
> by supper time
> we can boil our eyeballs
> & have visionary soup (77)

This last example also shows one of Pietri's most remarkable traits: his uncanny sense of humor, which is persistently sustained throughout the most terrible moments. Thus, when the drug addict in the poem "O/D" dies from an overdose, the poet comments:

> congratulations your imitation
> of another dead junkie

is so convincing that you will
be buried for the performance (52)

The half-humorous, half-tragic images and situations portrayed in the poems may often be fittingly described as fundamentally grotesque, giving to that term the meaning that Wolfgang Kayser gave it (as opposed to Bakhtin's somewhat more optimistic reading): the presentation of an "estranged world," "a play with the absurd," and, more precisely, "an attempt to invoke and subdue the demonic aspects of the world."[6] In Pietri's case, the "estrangement," "the absurd," and "the demonic" are firmly grounded in sociopolitical structures that keep Puerto Ricans trapped in cycles of inequality and prejudice; Pietri's humor invokes and precariously attempts to subdue those demons.[7]

The theme that dominates the book is the prejudice that Puerto Ricans consistently face in their dealings with official institutions of power and the white, Anglo-Saxon, Protestant establishment, including government agencies (and if I recur to the well-known "wasp" acronym, it is because race, language, cultural background, and religion all play important roles in Pietri's mapping of prejudice, including both individual and institutionalized forms of prejudice). To be sure, as I write these words (2006), one has to acknowledge that the situation of Puerto Ricans on the mainland has improved somewhat since Pietri published his book in 1973. From that point of view, *Puerto Rican Obituary* could be regarded above all as a vivid document of conditions prevailing in a very specific place and moment.[8] However, it is also true that many Puerto Ricans still face conditions of inequality and, above all, prejudice in their daily lives, both in New York and elsewhere in the United States.[9] In addition to that, newer immigrant groups are occupying the place at the bottom of the social ladder that Puerto Ricans used to occupy, and to them (making, of course, the necessary adjustments to fit their individual cultural idiosyncrasies) many of the issues that Pietri condemns are still enormously relevant.

In his protest, Pietri recurs to a tactic that gives urgency to his claims while also accurately portraying the paranoid state of mind of a marginalized group: instead of blaming impersonal forces or abstract social and economic structures, he formally denounces a "conspiracy" against Puerto Ricans. This approach, while certainly risky if taken as a literal statement of fact, should be regarded as a rhetorical strategy that in fact works as a call to action. After all, one important point to remember when reading Pietri's poetry is that many of his poems were designed for public readings and performances: elements of a collective "call to arms" are often evident in them.[10] In the book's main poem, "Puerto Rican Obituary," we read:

They knew
they were born to weep
and keep morticians employed
as long as they pledged allegiance
to the flag that wants them destroyed (5)

And in "The Broken English Dream" he declares:

To the United States we came
. . . .
To live where rats and roaches roam
in a house that is definitely not a home
. . . .
To dream about jobs you will never get
To fill out welfare applications
To graduate from school without an education
To be drafted distorted and destroyed
To work full time and still be unemployed (13)

Phrases like "democracy that raped our nation" (21) and "clean-cut white collar executioners" (20) abound in the poems. In "The Old Buildings" it is clearly indicated that

there is nothing
that frightens
this government more
than seeing people
living and loving
and breathing together
so they decided to
demolish the buildings
that could have been

saved by renovation
& eliminate the unity (53)

But certainly the best exposition of Pietri's "conspiracy theory" is the magnificent "Suicide Note from a Cockroach in a Low Income Housing Project." In that poem, a frenzied cockroach complains about how welfare and antipoverty programs have altered the lifestyles of minority groups in such a way that the old habitat of cockroaches has been destroyed:

why should our race be erased to make
america a beautiful place for everyone but us
. . . .
Why should we be denied co-existence??? (26)

The irony, of course, is that the cockroach, while complaining about the "progress" of minorities, stands precisely as a symbol for those minorities, who are alienated in a city where government programs do not prevent their life conditions from getting ever worse. However, the insect quite willingly positions itself against these minorities for the sake of its own advancement, allowing Pietri to characteristically denounce a lack of solidarity that he suggests is only too common among different marginalized groups. Finally, the cockroach moans:

THIS IS GENOCIDE
And what bothers me the most
is that nobody is protesting
No demonstrations or moritorium for our dead
Everybody's busy protesting this
Everybody's busy protesting that
Everybody's raising hell about the air strikes
But nobody is saying a damn word about the DDT strikes
Like nobody wearing STOP THE DDT STRIKE buttons (27)

These last accusations of the cockroach, that "nobody is protesting," are particularly significant. Who is it that is not protesting? As we have seen, Pietri's emphasis is mostly on portraying how the North American establishment despises and rejects Puerto Rican immigrants, relegating them to lives of marginality, unemployment, and degradation. And yet, one may also wonder about how the attitude of Puerto Rican immigrants toward American culture and institutions is presented in the poems. Are the Puerto Ricans of these poems protesting? Are they trying to "cast off" their Caribbean skins, as John Quincy Adams would have wanted them to? Or are they a postmodern self-affirming ethnic group? The answer, of course, is not simple and straightforward. But let us emphasize that this complexity cuts both ways: while we do not see in the poems a group of immigrants eagerly trying to "cling to the prejudices" of their new country, we certainly do not see a group celebrating their "difference" in multicultural fashion. In fact, in several poems we find Puerto Ricans trying to climb the social ladder by the route of cultural self-denial that official institutions conscientiously impose. In his insistence on chronicling this phenomenon (as opposed to simply celebrating "Latino difference" or condemning American prejudices), Pietri remains quite unique among his generation of writers.

Thus, in the central poem, "Puerto Rican Obituary," the Puerto Ricans who "died yesterday today and will die again tomorrow" are described as

Dreaming about queens
Clean-cut lily-white neighborhood
Puerto Ricanless scene
Thirty-thousand-dollar home
The first spics on the block
Proud to belong to a community
of gringos who want them lynched
Proud to be a long distance away
from the sacred phrase: Que pasa

These dreams
These empty dreams
from the make-believe bedrooms
their parents left them
are the after effects
of television programs
about the ideal
white american family

with black maids
and latino janitors (4–5)

And in "The Broken English Dream" he laments:

To the united states we came
To learn to misspell our name
. . . .
and stay drunk and lose concern
for the heart and the soul of our race
and the climate that produce our face (14)

In poems such as these we are offered an image of many Puerto Ricans trying desperately to "belong," to integrate themselves into a society that does not allow them entrance. Some of them are in fact quite willing to "cast off" their old skins, but it is to no avail. Pietri obviously disagrees with those attempts and is positively disgusted by some of them. In "The Dead Uniform," we are introduced to a Latino who has become a policeman, whom the poetic voice addresses in this way:

What the fuck is wrong with you mister?
making believe
that your problems are over
because you passed
the civil service examination
to become a hired killer
for the administration
that is killing your generation
and will do the same to you (72)

What is most degrading in these attempts to assimilate is that for the most part they *fail*, not as a result of the immigrant's inability, but because of open rejection by the institutions and structures that the Puerto Ricans are trying to become part of. These efforts are portrayed as the grotesque behavior of a prisoner begging his jailer to throw away the prison keys:

you try over & over to impress
the bastards that are burying you (89)

Even in a poem like "O/D," where a drug addict's death due to an overdose is brutally portrayed, Pietri's objection to the addict's lifestyle is not only that it is self-destructive but also that it ironically reinforces and buys into the logic of an economic and ideological system that, to use Pietri's words, "wants him destroyed."

Faced with these desperate and failed attempts to belong, Pietri evidently considered it his responsibility as a writer to inject a sense of rebellion and dignity into these Puerto Ricans. As I have already indicated, Pietri regarded himself as a fundamentally oral performer, and his live performances were usually quite impressive. There is a strong didactic element in his view of his role as a poet, and very often he humorously assumed the persona of an itinerant preacher (a posthumous exhibit honoring Pietri at New York's Museo del Barrio in 2006 was advertised as "an homage to Reverend Pedro Pietri")—in this case, a preacher of a Latino sense of worth. However, in *Puerto Rican Obituary*, pride and nationalist self-affirmation are not simply celebratory gestures that immigrants spontaneously bring to the new country but a highly politicized strategy that often emerges, as we have seen, *as a result* of the immigrant's encounter with the racism of the American establishment. This is an aspect of ethnic self-affirmation that multiculturalism, as celebrated by even the most conservative sectors of corporate America, often neglects. In order to achieve his emancipating goal, Pietri resorts to a very common strategy among Nuyoricans and other minority groups: the glorification of the lost homeland. At the end of "Puerto Rican Obituary," the poet complains that if Puerto Ricans had made "their Latino souls the only religion of their race," they

will right now be doing their own thing
where beautiful people sing
and dance and work together
where the wind is a stranger
to miserable weather conditions
where you do not need a dictionary
to communicate with your people
Aqui se habla Español all the time

Aqui you salute your flag first
Aqui there are no dial soap commercials
Aqui everybody smells good
Aqui tv dinners do not have a future
Aqui men and women admire desire
and never get tired of each other
Aqui Que Pasa Power is what's happening
Aqui to be called negrito means to be called LOVE. (11)

There are similarly paradisiacal images of Puerto Rico in several poems. In addition to the Spanish words that proliferate in those moments, African or indigenous aspects of Puerto Rican culture are sometimes privileged. When the drug addict in "O/D" is about to die

for a few seconds
all the buildings from
the hudson river
to the east river
become palm trees
there is enough grass
for everybody to walk on
drums are heard
thru-out the vicinity
elephants participated
the wind was scented
with coconut integrity
. . . .
a rainbow was present (50)

One does not have to be too cynical to realize that those images have little to do with the "real" Puerto Rico. On the island, like anywhere else, Dial Soap commercials and TV dinners have a great future, men do beat their wives, and there are instances when Spanish is just not enough. But, as critic Efraín Barradas has indicated, this mythical view of Puerto Rico that appears in the work of not only Pietri but also other Nuyorican poets refers, not to a geographical place, but to "a state of mind."[11] To take Pietri's conception of Puerto Rico in literal terms would attribute to him a naïveté that the rest of his poetry denies. Rather, Puerto Rico should be interpreted as that which Nuyoricans *must* assume in order to resist oppression.

There have been many debates, particularly on the island, regarding the real "Puerto Ricanness" of Nuyoricans. "Purist" insular Puerto Ricans often complain that Nuyoricans have been "Americanized": that their language has been "contaminated" by English and their culture deformed. This outlook, of course, does not take into account the extreme degree to which that is also happening to insular Puerto Ricans. In fact, some Nuyorican writers, such as the poet Miguel Algarín, highlight the fact that the Nuyorican identity, always redefining itself with regard to its Hispanic and Anglo-Saxon connections, is a more accurate indicator of what it means to be a Puerto Rican today than the seemingly (but only seemingly) more stable identities of Puerto Ricans from the island.[12]

Pietri's *Puerto Rican Obituary* points to what may be regarded as a semiotic or political "Puerto Ricanness" that is displayed as a challenge, as resistance. When used in this way, the more idyllic and utopic the Puerto Rico that is created, the better, whether it is related to the "real" Puerto Rico or not. Such a Puerto Rico is like a religious relic whose "authenticity" no one needs to question as long as it performs miracles. And Pietri wants his Puerto Rico to perform the miracle of returning a sense of dignity and pride to Nuyoricans, who for too long have been internalizing oppression and prejudice. Whether Nuyoricans are entitled or not to claim a "Puerto Rican identity" is no longer a meaningful question. They have been marginalized and disrespected for decades *because of their Puerto Rican descent.* That is the identity they are going to use as a weapon. Let us notice, however, that this seemingly absolute allegiance to the island is expressed in English (a language that most island Puerto Ricans still regard, for practical everyday purposes, as "other"). Moreover, the English in the poems is selectively "broken" in an attempt to capture Nuyorican speech, and except for almost numinous invocations of "the island," the space of the poems is decidedly that of New York City.[13] So when it comes to national identity, Pietri quite willingly dances between two waters: he wants to keep his "authentic" Puerto Rican cake and eat it too. This strategic use of national identity, which is of course not exclusive to Pietri, can also be regarded as an attempt to go beyond the limitations of traditional politics of identity in struggles of emancipation. After all, fixed identities cut both ways, operating as refuges against discrimination but also as sites of prejudice, as we can often see in the petty prejudices of Puerto Ricans against Dominicans and other Caribbean neighbors. The liminal space of Nuyoricanness (always appealing to the *seemingly* more stable space of island Puerto Ricanness, yet always subverting it) focuses on redefining the uneven relation to the agents of an oppressive order, rather than on "being authentic." As a result, identity yields its place to a relational ethics as the privileged tool for social change.

It is in this context that one better understands some of Pietri's poems that would otherwise appear as too ingenuous, for example, "Tata":

> Mi abuela
> has been
> in this dept. store
> called america
> for the past twenty-five years
> She is eighty-five years old
> and does not speak
> a word of English
>
> That is intelligence. (105)

Taken literally, this poem could appear dangerously naïve, perhaps reactionary. After all, as Pietri shows in another poem, "Beware of Signs," Puerto Ricans' ignorance of English usually works to their own disadvantage: it is often used by those who want to exploit them. In that poem we read:

> Beware of signs that say
> "Aqui se habla español"
> Do not go near those places
> of smiling faces that do not smile
> and bill collectors who are well train
> to forget how to habla español
> when you fall back on those weekly payments (18)[14]

One can only wonder: if "Tata," the grandmother, cannot speak a word of English, how will she avoid the trap of signs that say "Aqui se habla español," and moreover, how will she heed her grandson's warning, written in *English*? Pietri reaches here an impasse of sorts, one that can only be appreciated as *productive* by paying attention to his strategic, mobile view of identity. Tata, that "authentic" grandmother who has lived for twenty-five years in New York without speaking a word of English (i.e., without losing her "roots"), has to exist within every Nuyorican struggling with his or her "broken English." But at the same time Pietri requires from Nuyoricans the astuteness and sophistication of someone skilled in border crossing and code switching.[15] Requiring total allegiance to traditional roots while also commending well-developed survival skills adapted to the particular traps of New York City, Pietri's instructions to Nuyoricans create, in fact, a position impossible to sustain in actual practice. And it is this impossible situation, and its implications, that return us to our original line of inquiry.

Although John Quincy Adams's assumptions now seem quite inadequate, Pietri's poems suggest that naïve contemporary trends of multicultural enthusiasm are equally misguided when they celebrate *only* as spontaneous free choice what very often was the fragile and fragmented retrieval of a lost homeland, painfully conjoined with a stern will to survive surrounding prejudices. This does not necessarily mean that Puerto Ricans were always trying to assimilate themselves to mainstream America (though this was sometimes the case, even on, or perhaps particularly on, the island). It simply means that many of them (including second- and third-generation children of immigrants) were never allowed to "forget" or "cast off" their descent (their difference): they were consistently harassed and ostracized for it and confined to slums and ghettos. This does not mean that it would have been better if they had "assimilated," but it does mean that the multiculturalist "ideal" needs to rehistoricize its own political project: the "celebration" of difference that seems to dominate the American scene today often had its origins, as the history of Puerto Rican immigrants shows, in the days when *difference* was negatively valued and *imposed*. This should not stop us from celebrating difference and pluralism, but perhaps it should make us distinguish between the celebration of "difference" as the restitution of a simple fact of social life (albeit one that admittedly was repressed throughout many decades of "melting pot" rhetoric) and the cultivation of difference as a *discordant* site within the solidified structures of official power (as opposed to a mere *variation* of the same structures)—that is, as the calling into question of monological conceptions of the social sphere, and as the opening of a space for the dialogue of *truly different* perspectives. This second approach to difference seems quite threatening from the perspective of multiculturalism as a symphony of "different" voices all singing the same tune. Paradoxically, as Pietri's poetry suggests, such a contesting role may be more skillfully played from a fluid, seemingly unstable location than from fixed ethnic roles imposed from above by the media and other institutions. If multiculturalism is to remain, or become, an ethically committed position, a site of truly discordant (transgressive) differences, its work is not to celebrate impermeable, unchanging identities but to confront a society that often terrorizes immigrants into becoming stereotypes of themselves.

Here I return to Pietri's "impossible" situation (he is proud of his grandmother who was never "corrupted" by English, yet he expresses this in English and mistrusts American attempts to use Spanish; or, in other words, he celebrates total allegiance to traditional values, yet he promotes survival strategies that such *total* allegiance would not allow). Pietri's position becomes an "impasse" (and, consequently, a gesture of critical interrogation and defiance) only in a society where identity as a closed category is the main site of both oppression and resistance: Puerto Ricans suffer discrimination because they are Puerto Ricans; therefore, they take refuge in their Puerto Ricanness. Pietri's strategic Puerto Ricanness attempts to break with such tight categories and tries to create a more fluid space where the main impulse is not (in spite of all appearances) toward being "authentic" but toward breaking with structures of privilege and discrimination. What Nuyoricans want in Pietri's book *is* in fact impossible within the parameters of the system in which they exist: therefore, the system must be dismantled. Pietri's point is not to scold Puerto Ricans for wanting to assimilate but to highlight that, in fact, those who wanted to assimilate ran against the wall of prejudice and racism. That racist and prejudiced society must be dismantled, not for the sake of those who want to assimilate, but in order to guarantee the just participation of all, particularly of those who *do not* want to assimilate. That Pietri has been able to argue his positions through a poetry that consistently maintains such high levels of quality and originality constitutes a great achievement indeed.

NOTES

1. Quoted in Werner Sollors, *Beyond Ethnicity: Consent and Descent in American Culture* (Oxford: Oxford University Press, 1986), 4.

2. For an interesting critical assessment of the claims and theoretical assumptions of multiculturalism, see E. San Juan Jr., *Racism and Cultural Studies: Critiques of Multiculturalist Ideology and the Politics of Difference* (Durham, NC: Duke University Press, 2002).

3. For an overview of the developments of Nuyorican literature, see Efraín Barradas, *Partes de un todo* (Río Piedras, PR: Editorial de la Universidad de Puerto Rico, 1998); and Juan Flores, *Divided Borders: Essays on Puerto Rican Identity* (Houston: Arte Público Press, 1993).

4. Pedro Pietri, *Puerto Rican Obituary* (New York: Monthly Review Press, 1973). All quotations from Pietri's poems are from this edition; hereafter cited in text.

5. At the moment of his death in 2004, Pietri had published only three volumes of poetry (in addition to several plays and a short story): *Puerto Rican Obituary*; *Traffic Violations* (Maplewood, NJ: Waterfront Press, 1983); and the anthology *Out of Order/Fueri servizio*, ed. Mario Maffi (Cagliari, Sardinia: Cooperativa Universitaria Editrice Cagliaritana, 2001). However, it is well known that he had an enormous number of unpublished poems (Maffi states that the 330 poems of his anthology come from a manuscript of about 1,000). If the recent exhibition in honor of Pietri and the artist Lorenzo Homar at the Museo del Barrio in New York (Between the Lines: Text as Image; An Homage to Lorenzo Homar and the Reverend Pedro Pietri, 24 Feb.–10 Sept. 2006) is an indicator of renewed interest, one may hope that some of Pietri's unpublished poems will be made available to the public, as they deserve. The same applies to his recorded performances (both audio and video) of his poems.

6. Wolfgang Kayser, *The Grotesque in Art and Literature* (New York: Columbia University Press, 1981), 184, 187, 188.

7. An interesting application of Kayser's concept that could shed useful light on Pietri's use of the grotesque is Fritz Gysin's *The Grotesque in American Negro Fiction: Jean Toomer, Richard Wright, and Ralph Ellison* (Bern, Switzerland: Francke, 1975).

8. For a description and assessment of the Puerto Rican experience in the United States, and its evolution throughout the years, see Clara E. Rodríguez and Virginia Sánchez Korrol, eds., *Historical Perspectives on Puerto Rican Survival in the U.S.* (Princeton, NJ: Markus Wiener, 1996).

9. For the situation of Puerto Ricans in the nineties, see Edna Acosta-Belén et al., *"Adiós, Borinquen querida": The Puerto Rican Diaspora, Its History, and Contributions* (Albany: State University of New York Press, 2000).

10. Pietri left at least two recordings of his performances: *Loose Joints* (Folkways Records) and *Pedro Pietri en Casa Puerto Rico* (Coquí Records).

11. Barradas, *Partes de un todo*, 59.

12. Miguel Algarín and Miguel Piñero, eds., *Nuyorican Poetry: An Anthology of Puerto Rican Words and Feelings* (New York: William Morrow, 1975).

13. For an excellent examination of the stages and facets of Puerto Rican identity in the United States, see Juan Flores, "'Qué assimilated, brother, yo soy asimilao': The Structuring of Puerto Rican Identity in the U.S.," in his *Divided Borders*, 182–195.

14. For the importance and suspect status of written signs in Pietri's poetry, see Alessandro Portelli, "Beware of Signs; or, How to Tell the Living from the Dead: Orality and Writing in the Work of Pedro Pietri," in *Race and the Modern Artist*, ed. Heather Hathaway (Oxford: Oxford University Press, 2003), 201–208.

15. For an insightful examination of the aesthetic and political significance of code switching and bilingual games, see Doris Sommer, *Bilingual Aesthetics: A New Sentimental Education* (Durham, NC: Duke University Press, 2004).

BIBLIOGRAPHY

Acosta-Belén, Edna, et al. *"Adiós, Borinquen querida": The Puerto Rican Diaspora, Its History, and Contributions*. Albany: State University of New York Press, 2000.

Algarín, Miguel, and Bob Holman, eds. *Aloud: Voices from the Nuyorican Poets' Café*. New York: Owl Books/Henry Holt, 1994.

Algarín, Miguel, and Miguel Piñero, eds. *Nuyorican Poetry: An Anthology of Puerto Rican Words and Feelings*. New York: William Morrow, 1975.

Bakhtin, Mikhail. *Rabelais and His World*. Bloomington: Indiana University Press, 1984.

Barradas, Efraín. *Partes de un todo*. Río Piedras, PR: Editorial de la Universidad de Puerto Rico, 1998.

Cordasco, Francesco. *The Puerto Rican Experience: A Sociological Sourcebook*. Totowa, NJ: Rowman and Littlefield, 1973.

Duany, Jorge. *The Puerto Rican Nation on the Move: Identities on the Island and in the United States*. Chapel Hill: University of North Carolina Press, 2002.

Fitzpatrick, Joseph. *Puerto Rican Americans: The Meaning of Migration to the Mainland*. Englewood Cliffs, NJ: Prentice Hall, 1971.

Flores, Juan. *Divided Borders: Essays on Puerto Rican Identity*. Houston: Arte Público Press, 1993.

Gysin, Fritz. *The Grotesque in American Negro Fiction: Jean Toomer, Richard Wright, and Ralph Ellison*. Bern, Switzerland: Francke, 1975.

Hernández, Carmen Dolores. *Puerto Rican Voices in English: Interviews with Writers*. Westport, CT: Praeger, 1997.

Kayser, Wolfgang. *The Grotesque in Art and Literature*. New York: Columbia University Press, 1981.

Mohr, Eugene V. *The Nuyorican Experience: Literature of the Puerto Rican Minority*. Westport, CT: Greenwood Press, 1982.

Pérez y González, María E. *Puerto Ricans in the United States*. Westport, CT: Greenwood Press, 2000.Pietri, Pedro. *Out of Order/Fueri servizio*. Ed. Mario Maffi. Cagliari, Sardinia: Cooperativa Universitaria Editrice Cagliaritana, 2001.

———. *Puerto Rican Obituary*. New York: Monthly Review Press, 1973.

———. *Traffic Violations*. Maplewood, NJ: Waterfront Press, 1983.

Portelli, Alessandro. "Beware of Signs; or, How to Tell the Living from the Dead: Orality and Writing in the Work of Pedro Pietri." In *Race and the Modern Artist*, ed. Heather Hathaway, 201–208. Oxford: Oxford University Press, 2003.

Rodríguez, Clara E. *Puerto Ricans: Born in the USA*. Boston: Unwin Hyman, 1989.

Rodríguez, Clara E., and Virginia Sánchez Korrol, eds. *Historical Perspectives on Puerto Rican Survival in the U.S.* Princeton, NJ: Markus Wiener, 1996.

San Juan, E., Jr. *Racism and Cultural Studies: Critiques of Multiculturalist Ideology and the Politics of Difference*. Durham, NC: Duke University Press, 2002.

Sollors, Werner. *Beyond Ethnicity: Consent and Descent in American Culture*. Oxford: Oxford University Press, 1986.

Sommer, Doris. *Bilingual Aesthetics: A New Sentimental Education*. Durham, NC: Duke University Press, 2004.

9 "BORINKEE" IN HAWAI'I

Rodney Morales Rides the Diaspora Wave to Transregional Imperial Struggle

MARITZA STANCHICH

This essay situates Honolulu-based author Rodney Morales's short-story collection, *The Speed of Darkness*, and first novel, *When the Shark Bites*, in a post-Nuyorican, greater Puerto Rico rubric that recognizes contemporary diasporic Puerto Rican literature as emerging from a field of broader locations and more complex genealogies than the term "Nuyorican" allows.[1] The term "diasporic Puerto Rican" responds to critics who lament the lack of decisive terms to identify the Puerto Rican diaspora.[2] Decisive terms are perhaps more urgent now that the U.S. census has registered a Puerto Rican population in the United States greater than that of the island. I use "diasporic Puerto Rican" and "post-Nuyorican" instead of other terms, such as those coined by spoken-word poets, to demonstrate how Morales usefully contributes a *strategic heterogeneity* to calls for more flexible Puerto Rican national paradigms that fully account for the diaspora.[3] As part of a substantial corpus of post-1980s diasporic Puerto Rican literature, Morales's fiction historicizes and complicates the diasporic literary canon, avoiding reductive, essentialist categories by revealing broad and sometimes contradictory agendas among diasporic writers and myriad ways of being diasporic. Although diasporic Puerto Rican literature often engages circuitously with island discourses and events, it should not be annexed or hijacked by the insular canon or discourses, as Lisa

Sánchez González usefully inveighs against.[4] Rather, situating Morales's work as contemporary diasporic Puerto Rican literature attends to what Flores calls "the seams and borders of national experience [that] need to be understood not as absences or vacuums but as sites of new meaning and relations" (51).

The term "diasporic Puerto Rican" importantly retains the full identification of "Puerto Rican" while emphasizing the community's refusal of a hyphenated identity, as critics have pointed out and as the title of this collection highlights.[5] While I appreciate the popularity and theoretical usefulness of terms such as poets María Fernández's "DiaspoRican" and Tato Laviera's "AmeRícan," which point to other poetic neologisms, such as Willie Perdomo's "Porta-Reecan,"[6] my use of "diasporic Puerto Rican" strives for an even broader currency than scholarly, literary, or performance domains by simply describing the Puerto Rican community in the United States as diasporic. In preferring "diasporic Puerto Rican," I am not as preoccupied with defining and maintaining distinct or fluctuating locations as with recognizing a substantial inter-American community and a shared, if at times internally contested and diverse, cultural imaginary. While I do not mean to collapse the terms for literary canons or writers with those for communities, I keep both in mind, as well as multiple locations, in national as well as extranational contexts. While this term concurs with Sánchez González's argument for a diasporic literary history, "Puerto Rican" is preferred over her usage of "Boricua" to account for and critically interrogate agendas that may contradict an "organically resistant" definition of the diaspora (11). This terminological preference also avoids the differentiated use of the term "Boricua" in island contexts, which does not necessarily have the same connotations of a badge that "Boricua" carries stateside. In addition, the indigenizing impulse of "Boricua" can be critiqued, as Taíno and *jíbaro* romanticism has been, for eliding, rather than foregrounding, Afro-Caribbean heritage, even while affirming affiliations with African Americans in a U.S. context, whereas the term "diaspora" links massive Caribbean migration to Afro-Caribbean history. For while Suzanne Oboler's *Ethnic Labels, Latino Lives* shows how ethnic labels and categories are historically contingent, they are also geographically contingent, even within the United States, as diasporic Puerto Rican autobiographies as divergent as Piri Thomas's *Down These Mean Streets* and Esmeralda Santiago's *Almost a Woman* illustrate when their main pro tagonists are racially and ethnically marked in changing ways when they travel south and north from New York, respectively.[7]

Heeding such tendencies for labels to travel and shift, I also avoid "Nuyorican" as a catchall term, though maintain it to denote specific historical, geographic, and literary contingencies. As with "Boricua," I am concerned with how "Nuyorican" sometimes functions in an island context as an exclusionary, pejorative term, even though 1960s and 1970s Puerto Rican activists and artists recuperated it stateside as well as in particular insular contexts, such as in spoken-word circles.[8] More importantly, however, historicizing the term "Nuyorican," albeit as a tradition that continues today, delineates the micropolitics and multiple locations of diasporic Puerto Rican literature. In historicizing the term and the movement, I agree with Flores's assessment that "Nuyorican" has become anachronistic for a variety of reasons (186), among them that its continued usage as a broad term for the diaspora ignores important shifts that have occurred in the stateside community and its literary history. While the prefix may be tired, "post-Nuyorican" denotes the importance of previous "post-" prefixes, such as "post-Boom," as well as the importance of the political and cultural movement that preceded it.[9] Post-Nuyorican literature, then, more than merely another generational shift, suggests a literary expansion of language practices; thematic concerns; class, race, and sexual identities; and geographic locations. More specifically, post-Nuyorican literature marks shifts in terms of contestational politics, class mobility, textual ethnic markers, and new affiliations.[10] A diversification of agendas and practices may be the organizing principle of post-Nuyorican literature, not that a unifying one is necessary. In fact, "post-Nuyorican" may be a provisional term for diasporic Puerto Rican literary productions starting in the 1980s and 1990s, marking a shift in modalities and topographies and an emerging yet marked heterogeneity. Few post-Nuyorican texts, however, omit Puerto Rican identifications and ethnic markers altogether, though some nearly do, such as Diana Rivera's poetry collection *Bird Language* (aside from the book cover marketing her as a Puerto Rican poet and painter).[11]

Rodney Morales's writing, however, revisits a transregional imperial history of the diaspora in Hawai'i, with a pronounced Puerto Rican sensibility often crucial to plot, characterization, and themes of a cultural politics in Hawai'i that can still function as a frontal resistance to unrelenting commodification and gentrification of everything from working-class neighborhoods to indigenous sacred burial grounds.[12] Morales's novel *When the Shark Bites* demonstrates a tenacious insistence on the part of the novel's characters, who are of mixed heritage, Puerto Rican with other Hawaiian ethnic groups, to identify as Puerto Rican. The novel centers on the Rivera family, and is told alternately from the points of view of Hank, Kanani, and their sons Mākena and ʻAnalu, as they become entangled in a web of intrigue involving the corrupt and murderous interests vying for control of Hawaiian land for tourism development. In such an ethnically diverse society as Hawaiʻi, Mākena and ʻAnalu remain unclear about the extent to which their father is Puerto Rican, as he is rumored to have a great-grandfather who is part Japanese; their mother is Chinese and Hawaiian. When it comes time to deal with census forms, they are forced to decide. As Mākena recalls:

> One day, when me and ʻAnalu had to fill out the "ethnicity" box on the forms that the school gave us, we never know what fo' put. There was no box for "Puerto Rican." Only had "Other." Dad said, "Mark down 'Part-Hawaiian.' Gotta make dat count." This left three-fourths of what we were unaccounted for, so on the way to school me and ʻAnalu wen' also check off Chinese and Japanese. Next to "Japanese" box I wrote "suspect." Then we crossed out "Other" and I watched as ʻAnalu wrote in "Porto Rican." (123–124)

According to the 2000 census, Puerto Ricans in Hawaiʻi numbered 30,005, and this was when the census allowed for mixed-race and ethnic identifications for the first time. While the much ballyhooed introduction of such a category in the 2000 census acknowledges "mixity" as a historical reality as old as the nation itself, with Thomas Jefferson's living African American relatives as perhaps the most salient proof, the new category nevertheless implies trends worth noting for pan-Latin and interethnic identifications. Such a complex field of broader trajectories in part contributes to pan-Latin and new inter-ethnic alliances as well as more complex genealogies, all helping to historicize a phase of literary production that supersedes the category "Nuyorican."[13] Such "mixity" as a whole also complicates the categorization of literary productions and canons strictly along ethnic lines. And while Puerto Rico as a geographical location is important to the novel, at one point crucial to the intrigue plot when informant Sparky Lopez, marked for death, is given a one-way ticket to San Juan as a safe harbor, the affiliations between ethnic groups, especially concerning rights struggles, emphasize cross-cultural alliance and community, as implied by Hank's urging his sons to register a substantial number of Native Hawaiians, no doubt to support the Native Hawaiian sovereignty movement's pending land claims, in which Native Hawaiians have legally pressed for the federal recognition accorded to more than three hundred American Indian nations and for control of 900,000 acres of ceded lands, plus additional lands in restitution for the illegal overthrow of the Hawaiian kingdom in 1893.[14]

The forging of such community is not necessarily romanticized as harmonious in Morales's oeuvre, as is seen earlier in the novel when the boys' father, Hank Rivera, wrestles with the memories of his short-lived college stint on the U.S. West Coast, and how a blonde girlfriend and her McGovern-supporting parents started arbitrarily calling him Enrique without his permission (Morales seems to use this device to sarcastically differentiate liberals from radicals).

> Even though that has *never* been my name, she insisted on calling me that. Now, mind you, I didn't think I had a problem with my Latino identity, especially once I had *found* it, but Enrique never rang right. Maybe sounded too much like Borinkee, which always sounded like a putdown to me. Even though now I know where that word came from—the original name of Puerto Rico was Borinquen—in Honolulu in the 1960s it sounded pretty nasty:
>
> Hey, Borinkee!
> What you like, paké who look like one Jap.
> Shit, you like one kanaka-popolo
> Eh, fuck you.
> Fuck YOOOOOU!
>
> That's the thing with cultural politics in Hawai'i, hard to sort out what's derogatory and what's not. (82)

The characters' agency in identifying with particular ethnic groups is crucial to both passages cited so far, and here we have another example of the way terms, categories, or affiliations travel or do not travel. Not only does "Boricua" have a Hawaiian Creole English equivalent, spelled BRINkay by Ted Solis,[15] but it shifts meaning from badge of honor to potential slur, as is also implied in Morales's short story "Ship of Dreams," which opens his 1988 short-story collection, *The Speed of*

Darkness. Told from the masculinist, heteronormative perspective of Takeshi, an adolescent Japanese nursing a big crush on Linda, a Puerto Rican teen whose brothers apparently stole the largest squash from his father's garden to fashion a formidable *güiro*[16] for the Saturday night dance, the story opens with Takeshi's father complaining, "Had to be dose damn borinkees" (15).

The only work by Morales to be included in an anthology of Puerto Rican literature to my knowledge,[17] the story explores early-twentieth-century Puerto Rican, Japanese, and Native Hawaiian cultural interaction. Unlike the rest of Morales's work, which is set in the later twentieth century, "Ship of Dreams" is set in 1922 and harkens back to the history of the Puerto Rican diaspora in Hawai'i. The largest and earliest migration of about 5,000 Puerto Ricans arrived between 1900 and 1901, and Puerto Ricans in Hawai'i totaled more than 10,000 by 1914 (and this was before U.S. citizenship was instituted in Puerto Rico). This population increase illustrates the global imperial reach of the U.S. sugar industry, which from the 1850s in Hawai'i successively recruited new sources of plantation labor (Chinese, Portuguese, Japanese, Korean, Puerto Rican, Filipino, and others), often as strike breakers, unbeknownst to the workers.[18] The characters in "Ship of Dreams" are cognizant of being at the helm of the twentieth century, with "the many strikes on plantations by Japanese, Filipinos, and Puerto Ricans" (16). They test whether the new promise of democracy in Hawai'i would live up to its claims, in a labor history that deepens the breadth of the diaspora and its resistance, broadening historical affiliations that Bernardo Vega documented between highly politicized Puerto Rican *tabaqueros* (cigar makers) in New York and striking plantation workers in Puerto Rico. The focus of the story, however, is the history of the cross-cultural crucible of multiethnic Hawai'i, with intercultural affiliations portending the mixed genealogies later seen in *When the Shark Bites*. The story details Takeshi's observations of gender behavior, food preferences, and musical practices of the Puerto Ricans, the latter also documented historically, as well as in a more contemporary context, by scholars such as Norma Carr, Ted Solis, and others. The story ends with Takeshi's transculturation, as he is invited down from the tree from which he observes the Puerto Ricans' Saturday night dance while tentatively playing a *güiro* of his own and is welcomed to the helm of the band and urged to scratch along, thereby, of course, capturing Linda's attention.

As with the previously cited "borinkee" reference and copious use of Hawaiian Creole English in *When the Shark Bites*, the story and ensuing collection demonstrate Morales's sustained commitment to turning local language practices to a literary project, as do many contemporary Hawaiian authors, such as Joseph Balaz, Barry Masuda, Darrell Lum, Diane Kahanu, Gary Pak, and the controversial Lois-Ann Yamanaka. These authors are all part of a still-emerging literary movement in Hawai'i that began in the 1970s and that Rob Wilson characterizes as a "critical regionalism" committed to cultivating a sense of place through historical specificity and local traditions and images and often embodying "a literary heteroglossia of mixed voices and local tongues."[19] Morales's narrations drop plenty of 1970s popular-culture references to rock bands and vintage cars and chart cultural negotiations with U.S. consumerism marked by a regional cosmopolitanism referred to in Asian Pacific studies as Pacific Rim, yet customized for local readers with local language and local colloquial observations, practices and events. Morales's for the most part standard yet slang-riddled English prose repeatedly deploys Hawaiian Creole English, popularly referred to as pidgin, in dialogue, although occasionally whole chapters or sections depict characters thinking in local language. An example of this practice comes up in a poignant early chapter in *Shark*, when the youngest son, 'Analu, searches for his recently deceased grandfather in a mall pet shop, believing his grandfather's spirit has transferred to a bird.

Numerous instances of code switching also heighten the effect of deploying local language. In *When the Shark Bites*, Hank's son Mākena admires his father's verbal virtuosity: "And that heavy pidgin stuff, that's just something he turns on and off like one spigot. Seems like standard English is the cold water, and pidgin is when he get hot" (119). Derek Bickerton illuminates the functions and effect of code switching in the Hawaiian context, recalling Mervyn Alleyne's description of the way Creole continuums function in Jamaica:

> Like many stigmatized languages and dialects, Hawaiian Creole English is at one and the same time (and often by the same people!) despised as some kind of uneducated "broken talk" and admired as a bonding mechanism among the locally born as well as a mark of working-class toughness and anti-*haole* solidarity.[20] Under these circumstances, code switching . . . became a sine qua non in the Islands. The same people who were being berated by teachers

as substandard language speakers were in fact performing prodigies of linguistic virtuosity—repidginizing their creole for the benefit of immigrant grandparents, switching into standard English (or something close to it) at their white-collar jobs or in court, then returning with visible relief to their natural [*sic*] speech when they were with friends or younger relatives.[21]

Indeed, Morales's local-language usage functions to forge "working-class toughness and anti-*haole* solidarity," with *haole* in this case symbolizing not only white outsiders but an imposed, corporate-driven social order. Local and Native Hawaiian solidarity is crucial to Morales's work; in fact, the title and ensuing shark symbolism in the novel conjure important indigenous Polynesian traditions, and the chapters are often headed by Hawaiian words of deep significance. The distinction between local and Native traditions and language is important, for while Native Hawaiians may also be local, nonindigenous locals are a distinct group.[22]

Nevertheless, the linguistic tenets of Hawaii's local literature movement cannot be simply collapsed into or advanced from the Spanglish code switching that came to define the street poetics of the Nuyorican tradition. Rather, if considered alongside the recent works of authors such as Kansas-based poet Gloria Vando, England-based Alma Ambert, Victor Hernández Cruz, and Giannina Braschi, Morales's language practices function simultaneously to register distinct permutations of a broadly diasporic local language hybridity that, despite its clearly contestational politics, is post-Nuyorican in that Spanglish bilingual code switching can no longer be construed as a linguistic binary in monolithic terms. Though taken as a group, writers and works of the past couple decades who also break with or blur the bilingual language binary are not necessarily constitutive of a cohesive literary movement. For example, Vando's poetry is just as apt to break into Dutch, Hebrew, or French, along with Spanish, as in "On Hearing That a Potato Costs $70 in Sarajevo" (2002); Hernández Cruz has more recently turned to exploring Moorish influences on Spanish, dividing his time between Aguas Buenas and Morocco;[23] Ambert's first poetry collections were published in Greek/English bilingual editions in Greece; and Braschi's brash and adventurous bilingualism in *Yo-Yo Boing!* explodes previous code-switching theories.[24] Like that of these diasporic Puerto Rican authors, Morales's copious use of code switching complicates rather than reinscribes the Spanish/English bilingual binary, be it circumscribed by geography, class antagonism, strategic essentialism, or cultural nationalism. His work expands the linguistic panorama without Spanish or Spanglish but with a keen ear for and investment in local Hawaiian usage, invoking a colonial language history with parallels to the U.S. imposition of English in Puerto Rico.[25]

The Hawaiian language was made illegal in schools from 1896 to 1898, and educational institutions systematically tried to eradicate it from the 1920s to the 1970s, when the educational community finally formally acknowledged it as a distinct language. Hawaiian was later decreed Hawaii's second language by law in 1986.[26] Indeed Morales's fiction foregrounds key global U.S. imperial intersections that were the subject of many scholarly conferences marking the 1998 centennial of the so-called Spanish-American War and the annexation of Hawai'i. The literary project of deploying such local language, as with border languages in literatures elsewhere, reveals the fissures of language imposition, an act of "bilanguaging," to use Walter Mignolo's term, with potential for producing post-Occidentalist epistemologies. By bilanguaging, Mignolo does not mean bilingualism, though bilanguaging may or may not also be bilingual or plurilingual; rather the "bi" prefix opposes monolanguaging. Bilanguaging goes beyond the grammatical system of language to reveal "the ideology of monolanguaging (and particularly the idea of national languages in the imaginary of nation states), that is, of speaking, writing, thinking within a single language controlled by grammar, in a way similar to a constitution's control over the state."[27] Mignolo is concerned with the geopolitics of language, rather than the grammars of language, and with how national languages are consolidated in complicity with the state and regulating institutions, with both nations and national languages as persistently seeming "natural."[28] Hence, bilanguaging theory critiques English imposition as well as linguistic neonationalism in Puerto Rico, which traditionally sanctified only Spanish-language literature as fit for insular discourse, thereby excluding non-Spanish diasporic expression from insular engagements.

Such transregional imperial affinities demonstrate that, while Morales's work constitutes a post-Nuyorican and broad diasporic imaginary, it also intersects in crucial and specific ways with insular Puerto Rican history and national discourses and events, as has been the case with many diasporic Puerto Rican authors, such as Jesús Colón, Piri Thomas, Martín Espada, Tato Laviera, and Esmeralda Santiago.[29] Though Morales's location and linguistic project may seem exceptional in the context of Puerto Rican studies, central themes such as the demilitarization of Kaho'olawe Island, achieved in 1990 after nearly half a century of U.S. military bombing, resonate for the island of Vieques, as the environmental decontamination of Kaho'olawe, not to mention former U.S. military bases in the Philippines, has been an ongoing struggle, each site having varying degrees of leverage in Washington, D.C. In November 2003, ten years after the U.S. Congress authorized a $400 million cleanup, and less than six months after the historic handover of Vieques, the U.S. Navy officially handed over control of Kaho'olawe to the state of Hawai'i, though unexploded ordnance has still not been completely cleared as had been promised, according to newspaper reports.[30] The U.S. military still controls about 30 percent of O'ahu, the most populated of Hawaii's eight major islands, and controversy continues over military misuse of land on all the islands.[31] Morales nostalgically recuperates Hawaii's 1970s protest era, which mainland radical groups such as the Young Lords recognized and participated in, and which launched the protracted confrontation to end the bombing in Kaho'olawe as well as renewed native Hawaiian spiritual worship there. In 1990, after the mysterious and still-unresolved deaths of two beloved activists, George Helm and Kimo Mitchell, and the island's designation as a national historic site, the bombing was halted.[32]

Morales's novel recalls the 1970s in Hawai'i not only to nostalgically evoke the era and symbolically resolve some of its most unsettled questions, such as Helm and Mitchell's disappearance at sea, but to connect it to current jural and statist confrontations. These include land-use and eviction struggles, which have been ongoing for decades in response to the rapid development of rural areas that began in the late 1960s, largely for tourism development, as well as the aforementioned Native Hawaiian sovereignty movement.[33] Similarly, in Vieques at the time of this writing, the pointed question ¿Un Vieques Libre para quién? (A Free Vieques for whom?) is being asked by local activists witnessing *la isla nena* ("baby island," a term of endearment) being developed by outsiders for luxury tourism. Indeed, Morales's work emphasizes the demilitarization and consecration of such land. In another story from *Speed of Darkness*, entitled "Daybreak over Haleakala/Heartbreak Memories," an excursion of politically active students goes haywire when one named

Bud, who looks *haole* but has a Native Hawaiian grandfather who was an important indigenous leader, suffers an emotional collapse after coming across human bones that had been used as target practice by the military. Aside from exploring, through the character of Bud, what Rob Wilson characterizes as the "lurking fear" of becoming homogenized into a "whitewashed American,"[34] the story also concerns indigenous religiosity in connection to land use and contests the relegating of ongoing traditions and belief systems to museums. In *When the Shark Bites*, the proper burial of stolen, sacred bones in a cave is the culminating denouement, recalling a widely publicized lawsuit against Hawaii's Bishop Museum that ended with the bones being stolen, as well as symbolically laying to rest the remains of a disappeared activist named Keoni, whose legacy pervades the novel and may be a stand-in for George Helm, who, as mentioned earlier, was lost at sea during an attempted takeover of Kahoʻolawe to stop navy exercises there.

Morales's fictionalization of such ongoing rights struggle, while highly specifically located, nevertheless involves more than the fringes of the diaspora. Rather, it forcefully posits the deeply transcommunal concerns of a Greater Puerto Rico, or Puerto Rico Extendido.[35] Rather than transcending, collapsing, or erasing the distinct histories of heterogeneous sectors that compose such a Greater Puerto Rico, this extended imaginary navigates difference and conflicts as well as mutual material and intuitive exchange encompassing diasporic and insular communities. While the potential to contest hegemonic paradigms and binaries and, as Mignolo would have it, think outside them is important, my concerns are not only contestational, a point supported by Caribbean novelist and philosopher Wilson Harris's theories of the cross-cultural imagination, which eschew umbrella discourses for deeper mutual engagements that are profoundly interactive.[36] Borrowing from a key concept in Chicano studies, "Greater Puerto Rico" is derived from José Limón's use of the phrase, as taken from Américo Paredes. For Limón and Paredes, "Greater Mexico" refers to all Mexicans and all areas they inhabit on both sides of the border, in a cultural rather than official political sense, though not apolitically cultural.[37] Paredes coined the term for his work in folklore to indicate the unofficial heritage of people who may not speak an officially sanctified language but nevertheless produce and interrogate *lo mexicano*. I prefer the Spanish translation *un Puerto Rico*

Extendido to *un Gran Puerto Rico* because, while it widens territorialized conceptions of the Puerto Rican imaginary, it does not reify the notion that size matters, even via correctives.[38] I also acknowledge that, while Greater Puerto Rico is proposed as an affiliated border/broader community reflecting, and often contesting, Puerto Rico's status as a U.S. territory, the border as a trope and as a militarized zone is not quite the same for Puerto Rico, since for diasporic Puerto Ricans the burdens vis-à-vis the federal immigration bureaucracy and *la migra* differ greatly, though of course pose their own unique challenges (such as the lack of independent Puerto Rican citizenship or dual citizenship, with all that implies). Language, however, has long been characterized as a key affiliation for stateside Latin America–descended communities. Island affiliations are just as crucial, as Morales's linguistic and military transregional imperial affinities show, to convey the sense of an insular and diasporic circuit and imaginary that exceed notions of labor flows. As Jorge Duany has recently noted, the divided-nation thesis previously ascribed to the diaspora has shifted to acknowledge the fluid relationship between the diaspora and the island.[39] The phrases *brincando el charco* (puddle jumping), the "air bridge," and Luis Rafael Sánchez's famous metaphor *la guagua aérea* (the air bus), along with the Puerto Rican Spanish word describing the "revolving door" of a mobile citizenry, *el vaivén*, also expansively break with notions of geographical isolation, from *La charca* to *El charco*.[40] Recognizing the Puerto Ricanness of Rodney Morales's fiction, even as it performs "his own postmodern yet Pacific-oriented claim for place-bound identity," to use Wilson's phrase,[41] extends that imaginary puddle to the deep Pacific and forges discursive *vaívens* that contribute to reconfigurations of the Puerto Rican diaspora.

NOTES

I thank Norma Klahn, Isabel Velez, and especially Pam Kido, who shared with me pertinent articles from her own research on Hawai'i, for their generosity as interlocutors as I worked out the ideas and substance of this essay, though of course I am solely responsible for its contents. I would also like to state that, although I am not Puerto Rican, but of Croatian-Peruvian descent, I do not approach Puerto Rican studies as an object of study but rather hope to make contributions in deep dialogue and community with Puerto Ricans in various locations.

I dedicate this essay to Joel Cruz Martínez (1967–2003).

1. Rodney Morales, *When the Shark Bites* (Honolulu: University of Hawai'i Press, 2002); Rodney Morales, *The Speed of Darkness* (Honolulu: Bamboo Ridge Press, 1988). Hereafter references to both works are cited in text.

2. Carlos Pabón, "La imposible lengua apropiada," in his *Nación postmortem: Ensayos sobre los tiempos de insoportable ambigüedad* (San Juan: Ediciones Callejón, 2002), 92; Jorge Duany, *The Puerto Rican Nation on the Move: Identities on the Island and in the United States* (Chapel Hill: University of North Carolina Press, 2002), 28.

3. Juan Flores, *From Bomba to Hip-Hop: Puerto Rican Culture and Latino Identity* (New York: Columbia University Press, 2000). Hereafter cited in text. See also Duany, *Puerto Rican Nation on the Move*; Arcadio Díaz Quiñones, *El arte de bregar: Ensayos* (San Juan: Ediciones Callejón, 2000); Juan Duchesne Winter, "Puerto Rico y las lenguas de su soledad," in his *Ciudadano insano y otros ensayos bestiales sobre cultura y literatura* (San Juan: Ediciones Callejón, 2001), 39–48; Carmen Dolores Hernández, *Puerto Rican Voices in English: Interviews with Writers* (Westport, CT: Praeger, 1997); Frances Negrón-Muntaner and Ramón Grosfoguel, eds., *Puerto Rican Jam: Rethinking Colonialism and Nationalism* (Minneapolis: University of Minnesota Press, 1997).

4. Lisa Sánchez González, *Boricua Literature: A Literary History of the Puerto Rican Diaspora* (New York: New York University Press, 2001), 17–20. Hereafter cited in text.

5. For more on the Puerto Rican refusal to hyphenate, see Flores, *From Bomba to Hip-Hop*, 167–190; Ramón Grosfoguel, Frances Negrón-Muntaner, and Chloé S. Georas, "Beyond Nationalist and Colonialist Discourses: The *Jaiba* Politics of the Puerto Rican Ethno-nation," in Negrón-Muntaner and Grosfoguel, *Puerto Rican Jam*, 1–38.

6. Willie Perdomo, *Where a Nickel Costs a Dime: Poems* (New York: W. W. Norton, 1996), 19.

7. Suzanne Oboler, *Ethnic Labels, Latino Lives: Identity and the Politics of (Re)Presentation in the United States* (Minneapolis: University of Minnesota Press, 1995); Piri Thomas, *Down These Mean Streets* (New York: Knopf, 1967); Esmeralda Santiago, *Almost a Woman* (New York: Vintage, 1998).

8. For more on the negative connotation of the term "Nuyorican" in an insular context, see Efraín Barradas, *Partes de un todo: Ensayos y notas sobre literatura puertorriqueña en los Estados Unidos* (San Juan: Editorial de la Universidad de Puerto Rico, 1998); Arnaldo Cruz-Malavé, "Teaching Puerto Rican Authors: Identity and Modernization in Nuyorican Texts," *ADE Bulletin* 91 (1985): 45–51; Duany, *Puerto Rican Nation on the Move*; and José Lorenzo-Hernández, "The Nuyorican's Dilemma: Categorization of Returning Migrants in Puerto Rico," *International Migration Review* 33, no. 4 (1999): 988–1013. An obvious example of positive connotations in an insular context is the Nuyorican Café, the weekend hot spot and alternative art and performance space in Old San Juan.

9. In a recent essay titled "Towards a Post-Nuyorican Literature," I wrote that Juan Flores considers the term "post-Nuyorican" in *From Bomba to Hip-Hop* (187) but did not fully deploy it. However, he and coauthor Mayra Santos-Febres had recently used the term "post-Nuyorican," along with other terms, in the introduction to a *Hostos Review*

issue fittingly entitled "Nuevas literaturas Puerto/Neorriqueñas New Puerto/Nuyor Rican Literatures." See Maritza Stanchich, "Towards a Post-Nuyorican Literature," in *Sargasso: The Floating Homeland/La patria flotante*, ed. María Cristina Rodríguez (Río Piedras, PR: University of Puerto Rico II, 2005–2006), 113–124; Juan Flores and Mayra Santos-Febres, eds., introduction to "Open Mic/Micrófono abierto: Nuevas literaturas Puerto/Neorriqueñas New Puerto/Nuyor Rican Literatures," special issue, *Hostos Review/Revista Hostosiana* 2 (2005): xi.

10. These affiliations could be called postethnic, by which I mean, not an end to ethnic categories or an end to the continuing need for class struggle, but a recognition of other intergroup affiliations, as David Hollinger argues in *Postethnic America* (New York: Basic Books, 1995). Rubén Ríos Ávila saliently illustrates just such multiple affiliations between Puerto Rican and gay contexts in the essay titled "Rambling" in his *La raza cómica del sujeto en Puerto Rico* (San Juan: Ediciones Callejón, 2002), 311–318.

11. Diana Rivera, *Bird Language* (Tempe, AZ: Bilingual Press/Editorial Bilingüe, 1994).

12. In Hawaiian studies, the *okina*, or glottal stop, a single inverted apostrophe, is used to indicate Hawaiian words such as "Hawai'i." Adjectives and possessives, such as "Hawaiian" or "Hawaii's," are considered Anglicized words. See Candace Fujikame, "Between Nationalities: Hawaii's Local Nation and Its Troubled Racial Paradise," *Hitting Critical Mass: A Journal of Asian American Cultural Criticism* 1, no. 2 (Spring 1994), http://socrates.berkeley.edu/critmass/v1n2/fujikaneprint.html, 8.

13. Though some of these affiliations and genealogies may be new, they also include previously less emphasized ones, such as Nuyorican poet Sandra Maria Esteves's Dominican mother and Piri Thomas's Cuban father.

14. Haunani-Kay Trask, "Kupa'a 'Aina: Native Hawaiian Nationalism in Hawai'i," in her *From a Native Daughter: Colonialism and Sovereignty in Hawai'i* (Monroe, ME: Common Courage Press, 1993), 86–110; Fujikame, "Between Nationalities," 3.

15. Ted Solis, "Jíbaro Image and the Ecology of Hawai'i Puerto Rican Musical Instruments," *Latin American Music Review* 16, no. 2 (1995): 123.

16. A *güiro* is an instrument indigenous to Puerto Rico that is made of hardened calabash or a gourd and rhythmically scratched with metal prongs.

17. Joy L. De Jesús, ed., *Growing Up Puerto Rican: An Anthology* (New York: William Morrow, 1997).

18. Manuel Maldonado-Denis, *The Emigration Dialectic: Puerto Rico and the USA*, trans. Roberto Simón Crespi (New York: International Publishers, 1980), 60–61; Ed Vega, foreword to De Jesús, *Growing Up Puerto Rican*, xi–xii; Norma Carr, "Imágenes: El Puertorriqueño en Hawaii," in *Imágenes e identidades: El puertorriqueño en la literatura*, ed. Asela Rodríguez de Laguna (Río Piedras, PR: Ediciones Huracán, 1985), 105–118; Michael Haas, ed., *Multicultural Hawai'i: The Fabric of a Multiethnic Society* (New York: Garland Publishing, 1998); Solis, "Jíbaro Image."

19. Rob Wilson, *Reimagining the American Pacific: From South Pacific to Bamboo Ridge and Beyond* (Durham, NC: Duke University Press, 2000), 151. Wilson and Fujikame ("Between Nationalities") both cite and interrogate Stephen H. Sumida's groundbreaking study *And the View from the Shore: Literary Traditions of Hawai'i* (Seattle: Uni-

versity of Washington Press, 1991) in establishing such characteristics for this literary movement.

20. *Haole* is the popular and often pejorative term for a white person. In Hawaiian it means "stranger." Because of Hawaii's colonial imperial history, the word perhaps has similar connotations to "gringo."

21. Derek Bickerton, "Language and Language Contact," in Haas, *Multicultural Hawai'i*, 63–64.

22. Fujikame, "Between Nationalities."

23. Victor Hernández Cruz also treats the Puerto Rican migration to Hawai'i in *By Lingual Wholes* (San Francisco: Momo's Press, 1982).

24. Giannina Braschi, *Yo-Yo Boing!* (Minneapolis: Latin American Review Press, 1998). This statement characterizing Braschi's bilingual vanguardism, which I elaborate further elsewhere, analyzes her work in relation to cultural studies of code switching, more than linguistics or social linguistics (though there are affinities), such as the seminal essay by Juan Flores and George Yúdice, "Living Borders/*Buscando América*: Languages of Latino Self-Formation," in *Latinos in Education: A Critical Reader*, ed. Antonia Darder, Rodolfo D. Torres, and Henry Gutiérrez (New York: Routledge, 1997), 174–200.

25. Though Spanish is spoken in Hawai'i, including on Hawaiian television, it is a newer addition owing to the more recent influx of migrants from Mexico and Central America. See Bickerton, "Language and Language Contact," 65.

26. Wilson, *Reimagining the American Pacific,* 197; Bickerton, "Language and Language Contact," 62–66.

27. Walter Mignolo, *Local Histories/Global Designs: Coloniality, Subaltern Knowledges, and Border Thinking* (Princeton, NJ: Princeton University Press, 2000), 252.

28. E. J. Hobsbawm, *Nations and Nationalism since 1780: Programme, Myth, Reality* (Cambridge: Cambridge University Press, 1990), 13.

29. Though I have elsewhere observed specific links between works by these authors and particular insular discourses and texts, an extended and extensive diasporic imaginary does not necessarily require empirical evidence as proof of influence but rather encompasses myriad forms of material thought, such as remittances and ongoing musical and mass-media developments. Useful here is anthropologist Arjun Appadurai's concept of "ethnoscapes," which helps define parameters supplanting landscapes with group identities that are no longer spatially bound but correlate to a broader, global field of "traditions of perception and perspective" that have been dramatically altered by mass movement and influenced by mass media. Arjun Appadurai, "Global Ethnoscapes: Notes and Queries for a Transnational Anthropology," in *Recapturing Anthropology: Working in the Present*, ed. Richard G. Fox (Santa Fe, NM: School of American Research Press, 1991), 191–192.

30. Timothy Hurley, "Traditions Await Further Cleanup," *Honolulu Advertiser*, 2 Nov. 2003, http://www.HonoluluAdvertiser.com.

31. Trask, "Kupa'a 'Aina," 91–92.

32. Ibid., 92–99.

33. Ibid., 99.

34. Wilson, *Reimagining the American Pacific,* 122.

35. John Brown Childs, "Beyond Unity: Transcommunal Roots of Coordination in the Haudenosaunee (Iroquois) Model of Cooperation and Diversity," in *Places and Politics in an Age of Globalization*, ed. Roxann Prazniak and Arif Dirlik (Lanham, MD: Rowman and Littlefield, 2001), 267–296. Childs's "transcommunality" structurally acknowledges "constructive disputes," rather than suppression and assimilation, among a "widening scope of affiliations" characterized by shared interests and emphasizes mutual cooperation while accentuating distinctions and groupings (268–282). Necessarily flexible, transcommunality is both pragmatic and idealistic. Childs's study explicates a deeply historical indigenous practice to frame a contemporary dialogue among U.S. urban ethnic groups who come together to prevent violence and incarceration in their communities. Committed to profound dialogue, it is potentially transformative. Rather than simplistically "building bridges," transcommunality aims to solidly ground participants in a process that enables participation, unlike top-down models, for enrichment rather than impoverishment of being (270–271). I thank Annie Lorrie Anderson for bringing to my attention how his concerns usefully intersect with mine.

36. Wilson Harris, *The Womb of Space: The Cross-Cultural Imagination* (Westport, CT: Greenwood Press, 1983). Defined in *The Womb of Space* in cross-national and interregional terms, Harris's cross-cultural imagination locates counterhegemonic fissures in the writer's unconscious and intuitive cultural imagination. However, the cross-cultural imagination also intuits mutual exchanges or "gifts" that can barely be discerned on the threshold of cross-cultural contact. When Harris writes of thresholds and bridges, he seems to be formulating the approach, if not the first step, toward locating the gifts within the chasm, rather than prematurely assuming the bridge can be crossed.

37. José E. Limón, *American Encounters: Greater Mexico, the United States, and the Erotics of Culture* (Boston: Beacon Press, 1998), 3n1; Américo Paredes, *A Texas-Mexico Cancionero* (Urbana: University of Illinois, 1976). I again thank Norma Klahn, at the University of California, Santa Cruz, for bringing this particular parallel to my attention.

38. This Spanish translation of "Greater Puerto Rico" first occurred during an interview I conducted with Ramón Grosfoguel at the University of California, Berkeley, in spring 2002, for which I am grateful.

39. Duany, *Puerto Rican Nation on the Move*, especially chaps. 1, 7, and 9.

40. I am referring to shifts in insular/diasporic thought from Manuel Zeno Gandía's *La charca* (1894; San Juan: Instituto de Cultura Puertorriqueña, 1996) to *Brincando el charco,* directed by Frances Negrón-Muntaner (Independent Television Service and Corporation for Public Broadcasting, 1994), videocassette.

41. Wilson, *Reimagining the American Pacific,* 241.

BIBLIOGRAPHY

Alleyne, Mervyn C. "A Linguistic Perspective on the Caribbean." In *Caribbean Contours,* ed. Sidney W. Mintz and Sally Price, 155–179. Baltimore, MD: Johns Hopkins University Press, 1985.

Ambert, Alba. *The Eighth Continent.* Houston: Arte Público Press, 1997.

———. *A Perfect Silence.* Houston: Arte Público Press, 1995.

———. *Porque hay silencio.* Houston: Arte Público Press, 1998.

Appadurai, Arjun. "Global Ethnoscapes: Notes and Queries for a Transnational Anthropology." In *Recapturing Anthropology: Working in the Present,* ed. Richard G. Fox, 191–210. Santa Fe, NM: School of American Research Press, 1991.

Barradas, Efraín. *Partes de un todo: Ensayos y notas sobre literatura puertorriqueña en los Estados Unidos.* San Juan: Editorial de la Universidad de Puerto Rico, 1998.

Bickerton, Derek. "Language and Language Contact." In *Multicultural Hawai'i: The Fabric of a Multiethnic Society,* ed. Michael Haas, 53–66. New York: Garland Publishing, 1998.

Braschi, Giannina. *El imperio de los sueños.* 2d ed. San Juan: Editorial de la Universidad de Puerto Rico, 1999.

———. *Yo-Yo Boing!* Minneapolis: Latin American Review Press, 1998.

Brincando el charco. Directed by Frances Negrón-Muntaner. Independent Television Service and Corporation for Public Broadcasting, 1994. Videocassette.

Carr, Norma. "Image: The Puerto Rican in Hawaii." In *Images and Identities: The Puerto Rican in Two World Contexts,* ed. and trans. Asela Rodríguez de Laguna, 96–106. New Brunswick, NJ: Transaction, 1987.

———. "Imágenes: El puertorriqueño en Hawaii." In *Imágenes e identidades: El puertorriqueño en la literatura,* ed. Asela Rodríguez de Laguna, 105–118. Río Piedras, PR: Ediciones Huracán, 1985.

Childs, John Brown. "Beyond Unity: Transcommunal Roots of Coordination in the Haudenosaunee (Iroquois) Model of Cooperation and Diversity." In *Places and Politics in an Age of Globalization,* ed. Roxann Prazniak and Arif Dirlik, 267–296. Lanham, MD: Rowman and Littlefield, 2001.

———. *Transcommunality: From the Politics of Conversion to the Ethics of Respect.* Philadelphia: Temple University Press, 2006.

Colón, Jesús. *The Way It Was, and Other Writings.* Ed. Edna Acosta-Belén and Virginia Sánchez Korrol. Houston: Arte Público Press, 1993.

Cruz-Malavé, Arnaldo. "Teaching Puerto Rican Authors: Identity and Modernization in Nuyorican Texts." *ADE Bulletin* 91 (1985): 45–51.

De Jesús, Joy L., ed. *Growing Up Puerto Rican: An Anthology.* New York: William Morrow, 1997.

Díaz Quiñones, Arcadio. *El arte de bregar: Ensayos.* San Juan: Ediciones Callejón, 2000.

———. *La memoria rota.* Río Piedras, PR: Ediciones Huracán, 1993.

Duany, Jorge. *The Puerto Rican Nation on the Move: Identities on the Island and in the United States.* Chapel Hill: University of North Carolina Press, 2002.

Duchesne Winter, Juan. *Ciudadano insano y otros ensayos bestiales sobre cultura y literatura.* San Juan: Ediciones Callejón, 2001.

Espada, Martín. *A Mayan Astronomer in Hell's Kitchen: Poems.* New York: W. W. Norton, 2000.

———. *Rebellion Is the Circle of a Lover's Hands.* Willimantic, CT: Curbstone Press, 1990.

Flores, Juan. *From Bomba to Hip-Hop: Puerto Rican Culture and Latino Identity.* New York: Columbia University Press, 2000.

Flores, Juan, and Mayra Santos-Febres, eds. Introduction to "Open Mic/Micrófono abierto: Nuevas literaturas Puerto/Neorriqueñas New Puerto/Nuyor Rican Literatures." Special issue, *Hostos Review/Revista Hostosiana* 2 (2005): viii–xxv.

Flores, Juan, and George Yúdice. "Living Borders/*Buscando América*: Languages of Latino Self-Formation." In *Latinos in Education: A Critical Reader*, ed. Antonia Darder, Rodolfo D. Torres, and Henry Gutiérrez, 174–200. New York: Routledge, 1997.

Fujikame, Candace. "Between Nationalities: Hawaii's Local Nation and Its Troubled Racial Paradise." *Hitting Critical Mass: A Journal of Asian American Cultural Criticism* 1, no. 2 (Spring 1994). http://socrates.berkeley.edu/critmass/v1n2/fujikaneprint.html (accessed 10 July 2002).

Grosfoguel, Ramón, Frances Negrón-Muntaner, and Chloé S. Georas. "Beyond Nationalist and Colonialist Discourses: The *Jaiba* Politics of the Puerto Rican Ethno-nation." In *Puerto Rican Jam: Rethinking Colonialism and Nationalism*, ed. Frances Negrón-Muntaner and Ramón Grosfoguel, 1–38. Minneapolis: University of Minnesota Press, 1997.

Haas, Michael, ed. *Multicultural Hawai'i: The Fabric of a Multiethnic Society.* New York: Garland Publishing, 1998.

Harris, Wilson. *Selected Essays of Wilson Harris.* Ed. Andrew Brundy. London: Routledge, 1999.

———. *The Womb of Space: The Cross-Cultural Imagination.* Westport, CT: Greenwood Press, 1983.

Hernández, Carmen Dolores. *Puerto Rican Voices in English: Interviews with Writers.* Westport, CT: Praeger, 1997.

Hernández Cruz, Victor. *By Lingual Wholes.* San Francisco: Momo's Press, 1982.

———. *Panoramas.* Minneapolis, MN: Coffee House Press, 1997.

Hobsbawm, E. J. *Nations and Nationalism since 1780: Programme, Myth, Reality.* Cambridge: Cambridge University Press, 1990.

Hollinger, David A. *Postethnic America.* New York: Basic Books, 1995.

Hurley, Timothy. "Traditions Await Further Cleanup." *Honolulu Advertiser*, 2 Nov. 2003. http://www.HonoluluAdvertiser.com.

Landry, Donna, and Gerald MacLean, eds. *The Spivak Reader.* New York: Routledge, 1996.

Laviera, Tato. *AmeRícan.* Houston: Arte Público Press, 1985.

———. *The Oxcart: La Carreta Made a U-Turn.* Gary, IN: Arte Público Press, 1979.

Limón, José E. *American Encounters: Greater Mexico, the United States, and the Erotics of Culture.* Boston: Beacon Press, 1998.

Lorenzo-Hernández, José. "The Nuyorican's Dilemma: Categorization of Returning Migrants in Puerto Rico." *International Migration Review* 33, no. 4 (1999): 988–1013.

Maldonado-Denis, Manuel. *The Emigration Dialectic: Puerto Rico and the USA*. Trans. Roberto Simón Crespi. New York: International Publishers, 1980. (Originally published 1976.)

Mignolo, Walter. *Local Histories/Global Designs: Coloniality, Subaltern Knowledges, and Border Thinking*. Princeton, NJ: Princeton University Press, 2000.

Minerbi, Luciano. "Native Hawaiian Struggles and Events: A Partial List, 1973–1993." *Social Process in Hawaii: The Political Economy of Hawai'i* 35 (1994): 1–14.

Morales, Rodney. "Literature." In *Multicultural Hawai'i: The Fabric of a Multiethnic Society*, ed. Michael Haas, 107–130. New York: Garland Publishing, 1998.

———. *The Speed of Darkness*. Honololu: Bamboo Ridge Press, 1988.

———. *When the Shark Bites*. Honolulu: University of Hawai'i Press, 2002.

Negrón-Muntaner, Frances, and Ramón Grosfoguel, eds. *Puerto Rican Jam: Rethinking Colonialism and Nationalism*. Minneapolis: University of Minnesota Press, 1997.

Oboler, Suzanne. *Ethnic Labels, Latino Lives: Identity and the Politics of (Re)Presentation in the United States*. Minneapolis: University of Minnesota Press, 1995.

Pabón, Carlos. "La imposible lengua apropiada." In *Nación postmortem: Ensayos sobre los tiempos de insoportable ambigüedad*, 89–103. San Juan: Ediciones Callejón, 2002.

Paredes, Américo. *A Texas-Mexico Cancionero*. Urbana: University of Illinois, 1976.

Perdomo, Willie. *Where a Nickel Costs a Dime: Poems*. New York: W. W. Norton, 1996.

Ríos Ávila, Rubén. "Rambling." In *La raza cómica del sujeto en Puerto Rico*, 311–318. San Juan: Ediciones Callejón, 2002.

Rivera, Diana. *Bird Language*. Tempe, AZ: Bilingual Press/Editorial Bilingüe, 1994.

Sánchez, Luis Rafael. *La guagua aérea*. San Juan: Editorial Cultural, 1994.

Sánchez González, Lisa. *Boricua Literature: A Literary History of the Puerto Rican Diaspora*. New York: New York University Press, 2001.

Santiago, Esmeralda. *Almost a Woman*. New York: Vintage, 1998.

———. *América's Dream*. New York: HarperCollins, 1996.

———. "Island of Lost Causes." In *Boricuas: Influential Puerto Rican Writings—an Anthology*, ed. Roberto Santiago, 22–24. New York: Ballantine, 1995.

———. *The Turkish Lover*. Cambridge, MA: Da Capo Press, 2004.

———. *When I Was Puerto Rican*. Reading, MA: Addison-Wesley, 1993.

Sato, Charlene J. "Sociolinguistic Variation and Language Attitudes in Hawaii." In *English around the World: Sociolinguistic Perspectives*, ed. Jenny Cheshire, 647–663. New York: Cambridge University Press, 1991.

Solis, Ted. "Jíbaro Image and the Ecology of Hawai'i Puerto Rican Musical Instruments." *Latin American Music Review* 16, no. 2 (1995): 123–153.

Stanchich, Maritza. *Insular Interventions: Diasporic Puerto Rican Literature Bilanguaging toward a Greater Puerto Rico*. ATT 3098765. Ann Arbor, MI: University Microfilms, 2003.

———. "Towards a Post-Nuyorican Literature." In *Sargasso: The Floating Homeland/La patria flotante*, ed. María Cristina Rodríguez, 113–124. Río Piedras, PR: University of Puerto Rico II, 2005–2006.

Sumida, Stephen H. *And the View from the Shore: Literary Traditions of Hawai'i*. Seattle: University of Washington Press, 1991.

Thomas, Piri. *Down These Mean Streets*. New York: Knopf, 1967.

Trask, Haunani-Kay. "Kupa'a 'Aina: Native Hawaiian Nationalism in Hawai'i." In *From a Native Daughter: Colonialism and Sovereignty in Hawai'i*, 86–110. Monroe, ME: Common Courage Press, 1993.

Vando, Gloria. *Promesas: Geography of the Impossible*. Houston: Arte Público Press, 1993.

———. *Shadows and Supposes*. Houston: Arte Público Press, 2002.

Vega, Bernardo. *Memorias de Bernardo Vega*. Río Piedras, PR: Ediciones Huracán, 1984.

Vega, Ed. Foreword to *Growing Up Puerto Rican: An Anthology*, ed. Joy L. De Jesús, v–xii. New York: William Morrow, 1997.

Wilson, Rob. *Reimagining the American Pacific: From South Pacific to Bamboo Ridge and Beyond*. Durham, NC: Duke University Press, 2000.

Zeno Gandía, Manuel. *La charca*. San Juan: Instituto de Cultura Puertorriqueña, 1996. (Originally published 1894.)

10 TATO LAVIERA'S PARODY OF *LA CARRETA*

Reworking a Tradition of Docility

JOHN WALDRON

In 1979, Tato Laviera published his first book of poetry, titled *La Carreta Made a U-Turn.*[1] The poems there weave together thematic threads that Laviera will wind and unwind in subsequent collections. Generally speaking, most of his poetry is concerned with representing and criticizing the situation of Puerto Ricans and other disadvantaged groups living in the urban center of New York City. Along with his critique and portrayal of life in the United States, he also focuses some attention on the often-problematic relationship he and others of the Puerto Rican diaspora have with mainland Puerto Rican culture. That is, he writes about forms of exclusion or marginalization in the United States and at the hands of the mainland Puerto Rican public.[2] In fact, the term "Nuyorican," which many diasporic Puerto Ricans use to identify themselves, is a term that has its origins in a process of cultural othering effected by mainland Puerto Ricans. This term, as well as a catalog of cultural differences it points toward, is used to signify the existence of perceived "defects," with the ultimate result of excluding diasporic Puerto Ricans from the island's cultural imaginary. In his first book of poems Laviera confronts this problem by parodying a major work in the Puerto Rican canon, René Marqués's *La carreta.*[3] By taking on Marqués's work, and the tradition it represents, he also contends with the problems emanating from colonialism that affect all Puerto Ricans.

The focus of my study here is to show how Laviera destabilizes the foundational colonialist myth of docility.

By employing the literary trope of parody, Laviera critiques a tradition of docility even as he forms part of diasporic Puerto Rican culture. Parody is quite often understood as having a solely negative or critical relationship to the original text and the tradition it represents. However, as Linda Hutcheon has shown in her book on the subject, the relationship between parodic text and original is far more complex than that.[4] As the etymology of the word suggests, *parodia* is a countersong, but as much as it is a song against a previously existing text, it is also one sung beside or along with the original. This singing alongside or along with suggests an intimate knowledge and even at times an accord with the previous text (32). Parody, then, has a dual nature. As the parodic text sings against and with the original text, it inscribes itself into the cultural history and canon represented by the original text even as it criticizes both the text and the canon of which it forms a part. This points to a paradox inherent in much of parody; the parodic text subverts even as it conserves past texts and the tradition they represent. The complexities implied by this literary trope are similar to Laviera's relationship to Puerto Rican and U.S. cultural practices. Even as Laviera critiques his own exclusion from island Puerto Rican culture, he writes himself into it by intertwining his own text with a recognized landmark of Puerto Rican culture, *La carreta*.

Parody then is an effective way for Laviera to confront Puerto Rico's problematic past and present. By choosing to parody *La carreta* and its theme of docility, Laviera allows himself the possibility of conserving its critique of U.S. colonialism even as he proposes an alternative response to it—one that is more inclusive of diasporic and African elements of Puerto Rican culture. To understand how, and to what effect, his parody functions, it is necessary to analyze Marqués's critique of the Puerto Rican colonial situation and its attendant docility in his essay "El puertorriqueño dócil," followed by the portrayal of the ideas he develops there in *La carreta*.[5] Once this is done, it is possible to then show how and to what effect Laviera's parody works with and against Marqués's texts toward a new conceptualization of culture.

In "El puertorriqueño dócil," Marqués studies what he describes as a phenomenon caused by colonialism, the illness of docility. He criticizes psychologists and sociologists "[for] the recent determination to deny docility as a psychological phenomena in the Puerto Rican male" ([por] el reciente empeño de negar la docilidad como fenómeno psicológico del hombre de Puerto Rico) (156). After this admonishment, he holds forth as a shining example of the Puerto Rican participation in the Korean War the story by Emilio Díaz Valcarcel called "El soldado Damián Sánchez"[6] because "very infrequently has the mechanism of the weak and docile psychology of man been dramatized so sharply and with such accuracy" (pocas veces se ha dramatizado tan aguda y certeramente el mecanismo psicológico del hombre débil y dócil) (160). Later Marqués claims that the phenomenon of nationalism dramatizes the self-destructive illness related to docility (161). He lists historic examples, such as the attack on Blair House, in Washington, DC,[7] along with the tremendous number of suicides or "martyr complexes" he sees portrayed in Puerto Rican literature. His study is an analysis without answers. He seems to follow the argument put forward by Antonio Pedreira in his landmark book *Insularismo*, which contends that Puerto Ricans are by nature docile and if they try to do anything to free themselves they are simply deluded and suicidal.[8] Marqués analyzes the situation imposed on the island by colonialism, but similar to Pedreira and others before him, he sees no solution. Like Pedreira, Marqués analyzes docility as a malady particular to those who inhabit the land of Puerto Rico and justifies his assertion through historical examples. He repeats a trope, that of docility and isolation, that has formed part of the tradition making up Puerto Rican letters, and therefore the cultural imaginary, since well before 1898. Perhaps he is right to leave it simply as an objective study with no possible solution: perhaps there is no solution. Regardless of how both Pedreira and Marqués appear to use a scientific approach to their object of study in order to maintain what appears to be an objective distance, their studies are less than objective.[9]

Similar to his essay, Marqués's play *La carreta* dramatizes his vision of a docile, colonized culture with no way out except docility or suicide. *La carreta* portrays a *jíbaro* family that, due to financial difficulties, leaves their mountain home for the urban environment of San Juan, eventually ending up in the metropolis of New York City.[10] As they move from their mountain home to the urban landscape of "La Perla"[11] in Old San Juan and eventually the metropolis of New York City, they move toward modern culture with all of its technological advances and farther from the roots of Puerto Rican culture. As they distance themselves from *jíbaro* life in the mountains, their family gradually disintegrates and falls into moral decline. In neither the play nor his essay does Marqués offer a possible response to this decline.

In both texts Marqués astutely analyzes the relations of power and the effects of the colonial system. However, his representations of that system tend to repeat forms and tropes that confirm colonial status rather than look for alternatives. In Marqués's play we see an example of the docile Puerto Rican as a literary trope representing a philosophic understanding of Puerto Rican culture that exists without agency and with no real or imagined way out of the colonial dilemma. By repeating forms and tropes that are more than two hundred years old, Marqués, as much as he would resist it, becomes part of the archaic tradition in Puerto Rico, a tradition founded entirely upon colonialist discourse first imposed by the Spanish and then by the United States.[12] If it is the function of the archaic/canon to be largely pedagogical, what Marqués analyzes and teaches in his representation of the *jíbaro* family in *La carreta*, and in his essay, is that Puerto Ricans are docile by nature and there is really no way out except suicide in its various forms. In fact, looking for a way out is often characterized as a mode of suicide. For example, it seems that on one level the family's greatest crime in the play is following the dreams of the nervous, always-in-motion Luis and not remaining in the mountains. That is, rather than remaining docile, and in effect true to their "nature," they follow the mechanized dreams of Luis. Left with few options, they can either remain homeless and in poverty in the mountains or follow Luis. However, the latter path leads to moral decline and death.

The end of *La carreta* portrays the two female characters of the play contemplating their return home to the mountains of Puerto Rico. The financial problems that led them to leave Puerto Rico for New York have been solved by means of a modern-day *deus ex machina*. When all hope seems to be lost, they find out that Juanita's old boyfriend has won the money to buy them a piece of land which they can return to, saving them from further horrors in New York. However, this is a less-than-satisfying ending. The two women, Juanita and Doña Gabriela, are what is left of the family that we have watched slowly fragment onstage. Luis has died—in what Marqués would call a suicide—a victim of his own dreams of progress and belief in North American technology; he is literally devoured by a machine where he works. Chaguito, the younger sibling, was arrested in San Juan for stealing money so he could go watch North American movies. He, like Luis, both victims of U.S. materialism, have been punished for distancing themselves and their family from the land and the teachings of truth, nobility, and honesty spoken by the patriarch Don Chago, who remained behind in the mountains of Puerto Rico.

With the hyperactive Luis out of the way, the remaining family members can now contemplate a return to the stability of the homeland, their roots. In the final scene, as Juanita contemplates the circle she and Doña Gabriela will complete by returning home, she verbally unites the play by reiterating the words and philosophy Don Chago spoke so forcefully at the beginning of the play. Juanita says, "So we'll go back to the *barrio!* You and I, Mom, firm like *ausubo* on our land, and Luis resting in it!" (¡Así volveremoh al barrio! ¡Uhté y yo, mamá, firmeh como ausuboh sobre la tierra nuehtra, y Luis dehcansando en ella!) (172). However, she differs from Don Chago in that she sees the necessity for change: "it isn't a matter of going back to the land to live like the dead. It is we who change the world. And we'll help to change it" (no eh cosa de volver a la tierra pa vivir como muertoh. Que somoh nosotroh loh que cambiamoh al mundo. Y vamoh a ayudar a cambiarlo) (172). At the same time that she proposes their return as a possibility for positive change, she also reiterates Don Chago's statements about the necessity for stability and firmness.

Her words are rather optimistic given the overall pessimism of the play, especially if the viewer or reader remembers the country people's extreme poverty and deprivation shown at the beginning. The same Don Chago whose words Juanita mimics was left behind when they moved to La Perla. Presumably left in the care of someone in the village, he ends up dying alone in a cave. After the family leaves the mountains for La Perla, we see the image of Germana, who arrives vulture-like to pick over what the family did not take with them, eventually leaving with a broken-down table. Given this and the historical realities, a return to the country will be a return to less-than-idyllic circumstances. Doña Gabriela responds to Juanita's optimism by repeating Juanita's and Don Chago's words, but as she finishes speaking, she breaks down in tears.

One of the trajectories of the play has been the collapse of Doña Gabriela. In the "Primera estampa"[13] she is a strong matriarch who literally and metaphorically has a powerful voice (the play opens with her yelling for Chaguito). She is slowly silenced by the realities of life in La Perla in the "Segunda estampa." Though she initially resists the moral depravity surrounding her, as shown in her relationship with Lito, a young boy, events slowly wear her down and silence her. The hope of a return home does nothing to refortify her character. The stage directions at the end of the play, rather than show her regenerating into the strong woman she once was, *como ausubo*, repeat and even accentuate her decline. In the stage directions, she changes from kneeling to being curved in on herself and finally to something entirely insignificant: "And she remains kneeling, then sitting on her heels, then curved in on herself like a small ball, insignificant, shaking with sobs and stricken with pain, at the feet of her daughter who rises firm and decided" (Y queda arrodillada, luego sentada sobre los talones, luego encorvada sobre sí misma como un ovillo pequeño, insignificante, agitado de sollozos y transido de dolor, a los pies de la hija que se yergue firme y decidida) (172). It is possible that Marqués is saying that hope, if there is any, must come from the young. However, given all that has happened in the play and the fact that, as Juanita voices her words of hope, Doña Gabriela is reduced to nothing, the promise seems empty. Marqués leaves them and the audience in a state of hopeless docility.

Contesting this play and its hopeless ending is Laviera's *La Carreta Made a U-Turn*. Laviera's parody of Marqués's play is in itself an act of agency that contests the historical characterization of Puerto Ricans as necessarily docile. His act of parody, while accepting Marqués's critique of U.S. colonialism, also rejects the dead-end, either/or structure created by a colonialized reading of Puerto Rico's past. Laviera contests these choices by providing a third possibility, one that was silenced or "whitened" by Spanish colonialism and subsequent traditions. He does this in part by adopting strategies similar to those identified as being particular to the "Black Atlantic" and U.S. African American cultures. Edouard Glissant, Henry Louis Gates, and others study parody as forming part of an aesthetic of detour particular to cultures of the African diaspora and to colonized cultures in general. Since literary acts of detour require agency, they necessarily create tropes and modes that offer images contrary to those supportive of a colonialist cultural imaginary, namely, docility.

Laviera employs an aesthetic that is characteristic of African Caribbean diasporic cultures that he came into contact with in New York.

Tropes of detour play an important part in this aesthetic. This is most evident when he chooses parody, to speak the old texts in his own voice, converting them, in the words of Gates, to "the master's pieces" rather than repeating the "masterpieces."[14] Parodying Marqués's use of colloquial speech in *La carreta*, Laviera uses everyday language to break down both Spanish and English, the languages of the two colonial powers in Puerto Rico's history. Juan Flores says of this fragmenting of language and its affects that "colloquial Puerto Rican is characterized by its porousness, its undermining and breaking, of the authority of the monolingual discourse."[15] Whereas at this point in his argument Flores is looking at the effects of "colloquial Puerto Rican" on U.S. English, Laviera's writing asks that we also look at its effects on Spanish. As Coco Fusco would say, "English is broken here,"[16] but so is Spanish: in the case of Puerto Rico, both are colonizing languages. Laviera's language and poetry "break" and undermine the authoritarian, monolingual cultural imaginaries on both sides of *el charco*[17] and on both sides of the Atlantic. He confronts a tradition of exclusion at its roots by reformulating both the Spanish and English languages in his own way. This strategy is similar to what he does to Marqués's play and, by extension, to Puerto Rican tradition in general. By attacking language, he also challenges the tropes and forms that support, even as they criticize, colonization. In this way, he confronts and undermines the historical arguments that gave the weight of precedence to canonical writers such as Pedreira and Marqués.

That he attacks language is important to the context surrounding Laviera and Marqués and Puerto Rican culture in general. Especially in Spain and Latin America, notions of language purity have always been used as a means to create exclusionary hierarchies in attempts to assert and maintain power. This practice in the case of Puerto Rico extends from the fifteenth century to the present.[18] During the Spanish colonial period, in order to become part of the realm, one literally had to pass tests of linguistic purity. This once-codified practice, a shibboleth of sorts, became part of a culture that fostered an explicit desire for linguistic, as well as ethnic/racial, purity. Such practices served to marginalize diverse cultural elements, especially those of African origin. This *blanqueamiento,* or "whitening," of culture established by the Spanish colonial empire and based on Nebrija's grammar,[19] continues to the present day. According to Eleuterio Santiago Díaz: "In the particular case of

Puerto Rico, the black voice frequently appears codified in literature and other media as a defective linguistic zone. The black person is the one who does not know how to say and, in other circumstances, is the one who does not know what to say" (En el caso particular de Puerto Rico, la voz negra aparece frecuentemente codificada, en la literatura y en otros medios, como una zona defectuosa del idioma. El negro es aquél que no sabe decir y, en otras instancias, aquél que no sabe qué decir").[20] This practice continues as literary canons are constructed.[21] Seen in this context, a poem like Laviera's "graduation speech," in *La Carreta Made a U-Turn*, becomes one in which the shards of broken English and Spanish allow the poet to take control over language and the systems it supports by creating his own images and writing them and himself back into exclusionary canons on his own terms. Laviera is not just constructing a new identity for himself but is also bringing down the systems that have worked against him by attacking them at their roots.

Through parody, monolingual and monocultural language systems are broken, not to destroy them, but to reform them in a way that allows entry or recognition of previously excluded groups. Laviera breaks these languages and the systems they support to demand that he and those like him become recognized as part of the Puerto Rican cultural imaginary, an imaginary that speaks only Spanish. When he says, "I speak a killed English / I speak a killed Spanish" (hablo lo inglés matao / hablo lo español matao) (17), he repeats what the dominant culture tells him: "you cannot speak either English or Spanish well" (an assertion he disproves in his perfect use of Spanish and English elsewhere). But he has also in a sense "killed" them both and recombined them in his own way.

The difference between Laviera's experience of culture, with its added tones, sounds, and traditions of a largely oral, African tradition, and Marqués's experience is made evident by comparing the cover of Laviera's *La Carreta Made a U-Turn* with that of Marqués's *La carreta*. Though authors usually do not control the cover art, the pictures on the covers are emblematic of the different ways that each text imagines Puerto Rican culture. The cover on the seventeenth edition of *La carreta*, published by Editorial Cultural, has not changed in well over twenty years. On this cover, in orange and black, an ox cart (*una carreta* being pulled by an ox) is portrayed from behind at a forty-five-degree angle. Some changes have been made to the cover of Laviera's book since the first edition, including making the picture smaller, as though seen through a keyhole. However, in both editions the picture shows a more modern type of *carreta*, a shopping cart. In the cart, which no one is pushing and no beast of burden is pulling, is a timbal (drum), a guitar, a *pava* (a straw hat of the type tourists buy but also traditionally worn by *jíbaros*), and a machete on which we see some of the letters of the words "Puerto Rico" written. Though there is no background on the cover of Marqués's book, we can perhaps imagine the tropical, country setting where such a sight would have been seen years ago. Remaking that fantasy, now a part of the archaic tradition, the cover of Laviera's book shows the snowy streets of New York. Behind the cart is a worn-out traffic barrier, large enough to seem almost permanent, with a "Detour" sign pointing in the direction the cart/*carreta* is heading. To the cultural symbol of the mountain people, or *los jíbaros*, presented on the cover of and in the play *La carreta*, the cover of Laviera's book adds his own, updated version of what a *carreta* is along with cultural symbols that mix *jíbaro* culture (the hat and the machete) with the Spanish (guitar) and the African (the timbal and the machete). This picture creates a cultural "detour" that will continue throughout the book.

The detour is a sign telling the viewer/reader that this *carreta* is not just going to New York from Puerto Rico, but that a more complicated route of *diversión* (fr.) is about to be taken. It is this detour that adds difference to the monodirectional, circular route depicted in Marqués's text. Laviera does this through traditional, accepted linguistic and formal practices that reflect Glissant's understanding of Creole. Laviera's use of "Spanglish," or "Spanenglish" as he calls it, forms a *détour* proposing "diversity" (*le divers*). "Diversity which is neither chaotic or sterile but which corresponds to the human spirit's striving towards a transversal relationship which shuns all universalist forms of transcendence. . . . The Same requires Being, Diversity sets up Relation."[22] This detour of inclusion is signaled in Laviera's parody of *La carreta* by the arrangement and naming of the sections of his book. The *tres estampas* (three acts) in *La carreta* are "El campo," "El arrabal" (The Slum), and "La metrópolis." Contrasting with this rather linear order that progresses from the less "modern" to the most modern, from "cultural essence" to the gradual "pollution" of culture, the sections of Laviera's book are titled "Metropolis Dreams," "Loisaida Streets: Latinas Sing," and "El arrabal: El nuevo rumbón." Since the word "metropolis" appears in the first section of Laviera's text and the last in Marqués's text, it might be argued that this section is the initiation of a return. But the return is not via a direct route. All three of the sections in Laviera's book repeat different names for urban spaces, hinting at the fact that the book, in effect, wanders until it ends up with *el nuevo rumbón*, a new "rumba," a new "party," or a new "direction." The meaning can perhaps be all possibilities at once, since by providing a new sound, sung with a different voice, he also creates new directions.

The first section of Laviera's book contains poems dealing mostly with life in the barrio as well as the often-cited "graduation speech" and "fighting," which begin to define the poet and the interlingual, transcultural space he inhabits. Here he defines himself as existing outside and within both English and Spanish. He also argues against dominant symbols of hegemonic culture like monolingual language and the Catholic Church in "excommunication gossip." The naming of the second section bears the least resemblance to the titles of Marqués's *estampas*. The title of this section might make it appear that Laviera is ready to leave Marqués's text behind. However, in this section he foregrounds one of the many silences in the original text, that of the women. Unlike *La carreta*, where a central figure, Doña Gabriela, is silenced, in Laviera's work, he attempts to unsilence women and their roles in culture. In "virginity," the first poem of the second section, he foregrounds the topic of Juanita's rape, which was told in muffled language in *La carreta*. He also confronts the cultural practice of *el qué dirán*, which Juanita faces because of her out-of-wedlock pregnancy. In his poem "a message to our unwed women," he writes

> adiós, ¿y cuándo
> te casastes?
>   and they gave you
>   the half Mirada
>   and you bit the tears
>   from showing up
> you walked knowing eyes were talking. (36)

He is criticizing here a cultural practice that clearly serves to "keep women in their place" whether in Puerto Rico or the streets of New York.

The last poems of the second section form a thematic transition to the third and final section, “El arrabal: El nuevo rumbón.” The poems “palm tree in spanglish figurines” and “congas mujer” combine representations of women with recognition of the influences of African culture. The poem “palm tree in spanglish figurines” could even be read as a response to or parody of the canonical poem “Majestad negra” by Luis Palés Matos, albeit problematically, due to the sexist images in both poems.[23] In Palés’s poem an eroticized female, who is also an exoticized representation of Afro–Puerto Rican culture, is portrayed uniting Afro-Caribbean and African culture in a single image. Palés writes in his famous poem “Flor de Tortola, rosa de Uganda”: “Haiti offers you its pumpkin squash / fiery rums Jamaica gives you / Cuba tells you: go for it *mulata!* / Puerto Rico: *melao, melamba!*”[24] (Haití te ofrece sus calabazas: / fogosos rones te da Jamaíca / Cuba te dice: ¡dale mulata! / Y Puerto Rico: ¡melao, melamba!) (70). Alluding to Palés, Laviera also uses the object of a dancing woman as the site where native Caribbean and African cultures combine:

> swaying soul essences
> and latino salsa all
> intertwine within her
> . . . .
> inside the feelings of
> ancestral bomba and plena
> the maunabo indian emerged from her hips
> piñones was her face setting. (48)

To the traditional Afro-Caribbean rhythms of “bomba and plena” he adds the “maunabo indian.” To that, he adds sounds created when Afro-Caribbean cultures mix in New York, “latino salsa.” Here, he embraces and extends the efforts by Palés and others to recognize the Caribbean’s African roots to include not only the Caribbean but also the other diasporic cultures in New York and elsewhere.

With the title of his last section, “El arrabal: El nuevo rumbón,” Laviera echoes *La carreta*’s second section “El arrabal.” It is in *el arrabal* where things really begin to fall apart for the family in *La carreta*. Chaguito is imprisoned, we see scenes of child abuse and neglect, Juanita is raped and, after contemplating abortion (offstage), attempts suicide; at the end, they all follow Luis’ version of the American Dream and go to New York. Responding to this, Laviera brings these and other fragments together in his own *arrabal*, creating a *nuevo rumbón*. As the title indicates, we might expect to find a glorification of Afro–Puerto Rican culture, but Laviera also includes "white," or *jíbaro*, culture into the mix with the poem "la música jíbara."

Following a poetic tradition begun in the nineteenth century in Puerto Rico, this poem recounts the "mythic" life of *el jíbaro*.[25] In this way the poem once again links Laviera's text to the foundational fictions of Puerto Rico's literary tradition. However, he never completely assimilates that tradition, choosing always to speak it in his own terms. He alerts us to the fact that this myth is being retold through the Afro-diasporic eyes of Jorge Brandon:

> y jorge brandon nos dice:
> el jíbaro puertorriqueño
> que siente amor por su tierra,
> quiere vivir en la sierra(73)
> [and jorge brandon tells us:
> the Puerto Rican *jíbaro*
> who feels love for his land,
> wants to live in the mountains]

This is an oft-repeated tale told in a rhythm similar to the popular form of the *décima*. But, like the movement of the entire book, after reminding us of the canonical, accepted text, Laviera ends the poem with a detour, telling us of an inspiration Brandon had while retelling this myth:

> ¡oh! le vino en una inspiración, tal vez.
> pero qué mucho camello paseando por soles puertorriqueños ardientes (73)
> [oh! an inspiration came to him, perhaps.
> but what a lot of camels saunter beneath the ardent Puerto Rican sun]

It is precisely this "¡oh! le vino en una inspiración" that forms a detour away from a mere repetition of myth and allows for a new way of telling an old story. It is a deviation from what is written and accepted. Here, the old story is one of racial/ethnic and cultural purity that extends from Puerto Rico back to Spain, connecting the *jíbaro* to his Spanish roots. But here the inspiration also paints a dissonant image of *camellos* (camels) sauntering under the burning Puerto Rican sun. Through the dissonance created here comes a rupture with the past that creates a possibility for agency, allowing something new to be proposed. This image reminds those who would like to go back to "pure Spanish culture" that even back in Spain their blood was probably mixed with that of the Moors, who inhabited Spain for more than seven hundred years. Brandon, like Glissant, is saying that there is no such thing as purity. As Brandon's inspiration inserts itself into the old song of the *jíbaro*, it creates a new song, a *nuevo rumbón*, one that questions the hegemony of past models even as it includes them in the present creation.

It has been argued that, in the last section of his book, Laviera moves from Puerto Rico, almost bypassing it completely, to end up in Africa, where he will remain.[26] This argument ignores the fusion of cultures Laviera undertakes throughout the book, especially in this last section. Though he does privilege African elements of Puerto Rican culture in this text, he is always looking for how they come together on the island and in New York, creating culture in *el vaivén*. He opens the space of Puerto Rican literature to the voices and traditions that, up until that time, and even in many respects up until today, it has largely excluded. The cultural trope of docility, which has informed much of the cultural imaginary in Puerto Rico, is left in ruins. In its fragments, Laviera offers the possibility of new voices and directions.

NOTES

1. Tato Laviera, *La Carreta Made a U-Turn* (Gary, IN: Arte Público Press, 1979). Hereafter cited in text.

2. I use the term "mainland Puerto Rico" to refer to the Caribbean archipelago called Puerto Rico.

3. René Marqués, *La carreta: Drama en tres actos* (Río Piedras, PR: Editorial Cultural, 1983). Hereafter cited in text.

4. Linda Hutcheon, *A Theory of Parody: The Teachings of Twentieth Century Art Forms* (Chicago: Illinois University Press, 2000). Hereafter cited in text.

5. René Marqués, "El puertorriqueño dócil," in his *Ensayos, 1953–1971* (Barcelona, Spain: Editorial Antillana, 1972), 151–216. Hereafter cited in text.

6. Emilio Díaz Valcarcel, "El soldado Damián Sánchez," in his *Cuentos completos* (Guaynabo, PR: Alfaguara Ediciones Santillana, 2002), 127–133.

7. The event known as "the attack on Blair House" was carried out by Oscar Collazo and Griselio Torresola on 1 Nov. 1950. They tried to shoot their way into Blair House

when President Harry S. Truman was living there while the White House was being renovated. Torresola died from gunshots received during the attack. Collazo was given the death sentence, but Truman later commuted his sentence to life in prison; President Carter pardoned Collazo in 1979.

8. Antonio S. Pedreira, *Insularismo* (Río Piedras, PR: Editorial Edil., n.d.)

9. See Juan Flores's seminal essay on how the concept of Puerto Rican docility was written into the cultural imaginary: "The Insular Vision: Pedreira and the Puerto Rican Misère," in his *Divided Borders: Essays on Puerto Rican Identity* (Houston: Arte Público Press, 1993), 13–57.

10. *Jíbaro* is a term used for the people who live in the mountains of Puerto Rico.

11. La Perla is a section in Old San Juan that is notorious for its extreme poverty and lawlessness. Local urban myth has it that the police will not even enter there.

12. Homi K. Bhabha articulates the tensions between the archaic and innovative possibilities in the postcolonial context in his essay "Articulating the Archaic: Cultural Difference and Colonial Nonsense," in his *The Location of Culture* (New York: Routledge, 1994), 123–138.

13. Marqués purposely uses the word *estampa* to define the different acts since *estampa* refers to illustrations, pictures, or prints and recalls the pictures and woodcuts of folkloric Puerto Rico.

14. Henry Louis Gates, "The Master's Pieces: On Canon Formation and the Afro-American Tradition," in *The Bounds of Race: Perspectives on Hegemony and Resistance*, ed. Dominick La Capra (Ithaca, NY: Cornell University Press, 1991), 17–38.

15. Juan Flores, *From Bomba to Hip-Hop: Puerto Rican Culture and Latino Identity* (New York: Columbia University Press, 2000), 58.

16. Coco Fusco, *English Is Broken Here: Notes on Cultural Fusion in the Americas* (New York: New Press, 1995).

17. *El charco*, or "the pond," is a term that is often used to refer to the space of the Atlantic Ocean separating Puerto Rico from New York and other locations of the Puerto Rican diaspora.

18. An excellent study on the complexities of English and Spanish in Puerto Rico is Frances Negrón-Muntaner, "English Only *Jamás* but Spanish Only *Cuidado*: Language and Nationalism in Contemporary Puerto Rico," in *Puerto Rican Jam: Rethinking Colonialism and Nationalism*, ed. Frances Negrón-Muntaner and Ramón Grosfoguel (Minneapolis: University of Minnesota Press, 1997), 257–285.

19. Antonio Nebrija wrote the first grammar of the Spanish language, published in 1492. During that same year King Fernando and Queen Isabel completed the reconquest of Spain by defeating the Moors in Granada. Nebrija's reasons for writing the grammar were to identify and unify the Spanish people. He thought that language was the companion to empire.

20. Eleuterio Santiago Díaz, "El drama de la escritura afropuertorriqueña en el escenario de la modernidad: Carmelo Rodríguez Torres ante la ontología de la nación" (PhD diss., Brown University, Providence, RI, 2003), 77. He has a book on a similar topic in the process of publication: *Escritura afropuertorriqueña y modernidad* (Pittsburgh, PA: Instituto International de Literatura Iberoamericana, in press).

21. As Arcadio Díaz Quiñones reveals in his study of Marcelino Menéndez Pelayo's history of Latin American literature, despite the common opinion that the Cuban poet Plácido was by every measure exceptional, Menéndez Pelayo chose not to include him based almost entirely on racist reasoning. See Arcadio Díaz Quiñones, "1898: Hispanismo y guerra," in *1898: Su significado para Norte América y el Caribe; ¿Cesura, cambio, continuidad?*" ed. Walther Bernecker (Frankfurt am Main: Vervuert, 1998), 17–35.

22. Jean-Pierre Durix, "Edouard Glissant's Aesthetic Theories," in his *Mimesis, Genres and Post-colonial Discourse: Deconstructing Magical Realism* (London: Macmillan, 1998), 149–171.

23. Luis Palés Matos, *Tuntún de pasa y griferia* (San Juan: Biblioteca de Autores Puertorriqueños, 1974). Hereafter cited in text.

24. *Melao* can be understood as either "thick cane syrup" or an adjective referring to something that is overly sweet. *Melamba* is either a place in Angola or the skirts women wear when dancing.

25. See Arcadio Díaz Quiñones, "Luis Palés Matos en la Biblioteca de Ayacucho," *Sin Nombre* 10, no. 2 (1979): 7–13.

26. Israel Ruiz, "Tato Laviera, a Puerto Rican Poet and His African Heritage," in *Marvels of the African World: Cultural Patrimony, New World Connections, and Identities*, ed. Omoniyi Afolabi (Trenton, NJ: Africa World Press, 2003), 545–578.

BIBLIOGRAPHY

Bhaba, Homi K. "Articulating the Archaic: Cultural Difference and Colonial Nonsense." In *The Location of Culture*, by Homi K. Bhaba, 123–138. New York: Routledge, 1994.

Díaz Quiñones, Arcadio. "1898: Hispanismo y guerra." In *1898: Su significado para Norte América y el Caribe; ¿Cesura, cambio, continuidad?*" ed. Walther Bernecker, 17–35. Frankfurt am Main: Vervuert, 1998.

———. "Luis Palés Matos en la Biblioteca de Ayacucho: On the Mythic Qualities of the Jibaro." *Sin Nombre* 10, no. 2 (1979): 7–13.

Díaz Valcarcel, Emilio. "El soldado Damián Sánchez." In *Cuentos completos*, 127–133. Guaynabo, PR: Alfaguara Ediciones Santillana, 2002.

Durix, Jean-Pierre. "Edouard Glissant's Aesthetic Theories." In *Mimesis, Genres and Post-colonial Discourse: Deconstructing Magical Realism,* by Jean-Pierre Durix, 149–171. London: Macmillan, 1998.

Flores, Juan. *From Bomba to Hip-Hop: Puerto Rican Culture and Latino Identity*. New York: Columbia University Press, 2000.

———. "The Insular Vision: Pedreira and the Puerto Rican Misère." In *Divided Borders: Essays on Puerto Rican Identity,* by Juan Flores, 13–57. Houston: Arte Público Press, 1993.

Fusco, Coco. *English Is Broken Here: Notes on Cultural Fusion in the Americas*. New York: New Press, 1995.

Gates, Henry Louis. "The Master's Pieces: On Canon Formation and the Afro-American

Tradition." In *The Bounds of Race: Perspectives on Hegemony and Resistance*, ed. Dominick La Capra, 17–38. Ithaca, NY: Cornell University Press, 1991.

Glissant, Édouard. *Poetics of Relation*. Trans. Betsy Wing. Ann Arbor: University of Michigan Press, 1997.

Hutcheon, Linda. *A Theory of Parody: The Teachings of Twentieth Century Art Forms*. Chicago: Illinois University Press, 2000.

Laviera, Tato. *AmeRícan*. Houston: Arte Público Press, 1985.

———. *La Carreta Made a U-Turn*. Gary, IN: Arte Público Press, 1979.

Marqués, René. *La carreta: Drama en tres actos*. Río Piedras, PR: Editorial Cultural, 1983.

———. "El puertorriqueño dócil." In *Ensayos, 1953–1971*, 151–216. Barcelona, Spain: Editorial Antillana, 1972.

Negrón-Muntaner, Frances. "English Only *Jamás* but Spanish Only *Cuidado*: Language and Nationalism in Contemporary Puerto Rico." In *Puerto Rican Jam: Rethinking Colonialism and Nationalism*, ed. Frances Negrón-Muntaner and Ramón Grosfoguel, 257–285. Minneapolis: University of Minnesota Press, 1997.

Palés Matos, Luis. *Tuntún de pasa y grifería*. San Juan: Biblioteca de Autores Puertorriqueños, 1974.

Pedreira, Antonio S. *Insularismo*. Río Piedras, PR: Editorial Edil., n.d.

Ruiz, Israel. "Tato Laviera, a Puerto Rican Poet and His African Heritage." In *Marvels of the African World: Cultural Patrimony, New World Connections, and Identities*, ed. Omoniyi Afolabi, 545–578. Trenton, NJ: Africa World Press, 2003.

Santiago Díaz, Eleuterio. "El drama de la escritura afropuertorriqueña en el escenario de la modernidad: Carmelo Rodríguez Torres ante la ontología de la nación." PhD diss., Brown University, Providence, RI, 2003.

———. *Escritura afropuertorriqueña y modernidad*. Pittsburgh, PA: Instituto International de Literatura Iberoamericana, in press.

PART IV *Home*

11 WRITING HOME

Mapping Puerto Rican Collective Memory in The House on the Lagoon

KELLI LYON JOHNSON

When Rosario Ferré chose to publish her novel *The House on the Lagoon* in English, her choice drew sharp questions from other Puerto Rican and Caribbean writers and critics.[1] Several of her previous works had appeared in English—*Sweet Diamond Dust* and *The Youngest Doll* among them—but only after having been translated by Ferré herself from the initial Spanish-language versions.[2] The publication of the first edition of *The House on the Lagoon* in English reopened the debate among literary critics about the political and intellectual significance of selecting English as the language in which to encode the complexity of Puerto Rican history and literature. Writer and critic Lizabeth Paravisini-Gebert describes Ferré's choice as "an unthinkable heresy," Ferré's decision "a most regrettable error in judgment, a seduction, a responding to the siren song of a multicultural, postcolonial book market."[3] Paravisini-Gebert's indictment of Ferré's "heresy" highlights the extent to which identity has been constituted through language.

A primary marker of identity, language has emerged as paramount in delineating categories of ethnic, exile, and diaspora writing. Language constitutes contested space for processes of assimilation, resistance, and cultural reclamation; as such, language provides new territory for elaborations of identity for those in exile or diaspora. Those who continue to speak the language of their culture of origin are seen as more closely connected to that culture and, thus, more authentic. In her frequently cited article, "Displacements and Autobiography in Cuban-American Fiction," Isabel Álvarez-Borland argues that with the adoption of the language of the exile's new country, the writer becomes an ethnic writer—not a writer in exile, as Ferré has sometimes referred to herself.[4] Critics such as Álvarez-Borland generally present this linguistic transformation as progress, a desired evolution in identity that presupposes acceptance, assimilation, and integration. In her work on Cristina García's *Dreaming in Cuban*, for example, Álvarez-Borland suggests that because García's childhood "occurred in English," García "integrate[s] issues of past and present more easily. As one of the first ethnic Cuban-American writers, García envisions questions of identity and heritage with less anxiety and thus greater distance from her material," giving her the ability to "walk the path from exile to ethnicity."[5] For Álvarez-Borland, this path from exile to ethnicity creates a psychological wholeness unfettered by issues of biculturalism—linguistic or otherwise. In *After Exile* Amy Kaminsky similarly envisions the transition from Spanish to English as psychologically and culturally salubrious, suggesting that "[i]n today's United States this embrace of ethnic identity does not mean a denial of origins, but rather a fuller participation in the cultural life of the new country."[6] Such a construction of linguistic identity leads in one direction only—movement toward the future—and fails to account for a crucial element of ethnic identity: history, memory, and the collectively shared past. The connection between language and movement toward or away from the cultural past emphasizes the importance of translation for Rosario Ferré and for Puerto Rican identity in diaspora. Ferré translates her works from Spanish into English and from English into Spanish, allowing her to move not in a single direction but back and forth between languages, countries, and cultures. As a result, Puerto Rico and Puerto Rican history emerge as fluid and changeable, contingent on evolving constructions of the past as it transforms the future.

Despite accusations about her desire to break into the literary market of the United States by writing in English, Ferré has pointed out in several interviews that she is more interested in (absent) memory than markets. Rather, she has said that she writes or translates her own work into English in order to include Puerto Ricans living in the United States as part of her audience and to provide them with memories of the island.

In her essay "On Destiny, Language, and Translation; or, Ophelia Adrift in the C. & O. Canal," Ferré evokes the problem of "absent memory," asserting her belief that "it is the duty of the Puerto Rican writer, who has been privileged enough to learn both languages, to try to alleviate this situation, making an effort either to translate some of her own work or to contribute to the translation of the work of other Puerto Rican writers."[7] For Puerto Ricans born in the United States, their experience of the island parallels the Cuban American experience, which Caroline Bettinger-López characterizes as "an unlived one." For those who have left the Caribbean, their national and ethnic identity is often tied to "images they take from the stories of their parents and others who once lived on the island, images from various cultural and political institutions with connections to Cuba. This is a process of imagining history through 'knowing' unfamiliar and distant experiences."[8] Ferré's publications and translations both create and transmit knowledge and memory to fill the void—*el olvido*—left by displacement.

Memory, Ferré writes, can be carefully maintained by those of the privileged classes who have left the island. In contrast, "[t]hose who come [to the United States] fleeing poverty and hunger are often forced to be merciless with memory, as they struggle to integrate with and become indistinguishable from the mainstream." Ferré translates her work particularly for "the children of these Puerto Rican parents [who] often refuse to learn to speak Spanish, and [who] grow up having lost the ability to read the literature and the history of their island." Ultimately, what results is a "cultural suicide," a fundamental loss of Spanish, "which is the mainroad to their culture."[9] Ferré's metaphor of language-as-road suggests that translation is a "road map" to Puerto Rican collective memory. For those in the Puerto Rican diaspora, collective memory has been interrupted, and Ferré seeks to re-create unlived experiences through fiction and through translation. Translation ensures that the road of language moves in multiple directions and not merely away from the island, its culture, and its memories. She hopes that memory, "which so often erases the ache of the penury and destitution suffered on the island, after years of battling for survival in the drug-seared ghettos of Harlem and the Bronx, can, through translation, perhaps be reinstated to its true abode."[10]

The "true abode" of memory has been much debated by historians and other scholars of collective memory. Pierre Nora, in his well-known work *Les lieux de mémoire*, suggests that memory "attaches itself to sites" and is invested in place-names, monuments, markers, and other commemorative practices or locations.[11] Susan Crane argues that collective memory is ultimately located not in such sites but in the individuals who do the work of remembering.[12] In *The House on the Lagoon*, Ferré engages this debate about sites of memory through the house of the novel's title. As a "true abode," the house on the lagoon serves as a site for both family and national memories. Also the title of the narrator's novel-within-the-novel, the house on the lagoon creates space for the inscription of the domestic into official versions of history, thus including women in Puerto Rico's national story. While the house recalls Nora's *lieux*, the narrator, Isabel Mendizabal, serves as a facilitator of collective memory as she records and transmits it for others; she is the individual in whom Crane insists memory is located. In Ferré's novel, collective memory is both mutable and flexible in its location and incarnation. Throughout the course of the novel, the house on the lagoon is destroyed and re-created several times, suggesting various visions of history and memory, and each new vision of the house, in Ferré's words, "recoge un símbolo de Puerto Rico."[13] The house is situated "where the mangrove swamp met the private beach of the lagoon" (9), a site that Ferré sees as "halfway territory: half earth, half water," similar to Puerto Rico, "a borderline country."[14] The mangrove "es un arbusto con una raíz muy alta y el follaje se encuentra fuera del agua pero las raíces están debajo de ella. Es, pues, una planta tibia, semiacuática y semiterráquea."[15] Ferré's metaphor suggests the island roots of Puerto Ricans in diaspora and of herself as a writer; the mangrove represents what Ferré has called "the water of words," which is "my true habitat as a writer."[16] As Isabel asserts in the novel, however, the swamp "was a strange territory to navigate in" (10), much like the territory of womanhood, authorship, and Puerto Rican diaspora. A terrain that is fluid and amorphous, the mangrove swamp forges a connection among the various Puerto Rican communities both in diaspora and on the island. As an aid to the navigation of such territory, the novel provides a roadmap of the island's history for those whose mainroad to the culture has been disrupted through migration.

In *La memoria rota*, Arcadio Díaz Quiñones points to the dis-junction among these communities, a dis-junction that creates a "break" in Puerto Rican memory: "Las categorías nacionales y culturales dominantes en los Estados Unidos y en Latinoamérica, y la situación colonial puertorriqueña, llevan con frequencia a negar la memoria histórica," resulting in "una memoria muchas veces negada, y rota."[17] Puerto Rican memory has been broken not only historically but also geographically. Following the work of Díaz Quiñones, Juan Flores has persuasively argued that "perhaps the most pronounced break in collective memory [is] the emigrant Puerto Rican community in the United States."[18] Ferré is poignantly aware of this geographical break, so she focuses her efforts in writing and translating toward repairing it. For Flores, however, "[i]t is not enough to point to the break and glue the pieces back together by mentioning forgotten names and events. The seams and borders of national experience need to be understood not as absences or vacuums but as sites of new meanings and relations."[19] Ferré has written these new meanings and relations in both English and Spanish, a translation that she insists is "not only a literary but also a historical task."[20] The connections among history and translation, language and identity, memory and geography, come together in the house on the lagoon and its swampy surroundings.

In order to write into being a new collective memory, Ferré first destabilizes traditional constructions of both history and truth. Through an ongoing dialogue between Isabel Mendizabal and her husband, Quintín, Ferré recapitulates classic gendered divisions of history and literature. Isabel is writing a manuscript, titled *The House on the Lagoon*, about their family histories, which are also the (multiple) histories of the island. Quintín, however, "preferred history to literature; literature wasn't ethical enough for him." Writing fiction, for him, is not "a serious occupation, like science or history," which require intellectual vigor and commitment to what Quintín sees as the "nucleus of truth" (72) in every story. He believes that Isabel "had consciously altered the facts of history to serve her story" (74) in her manuscript. Ultimately, "[w]hat troubled Quintín the most was Isabel's blatant disregard of history" (151), and he finally concludes that "history is much more important than literature" (312).

In contrast to Quintín's certainty that "[t]here was a true and a false, a right and a wrong," Isabel believes that "[n]othing is true, nothing is false, everything is the color of the glass you're looking through" (106). As Isabel tells Quintín: "History doesn't deal with the truth any more than literature does. From the moment a historian selects one theme over another in order to write about it, he is manipulating the facts. The historian, like the novelist, observes the world through his own tinted glass, and describes it as if it were the truth. But it's only one side of the truth, because imagination—what you call lies—is also part of the truth" (312). In these discussions on the nature of truth, history, and memory, Isabel and Quintín are trying to work out what Julie Barak sees as the focus of *The House on the Lagoon*, "the connections and disconnections between history and literature," which they posit "in gendered terms."[21] Ferré identifies Quintín with traditional masculine and privileged discourses of fact, history, and nation, whereas she associates Isabel with memory, family, and the house—gendered spaces of female identity and experience. Ferré uses those connections and disconnections to privilege literature—specifically, women's literature—over history as a wellspring of collective memory for the Mendizabales and for Puerto Ricans.

Ferré reveals writing to be essential in the creation of this new, more inclusive collective memory. In writing *The House on the Lagoon*, Isabel Mendizabal and Rosario Ferré engage in world building; they are writing home as they both reconstruct it in their novels and address it to their compatriots across space (for Ferré) and time (for Isabel). For them, "home" is the site of both family and nation—a house, an island, and an identity that transcends borders on maps. An act of creation, the power to write home threatens male dominance in domestic and intellectual spaces, and Ferré represents the male reaction to such a threat through Quintín's additions and deletions to and contestations of Isabel's writing of home, particularly as he views them possessively—his family, his house, his nation. When he discovers Isabel's writing, Quintín sees his first duty as a decision to "create a distance between what he was reading and his own personal feelings, and he would do that by adopting a critical attitude. He would read the manuscript as if he were a conscientious literary critic" (107). Ferré here uses the irony for which she is well known, scorning the artificial distance adopted by the literary critic; Quintín cannot distance himself from "what he was reading" because the subject is Quintín himself and his own family. Quintín, however, as with other historians of the Puerto Rican past, believes in that critical distance. A self-appointed literary critic, Quintín begins writing in the margins of Isabel's story, inverting postcolonial concepts of center and margin. Ferré locates Isabel and her writing at the center and

Quintín—historian and descendant of the Spanish conquistadors—in the margins of the text.

As Ferré herself has attested in an interview, "Nadie tiene el monopólio de la verdad." "La historia y la ficción," she writes, "son dos caras de una misma realidad; no se puede entender la historia de un determinado periodo si no leemos tanto las novellas como libros de historia que se escribieron sobre él."[22] *The House on the Lagoon* serves as just such a novel, focused on the period between 4 July 1917—the day on which President Woodrow Wilson signed the Jones Act into law, granting Puerto Ricans status as citizens of the United States—and a plebiscite in 1982 in which Puerto Ricans voted to remain a commonwealth of the United States. She presents contradictions between literature and history by contrasting Isabel's account in her novel-within-the-novel and Quintín's reinterpretation of that account. Such a structure again inverts the traditional perspective that literature is a reinterpretation of history, and Ferré thus privileges literary discourse over historical writings.

Isabel weaves historical events into the family history that she is ostensibly writing in *The House on the Lagoon*, events with which Quintín takes issue in his role as critic and editor. In her story of Quintín's grandmother, for example, Quintín finds that "Isabel had attributed his grandmother's failed marriage to the fact that she had never learned to speak Spanish." In his role as guardian of national history, Quintín feels obligated to point out that "Commissioner Easton's ordinance making English the official language at school seventy-nine years ago was a historical fact, and everyone agreed today that it had been a mistake. But the truth was that learning English had given the island a great advantage over its Latin American neighbors" (150). Quintín addresses this important element of Puerto Rican identity—language—through personages, dates, and accepted historical interpretations, while Isabel's perspective addresses the language issue through his grandmother's personal story. The family and marriage metaphor serves here to undermine historical accounts of Easton's ordinance and make it relevant to women, who have traditionally been excluded from historical texts. The marriage metaphor, in fact, appears frequently throughout the text, pointing to the correlation between the dependence of women within traditional marriage and the island's relationship to other countries. "The way I see it," Isabel writes, "our island is like a betrothed, always on the verge of marriage" (184). As it would for women, "marriage" to the United States for Puerto Rico would result in loss—of language, culture, and self-determination—while remaining "single" would mean poverty and sacrifice (184).

Such connections between marital status and the nation's commonwealth status allow Ferré to write the family back into Puerto Rican collective memory. She does so by drawing the private, or domestic, concerns of the family into the public realm of national history. For his part, Quintín calls it "a silly novel" (249), dismissing women's writing and telling her that it is "not a work of art. It's a feminist treatise, and Independentista manifesto; worst of all, it distorts history" (386). Quintín's condemnation of *The House on the Lagoon* reiterates traditional patriarchal claims of objectivity and aesthetic value, as if they themselves were free from any political message or bias. Isabel responds to such condemnation by telling Quintín, "'My novel is about personal freedom,' I said calmly. 'It's about my independence from you'" (386). Isabel's quest for self-determination mirrors the island's struggle for the same, a parallel that Ferré draws in *El coloquio de las perras*, in which she identifies "el colonialismo de estado" in Puerto Rico with "el colonialismo de la mujer, que vive una vida fragmentada y dependiente del orden patriarchal."[23] Like women, Puerto Rico is "a country that in five hundred years of existence has never been its own self" (341). Isabel is writing her own freedom, prompting Quintín to suspect that Isabel was "writing this novel because she wanted to have control of their lives" (108). The connection between writing and self-determination emerges clearly in Ferré's construction of the writing process and its effects on the family and on the nation. Quintín's anger that Isabel "insisted on baring his family's secrets to the world" (247) in her novel ignores the fact that Isabel is also revealing the country's "secrets" as seen from Isabel's perspective.

Such claims of independence for Isabel reveal family stories as parallel to—and as important as—the history of the nation, a means of "writing home" for those who have never lived there but continue to identify with the island. Isabel follows the advice of Quintín's mother, Rebecca, that "[e]very woman should be a republic unto herself!" Rebecca's personal circumstances within the Puerto Rican family also inform her political beliefs: "If she couldn't be independent herself, she would say, at least her country should have control over its own destiny" (97). She is an Independentista, a term for an advocate of national independence for Puerto Rico; the word "independent" here refers to Rebecca's personal freedom. Inverting the traditional U.S. feminist call that "the personal is political," Ferré makes the political personal for Rebecca Mendizabal. Ferré is calling for both an independent Puerto Rico and independent Puerto Rican women.

Ferré genders Puerto Rican collective memory by focusing the events —the history—of the novel on the house on the lagoon itself, a symbol, as Ferré has said, of Puerto Rico and also of female space. The house is situated on the Morass Lagoon, so named by the Spanish conquistadors. The name reappears in Isabel's description of the conquistadors themselves, and the violent colonial heritage of Puerto Rico, when she decries "the morass of heredity" that contributes to Quintín's own violence. Before the first house on the lagoon, Buenaventura Mendizabal, Quintín's father, had built a small cottage near a public spring, a spring that he appropriates for himself and his family in the tradition of the colonial invaders from whom he is descended. There are three successive houses on the lagoon, and each in turn represents a redefinition of the Mendizabal family and the country; each incarnation is influenced by factors outside the family that contribute to its evolution; each is an endeavor of creativity; and each house is destroyed in the name of an ideology that the (male) characters are unwilling to adapt to changing traditions and mores in Puerto Rican culture.

Buenaventura commissions the first house on the lagoon, which is designed by Milan Pavel, a Czech émigré who had worked with Frank Lloyd Wright in the United States before fleeing to Puerto Rico in disgrace after accusations of plagiarism. The similarity between Wright's work and Pavel's work parallels the relationship between the United States and Puerto Rico. Pavel uses "one of Wright's masterpieces as his model" (48) for the first house on the lagoon, which represents the growing influence of the United States on Puerto Rican culture and politics. The architecture is ornate and extravagant, as Pavel takes Wright's work and extends it. He adds "new elements which would make the house more in keeping with life in the tropics" and designs ceilings "twice as high as those of Wright's houses" and a terrace made of gold. When he accepts Buenaventura's commission, Pavel feels as if "[i]t was the first time in his life [that] he had designed something truly original. He created the house on the lagoon as one would create a poem or a statue, breathing life into its every stone" (49). Ferré deliberately links art, architecture, and commemoration in order to suggest artistic creation—statues, poetry, and even novels—as sites of collective memory. Rebecca herself is an artist, a dancer and a poet who, largely because she is a woman, is unable to perform in public and therefore seeks to construct a home as a venue for her artistry. The house must stand in proxy for the national space to which Rebecca is denied access.

Buenaventura, for his part, does not support the artistic community that Rebecca attempts to foster in the house on the lagoon and instead seeks to improve his business by entertaining clients. Rebecca herself "had wanted a Temple of Art, and instead they lived in a Temple of Commerce and Diplomacy where her husband reigned supreme" (51). Ferré here points to the assertion long made by feminists about the doctrine of "separate spheres" that emerged in the nineteenth century: although the house was supposed to be the domain of women, they seldom enjoyed any real autonomy in the household. In the novel, "Rebecca maintained that a man's kingdom is his business and a woman's is her home, but Buenaventura wouldn't take her seriously. 'A man's home is like a rooster's coop: women may speak out when chickens get to pee,' he said to Rebecca, giving her a pat on the behind" (51). That pat on the behind reveals Buenaventura's sense of ownership of both the house and Rebecca, undermining her own autonomy and dismissing her political and personal convictions about independence. Unlike Isabel, Rebecca is unable to construct a home in which she can define herself, her family, and her country.

Buenaventura's sense of ownership devolves into violence and destruction. When he catches Rebecca at one of her artistic "soirées" dancing the Dance of the Seven Veils, he beats her severely. After that evening, Buenaventura realizes that the house had been the site of Rebecca's aspirations to a life of art and of her ideas of an independent Puerto Rico and, as such, represents for Buenaventura the danger of freedom—in art, in thought, and in politics. As further punishment and to assert his control over his home, his wife, and his nation, Buenaventura razes the first house on the lagoon.

The second house on the lagoon recalls the island's Spanish colonial heritage, moving backward into the past. On the same land that merged the lagoon and the swamp, "Buenaventura built a Spanish Revival mansion with granite turrets, bare brick floors, and a forbidding granite stairway with a banister made of iron spears. From the ceiling in the entrance hall he hung his *pièce de résistance*, a spiked wooden wheel that had been used to torture the Moors during the Spanish conquest, which he ordered made into a lamp" (67). This lamp, along with the architecture of this second house, sheds light on both Buenaventura's and Puerto Rico's colonial heritage; he continues to colonize the public spring beneath the house, the Spanish products that he imports to Puerto Rico, and Rebecca. What this second house has in common with the first is its cellar. It belongs to the servants, with a common room where Petra, the oldest of the servants, rules their existence. Petra also has significant influence upstairs with the Mendizabal family. The character of Petra allows Ferré to introduce the African influence into Puerto Rican culture, an influence that is often denied among the upper classes, who stress their Spanish heritage. Yet Petra's family and the Mendizabal family are in fact blood relations, revealing the multiplicity of nations, cultures, and peoples that characterize Puerto Rican history and, thus, identity.

The space of the cellar bespeaks the class stratification that Ferré carefully delineates throughout the course of the novel, distinctions based not only on money but also on race. Petra's grandfather came from Africa, and their descendants populate nearby Locumí Beach, an entire community of Puerto Ricans of African descent. The cellar also "gave the house much of its mystery, the feeling that events weren't always what they seemed but could have expected echoes and repercussions" (235), much like history itself. In the house on Aurora Street, where Isabel and Quintín live together, "events were easy to classify: there was a right and a left, a front and a back to everything—there was little room for ambiguity or doubt. But at the house on the lagoon, things were often misleading" (235). If the house on the lagoon, in its many incarnations, symbolizes Puerto Rico, as Ferré suggests, then she emphasizes here the complexity of Puerto Rican history and the multiple migrations that preceded those of the twentieth century. Moreover, Isabel finds, "[t]rying to get away from the house on the lagoon was like trying to get out of a brier patch; when you pulled away, you took part of it with you, and it pulled you right back" (255). Isabel's description of the house resonates with Ferré's description of the mangrove swamp, both of which suggest a rootedness in the island, however tangled, unbroken by linguistic difference or spatial difference. Moreover, some of those tangled roots reach back to Africa and Puerto Rico's colonial history of slavery and violence.

Isabel and Quintín ultimately return to live in this second house on the lagoon, which Quintín transforms into the third house on the lagoon. Concerned that he will not be "remembered" and his "memory will be erased from the face of the earth," Quintín decides to turn the house into a museum, restoring it to its original plan as Pavel designed it. Although he imagines it to be a museum to house his considerable art collection, it will also serve to commemorate Pavel, Rebecca, Puerto Rican history, and, of course, himself. He hires a demolition crew that "leveled Buenaventura's Gothic arches and granite turrets. Slowly a fairy-tale palace began to rise from its rubble." When construction is finished, the house looks exactly as it had "in Rebecca's time" (299). With the new house as a museum, Quintín "would always be remembered" (326). What haunts Quintín, however, is that he can never faithfully re-create the original house; the re-membered house on the lagoon will only resemble Quintín's childhood memories of the first house. The new house and its history eclipse its previous incarnations, the risk of such layers of memory. For those in diaspora, additional layers of experience—new terrains, new languages, new cultures—create further distance. For Quintín and his new house, and for Puerto Ricans in diaspora, the remembered home does not exist. As Ferré has said in an interview, "You never see things the way they really are, but how you remember them. This worries me because I don't want to start writing about a Puerto Rico that doesn't exist anymore."[24] Living in Washington, D.C., at the time she wrote the novel, she has thus experienced Quintín's anxiety, caused by the distance between the island and herself.

But much has changed since the construction of the first house on the lagoon, which Ferré makes clear in Isabel's discussion of her manuscript. Isabel tells Quintín: "Between the writing and the reading of a text, things change, the world goes round, marriages and love affairs are made and unmade." In her view of art—fiction, architecture, history—"[e]ach chapter is like a letter to the reader; its meaning isn't completed until it is read by someone" (311). The meaning of the Mendizabal story is completed by the final act of the novel, in which Quintín's son Manuel, an activist for independence, destroys the third house on the lagoon. The culmination of the violence of the nation's colonial history, reflected in the lives of the Mendizábales, results in the destruction of the house on the lagoon, suggesting repeated annihilations and reconstructions of Puerto Rican national identity since the Spanish invasion.

The fourth house on the lagoon is Isabel's manuscript, which is Ferré's novel. Through this book, Isabel will be able to gain the recognition—and a place in the culture's collective memory—that Quintín seeks with his museum on the lagoon. While Ferré clearly depicts the house on the lagoon as a space that constrains the experience and self-determination of its female inhabitants—particularly Rebecca and Isabel—Quintín sees the house as a place of freedom for women, free of the responsibility of economically supporting the household. Quintín laments the fact that "[h]e never had the opportunity to sit around doing nothing, fanning himself on the terrace as Isabel did, watching the pelicans dive into the lagoon and waiting for ideas to come to him so he could capture them in beautiful words." He resents Isabel's writing, believing that "[h]e could have been an artist, too. After all, a good historian is as creative as a good novelist. But he simply never developed that part of himself. There were too many people to feed, too many obligations to attend to" (187). At issue for Quintín is not merely his failure to develop "that part of himself"; what worries Quintín is memory, that he will not be "remembered" within the collective memory of the island, in the same way that women's experiences have been excluded from traditional histories of the island. Quintín "had never been able to create anything, and he feared that when he died his memory would be erased from the face of the earth" (326). On the other hand, Isabel "would be remembered as the author of *The House on the Lagoon*, a 'work of art'" (188). Quintín's reasoning follows traditions of historical commemoration; he invests his faith in documents, photographs, archives, church records, and other material evidence of the past—the data of the historian.

Ferré's concern with the interconnections of race, faith, memory, and material history is perhaps most apparent in her descriptions of the Bloodline Books, which "had been instituted to keep the blood free of Jewish or Islamic ancestry, and separate records of all white and nonwhite marriages were kept in them" (22). In Puerto Rico, they were used to record marriages free of African blood as well. Considered "unworthy of American citizens" (23), the Bloodline Books were abandoned when the Americans arrived on the island at the turn of the twentieth century. These books, however, maintain their value in many of the upper-class families on the island, often secretly consulted before marriages were approved by the patriarchs of these families. Such records emphasize not only the tradition of material history that Quintín supports but also the national, class, and gendered hierarchies inherent in archival traditions of recording history.

Traditionally, material history has replaced memory in the (re)construction of the past, often of a past that never existed. In *The House on the Lagoon*, Ferré interrogates this tradition in her treatment of material history. She describes early photographs of the island, commissioned by Governor Winship, that reveal that the photographer "captured the island in all its splendor: there were angel-hair waterfalls, cotton-candy clouds, sugar-white beaches, cows pasturing up and down velvet-green hills—and not a single starving peasant to mar the beauty of the landscape" (125). Ferré ironically acknowledges the selectivity of the traditional materials of history, and she seeks to expand that history to include the starving peasants, the Independentista movement, and women's lives in Puerto Rico. She expresses similar doubts about the veracity of material documents of family heritage. The Mendizabal family story is largely centered on Quintín's father, Buenaventura, and the story, as Quintín prefers it, serves "to remind [his sons] of who they were and where they come from" (14). Part of that story is based on material history, specifically "an old parchment in which his family pedigree was inscribed" (22). Isabel, however, imagines that Buenaventura's "parchment"—as well as his coat of arms—had all been a hoax. "I always suspected Buenaventura, like many of the Spanish Conquistadors, was really of humble origin, though that was one of the secrets he took with him to his grave" (253). Such secrets are the very ones that are invisible in history but can be written into Puerto Rican collective memory through Isabel's art.

While Isabel herself is concerned with memory, she remains uncertain of the role her book will play in the collective memory of Puerto Ricans. She wonders, "Why should I keep painful memories alive, when the rest of the world has forgotten?" (328). With *The House on the Lagoon*, Ferré answers Isabel's question by insisting that the world not forget about the Caribbean, about Puerto Rico, or about Puerto Ricans in diaspora. Ferré's novel becomes a site of memory as she repairs in that narrative space the broken memory of Puerto Ricans. Drawing them from the margins into the center of the narrative, she relegates traditional colonial history to the margins of the text. The writing of collective memory lends it a validity that belies Quintín's insistence that "literature never changes anything, but history can alter the course of events" (311). Literature, as Ferré demonstrates in her English-language and Spanish-language work alike, can indeed change the course of events, as both Puerto Rican and Anglo readers participate in the memory community that Ferré constructs in *The House on the Lagoon.*

As Ferré's work suggests, literature can reinstate collective memory and thus cultural identity for those in diaspora. Since World War II, we have witnessed the mass migrations caused by genocide, civil wars, and economic and political imbalances throughout the world. The irony of these migrations and the concomitant phenomenon of globalization is the increasing isolation of many postmodern societies. Collective memory allows us to overcome that isolation, and the recuperation of collective memory creates both historical continuity and community across both space and time. Translation provides a means not only of navigating across space and time but also of expanding the memory community and creating a more inclusive "mainroad" for diasporic literature and culture.

NOTES

1. Rosario Ferré, *The House on the Lagoon* (New York: Plume, 1995). Hereafter cited in text.

2. Rosario Ferré, *Sweet Diamond Dust* (New York: Ballantine, 1988); Rosario Ferré, *The Youngest Doll* (Lincoln: University of Nebraska Press, 1991).

3. Lizabeth Paravisini-Gebert, "Women against the Grain: The Pitfalls of Theorizing Caribbean Women's Writing," in *Winds of Change: The Transforming Voices of Caribbean Women Writers and Scholars,* ed. Adele S. Newson and Linda Strong-Leek (New York: Peter Lang, 1998), 162.

4. Rosario Ferré, "On Destiny, Language, and Translation; or Ophelia Adrift in the C. & O. Canal," in Ferré, *Youngest Doll,* 163.

5. Isabel Álvarez-Borland, "Displacements and Autobiography in Cuban-American Fiction," *World Literature Today* 68 (1994): 48.

6. Amy K. Kaminsky, *After Exile: Writing the Latin American Diaspora* (Minneapolis: University of Minnesota Press, 1999), 134.

7. Ferré, "On Destiny, Language, and Translation," 163.

8. Caroline Bettinger-López, *Cuban Jewish Journeys: Searching for Identity, Home, and History in Miami* (Knoxville: University of Tennessee Press, 2000), 163.

9. Ferré, "On Destiny, Language, and Translation," 163.

10. Ibid., 164.

11. The English translation of the introduction to this seven-volume work appeared in Pierre Nora, "Between Memory and History: *Les lieux de mémoire*," *Representations* 26 (1989): 22.

12. Susan Crane, "Writing the Individual Back into Collective Memory," *American Historical Review* 102 (1997): 1381.

13. Begona Toral Alemañ, "Entre Puerto Rico y Estados Unidos: Entrevista a Rosario Ferré," *Caribe* 3 (Winter 2000): 59 ("takes in a symbol of Puerto Rico").

14. Bridgit Kevane and Juanita Heredia, "A Side View: An Interview with Rosario Ferré," in *Latina Self-Portraits: Interviews with Contemporary Women Writers,* by Bridgit Kevane and Juanita Heredia (Albuquerque: University of New Mexico Press, 2000), 66.

15. "[The mangrove] is a bush with a very long root and the foliage remains out of the water but the roots are still beneath it. It is, then, a tepid plant, semiaquatic and semiterrestrial." Toral Alemañ, "Entre Puerto Rico y Estados Unidos," 59.

16. Ferré, "On Destiny, Language, and Translation," 155.

17. "The dominant national and cultural categories in the United States and in Latin America, and the Puerto Rican colonial situation, frequently serve to negate historical memory," resulting in "a memory many times negated and broken." Arcadio Díaz Quiñones, *La memoria rota* (Río Piedras, PR: Ediciones Huracán, 1993), 79.

18. Juan Flores, "Broken English Memories," in *Postcolonial Theory and the United States: Race, Ethnicity, and Literature*, ed. Amritjit Singh and Peter Schmidt (Jackson: University Press of Mississippi, 2000), 339.

19. Ibid., 340.

20. Ferré, "On Destiny, Language, and Translation," 155.

21. Julie Barak, "Navigating the Swamp: Fact and Fiction in Rosario Ferré's *The House on the Lagoon,*" *Journal of the Midwest Modern Language Association* 31 (1998): 32, 35.

22. "Nobody has a monopoly on the truth"; "History and fiction are two sides of the same reality; we cannot understand the history of a particular period if we do not read novels like history books written about that period." Gloria Díaz Rinks and Elisabeth Sisson-Guerrero, "Rosario Ferré entre el inglés y el español: 'Let oneself be the meeting place of both,'" *Dactylus* 16 (1997): 68.

23. Ferré identifies "the colonialism of the state" in Puerto Rico with "the colonialism of the woman, who lives a fragmented and dependent life in a patriarchal order." Rosario Ferré, *El coloquio de las perras* (San Juan: Editorial Cultural, 1990), 109.

24. Donna Perry, "Rosario Ferré," in *Backtalk: Women Writers Speak Out,* by Donna Perry (New Brunswick, NJ: Rutgers University Press, 1993), 95.

BIBLIOGRAPHY

Álvarez-Borland, Isabel. "Displacements and Autobiography in Cuban-American Fiction." *World Literature Today* 68 (1994): 43–48.

Barak, Julie. "Navigating the Swamp: Fact and Fiction in Rosario Ferré's *The House on the Lagoon*." *Journal of the Midwest Modern Language Association* 31 (1998): 31–38.

Bettinger-López, Caroline. *Cuban Jewish Journeys: Searching for Identity, Home, and History in Miami*. Knoxville: University of Tennessee Press, 2000.

Crane, Susan. "Writing the Individual Back into Collective Memory." *American Historical Review* 102 (1997): 1372–1385.

Díaz Quiñones, Arcadio. *La memoria rota*. Río Piedras, PR: Ediciones Huracán, 1993.

Díaz Rinks, Gloria, and Elisabeth Sisson-Guerrero. "Rosario Ferré entre el ingles y el español: 'Let oneself be the meeting place of both.'" *Dactylus* 16 (1997): 61–69.

Ferré, Rosario. *El coloquio de las perras*. San Juan: Editorial Cultural, 1990.

———. *The House on the Lagoon*. New York: Plume, 1995.

———. "On Destiny, Language, and Translation; or Ophelia Adrift in the C. & O. Canal." In *The Youngest Doll,* by Rosario Ferré, 153–165. Lincoln: University of Nebraska Press, 1991.

———. *Sweet Diamond Dust*. New York: Ballantine, 1988.

Flores, Juan. "Broken English Memories." In *Postcolonial Theory and the United States: Race, Ethnicity, and Literature*, ed. Amritjit Singh and Peter Schmidt, 338–348. Jackson: University Press of Mississippi, 2000.

García, Cristina. *Dreaming in Cuban*. New York: Ballantine, 1992.

Kaminsky, Amy K. *After Exile: Writing the Latin American Diaspora*. Minneapolis: University of Minnesota Press, 1999.

Kevane, Bridgit, and Juanita Heredia. "A Side View: An Interview with Rosario Ferré." In *Latina Self-Portraits: Interviews with Contemporary Women Writers,* by Bridgit Kevane and Juanita Heredia, 59–68. Albuquerque: University of New Mexico Press, 2000.

Nora, Pierre. "Between Memory and History: *Les lieux de mémoire*." *Representations* 26 (1989): 7–24.

Paravisini-Gebert, Lizabeth. "Women against the Grain: The Pitfalls of Theorizing Caribbean Women's Writing." In *Winds of Change: The Transforming Voices of Caribbean Women Writers and Scholars*, ed. Adele S. Newson and Linda Strong-Leek, 161–168. New York: Peter Lang, 1998.

Perry, Donna. "Rosario Ferré." In *Backtalk: Women Writers Speak Out,* by Donna Perry, 83–103. New Brunswick, NJ: Rutgers University Press, 1993.

Toral Alemañ, Begona. "Entre Puerto Rico y Estados Unidos: Entrevista a Rosario Ferré." *Caribe* 3 (Winter 2000): 51–62.

12 TRANSLATING "HOME" IN THE WORK OF JUDITH ORTIZ COFER

JOANNA BARSZEWSKA MARSHALL

The narrator of Judith Ortiz Cofer's first novel, *The Line of the Sun*, is Marisol. When her father, Raphael, joins the navy, she moves from Puerto Rico to New Jersey with her mother, Ramona, and her younger brother, Gabriel. They live in an apartment house in Patterson with other Puerto Rican migrants, as well as her father during his visits home. In this place, known as "El Building," the residents create a community that reminds Marisol of a "vertical pueblo" where life is lived at a "high pitch."[1] Believing that "all could be kept the same within the family as it had been on the Island," the residents produce a "microcosm of Island life" in which they re-create "every day the same routines they had followed in their mamá's houses so long ago" (170, 223). Marisol details the similarities of El Building's sounds and smells, its staple foods (chiefly rice and beans), its typical decor (with the Sacred Heart over the kitchen table and Mary "smiling serenely from walls"), its gestures of hospitality (such as open doors), its recourse to spiritists and the cleansing power of *agua florida*, its beehive-like activity, intrigues, gossip groups, and domestic quarrels, its fights, separations, and reconciliations, to those of a barrio on the Island.

Yet Marisol concludes that the Island way of life has been "lost" and that the attempt to re-create it in cold rooms above frozen ground is evidence of a "cultural schizophrenia" that only enhances a "fantasy" of living as a Puerto Rican and even turns that way of life into a "parody" (170, 223). Although she feels "deprived" of the Island, she feels embarrassed about living in a "crowded, noisy tenement, which the residents seemed intent on turning into a *bizarre facsimile* of an Island barrio" (220, italics added).

To some extent, Marisol is simply a typical adolescent—struggling for independence and confused, simultaneously identified with and embarrassed by her parents and their way of life. For example, Marisol thinks that a spiritist meeting she helps Ramona organize is a "silly game"; like the life of El Building in general, this game is not only a "fantasy" but also "absurd." But when Ramona excludes Marisol from the "fun" part, Marisol shouts her fury; when Ramona then slaps her, Marisol ends up trembling "from the pure hatred of a mother only a teenager can feel" (253–254). The context of their struggle, however, indicates that something more than typical adolescent feelings are involved. For Marisol is similarly embarrassed by her mother's "wild beauty" that makes her akin to a "circus freak" and also by the fears that Ramona advertises in a foreign language (174, 220). Like the children in *Silent Dancing,* Ortiz Cofer's memoirs, Marisol would prefer to be a cultural "chameleon" who blends in with her surroundings.[2] Instead, she feels that she does not "fit" her environment; and she resents her parents, blaming them for the choices that put her in this position.

Marisol believes her life would be more normal, more natural, if she had been raised on the Island, where the children use the weirdness of pueblo eccentrics to measure their own normalcy (*SD*, 17). But what seems normal and natural to children on the Island seems strange and "out of place" in New Jersey, where Marisol uses middle-class normalcy to measure Puerto Rican weirdness. So what seems bizarre to Marisol about Puerto Rican life in the States is related, not so much to its being a fantasy or a facsimile, but to its being Puerto Rican.

The characters' struggles over their way of life, over what and where home should be, are not simply generational ones. The idea that Puerto Rican homes and Puerto Rican behavior belong to the Island, that they are natural there and unnatural elsewhere, is part of a wider, politically charged discourse. As Jorge Duany observes in *The Puerto Rican Nation on the Move*, an island-centered canon has historically "promote[d] the idea that islanders were more culturally authentic"; and the founding myth of Puerto Ricanness as a mix of the Spanish, the African, and the

Taíno shuns anything American as a corrupting "foreign influence."[3] Marisol, the character in Ortiz Cofer's first novel, seems to echo these sentiments. Countering these assumptions, Duany argues that the "discourse of Puerto Ricanness needs to be expanded to include nearly half of the Puerto Rican people, who now live outside the Island" (207). Ortiz Cofer, the author, concurs. In an interview with Raphael Ocasio, she insists that the Puerto Rican experience exists in New York and other U.S. cities as well as on the Island. And the variety of that experience is not "corrupting" but "beautiful" and "delightful."[4]

The Puerto Rican diaspora is part and parcel of the Puerto Rican nation described by Duany, Ortiz Cofer, and Juan Flores, among others. In making this claim, Duany urges scholars to pay attention to the "performative aspects" of people's sense of who they are and to "document which cultural practices travel between the Island and the mainland and how they move" (34). He also suggests that bidirectional flows will challenge conventional views of the distinction between sending and receiving cultures; for Puerto Ricans in the diaspora are not only members of the nation but also shapers of the culture. The work of Ortiz Cofer demonstrates that, despite Marisol's reservations, home-making is one of those practices that travel. Because it travels as and through translation, however, it is subject to much of the same controversy and the same obsessions that have attended linguistic translations.

The adolescent Marisol seems to believe that a Puerto Rican home is "untranslatable"—unable to exist outside the borders of the Island without becoming a "bizarre facsimile" of the source. Her resistance to the possibility of translation fits with an initial stage that Martha Cutter has identified as a transethnic tendency in the work of contemporary ethnic American writers. In the Asian American, Native American, African American, and Chicano/a texts that Cutter analyzed, this resistance is accompanied by a rejection of the parent or ethnic culture; because this culture lacks cultural capital, it is not worthy of transmigration or relocation to the new context.[5] But characters in this body of literature eventually develop facility as translators, and their attitudes about both source and target cultures change. As they begin to appreciate translation, they transcode ethnicity as a valuable position *within* the discourse of the "American" and understand ethnicity as a constituent part of that culture. They also value the changes that simultaneously re-create both the ethnic and the "American" when ethnic customs transmigrate.[6]

As I will later explain, Marisol's resistance to translation, like that of the characters that Cutter studied, is linked to her experience with language. But focusing on other types of cultural translation in Ortiz Cofer's novel reveals other features of the practice and the role of translation in contemporary ethnic society, features that may be highlighted in the Puerto Rican diaspora because of the unique position of Puerto Rican migrants—as citizens who commonly travel back and forth in a pattern of circular migration—among the various groups who make up "ethnic America."

Although Marisol is embarrassed when residents of El Building attempt to relocate Puerto Rico to New Jersey, for example, the novel makes it clear that she does value their culture; her resistance to translation, however, means that the Island is the place where she believes it should be preserved. The Marisol who narrates the story of her adolescence and her family after the fact demonstrates that she has developed a facility for the translation of cultural stories. In those narratives, her focus on the homes that are most significant for these stories highlights another important feature of translation in the Puerto Rican diaspora—the fact that translation re-creates not only the diasporic ethnic culture and the "American" culture in the States but also the "source" culture. For "Puerto Rican," or "Island," culture has itself been created through a series of translations and retranslations. The extent to which Puerto Ricans resist, accept, or embrace these various features of translation is linked to fundamental differences in their attitudes about the way translation is or should be practiced and thus, as previously noted, to controversies and obsessions that have marked the field of translation studies.

When Duany refers to the concept of sending and receiving cultures to argue that Puerto Ricans in the diaspora shape culture in the United States and on the Island, he highlights an intersection between diaspora studies, cultural anthropology, and translation studies. The three fields have been caught up in similar obsessions—obsessions that are deeply involved in a history of domination and resistance, of colonialism and anticolonial struggle. As Tejaswini Niranjana observes in *Siting Translation*, ethnography, or cultural anthropology, has "always conceived of its project as one of *translation*."[7] The discipline developed in a context of asymmetrical relations of power, and its knowledge depended on notions of translation that served an idiom of domination. And the *model* of translation that produced this knowledge and colonial approaches to cultural understanding was one that attempted to make the culture under study fully intelligible and transparent in the language of the colonizer. In a humanistic attempt to bridge the gap between peoples, ethnography strove for a translation based on "exchange without loss" and ended up making the source culture seem "natural" to the receiving culture by erasing all sense of what was foreign (47, 68).

According to midcentury translation theory, the "cardinal fault" of translation was to make a reader aware that a work is a translation.[8] Theory focused on the need for and the means to equivalence. As Niranjana explains it, the traditional discourse of translation studies and ethnography was "caught in an idiom of fidelity and betrayal" and became obsessed with oppositions between the faithful and the unfaithful, freedom and slavery, truth and falsehood, the adequate and the inadequate (4, 50). The ultimate oppositions focused on distinctions between the source and the target, the original and the copy, and the notions of authenticity and imitation or purity and corruption. A preoccupation with the undesirability, yet inevitability, of loss was so strong that the idea that something is "lost in translation" became part of "common sense," especially in the mind-set of migrating cultures.

Since "successful" translation rendered the source invisible, symbolically and sometimes literally erasing it, translation, from the perspective of a colonized and translated culture, was always betrayal. As Casteñeda explains, the charge of betrayal began with the experience of a young female translator, Malintzín, also known as La Malinche. A fourteen-year-old Mayan who was selected to translate for the Spaniard Cortés, she became the ultimate symbol of a traitor and whore in patriarchal Mexicano/Chicano culture.[9] Within the norms of classical theory, translations are unsuccessful if they do not blend in or seem natural in their new surroundings. In the trajectory of migrants to a dominant culture, then, translation was equivalent to assimilation (melting into the dominant culture) or at least acculturation (adapting to that culture) and was marked chiefly by a sense of loss or of corruption. Reactions intended to stem the spread of such loss and corruption privileged the "original" and focused on desires to maintain the purity of the source culture.

Meanwhile, ethnography and translation studies, as well as studies of migration, have undergone an internal critique that takes their norms and their ideology in an opposite direction. The translations favored by colonial projects had been responsible for "*fixing* colonized cultures, making them seem static and unchanging." New ethnography, by contrast, emphasizes that translation neither imitates nor reflects; it produces. Niranjana writes that the supposed "purity" of the "original" never existed but was brought into being by translation—by translation practiced as a strategy of containment (3, 54). She argues that continuing notions of fidelity to an "original" have held translation theory back "from thinking through the *force* of a translation" (58, italics added). Her goal is to reclaim the notion of translation and its potential as a strategy of resistance in anticolonial or postcolonial struggle. This kind of translation would disturb and displace cultural truths. The earlier, but long-standing preference for "natural-seeming" translations of supposedly "authentic" texts also effaced the fact that several languages or cultures are superimposed in any "original," or source, language or culture. A "deliberate roughness," by contrast, can resist containment and fixity of meaning while exposing "the instability of the 'original'" and the arbitrariness of what is posited as "natural" (185, 186).

What Niranjana proposes corresponds to a resistant kind of translation long advocated by Lawrence Venuti. If the "cardinal fault" of traditional translation was to make the reader aware of translation, the "basic error" of translation according to Venuti and much recent theory is not allowing the language of translation to be affected by the foreign tongue. As Dingwaney explains, Venuti identifies the long-standing preference for fluency as a "domesticating method." He counters this preference with a "foreignizing method" that allows the alien to interrogate and disrupt accepted ways of life. For this to occur, Venuti insists that the *translation* in a translation must be *visible*.[10] As Mary Lanyoun puts it, a transgressive translation would emphasize the distance between the source and the destination and would make the apparently familiar strange.[11]

Frances Aparicio comes to a similar conclusion when she analyzes the "new English" that characterizes the writing of U.S. Latinos and Latinas. She values the so-called interference of Spanish in English as positive and creative. Her discussion of linguistic *calques* is especially significant for this study. *Calques* are literal translations of colloquial phrases or proverbs and have been associated with uneducated speakers of a new language. Although they have been used to stereotype a Hispanic who is losing his or her mother tongue, Aparicio argues that they may be an original strategy and a vehicle for formulating new images and metaphors. Although these displacements may be read as "funny, surrealist, or absurd" in English, a bicultural and bilingual reader may recognize them as "repetition with a difference."[12] At the same time as the originality and surprise of the *calques* transform and affect English, however, they also encourage a "more distanced re-reading of the original cultural text" and open up the possibility of new expressions in that culture.[13]

In an attempt to define a "theoretical practice for cross-cultural translation," Carol Maier, like these other theorists, associates the "loss" of translation with the attempt to fix one meaning out of many possibilities. But she also suggests that we might expand the unit of translation from words to texts to entire cultures.[14] "Home" has been one of the key units in the cultural translations of anthropology. Like language, ideas about "home" are closely identified with the concept of "roots" and with the notion of "origins" or the "original" text of a culture. As James Clifford observes, the traditional belief was that "dwelling" is the "local ground of collective life" and that "travel [was simply] a supplement."[15] "Home" was strictly "local" and referred to the place and the related practices that were defined within, by, and for the culture. As with the other key terms in translation and diaspora studies, ideas about "home" have also undergone a revolution in anthropology. Clifford claims that traditional ethnography "localized what is actually a regional/national/global nexus," and "homelands" were "kept small, local, and powerless by forces of domination."[16] Ethnographers now emphasize that any culture may be as much a site of travel as of dwelling and that notions of "home" are constituted *through* contact and also through travel and dwelling elsewhere. In terms of translation theory, this revised notion means that the "original," or "source," culture, even its sense of "home," is already heterogeneous and "contaminated" by foreign cultures, perhaps even the "target" cultures into which they are then retranslated. As Duany does, Clifford calls on scholars to examine how cultures travel. Especially significant are the ways that people leave and return home and also how "home" is conceived and lived in relation to practices of coming and going. These developments in ethnology, together with new emphases in translation theory, suggest that customary distinctions between sending and receiving cultures, between the source and the target, between the "original" or "authentic" experience and the "translated" one, will be blurred.

Changes similar to those in ethnology and translation studies have led diaspora studies beyond long-standing concerns with assimilation and toward a focus on transformation and transculturation.[17] These developments have produced a new vocabulary and a way to reframe issues that arise in spaces—even those associated with "home"—where one culture encounters and intersects with another. These may be seen as "spaces of translation" that are both disquieting and fertile.[18]

When Marisol criticizes El Building as a bizarre facsimile of homes on the Island, she echoes a classical refrain in which British imperialists, for example, berated Indians for not being true to their "origins"—meaning not true to the fixed, "pure" models in which British translators sought to contain that culture.[19] It is not surprising that Marisol would mimic such gestures. For one thing, having left the Island at age two and having been schooled apart from other Puerto Rican immigrants, in a system that treated Puerto Rico as a colony that needed to be "Americanized," she is a product of a colonizing education. For another, her father encourages her to replace Puerto Rican habits with American ones. Finally, her own experiences with linguistic translation are distressing ones.

Like many children of immigrants who do not learn English, Marisol becomes her mother's interpreter with the "world" outside the Puerto Rican community and she is embarrassed by her role. These acts of translation usually occur under conditions of conflict and stress: for example, when her father is incommunicado during the Cuban Missile Crisis or after El Building is destroyed in a fire. The authorities with whom she must interact on an unequal footing make no effort to hide their prejudices during the latter encounter. When the family requests assistance from the Red Cross, Mrs. Pink is pleased that an "eyesore" has been removed and assumes that the fire was caused during a "wild party" with "dozens of people drinking and carrying on *like they do*" in such places (274, 275, italics added).

But if Marisol the adolescent translator is susceptible to traditional thinking about translation, Marisol the narrator after the fact engages in more complex acts of translation that correspond closely with recent concepts. The translations she performs in the novel illustrate and are illuminated by recent theory.

What Marisol translates is the story of her uncle Guzmán and the town in which he and her parents were raised. In a 1994 interview, Ortiz Cofer responds to reviewer comments that the first half of the novel, the section that is set in Salud before Marisol's birth, "sounds like translation." Ortiz Cofer concedes that, as she composed the novel, the characters in Salud spoke to her in Spanish and that she translated what she heard into English. She also explains that she wanted to retain the impression that these were Spanish-speaking people, with a different syntax, even as she translated their story for an English-speaking audience.[20] In the novel, Marisol the narrator performs a similar linguistic translation. Much of the story that she heard as a child and as an adolescent was told in Spanish. For example, when Guzmán updates his adventures for Ramona at her New Jersey kitchen table, he speaks in Spanish (191). Ill in bed, Marisol overhears much of the story and dreams the rest. When she then translates that story into the narrative of the novel, she translates from Spanish to English. But she also translates the story in another way, in a way of translating that Ortiz Cofer and all the storytellers that she writes about use.

When Ramona told the story of Guzmán and Salud in ongoing installments, there were different versions of the story, "each one suited to its audience" (177). The telling of Guzmán's story, then, follows the pattern of all the stories that Ortiz Cofer and her foremothers have been telling. *En casa*, her Mamá, like the generations of women who preceded her, told certain *cuentos*, or morality and cautionary tales. As they repeated these stories, they changed the telling to suit the circumstances of the listeners who were their intended audience. As Ortiz Cofer explains, many of these stories were based on even earlier tales brought to the Island by Spaniards, who themselves had translated Greek and Roman myths; the women then "modified [them again] in clever ways to fit changing times" (*SD*, 76). Ortiz Cofer continues this process with her own translations of these stories—for example, in a collection of essays on "becoming a writer," which she titled *Woman in Front of the Sun*. In "The Woman Who Slept with One Eye Open," she returns to the tales of María Sabida and María La Loca in order to re-vision the roles of women in and out of the home.[21] Similarly, when Marisol listens to the adult stories in El Building, she assigns Guzmán the role of Zorro in her imagination; and when she narrates *The Line of the Sun*, she fills in the silences and omissions of those stories and modifies Guzmán's story to serve her own purposes—to teach herself "how to rebel, how to prepare for escape, how not to fear anything or anyone" (233). Both Ortiz Cofer and Marisol the narrator do what Carol Maier says that successful translators should do: they render translation visible by recording the choices made in translation rather than just the result.[22]

In the narrative Marisol retells, all the homes created by Puerto Ricans, like the stories told within them, are shown to be products of translation. And they are all products of one or another fantasy. In this context, El Building's strangeness in the New Jersey landscape and its status as "fantasy" or "illusion" make it a "successful" translation. It allows the reader to question the naturalness of the middle-class dream home, where, from Ramona's perspective, each house is an "island" devoid of community (285). And even as it exposes the illusory nature of the United States imagined as a paradise of snow and freedom, it also allows the narrator to uncover and describe the fantastic and translated nature of the Island "home" that has been remembered as paradise.

Even when Marisol feels deprived of the Island, she recognizes that the adults in El Building are describing an "illusory Eden" whose poverty and flaws have been romanticized (174). What she does not recognize at the time is the illusory basis of her own longing. She is almost fifteen but restricted in her movements by her parents' fears and her own difference from those around her. She imagines that on the Island she would be more free and seen as an adult—"respected as a woman of marriageable age" (222). When she retells the stories of her uncle and her mother, however, she reveals the irony of her assumptions. For Guzmán and Ramona, during their own adolescence, had felt imprisoned by the Island's judgments and expectations and had each dreamed of the United States as a place of escape from the Island's vigilance.

The Salud that Marisol describes in the first half of the novel is more a place of gossip, morals, and survival than of romance. The neighborhood is El Polvorín—translated by Marisol as "Dustdevil" but also and appropriately signifying a "powder keg." It exists in the "drab, dirty hamlet" of Salud, a vindictive small town that feeds on rumor and scandal. At its worst, it is a "snake's nest" (102). Her uncle Guzmán, who is the focus of much scandal, imagines that an earlier paradise was destroyed by the Spanish when they invaded the Taíno home. Ironically, one of the places that seems to retain some of the freedom and abundance that he yearns for is an experimental farm, also known as the Granja. Marisol the narrator then corrects this impression, admitting that he is actually on the border between this farm and a "no-man's-land where vegetation was allowed to grow freely as a natural boundary" (134). The remnants of this earthly paradise now exist mainly in "no-man's-land."

Looking at Salud as she imagines Guzmán would have, Marisol the narrator also sees Puerto Rican homes in ways that accord with the concepts of recent translation theory. Despite their proximity to each other on a hill near the church, the homes of Guzmán's neighborhood reveal that Island homes are themselves varied. Guzmán observes the sky-blue house that his Papá Pepe built; the house of Doña Lula, who is "an impeccable housekeeper" but harbors whores in the attic; the house of Doña Julia, who wears only mourning clothes and encourages witch-hunts against those who violate the pueblo's conventions; the house of Franco El Loco, crippled in a fight sparked by jealousy, who lives locked (from the outside) in a dirt cellar; the house of Doña Melina, a scorned wife who "wrought a different life for herself" and became the first female superintendent of schools; the house of Doña Saturnino, an aging matriarch who lives with her unmarried children and turned away all suitors for her daughter, Rosario; and the house of Doña Amparo, a shrewd businesswoman who also owns the domino hall, where cockfights are held, and who never wears dark colors but prefers "imported costumes" like "a Hawaiian print muumuu" or "a fringed skirt of American Indian design" (106–131).

As Doña Amparo's costumes suggest, these "Island" homes also reveal the "superimposition of languages and cultures" that characterize any "home," and they also serve to blur the distinction between native and foreign, original and copy, sending and receiving, or source and target cultures. This presence of the "foreign" (including the "American") in the "original" is perhaps more clearly recognized in the essays Ortiz Cofer includes in *Silent Dancing*. In her bedroom, Mamá Cielo, Ortiz Cofer's grandmother, took "care of the obligatory religious decoration with a crucifix" over the bed. But Mamá then elected to cover the other walls with objects from the States, objects received from her children: "*Los Nueva Yores* were represented by, among other things, a postcard of Niagara Falls from her son Hernán, postmarked, Buffalo,

NY. In a conspicuous gold frame hung a large color photograph of her daughter Nena, her husband, and their five children at the entrance to Disneyland in California. . . . [And] each year more items were added as the family grew and dispersed" (25). And because "every object in the room had a story attached to it, a *cuento* which Mamá would bestow on anyone who received the privilege of a day alone with her," the significance is not just that objects from the States entered the home but also that stories from the States entered the repertoire of Puerto Rican *cuentos* told on the Island.

The presence of the "foreign" in the "original" is also visible in *The Line of the Sun.* The house of the Saturninos, for example, illustrates that Island homes may even possess a certain "tradition" of translation. The Saturninos come from an aristocratic Spanish line and their old, elegant, dark house has windows "in the French style"—"long as doors and latticed" (115). What the novel also reveals, however, is the extent to which the Island attempts to reject the "interference" of the "foreign." This rejection of the "inauthentic" by Island residents is represented by the experience of the family of Marisol's father. Raphael Santacruz, whose ancestors came to Puerto Rico from Spain, is fair-skinned and blond. Judged to be as "fair as a gringo," he stands out everywhere he goes in Salud, and his family receives few visitors (57). They live in a caretaker's cottage at the gates of an American estate—an experimental farm. Their home is "built to the American's specifications" with indoor plumbing and mosquito screens and beautiful mahogany furniture that seems "out of place" to Guzmán when he visits the house. Just as Marisol believes that what she thinks of as Island décor does not "belong" in El Building, some residents of Salud believe the Santacruz furnishings do not "belong" on the Island. Each belief represents a refusal of translation and an attempt to fix ideas about what is culturally appropriate by insisting on what is conventional or dominant at a particular time—rejecting past and potentially emergent forms of identity and home-places.

The home of Rosa, La Cabra, however, may be the most significant for understanding the trajectory of translation in the novel. When Guzmán tells Marisol about Rosa, he speaks "as if she were the embodiment of all that was beautiful, strange, and tempting about his homeland" (220). Like its owner, her house is the one that Guzmán and Raphael associate most closely with the beauty of a quintessential island paradise.

In Marisol's narration, it is the place where "the beauty of the island [is] all concentrated into a few acres with river, valley, hill, and turquoise-blue sky" (91). Here is truly the romantic fantasy of the Island paradise that turns the adults in El Building "misty and lyrical" (174). In part, Rosa's home is significant because it, like the apartment of Elba La Negra in El Building, is also a "spiritual center." The district's most sought-after medium, Rosa challenges the dominance of the church in the pueblo. While the church "sits like a great white hen" on the Holy Hill and spreads its "marble wings over the town," Rosa's house, with a white boat under its stilts, looks "like a brown hen sitting on an egg" the first time Guzmán sees it (23, 46). While the houses of Salud surround the Holy Hill, however, they are separated from Rosa's house by the Red River and three miles of an overgrown coffee plantation supposedly established on Taíno burial grounds.

The women of the community visit Rosa for "almost any female trouble, including jealousy and infertility." But the "evil tongues" of Salud rechristen her La Cabra, which Marisol translates literally as "she-goat"; on the Island, however, the epithet is part of an expression that would also imply that Rosa is crazy. The churchwomen eventually drive Rosa away. In part, Rosa's house offends the likes of Doñas Julia, Tina, Corina, and other churchwomen because it is an impure place where Rosa sees men of the community with "discretion" (20). But it also violates the conventions of "Salud"—or, to translate, it threatens the community's sense of its own "health"—because it "represents a new way" (37).

Rosa has inherited this house from her mother, Doña Lupe. She, like Mamá Cielo, changes what she inherits. Mamá Cielo, for example, distrusts her domineering mother-in-law and banishes a rocking chair that she inherits from the living room to the porch. The new ways that Rosa introduces, however, are "foreign" and "originate" in the United States. Her Island home, the place that concentrates the beauty of the Island, is a translated home that strongly blurs the distinctions between the Island as source and the States as target. So Rosa, like La Malinche, is condemned as both traitor and whore.

To the town that was founded on a miracle, Rosa brings such "miracles" from New York as a flashlight and a TV that plays the American national anthem when it goes off air at night. The *centro* where she works her causes also differs from the setting of the *Mesa Blanca* practiced by Papá Pepe; for the spiritism that she brought to the Island was learned in New York from El Indio and is denounced by Papá Pepe. When churchwomen finally come to run Rosa out of town, she decides to give them something to remember, burning frankincense in every room and lighting a candle that burns with intoxicating fumes. When obstacles become overwhelming, she tells herself, "one could choose to go down in flames" (95). The encounter is less spectacular than she predicts, but the symbolic fire that she prepares prefigures the literal fire that will destroy Elba, her *centro,* and El Building in one sweep.

Unlike the single-family homes in Salud, El Building is obviously more than a single dwelling. It concentrates house, barrio, and retranslations of Rosa's *centro* all in one location. It is also a place that suits Guzmán so well that it seems to be his "natural environment" to Marisol. Like the *calques* that Aparicio examines, the translations of Puerto Rican culture produced in El Building may appear odd in a monolingual setting. But bilingual, bicultural "insiders" can recognize the subversive and creative potential of *calques* as a form of translation.[23] Similarly, readers conversant with a history of translation can recognize the creative and subversive potential of El Building and particularly its *centro*. For the form of spiritism practiced in Elba's apartment is a quintessential product of translation that makes visible the superimposition of cultures. Elba is a *Santera*, who combines "Catholic symbol and ritual with ancient African rites" (238). Santa Bárbara, the patron saint of both Elba and Rosa and a favorite guide among young women, is widely known to be Changó, the spirit of fire, in her African manifestation (261). In the trajectory of the novel, Elba's *centro* in El Building is a translation of Rosa's *centro* in Salud, which is itself a translation of spiritual centers first encountered in New York. These home-based *centros* of the novel illustrate the circular migrations of the Puerto Rican culture, the circular process of translation and retranslation, and the blurring between sending and receiving cultures. Yet these spiritual centers travel with a difference. Ortiz Cofer explains in her interview with Ocasio: *espiritismo* and *santería* in the States have a different role than that of the traditional Island-based *santería*. In the States, they serve the purposes of a psychologist, and people go to them for "comfort and support" and also "to feel some connection with and some control over a world that was extremely confusing" (737). When El Building is destroyed in the fire that begins during a spiritual meeting held by the women, the uses of this spiritual translation—the comfort, support, and fantasy of control—are also destroyed.

A comment from Santiago, one of the male residents, illustrates the ties between Marisol's adolescent judgments of the building and of the spiritual center. When he speaks with Marisol while preparations for the meeting are under way, he warns that "here in America their hocus-pocus only complicates things." While belief in "invisible friends" might seem reasonable on the Island, he advises, it creates problems if the purpose of the meeting has to be explained to "crewcut *policía*" (246). As attached as Marisol is to Elba, her adolescent judgment of spiritism is ultimately the same as her judgment of El Building; the fact that its attempt at control was vanquished is evidence that it is "pathetic" and "absurd" (268). What seems lost in Marisol's understanding is the fact that Santiago's judgment was a gendered criticism of the ways of Island women, who are holding the meeting to counter the men's plans to hold a *huelga,* a strike, because of increasing layoffs at Patterson's factories.

By the end of the novel, the potential of translation has been contained in the States and also on the Island. For Rosa's house has been inherited by her daughter Sarita, a product of convent education on the Island. A "shrew" and a "moralizer," she is the new self-appointed "guardian of Salud's morals." She is also married to Guzmán, whose youthful rebellion has also been quelled. The concentrated beauty that once marked Rosa's translated home has been returned to a state of "purity" that is now odious to Mamá Cielo. The "roughness" and "out-of-place" quality that characterize potentially transgressive translations have been eliminated on both sides of the big pond that separates the Island from the States. "Foreign" differences that threaten "native" culture have been erased.

With the return of Rosa's house to a state of purity and the destruction of El Building, the translations of "woman" and "mother" that Ortiz Cofer herself struggles over with her own mother, and that are intimately tied to translations of "home," are also put on hold. The struggle against containment and a fixing of culture is left to continue in another time and space.

In her reflections on the events of the narrative, Marisol underplays the extent to which her own actions and attitudes were responsible for the destruction of the building she found so embarrassing and absurd.

After all, it was her insistence on opening the windows during the meeting that pulled the smoke from the room and began the chaos that ended in conflagration (264–266). But Marisol, like Guzmán and Ramona and Raphael before her, does not want to be contained by the conventions of Salud, and she is translating the story of Guzmán to support her own attempts at freedom. Perhaps the narrative that then brings El Building back to life and repositions it in the history of Puerto Rican home-making is also an indirect attempt to mourn its loss, to compensate for its destruction, and to recover some of its potential for translating concepts like woman, mother, and home, both in the States and on the Island. Despite Marisol's reservations, the narrative that prompts readers to mourn the loss of El Building to flames, and of Rosa's house to the guardians of purity, seems to align itself with diasporic attempts to recuperate "home" as a space of translation.

NOTES

1. Judith Ortiz Cofer, *The Line of the Sun* (Athens, GA: University of Georgia Press, 1989), 207. Hereafter cited in text.

2. Judith Ortiz Cofer, *Silent Dancing: A Partial Remembrance of a Puerto Rican Childhood* (Houston: Arte Público Press, 1991), 17. Hereafter cited in text; whenever it is unclear which text is being cited, the abbreviation *SD* will be included in the parenthetical citation.

3. Jorge Duany, *The Puerto Rican Nation on the Move: Identities on the Island and in the United States* (Chapel Hill: University of North Carolina Press, 2002), 135, 184. Hereafter cited in text.

4. Judith Ortiz Cofer, "The Infinite Variety of the Puerto Rican Reality: Interview with Raphael Ocasio," *Callaloo* 17, no. 3 (Summer 1994): 735–736.

5. Martha J. Cutter, *Lost and Found in Translation: Contemporary Ethnic American Writing and the Politics of Language Diversity* (Chapel Hill: University of North Carolina Press, 2005), 3. Although Cutter focuses primarily on an analysis of linguistic translations, her conclusions refer broadly to various types of cultural translation, including the translation of ideas, values, and customs; because of this, they serve as a useful point of comparison for the cultural translations of home and home-making in Ortiz Cofer's work.

6. Ibid., 6–7.

7. Tejaswini Niranjana, *Siting Translation: History, Post-structuralism, and the Colonial Context* (Berkeley and Los Angeles: University of California Press, 1992), 68. Hereafter cited in text.

8. Eugene Nida, "Principles of Correspondence," in *The Translation Studies Reader*, ed. Lawrence Venuti (New York: Routledge, 2000), 126–140.

9. Antonia I. Casteñeda, "Language and Other Lethal Weapons: Cultural Politics and the Rites of Children as Translators of Culture," in *Mapping Multiculturalism*, ed. Avery F. Gordon and Christopher Newfield (Minneapolis: University of Minnesota Press, 1996), 210.

10. Anuradha Dingwaney, "Introduction: Translating 'Third World' Cultures," in *Between Languages and Cultures: Translation and Cross-Cultural Texts*, ed. Anuradha Dingwaney and Carol Maier (Pittsburgh: University of Pittsburgh Press, 1995), 7, 9.

11. Mary N. Lanyoun, "Translation, Cultural Transgression and Tribute, and Leaden Feet," in Dingwaney and Maier, *Between Languages*, 269, 270.

12. Frances R. Aparicio, "On Sub-versive Signifiers: Tropicalizing Language in the United States," in *Tropicalizations: Transcultural Representations of Latinidad*, ed. Frances R. Aparicio and Susana Chávez-Silverman (Hanover, NH: University Press of New England, 1997), 204.

13. Ibid., 206.

14. Carol Maier, "Toward a Theoretical Practice for Cross-Cultural Translation," in Dingwaney and Maier, *Between Languages*, 21–38.

15. James Clifford, *Routes: Travel and Translation in the Late Twentieth Century* (Cambridge, MA: Harvard University Press, 1997), 2.

16. Ibid., 28, 36.

17. Jorge Duany, for example, contends that Puerto Ricans in the United States tend to "transplant" their culture; they "selectively appropriate the discursive practices traditionally associated with being Puerto Rican" rather than assimilating (Duany, *Puerto Rican Nation on the Move*, 186). Juan Flores also insists that the transformation of Puerto Rican culture in the United States is not assimilation; it leads neither to "accommodation nor to 'cultural genocide.'" What is "mistaken for assimilation" exemplifies the partial "growing-together" that is characteristic of transculturation and interaction. See Juan Flores, "Qué assimilated, brother, yo soy asimilao," in *Divided Borders: Essays on Puerto Rican Identity*, by Juan Flores (Houston: Arte Público Press, 1993), 186, 192.

18. Dingwaney, "Introduction," 8.

19. Niranjana, *Siting Translation*, 19–20.

20. Judith Ortiz Cofer, "The Infinite Variety of the Puerto Rican Reality," 734.

21. Judith Ortiz Cofer, *Woman in Front of the Sun: On Becoming a Writer* (Athens, GA: University of Georgia Press, 2000), 73–90.

22. Maier, "Toward a Theoretical Practice for Cross-Cultural Translation," 21.

23. Aparicio, "On Sub-versive Signifiers," 204.

BIBLIOGRAPHY

Aparicio, Frances R. "On Sub-versive Signifiers: Tropicalizing Language in the United States." In *Tropicalizations: Transcultural Representations of Latinidad*, ed. Frances R. Aparicio and Susana Chávez-Silverman, 194–212. Hanover, NH: University Press of New England, 1997.

Casteñeda, Antonia I. "Language and Other Lethal Weapons: Cultural Politics and the Rites of Children as Translators of Culture." In *Mapping Multiculturalism*, ed. Avery F. Gordon and Christopher Newfield, 201–214. Minneapolis: University of Minnesota Press, 1996.

Clifford, James. *Routes: Travel and Translation in the Late Twentieth Century*. Cambridge, MA: Harvard University Press, 1997.

Cutter, Martha J. *Lost and Found in Translation: Contemporary Ethnic American Writing and the Politics of Language Diversity*. Chapel Hill: University of North Carolina Press, 2005.

Dingwaney, Anuradha. "Introduction: Translating 'Third World' Cultures." In *Between Languages and Cultures: Translation and Cross-Cultural Texts*, ed. Anuradha Dingwaney and Carol Maier, 3–15. Pittsburgh: University of Pittsburgh Press, 1995.

Dingwaney, Anuradha, and Carol Maier, eds. *Between Languages and Cultures: Translation and Cross-Cultural Texts*. Pittsburgh: University of Pittsburgh Press, 1995.

Duany, Jorge. *The Puerto Rican Nation on the Move: Identities on the Island and in the United States*. Chapel Hill: University of North Carolina Press, 2002.

Flores, Juan. "Qué assimilated, brother, yo soy asimilao": The Structuring of Puerto Rican Identity." In *Divided Borders: Essays on Puerto Rican Identity,* by Juan Flores, 182–195. Houston: Arte Público Press, 1993.

Layoun, Mary N. "Translation, Cultural Transgression and Tribute, and Leaden Feet." In *Between Languages and Cultures: Translation and Cross-Cultural Texts*, ed. Anuradha Dingwaney and Carol Maier, 267–289. Pittsburgh: University of Pittsburgh Press, 1995.

Maier, Carol. "Toward a Theoretical Practice for Cross-Cultural Translation." In *Between Languages and Cultures: Translation and Cross-Cultural Texts*, ed. Anuradha Dingwaney and Carol Maier, 21–38. Pittsburgh: University of Pittsburgh Press, 1995.

Nida, Eugene. "Principles of Correspondence." In *The Translation Studies Reader*, ed. Lawrence Venuti, 126–140. New York: Routledge, 2000.

Niranjana, Tejaswini. *Siting Translation: History, Post-structuralism, and the Colonial Context*. Berkeley and Los Angeles: University of California Press, 1992.

Ortiz Cofer, Judith. "The Infinite Variety of the Puerto Rican Reality: Interview with Raphael Ocasio." *Callaloo* 17, no. 3 (Summer 1994): 730–742.

———. *The Line of the Sun*. Athens, GA: University of Georgia Press, 1989.

———. *Silent Dancing: A Partial Remembrance of a Puerto Rican Childhood*. 1990. Houston: Arte Público Press, 1991.

———. *Woman in Front of the Sun: On Becoming a Writer*. Athens, GA: University of Georgia Press, 2000.

Venuti, Lawrence, ed. *The Translation Studies Reader*. New York: Routledge, 2000.

13 GETTING THERE AND BACK

The Road, the Journey, and Home in Nuyorican Diaspora Literature

SOLIMAR OTERO

The experiences of home, journey, and resettlement are perpetual tropes for understanding the affinities that shape cultural production in diasporic communities. Between Nuyorican and Yoruba diasporas in the Americas, these tropes are shared on a "real" historical and cultural basis through the legacy of colonialism and slavery in the Caribbean and the United States. The literary scapes of the neighborhood/*barrio*, the marketplace/*bodega*, and the religious storefront/*botánica* frame how I present Nuyorican tendencies in constructing, negotiating, and ritualizing diasporic identity and memory. Nuyorican diaspora literature provides a rich tapestry that remembers, rebuilds, and dreams home from both Caribbean and Yoruba shores.

The Journey

Before discussing the neighborhood, I want to address Yoruba and Nuyorican literary descriptions of diaspora. Yoruba and Nuyorican concepts of the road, the journey, and the neighborhood are central tropes for understanding the affinities that shape public space for these communities. These shared stylistic tendencies, or aesthetics, are based on historically shared diasporas in the Americas and in Africa, and the descendants of Africa—as Nuyoricans and as African Americans—have written about living and working together in these contested domains.[1]

In Yoruba writing about home and memory, there is a connection between the intimate familiarity of the home compound, the *ode*, and the external wonders of the road, the *ona*. These concepts create two foundational motifs for Yoruba literature, as they stem from a Yoruba "aesthetic epistemology."[2] The *ode* is a compound where the extended family and community live together. The world of the *ode* includes friends, rivals, neighbors, and tenants. In an *ode*, personal politics and differential social networks combine with group living, making these sites interesting and rife with human drama. The road, the *ona,* extends out from the *ode*, from the living-compound gates out into the world.

The journey, *iranjo*, to the world outside the *ode* includes the potential for wonder, opportunity, and danger. Extraordinary and strange people and beings are often found along the *ona*, and crossroads and places near the *igbo* (forest) are significant focal points of encounter. Indeed, ports and crossroads are spaces in diasporic literature where destinations meet and converge. In diasporic literature, these spaces of encounter meet multiple and overlapping needs: as portable homes, moving marketplaces, and shifting spiritual centers. Below, I will explore how Wole Soyinka and Bernardo Vega provide two lucid descriptions of points of departure and entry for the journey from home onto the road beyond.

Contemporary diasporic Yoruba memoir and fiction focus on how physical and metaphysical wandering navigates childhood. The foray onto the road becomes a central motif in how an emerging self is remembered, related, and constructed. In an imaginative and gripping way, Soyinka's *Aké: The Years of Childhood* provides a detailed account of a young Soyinka embarking on "the road":

> Simply by following the rush of feet, I knew where to go whenever the sounds carried into the house of Aké. . . .
>
> I followed the group of dancers from the road which went past the cenotaph, behind the church, then disappeared in the direction, Joseph said, of the palace. . . .
>
> We marched [past] the bookshop and I felt vindicated. The frontage was exactly where I had gauged it while seated on Joseph's shoulder. But then the

> curious thing happened: after the bookseller's, the wall rolled away into a different area I had never seen before. . . . It upset my previous relationship between the parsonage and Aké. . . .
>
> There was a market before we got to Ibara. There, women were waiting by the road, more were flocking from their stalls by the time we got there. Their stalls stretched endlessly from the right side of the road, goods piled up on low stools or on specially laid trestles. . . .
>
> The butcher was as magical in his own field as the policeman who performed the juggling with his mace.[3]

Soyinka's child keeps moving along the road, marching into market stalls, meeting strangers, getting lost. He eventually makes it back home to Aké, where he is received with both joy and relief by the *ode*.[4] It is a significant detail that Soyinka's family does not originally hail from Aké's part of Yorubaland. Rather, his father is an Ijebu Yoruba from the Isara region; some of his mother's people are Brazilian and some come from Igbe Province near Abeokuta.[5] Thus, it is understood that the "core" community of the Aké compound is infused with arrivals and departures that converge around the school and parish to settle. It is a quintessential diasporic, migrant community in an African, Yoruba context.

It is important to remember that Yoruba writers like Soyinka focus on the *experiential* quality of knowledge. In the example above, young Soyinka takes his caretaker Joseph's word about the road leading to the Oba's palace, as just that, a description. He embarks, at the peril of getting lost or being punished, on his own investigation of the world not only outside but flowing out from the compound of Aké. Soyinka's existential sense of awe, which he encounters by wandering on the road, into the world, *firsthand*, is echoed by Bernando Vega in his *Memoirs of Bernardo Vega*.[6]

The journey is a major component of "writing" the diaspora, of the spreading of seed, as the Greek roots of the word "diaspora" suggest.[7] The journey has both individual and communal aspects to its experiential quality. These aspects merge in Yoruba and Nuyorican writing about the journey from "home" to the road. In *Memoirs of Bernardo Vega*, we get some of the earliest impressions of the journey from Puerto Rico to New York City penned for this diaspora. This is how Vega remembers leaving home and embarking on his journey:

> Early in the morning of August 2, 1916 I took leave of Cayey. I got on the bus at the Plaza and sat down, squeezed in between passengers and suitcases. . . . I hadn't the slightest idea what fate awaited me. . . . Sunrise of the first day and the passengers were already acting as though they belonged to one family. It was not long before we came to know each other's life stories. The topic of conversation, of course, was what lay ahead: life in New York. . . . All of us were building our own little castles in the sky.[8]

Here, Vega's individual journey transforms into a community in the making. The process of moving out and away from one's home creates a set of individuals faced with the same dilemma who decide to share the experience through stories. This retelling, recontextualizing of one's place, vis-à-vis home, is part of the portable skills most diasporas encourage. People on the move situate themselves in terms of time and place. Thus, diaspora is what people carry—ways of connecting, relating the inside of stories, outside of individuals. For Vega and Soyinka, the journey from home is relational; home behaves as a frame of reference that *allows* them to move beyond the gates of Aké or the town of Cayey.

The marketplace is a vital "pit stop" in making these diasporas livable as "portable homes" for both Soyinka and Vega. Vega goes on to describe his first impressions of arriving in New York.[9] Dismal and gray, Vega is not impressed by his surroundings. However, there emerges in his *Memoirs* a growing sense of identification and wonder for the place known as the "barrio." As with Soyinka's memoir, the literal marketplace becomes the place where different communities merge with each other. Different diasporas, strange and familiar people and objects, and activity all abound in most major open-air markets. The marketplace described in *Aké* is no exception. Neither is Vega's memory of the market under the elevated train in the neighborhood:

> On Park Avenue there was an open-air market where you could buy things at low prices. Early in the morning the vendors would set up their stands on the sidewalk under the elevated train, and in the afternoon they would pack up their goods for the night.
>
> . . . On makeshift shelves and display cases, hanging from walls and wire hangers, all kinds of goods were on display. You could buy everything from the simplest darning needle to a complete trousseau.[10]

For our two travelers thus far, the marketplace is a place to stop, look, and listen. It is a signpost of one of many arrivals in descriptions of diaspora in writing about the journey. The marketplace is a place of danger and of respite, a place of wonder, and a place that is also familiar. It is a place full of possibilities where many disparate peoples and objects meet. Marketplaces also are found where main roads meet, where they are easy to get to. Under the El, at a crossroads, near a dock. For Puerto Rican and Yoruba diaspora writers remembering their journeys away from home, the marketplace is a significant gateway to new experiences and new lives.

Movement away from home, even when forced to a certain extent by circumstances beyond one's control, nevertheless involves a force of *voluntad*, force of volition. A person moves, and with this movement we discover ourselves, others, and the world. The journey itself is the ontological rite of passage, the way that process becomes being on an individual and communal level. As Soyinka and Vega write from a diasporic place of remembering youth and the journey from home, they are attuned to the significance of movement in making home. A sense of expectancy and the willingness to assimilate new experiences into one's ontological repertoire are part of the "portable" home that individuals creating literature about diasporic journeys share. That they later revisit these moments on the road, by writing about the wonder and expectation of the journey, helps to provide both personal and communal road maps for other sojourners.

The Portable Home

Nuyorican writing about the barrio describes the scapes of diaspora as contested domains.[11] The battle over symbolic terrain in the public sphere is waged by many immigrant and exile groups settling in "new" territories. In second or third diasporas and relocations, the experience of remembering and writing "the journey" from "home" textually shapes new environs into livable habitats by creating and narrating history as memory. This means reimagining and building literary spaces in familiar ways. Nuyorican authors' depictions of immigrant and second-generation diasporic experiences of the barrio are ripe with images from the "streets" and "home" that merge on physical, cultural, and historical terrains.

Recently, authors have been locating "Latino" and Puerto Rican diasporas in writing and cultural production that account for Boricuas' multiple "centers." Sánchez González's *Boricua Literature* and Flores's *From Bomba to Hip-Hop* are works that grapple with the layered and fluctuating identity of Puerto Ricans in the United States.[12] A recurring theme is that Nuyorican writers have been prolific in situating themselves, especially as poets, since the 1960s civil rights era as a group with a political stake and a self-awareness, creating a kind of "mass" cultural production. Willie Perdomo's poetry in *Where a Nickel Costs a Dime*, for example, poignantly celebrates an "urban diasporic" Nuyoricanness.

In *Magical Urbanism*, Davis charts the transformation of U.S. cities into ports of entry for a transnational, maybe oversimplified, "Latino" nation.[13] "Magical urbanism," within the milieu of the United States, becomes a trope that pinpoints the unbounded, conceptual, and shifting nature of the multinational Latino presence in a city's landscape. These diasporic cities become as textually mutable and porous as "Latino," especially as Nuyorican authors, activists, and poets reinvent cosmopolitanism in literal and symbolic ways. By "cosmopolitanism," I mean a non-Eurocentric notion of itinerant urbanity that is connected to a Yoruba aesthetic of decorum aptly described by cultural theorists writing about Yoruba movement, knowledge, cultural openness, and sophistication.[14]

The physical demarcation of Nuyorican space in an urban environment is noted in writing that describes the flourishing of mural art, bilingual advertisements, and bodegas along New York's city streets. For example, Vega takes us back to the late 1920s, to a retrievable Puerto Rican imaginary, a barrio remembered when he writes,

> By now [1927–1930] the Puerto Rican neighborhood extended from Lexington Avenue between 96th and 107th streets over to the beginning of the Italian section on First Avenue. Through this entire area, life was very much like it was back home. Following the example set by the *tabaqueros*, whites and blacks lived together in harmony. There were many Hispanic *bodegas*, barbershops, and butchers. Branches of green plantains hung in store windows, and the sidewalks were lined with food and vegetable stands. In the stores and in the streets all you heard was Spanish.[15]

Describing the barrio requires the use of the language of memory, the ability to imagine the streets onto the page. In diasporic fashion, Nuyorican authors move within multiple temporal, cultural, and linguistic codes.

The concept of the marketplace as detailed above is encapsulated by Vega's bodega. Literally, the marketplace is moved indoors and becomes a domesticated space for consumption and the gathering of folk. Vega's remembered barrio and bodega in Spanish Harlem operate to give the reader a sense of how variegated street life spills in and out of enclosed spaces in marked racial, cultural, and linguistic ways. The politics of the street marks the page in liberated semiotic codes that seem almost Bakhtinian in their carnivalesque populism.[16] Here, memory and description are also framed by a border that references this kind of living as being like "home." Thus, Vega ties nostalgia and insurgency in a subtle and characteristically diasporic manner in writing about his culture as portable, political, and progressive.

Writing about the bodega and the barrio in Nuyorican fiction is a legacy that begins with Vega but is also manifested in recent works, such as Quiñonez's *Bodega Dreams*. Here, we must note that the idea of a "Nuyorican" identity is constructed against any easy essentialism based on biological "blood count" or a restrictive form of Puerto Rican nationalism. As has usually been the case for those speaking across *latinidades*, or modes of being "Latino," there is a tendency to see, accept, and incorporate national differences in reference to historical and political affiliations vis-à-vis the larger project of establishing social agency for people of Latin American heritage, especially in the context of North America.[17] Though Quiñonez is half Ecuadorian and half Puerto Rican in his ancestry, his depiction of Spanish Harlem as Nuyorican also necessarily includes the transnationality inherent in the construction of incorporative identities stemming from the very world of the barrio. A good example of how Quiñonez describes the mitigation of these international "Latino" identities comes from *Bodega Dreams*. In the two passages related below, our narrator, Julio, aka "Chino," speaks about growing up in Spanish Harlem as a "halfsie" (half Puerto Rican and half Ecuadorian), and also earning a "rep" for it: "And since I was born with high, flat cheekbones, almond-shaped eyes, and straight black hair (courtesy of my father's Ecuadorian side of the family), and because kung fu movies were very popular at the time, when I was in eighth grade, I was tagged Chino."[18] Later in the text, Chino speaks to Willie Bodega:

"I'm only half Rican, my father is from Ecuador," I felt compelled to tell Bodega.

"So what? You Spanish, this is your neighborhood. You grew up here, got beat up here, and I hope beat someone up too. Sapito tells me you used to paint R.I.P.'s?"

"Yeah, so?"

"Thass [*sic*] good, bro. People remember you as someone who tried to make the neighborhood a better place."[19]

Here we learn that Julio "earns" the name Chino for being different from the "other" Puerto Ricans at his school in Spanish Harlem. The name "Chino" may be exoticizing, the name literally meaning "Chinese" in Spanish. However, he receives this name as a sign of belonging to the barrio and his cohort group. As Quiñonez deftly explains in the rest of this introductory chapter to *Bodega Dreams*, naming in Spanish Harlem is an important way of both incorporating members into the community and also recognizing the unique characteristics of certain individuals.[20] The fact that it does not matter that Julio is a "halfsie" becomes a moot point when we begin to realize that a strict biological and national essentialism cannot operate in a cultural context that is based on the more open social epistemologies that are set in place in Spanish Harlem.

In the second quotation from *Bodega Dreams* above, we see how Willie Bodega responds to Chino's confession about being "only half Rican." After his response "So what?" Bodega goes on to explain that, in his eyes at least, there is some level of shared identity through the common cultural marker of "Spanish" (used colloquially in the northeastern United States to refer to Latinos of all nationalities). But, more importantly, it is Chino's contribution to the neighborhood that "counts" toward his "Nuyorican" identity. The public artwork of his R.I.P. murals commemorating the dead of the barrio, and his own upbringing, make him part of Spanish Harlem. That the community will recognize his belonging to the space of the barrio, regardless of how he performs his *latinidad* in terms of national origins, is the point that I want to emphasize here from Bodega's response to Chino. In the literature that displays aspects of the "Latino imaginary" being discussed here, "Nuyoricanness" is about performing and participating in an incorporative and creative social endeavor that feeds that imaginary. It is also clear that the underlying political motivation for the construction of texts like *Bodega Dreams* is to include the social imagination as a guidepost for formulating lived instances of social agency for the communities being depicted on the page.

It is no accident that Chino is celebrated by Bodega for painting R.I.P.'s, because these cultural productions distinctly "mark" the way that the barrio is remembered in contemporary Nuyorican fiction. The descriptions of these murals in literature represent a Puerto Rican imaginary that is built on diasporic aesthetics. In the ultimate tribute to urban ancestors in neighborhoods all over America, the mural R.I.P. paints dreams and histories like that of the Egungun, Yoruba ancestors, of the barrio. In Quiñonez's *Bodega Dreams*, our narrative voice, Chino, envisions this tribute to Young Lord Willie Bodega and the "ancestors," great and small, of Spanish Harlem:

> Alone on the fire escape, I looked out to the neighborhood below. Bodega was right, it was alive. Its music and people had taken off their mourning clothes. The neighborhood had turned into a maraca, with men and women transformed into seeds, shaking with love and desire for one another. Children had opened fire hydrants, and danced, laughing and splashing water on themselves. Old men were sitting on milk crates and playing dominoes. Young men left their car doors wide open, stereos playing full blast. Young girls strutted their stuff, shaking it like Jell-O, proud to be voluptuous and not some bony Ford models. Old women gossiped and laughed as they sat on project benches or tenement stoops, where they once played as children with no backyards—yes, they were happy too. Murals had been painted in memory of Bodega. . . . Some had him as a Young Lord. . . . Others had painted him among the greats: Zapata, Albizu Campos, Sandino, Martí, and Malcolm, along with a million Adelitas. But they were all saying the same thing: "Here once walked Bodega; these were the things he left for us."[21]

Here, community history is a public, lyrical, and sensual affair. By sensual I mean perceived by all of the senses. However, a level of Nuyorican competency is needed to fully appreciate what is being paraded across the page. One needs to be educated to read and unpack the semiotically charged cultural codes found in Quiñonez's description above. Thus, "public space" on the page here is a portable and flexible notion in that only a select group can fully view and appreciate the literary Nuyorican barrio imaginary being painted here. This kind of writing utilizes a methodology of community protection in that the very public, "mass" tribute of the novel may also be privately consumed in semiotically dense ways. For Nuyorican writers like Quiñonez, these "guerilla" semiotics are locked right into a very particular, localized understanding of community history encapsulated by writing the barrio. The process is not static, however, as the very walls of R.I.P.'s are repainted, contested, and reinterpreted within communities "in the know" as well.

Finally, Quiñonez's visual images of shared streets echo those of Soyinka's and Vegas's textual memory. The road again becomes a palette for experiencing a kind of existential and experiential awakening based on witnessing, *eti*, one's surroundings. The maraca here recalls the *igba*, or gourd, of the Yoruba. The use of this allegory is apt here in seeing how people can merge together in a physical way that semiotically recalls the performance of (Afro) Puerto Rican song and celebration. Again, we see that, through the images of children and busy streets, Yoruba and Nuyorican authors use an aesthetics of community as "family" and "hope," which prevail in the midst of economic despair. Like Soyinka and Vega, Quiñonez paints a street teeming with activity. Nuyoricans write the "island-in-the-'hood" to show how diasporic communities claim the public sphere by *being*. Again, the ontological journey from home emerges as a literary trope for carrying and layering the self. In writing about how the road is marked by individual travelers, remembering becomes an act of insurgency.

Insurgent Memories: Diaspora as "Home"

In the early twentieth century, Nuyoricans were struggling to find their place in a diaspora through writing and singing about their experiences of dislocation and community building.[22] Part of Nuyorican nostalgia comes from remembering earlier politicized instances of diaspora as community, especially in excavating the precursors to the Young Lords movement of the 1970s. As Vega asserts in his memoir, writing about a place and space in the United States becomes central to diasporic literature by mainland Puerto Ricans early on.

Remembering by writing *la isla* in the barrio is an act of self-defense, self-representation, and insurgency. Nuyorican communities, written and lived, confound the dichotomies of U.S. social stratification: they are both black and white, new and old, *machista* and *feminista*. The moment then becomes one of synergy between writing and political activity—of living and writing about that life. This kind of flux is found in diasporic writing in general, but an affinity is especially seen between Yoruba and Nuyorican memoir. The politicization of the workplace is a portable affair as well, as Yoruba market women and Nuyorican *tabaqueros* use space in ways that make them self-aware. As Vega writes, "A few days later I found work at another cigar factory, 'El Morito.' . . . At that wonderful place I struck up friendships with a lot [of] Cubans, Spaniards, and fellow countrymen, all of whom awakened in me an eagerness to study. . . . With workers of this caliber, 'El Morito' seemed like a university."[23] It is important to note that *tabaqueros* and *lectores* (readers in tobacco-rolling factories) were an especially politicized sector of the working class in both New York and Puerto Rico. Diasporic Puerto Rican activists like Vega and Luisa Capetillo became politicized on the tobacco-rolling floor.[24] Most literary descriptions of the practice of reading in tobacco factories mention the *tertulia*, or roundtable discussion, that occurs after the news and literature of the day has been heard. Thus, we have a merging of space and purpose described by diasporic Nuyorican writers and activists that confounds neat notions of compartmentalized living. The workroom and the classroom come together in Nuyorican writing about labor in significant, empowering ways. This kind of confounding of space is found in the ways that insurgency is remembered on the page, and remembering becomes insurgency in Yoruba memoir as well.

In Soyinka's *Aké*, remembering his childhood ends in the memory of a political strike. The market women, the *iyalojas* of Aké, band against the local monarch to protest unfair taxation. He remembers how the itinerant market women turn the palace grounds into their own space. "They came from the direction of Iporo, Iberekodo, Ibara, Lantoro and Adatan, from other byways within the city itself. The lines of humanity curled through the hidden *agbole* to swell the other throngs on the final approach along the road that led to the gates of the palace. There began a transformation, not only of the physical terrain, but of the shapes and motions of the gathering."[25] The market women gather on the king's lawn with their children and wares until their demands are heard. Furthermore, there is no market without them. They inhabit space in ways that mark their presence. Soyinka's description of their formidable grass-roots organization and collective voice resembles Vega's memories of the kind of space inhabited by organized tobacco workers.

Yoruba and Nuyorican authors remember how people become politicized in their daily lives by describing how and where they do their politics, and this is tied to *being* at work. In these instances, songs, children, wares, food, and voices as read aloud or sung are carried deep within these descriptions about politics as life. In both Soyinka's *Aké* and Vega's *Memoirs*, communities are remembered as coming together in ways that confound the boundaries of work, play, family, and friends. The very spaces where politics are lived are also versatile places of habitation and action.[26] The king's yard and the tobacco factory are domains that become malleable, and the community transforms what happens there. Furthermore, the similarity between Nuyorican and Yoruba diaspora writing on legacies of community as a remembered portability has its historical roots in a shared Afro-Atlantic cultural legacy.

"Botanica Dreams": Remembering Puerto Rican African Things

More than dreaming, imagining, and remembering the bodega, locating the botanica in Nuyorican writing and imaginary is our direct link to Yoruba cultural legacies in the U.S. diaspora. Very much like the marketplace described above, the botanica specializes in bringing together and making available the variegated elements of Boricua spirituality. Writing about the Yoruba, Congo, Taíno, Catholic, Gitano, and Chinese—among other—influences that make up Nuyorican spiritual life takes center stage in pinpointing the roots to the routes of deeper historical diasporas. The Nuyorican authors being investigated here grapple with a circum-Atlantic movement of spiritual beliefs, practices, and ways of telling about these traditions in new ways. The road and the journey include the portability of gods, especially the Yoruba *orishas*, from Africa to the Caribbean and then onto the streets and barrios of Spanish Harlem in New York City. The botanicas found on these roads give multiple spiritual diasporas supplies and guidance, a flexible resource catering to a fluctuating population. As with Soyinka's description of the herbalists' stalls in Aké's marketplace,[27] the Nuyorican diaspora author writes about his or her botanica as a place where one can connect to "home"—however signified—and begin a journey.

In *Santería Garments and Altars: Speaking without a Voice*, Ysamur Flores-Peña and Roberta J. Evanchuck aptly demonstrate how the semiotics of altar making in Puerto Rican Santería is both an intimate and public affair. Indeed, the *oju aiye*, the "face to the world" that makes a Yoruba religious altar, is laden with symbolic properties created to simultaneously shield from and draw in different magical elements and people. The logic makes sense because an "altar" brings together those in your spiritual family, in your spiritual genealogy, including the beings and spirits represented by the ancestors, or *egun*. Thus, the Santería altars found in the windows of botanica storefronts are open enough, public enough, to draw in the vital forces needed to bring communities together. Yet, they are semiotically dense in ways that mimic Nuyorican authors' sense of (E)spanglish in describing the barrio, bodega, and botanica. The meaning of the layered language and descriptions, like the objects placed on an altar in a botanica storefront, can be dismantled only by those who can successfully "read" the codes.

In *Bodega Dreams*, Quiñonez touches upon this Nuyorican botanica aesthetic. Below, Sapo brings Enrique on a spiritual errand for Willie Bodega. Note how the Santera, Africanness, and power are presented in quotidian, familiar ways, eschewing any exoticism. These spiritual practices and people *are* Nuyorican and African all at once. They belong.

> When we reached the botanica on 166th between Park and Madison, San Lázaro y las Siete Vueltas, Sapo parked his car and asked me and Nene to carry the box. . . . Doña Ramonita was a heavy woman with strong African roots from Puerto Rico's Loiza Aldea. With her hair pulled back in a pink bandanna and her hands on her hips, she looked like Aunt Jemima from the pancake boxes. She was standing next to a life-sized statue of San Lázaro with all of his boils and diseased skin. Incense was burning all around the botanica and the shelves were crowded with teas and potions and smaller saints. . . . "Doña Ramonita," Sapo said, "Willie Bodega would like for you to make an offering to Changó on his behalf, 'This is for him,'" Sapo said.[28]

Vega also remembers the botanica: "Small pharmacies and *botánicas* sprang up throughout the neighborhood. . . . Doctors, witches, druggists, mind readers, dentists, spiritualists, palm readers, all shared the same clientele."[29]

Both Quiñonez and Vega describe the botanica and those participating in botanica spirituality as part of the barrio. Nuyorican authors write the botanica, like the bodega, onto the streets of the neighborhood. Specialists and clientele come from a myriad of racial, cultural, and social backgrounds, yet they are especially associated with "African" beliefs, practices, and goods. These are descriptions of diasporas twice or three times removed, because they are located in a particular *isla* remembrance of the (Afro) Puerto Rican. In mentioning places like Loiza Aldea or describing Santeros as distinctly having "black" features, Nuyorican authors, not unproblematically, locate the spirituality of the African diasporas, or African *cosas* (things), in a racialized context.

These racial codes are borrowed from the *isla* and transformed in the barrio. Writers attempt to reflect the tension of bringing a Boricua kaleidoscopic vision of race into focus for the bifurcated social lens found in the United States. Thus, in recovering "African things" that are also Puerto Rican, Nuyorican authors create their own claims to African ancestry by situating the botanica on the streets of their urban imaginary. The botanica brings the African part of the *isla* into the 'hood; it brings *el monte* (the forest) into the city in ways that are also specifically coded as "Boricua African" rather than "black."

Botanica storefronts, altars, and sacred objects are cluttered and coded in just the right way so that they do not trickle into *where they do not belong*. Like the barrio and the bodega, descriptions of botanicas in Nuyorican diasporic literature serve to locate a semiotics of remembrance that resonates in the perception of symbolic markers. As with the "protective methodology" of reading the barrio, reading the botanica also has to do with accessing the knowledge necessary to decipher certain African or Yoruba codes. Sapo's request above makes little sense if one does not know about the Yoruba deity Changó or rituals found in Nuyorican Santería. In order to make sense of the African Nuyorican codes that Quiñonez references, one has to be schooled in specialized kinds of spiritual, Yoruba-based cultural practice. For Nuyorican authors utilizing this kind of botanica imaginary, the mediation of the Yoruba in Puerto Rican spirituality is often achieved in textual spaces that simultaneously traverse the urban and the rural, the sacred and the secular, inside and outside the botanica, in a semiotic collaboration with the reader. That some audiences do not "get it" is implicit in the work.

Anthropologist Margaret Drewal works extensively with Yoruba ritual and play in *orisha* worship, a main aspect of the practice of Nuyorican Santería.[30] She observes how the high priest Ositola makes a sacred grove at home, in his own backyard, in Nigeria. The high priest has this to say about the construction of this special site: "If you were to see it [the inside of the grove] you would know it is a strange place. It is not common. It is not the gate to Mecca or the barracks, but to the holy land igbodu. I have my own igbodu. You can prepare your own igbodu at your place as well."[31] Here, Ositola affirms the conceptual component of zones like the *igbodu*. The sacred scape of the grove is portable like the *isla* in the barrio. These spaces are diasporic zones of commemoration, and writing about them is one way of bringing them back into being. As Nuyorican authors like Vega and Quiñonez encode it, the presence of the botanica on a street in a Nuyorican barrio re-creates the *igbodu* in a new space.

The act of building an altar is also an insurgent act of commemoration. Puerto Rican Santeros are said to *armar un altar*, that is, to build or "arm" an altar. The creation of the sacred space, the *igbodu* of the altar in *Santería,* often involves a guerilla symbolism used to protect a spiritual community from its enemies. Nuyorican literary descriptions of "African Puerto Rican things" are similarly *armado*, construed to be read in multiple layers by varied audiences. These botanica dreams are indeed revived by authors in sacred textual spaces that shine in a distinctly Nuyorican relief.

El Collar de la Memoría: *Memory Necklace in Nuyorican Diaspora Literature*

Nuyorican writing about experiences of diaspora inherits much more than a rhythmic *tumba'o* from the Yoruba culture brought to the Americas during the slave trade. The sensibilities I have been speaking about in this essay display a sophisticated and subtle legacy that is characteristic of a distinct urbanity and cosmopolitanism. The cultural expression, especially the use of lyricism, of writing about memory in the context of a diaspora is a legacy that Yoruba and Nuyorican authors share. My hope has been to more accurately depict how bifurcated notions about the quality of African and European expressions that come together in Nuyorican literature and cultural expressions are forced, are a farce. These categories constitute conceptual roadblocks that distort our own realities and cultural expressions of writing, music, and quotidian practice.

Ngugi wa Thiong'o, in *Moving the Centre*, grapples with a similar problem in a postcolonial African context. He points to the issue of language in the formation of "national literatures" that relate the experiences of Africans in postindependence contexts. He supports the use and development of "literatures" in indigenous African languages in lieu of developing more Europhone texts. Though controversial among postcolonial African writers, Ngugi wa Thiong'o rightly describes how the very terms, the etymology of the words, that authors use to explain their worlds should reflect their epistemologies. Thus, the densely coded use of language in writing the barrio, the bodega, and the botanica shows that Nuyorican authors indeed can "move the center" in the site for producing meaning and knowledge in their texts. Further, the use of (E)spanglish and code switching in Nuyorican literature reflects Ngugi wa Thiong'o's sense of literary self-representation for writers describing a postcolonial situation.

The Nuyorican diaspora writing discussed in this essay displays a sense of "belongability" that is able to contain all the complexities of verbal contradiction through itinerancy as language. Remembering as insurgence helps to hold these "wonder/full," disparate tensions together in what is understood to be a complicated, conflicted, and portable rhetoric of home and group identity. Nuyorican writing reflects this linguistic tension that holds the island's and the city's diasporic boundaries in place. They merge like the shores that begin and end the perpetual journey. Each of us is a microcosm of how we get there and back. Using the semiotics of the barrio, bodega, and botanica, Nuyorican diasporic authors enunciate that tradition is portable and that remembering is revolutionary.

NOTES

1. See Juan Flores, *From Bomba to Hip-Hop: Puerto Rican Culture and Latino Identity* (New York: Columbia University Press, 2000), 167–188; Piri Thomas, *Down These Mean Streets* (New York: Vintage Books, 1997), 95–119; and Willie Perdomo, *Where a Nickel Costs a Dime* (New York: W. W. Norton, 1996), 19–21.

2. Olabiyi Babalola Yai, "In Praise of Metonymy: The Concepts of 'Tradition' and

'Creativity' in the Transmission of Yoruba Artistry over Time and Space," in *The Yoruba Artist*, ed. Roland Abiodun et al. (Washington, DC: Smithsonian Institution Press, 1994), 107–115; 'Wande Abimbola, "Lagbayi: The Itinerant Wood Carver of Ojowon," in Abiodun et al., *Yoruba Artist*, 137–142.

3. Wole Soyinka, *Aké: The Years of Childhood* (London: Rex Collins, 1981), 36–42.

4. Ibid., 49–50.

5. Ibid., 155.

6. Bernardo Vega, *The Memoirs of Bernardo Vega: A Contribution to the History of the Puerto Rican Community in New York*, ed. César Andreu Iglesias, trans. Juan Flores (New York: Monthly Review Press, 1984).

7. Solimar Otero, "Rethinking the Diaspora: African, Brazilian, and Cuban Communities in Africa and the Americas," *Black Scholar* 30, nos. 3–4 (2000): 54–56.

8. Vega, *Memoirs*, 3–6.

9. Ibid., 7–9.

10. Ibid., 10.

11. Ibid., 9–11, 151, 157; Thomas, *Down these Mean Streets*, 24–38, 81–87.

12. Lisa Sánchez González, *Boricua Literature: A Literary History of the Puerto Rican Diaspora* (New York: New York University Press, 2001); Flores, *Bomba.*

13. Mike Davis, *Magical Urbanism: Latinos Reinvent the U.S. Big City* (New York: Verso, 2000), 13–15.

14. Abimbola, "Lagbayi"; Yai, "In Praise of Metonymy."

15. Vega, *Memoirs,* 151.

16. Mikhail Bakhtin, *Rabelais and His World*, trans. Helene Iswolsky (Bloomington: Indiana University Press, 1988), 145–146, 152–153.

17. Juan Flores, "The Latino Imaginary: Dimensions of Community and Identity," in *Tropicalizations: Transcultural Representations of Latinidad*, ed. Frances R. Aparicio and Susana Chávez-Silverman (Hanover, NH: University Press of New England, 1997), 190–191.

18. Ernesto Quiñonez, *Bodega Dreams* (New York: Vintage Books, 2000), 8.

19. Ibid., 36.

20. Ibid., 3–11.

21. Ibid., 212–213.

22. Vega, *Memoirs*, 83–142; Sánchez González, *Boricua Literature*, 42–70, 102–133; Ruth Glassier, *My Music Is My Flag* (Berkeley and Los Angeles: University of California Press, 1995), 52–83.

23. Vega, *Memoirs,* 20–21.

24. Sánchez González, *Boricua Literature*, 24–25.

25. Soyinka, *Aké*, 216–218.

26. Mark Anthony Neal, *Songs in the Key of Black Life* (New York: Routledge, 2003), 104.

27. Soyinka, *Aké,* 42–43.

28. Quiñonez, *Bodega Dreams*, 31–33. San Lázaro is the Catholic representation of the Yoruba deity of smallpox, Baba Lu Aiye, in Santería. Loiza Aldea is a town in Puerto

Rico known for its African cultural roots. Changó is the Yoruba god of lightning associated with the Catholic image of Santa Bárbara.

29. Vega, *Memoirs,* 155.

30. Margaret Thompson Drewal, *Yoruba Ritual: Performers, Play, Agency* (Bloomington: Indiana University Press, 1992), 62–65.

31. Ibid., 66.

BIBLIOGRAPHY

Abimbola, 'Wande. "Lagbayi: The Itinerant Wood Carver of Ojowon." In *The Yoruba Artist,* ed. Roland Abiodun et al., 137–142. Washington, DC: Smithsonian Institution Press, 1994.

Bakhtin, Mikhail. *Rabelais and His World.* Trans. Helene Iswolsky. Bloomington: Indiana University Press, 1988.

Davis, Mike. *Magical Urbanism: Latinos Reinvent the U.S. Big City.* New York: Verso, 2000.

Drewal, Margaret Thompson. *Yoruba Ritual: Performers, Play, Agency.* Bloomington: Indiana University Press, 1992.

Flores, Juan. *From Bomba to Hip-Hop: Puerto Rican Culture and Latino Identity.* New York: Columbia University Press, 2000.

———. "The Latino Imaginary: Dimensions of Community and Identity." In *Tropicalizations: Transcultural Representations of Latinidad*, ed. Frances R. Aparicio and Susana Chávez-Silverman, 183–193. Hanover, NH: University Press of New England, 1997.

Flores-Peña, Ysamur, and Roberta J. Evanchuck. *Santería Garments and Altars: Speaking without a Voice.* Jackson: University of Mississippi Press, 1994.

Glassier, Ruth. *My Music Is My Flag.* Berkeley and Los Angeles: University of California Press, 1995.

Lawal, Babatunde. "From Africa to the Americas: Art in Yoruba Religion." In *Santería Aesthetics in Contemporary Latin American Art*, ed. Arturo Lindsay, 3–37. Washington, DC: Smithsonian Institution Press, 1996.

Lindsay, Arturo. "Orishas: Living Gods in Contemporary Latin Art." In *Santería Aesthetics in Contemporary Latin American Art*, ed. Arturo Lindsay, 201–223. Washington, DC: Smithsonian Institution Press, 1996.

Neal, Mark Anthony. *Songs in the Key of Black Life.* New York: Routledge, 2003.

Ngugi wa Thiong'o. *Moving the Centre: The Struggle for Cultural Freedoms.* Portsmouth, NH: Heinemann, 1993.

Otero, Solimar. "Rethinking the Diaspora: African, Brazilian, and Cuban Communities in Africa and the Americas." *Black Scholar* 30, nos. 3–4 (2000): 54–56.

Perdomo, Willie. *Where a Nickel Costs a Dime.* New York: W. W. Norton, 1996.

Quiñonez, Ernesto. *Bodega Dreams.* New York: Vintage, 2000.

Sánchez González, Lisa. *Boricua Literature: A Literary History of the Puerto Rican Diaspora.* New York: New York University Press, 2001.

Soyinka, Wole. *Aké: The Years of Childhood.* London: Rex Collins, 1981.

Thomas, Piri. *Down These Mean Streets.* New York: Vintage Books, 1997.

Vega, Bernardo. *The Memoirs of Bernardo Vega: A Contribution to the History of the Puerto Rican Community in New York.* Ed. César Andreu Iglesias. Trans. Juan Flores. New York: Monthly Review Press, 1984.

Yai, Olabiyi Babalola. "In Praise of Metonymy: The Concepts of 'Tradition' and 'Creativity' in the Transmission of Yoruba Artistry over Time and Space." In *The Yoruba Artist*, ed. Roland Abiodun et al., 107–115. Washington, DC: Smithsonian Institution Press, 1994.

PART V *Gender*

14 IDENTITY OF THE "DIASPORICAN" HOMOSEXUAL IN THE LITERARY PERIPHERY

ENRIQUE MORALES-DÍAZ

Scholars such as Judith Lorber, Annamarie Jagose, and Donald E. Hall argue that gender, as well as sexuality, is a social construct.[1] As in many societies, beliefs, attitudes, and expectations as to how individuals should behave are often imposed specifically on groups that are "peripheral" because in some way or another they do not conform to societal expectations. Jagose argues that individuals behave according to how society expects them to: "For gender is performative, not because it is something that the subject deliberately and playfully assumes, but because, through reiteration, it consolidates the subject. In this respect, performativity is the precondition of the subject."[2] People in Western societies "perform" their gender as dictated by their societies—because conforming to the ideals imposed by the concept of two genders maintains the status quo. Among the groups often marginalized and expected to "fall in line" with the rest of society are homosexuals. The expectations placed upon the homosexual are often those associated with specific gender behavior; everyone must act according to his or her "assigned" gender; a man must be masculine and "take a woman" and vice versa. As Rafael Ramírez writes, "In Puerto Rico . . . the masculine ideology stresses sexuality. The male is an essentially sexual being, or at least he should look and act like one. He should enjoy his sexuality, declare it, boast about it, feel proud of it and, above all, show it."[3]

However, what happens when individuals do not conform to what society expects of them? What happens when homosexuals refuse to accept that, in order for them and their identity (which may include ethnic and even sexual affiliations) to be accepted by society, they must behave according to prescribed notions of proper conduct? Why must a man always be "masculine" and a woman "feminine"? This essay seeks to answer these questions, specifically as they pertain to the Diasporican homosexual experience as represented by three contemporary gay writers.

What makes the Diasporican homosexual condition especially challenging are the "extra" expectations placed on Puerto Rican men, who traditionally have had to conform to the stereotypical and dated notion of machismo, which is the belief that the role of the "macho," or "real man," is to conquer, possess, and dominate. As a result, an integral element that homosexuality adds to the transformative identity of the Diasporican experience has been marginalized. The notion that machismo must be present within every man of Latin American and Spanish descent is expressed by Steven Kurtz, who states that "the sexual and gender identities (and behaviors) of homosexual men tend to conform to the tenets of the systems within which they live."[4] Thus, for Diasporican homosexuals, the task is a challenging one, as they are forced to conform to both a North American and a Puerto Rican ideology of masculinity devoid of a homosexual identity.

To undertake the proposed venture, I will focus specifically on the literature of three contemporary U.S. Puerto Rican gay writers, or Diasporican homosexuals: Robert Vázquez-Pacheco, Emanuel Xavier, and Larry La Fountain-Stokes, whose experiences center on their ethnic/sexual identity, which in turn plays an important role in their identity as Diasporican men. It can be argued that their writing represents an attempt at interpolating themselves within the "fixed" definition of what it means to be Puerto Rican and a man, both in the United States and in Puerto Rico, in order to establish themselves as part of the diasporic experience. At the same time, they are trying to break with the imposed dichotomy masculine man/feminine woman, which they do not conform to, and this often leads to their attempts to redefine *puertorriqueñidad* being ignored by scholars. These three writers differ in terms of experiences and expression. However, their writing shares an autobiographical tone, since a Puerto Rican writer (and, by extension, a Latino writer) is, according to Katherine Gatto, "an autobiographical writer."[5] The stories by La Fountain-Stokes, Vázquez-Pacheco, and Xavier also "serve to create a discourse that counteracts established heteropatriarchal norms."[6] Edna Acosta-Belén writes that identity within the Diasporican communities must be reaffirmed through cultural productions that will demystify mainstream society's understanding of what a Puerto Rican is and is not.[7] Consequently, the process of interpolation for these Diasporican homosexual writers is important because, as a new generation of Puerto Rican writers in the United States, they must attempt to define themselves in order for those establishing a more cohesive interpretation of *puertorriqueñidad* to acknowledge their presence and contributions to the enhancement of the mainland diaspora.

The process of constructing an identity within the Puerto Rican diaspora (Diasporican) on the part of Vázquez-Pacheco, La Fountain-Stokes, and Xavier can be considered a postcolonial attempt at deconstructing fixed characteristics that marginalize them with respect to the concept of *puertorriqueñidad*, particularly because they do not necessarily conform to "universal" notions of what a Puerto Rican man is. They present a counterdiscourse that "defines them" both ethnically and sexually without forcing a dichotomy that requires them to choose one identity over another. As Acosta-Belén postulates, the constructivist process of these writers to establish themselves within the "definition" of Puerto Rican identity in the United States is a way to counteract how Puerto Ricans are "understood" on the mainland by U.S. mainstream culture.[8] The texts that will be discussed in this essay can be considered "rites of passage that figure the Nuyorican subject's attempt to gain authority, to emerge, as it were, as a passage into maturity and maleness," since "homosexual practices occupy that zone of reversibility where the Nuyorican author's struggle to emerge from the spectral state of abjection to which he is subjected by 'internal colonialism,' by 'the System,' by 'the Man,' always inevitably falls back on contested territory."[9]

In "My Name, Multitudinous Mass," Larry La Fountain-Stokes writes: "By profession I tell, I am a teller of stories . . . I write myself, I write my body on many pages as if an indelible tattoo on your buttocks."[10] Here the author describes the role of every writer: to write in the hope that the reader will connect with the words on the page. Also important here is that the writer refers to himself, or the narrative voice, as a "multiple" writer, that while he writes because that is what he does, he may also write on behalf of others, perhaps those whose lack of agency does not allow them to share their experiences with the reader, who will possibly relate to their words. However, although "multitudinous mass" may bring to mind an undifferentiated conglomeration, that is not the intent here since the writer is attempting to acknowledge, not just a collective sensibility, but an individual one as well. La Fountain-Stokes's strategy seems to be to announce to his reader that his is a voice through which others can express themselves, and yet his voice is also individual and unique. His act of "self-identification" coincides with Donald Hall's idea that "self-identification, explicit or potential, should *not* limit us in the ways we theorize about desire, that self-identification is a potentially powerful political position, but that it is also an intellectual problem."[11]

Emanuel Xavier also describes his writing as a form of self-identification: "I write about the gay Nuyorican experience because it is what I know, and somewhere along the line I also represent the gay Ecuadorian community because of the mix in my blood. In itself, these are two very different cultures, which become blended with the New York experience because it is my life, my history."[12] Hence, as a Nuyorican and Ecuadorian, as well as a Latino gay man, Xavier writes with a multitude of voices but shares the experiences with which he is familiar: his own.

This approach by the writers differs from the notion of uniform categorization, which creates labels such as Hispanic or Latino/a and ignores the cultural, linguistic, and historical experiences and differences of those whom it "lumps" together within its definition. The same argument is made for homosexuality and the idea that the experience is the same for all Latinos and, by extension, all people of color in the United States. Hall's assertion is that identity cannot be defined—there is no fixed method to determine how a group of people with shared beliefs and practices will conduct themselves.[13] In relation to homosexuality in Puerto Rico, Rafael Ramírez writes that the negative connotations associated with sexual orientation depend upon the time, place, and belief system shared by any given community.[14] John C. Hawley affirms that the idea of "the global gay" has become a way to explain homosexuality, as if all individuals who share an attraction to the same gender are the same.[15] It can be argued, then, that the goal of these three writers is "the formation of a shared consciousness . . . that transcends the specific national and cultural specificities . . . in favor of embracing a broader collective identity," while maintaining a sense of individuality that avoids a need for uniform categorizations.[16] "My Name, Multitudinous Mass," for instance, works as a funnel, introducing broader themes than the stories by Vázquez-Pacheco and Xavier, yet providing the leitmotif necessary to connect all three writers. As La Fountain-Stokes writes, "I am one and a thousand persons and no one knows who I am. . . . I have been a john, bisexual, queen, man, woman, my name is desire and yours is hope" (66).

He opens his story with the assertion that the person speaking is Manuel Ramos Otero: "My name, Manuel Ramos Otero, my parents called me but I respond to other secrets, other voices from within as well as to your name, the greatest mystery of all time" (61). The narrative voice's claim that "he" is the exiled Puerto Rican writer who speaks exposes a number of ideas. First, as a Puerto Rican/Nuyorican writer in exile, Manuel Ramos Otero can represent all those who left the island, either by force or voluntarily because they did not conform to the behavioral expectations established by Puerto Rico's mainstream society. Second, another reason for the affirmation of the narrative voice refers to the life that Diasporican homosexuals live and the obstacles they face by being placed into categories based on their "improper conduct," since according to Ramírez, "sexism and homophobia are manifested daily in Puerto Rican society and that collectively, homosexuality is not accepted as a legitimate sexual orientation or preference."[17] Third, the idea of responding to "other secrets" can refer to the need of some homosexuals to remain "in the closet" and hide an aspect of who they are in order to avoid repudiation by the rest of society, given that "[b]eing looked upon as a sinner, a criminal, or a person who is mentally ill means dealing with rejection, ridicule, a sense of guilt, contempt, and even physical violence on a daily basis."[18] Thus, it seems as though the individual's sexuality cannot merge with the ethnic part of the entire identity, not by personal choice, but due to expectations and requirements imposed by society.

Manuel Ramos Otero's name is not the only one present in this story. As part of his strategy, the author introduces other personalities/intellectuals, not just from Puerto Rico but the United States as well, and their presence in the narrative corresponds to the statement regarding "other voices from within as well as to your name." La Fountain-Stokes writes, "Sometimes, when I walk down the street, I become other people. . . . And I write and think, what is there left to say that my many divine incarnations have not already said?" (62). The affirmation "my many divine incarnations" claims that there are many voices within one individual, which can be interpreted as an embracing of past lives or of those individuals who, like the writer, either have lived secret lives or have played a part in *"el ambiente,"*[19] and at the same time acknowledges a gay/queer diaspora that homosexuals are a part of. This claim can be juxtaposed to those that affirm that there cannot be a homosexual diaspora because sexuality as a form of identity, as Hawley states, has not yet been accepted. For the purposes of this essay, however, this diaspora not only is "universal" but is a Hispanic Caribbean gay/queer diaspora.

La Fountain-Stokes's acknowledgment of the existence of such figures as Manuel Ramos Otero, William Burroughs, René Marqués, and Truman Capote, and later Reinaldo Arenas, Severo Sarduy, José Lezama Lima, Federico García Lorca, Walt Whitman, and Nan Goldin, has various purposes. First, as Hawley states, it is a reflection of a global gay identity, proposing that homosexuality is not a phenomenon of just one specific place or time but is a characteristic shared by many across cultural and ethnic borders. As Oscar Montero explains, homosexuals are not limited to any specific time or space. Although the idea of homosexuality may be a nineteenth-century concept to explain a particular form of behavior, Montero argues that not one homosexual is the same as another one, and this includes the very nature of an individual's sexual desires.[20] By employing this approach, it is as though La Fountain-Stokes is responding to Hawley's own arguments regarding a "universal gay identity," the idea that "identities based on sexuality will be as strong as those based on race or religion."[21]

This idea is again affirmed in the story when the author writes: "I am everything and nothing, I overflow my memory of transatlantic cruise ships, of migratory waves, of Hawaiian fields in which I am called mountain jíbaro, an old citizen of such illustrious cities, of snivelly and ragged dens of perdition where we learned to kiss each other on hot August nights" (65). Here La Fountain-Stokes affirms both an ethnic and a sexual identity—one is not separate from the other. What this statement also does is introduce another strategy that will be shared with the other two writers whom I will discuss, but not with other Nuyorican/Diasporican writers: La Fountain-Stokes is not asking to be recognized as a Puerto Rican but instead, is stating the fact that he is Puerto Rican, an assertion also made by Salsa singer Marc Anthony in his remake of

Rafael Hernández's "Preciosa," in which he affirms that, regardless of where he is, he will always be Puerto Rican because of his parents and the blood that flows through his veins. In this case, it is as José Torres-Padilla states, "the ethnic project needs memory for validation."[22] This fact is also present in the line "Manhattan is a town in Puerto Rico, except that it's a couple of hours away by plane" (64). However, one statement that the writer makes to solidify this ethnic identity is perhaps the most important because of what he is acknowledging. His pronouncement "My name is Lawrence Martin La Fountain-Stokes" becomes a reaffirmation of his identity as an individual, as a homosexual, and as a Puerto Rican, thus suggesting that none of these individual characteristics weakens any of the others. Thus, he is a Diasporican homosexual.

La Fountain-Stokes describes himself as a "Puerto Rican writer, academic, and activist."[23] Robert Vázquez-Pacheco is described as "a Nuyorican gay writer and longtime community activist."[24] Emanuel Xavier considers himself "to be American—but Latino; Latino—but gay; Nuyorican—but Ecuadorian; revolutionary—but not an activist."[25] Charlie, the protagonist in Vázquez-Pacheco's "Brujo Time," does not make any of these claims. He does not consider himself a Puerto Rican, or a Nuyorican for that matter, but sees himself and his success connected to his acceptance of an American identity. In Emanuel Xavier's "Banjee Hustler," an excerpt from his 1999 novel *Christ-Like*, Mikey, the protagonist, is acknowledged as being half Puerto Rican by his friends: "Just bring your tired half Puerto Rican ass over, ah-ight?"[26] He never makes reference to this fact himself, and while the story is a semi-autobiographical account of the author's experiences, it is in his poetry that assertions of his ethnic background are made clearer. For example, in the first stanza of his poem "Americano" he writes: "I look at myself in the mirror / trying to figure out what makes me an American / I see Ecuador and Puerto Rico."[27] Again, in the fourth stanza of the poem, Xavier acknowledges the presence of the Puerto Rican/Nuyorican culture that surrounds him: "I see Don Rosario in his guayabera / sitting outside the bodega / with his Puerto Rican flag / reading time in the eyes of alley cats."[28] The *guayabera*[29] and flag are exterior symbols that tell a passerby how Don Rosario defines himself ethnically. On the other hand, the images Xavier sees of Ecuador and Puerto Rico in the mirror are an affirmation of his ethnic identity, which he accepts and acknowledges as forming a part of who he is. Consequently, the struggles, not only of individuals who are constantly reclaiming their heritage, but also of those who must establish themselves as "men" in a society that considers their behavior abnormal, non–Puerto Rican, and unacceptable must be explored in order to enhance the understanding of the diversity present within the U.S. Puerto Rican diaspora. This case is important for the Diasporican homosexual, who is opposing the belief that being homosexual makes an individual less than a man.

For decades Puerto Rican scholars have attempted to modify the concept of *puertorriqueñidad*, Puerto Ricanness, as a way of breaking with a colonialist/neocolonialist view of fixity in reference to Puerto Rican national identity. Acosta-Belén states that Puerto Rico has been in a continuous struggle against a process of "denationalization" by the United States, which has sought to impose a uniformity that threatens "the process of development of a strong sense of national identity and consciousness that might threaten U.S. control over the island."[30] The very struggle that exists in Puerto Rico has migrated with the diaspora as a concern to recapture or redefine what it means to be Puerto Rican within the confines of the United States and in relation to the island itself. This struggle by those in Puerto Rico as well as their counterparts on the mainland who are attempting to redefine *puertorriqueñidad* has led, whether consciously or not, to the displacement of one "element" of the diaspora—it has meant continued marginalization of the periphery, in this case homosexuals, in an already peripheral society (the U.S. Puerto Rican diaspora).

For example, the reader of Robert Vázquez-Pacheco's "Brujo Time" learns at the beginning that Charlie is homosexual and that he is in a botanica. This is important for two reasons: first, the fact that the "businesswoman" assumes that he is there because of problems with his girlfriend suggests the possibility that his sexuality will not be accepted. However, he does accept his sexuality, since he is there because of problems with his boyfriend. Second, the botanica is a direct reference to a cultural practice that his family has denied him. However, as the story unfolds we learn that Charlie, although "Puerto Rican" is not exactly what he seems:

> He had grown up knowing very little about this stuff. His family had raised him to be a good boy, to be an American success so they didn't weigh him

down with the burdens of their culture. He spoke Spanish badly. He knew little of his people's history, habits, or culture. They had decided that he didn't need them to be an American success. Charlie was better off free from his Puerto Rican identity, from the loudness, tackiness, and superstition that ruled the lives of his family members. He would not have embarrassing statues or mysterious substances around his apartment. . . . He would simply do well, unencumbered by the past, becoming a modern day Hispanic. He was the carefully constructed repository of his family's American dream.[31]

One of the important points here is not Charlie's denial of his ethnic and cultural identity, but the fact that that identity was denied to him. This denial and loss of an ethnic identity is due to "a loss of the culture of origin which is gradually replaced by the adoption of the dominant culture of the nation to which they emigrated," although rather than one culture replacing another it has been a process of incorporation, which allows for the evolution of the two cultures into something that goes beyond national identity; it represents "alternative ways of cultural adaptation, innovation, and resistance."[32] This denial is also reminiscent of the idea that a "real man" cannot be a homosexual—a real man is masculine; he conquers and dominates others.

However, no matter how much his family denies him his Puerto Rican identity, and no matter how much Charlie has assimilated into North American mainstream society, there are those who recognize it in him. For example, Brett, the man Charlie is in love with, says, "That's what I like about you, Charlie. You're so Porto Rican," which is ironic given that Charlie does not see himself in the same way; and even as Charlie finds this statement offensive, since he thought that he was able to escape his family's "powerlessness" based on their ethnic identity, Brett responds, "You just remind me of the Portorican guys I know. You all get so touchy about family stuff" (108). This statement by Brett confirms to Charlie that perhaps he cannot hide who he is, because regardless of what he does and how he acts, society will see him and know where he comes from, just as Cruz-Malavé writes about homosexuality in Puerto Rico, "the specter of homosexuality haunts Puerto Rico's hegemonic discourse of national identity, . . . homosexuality is not only its excluded other but its abjected self."[33]

Brett's recognition of the identity that Charlie attempts to hide diminishes some of the beliefs Charlie has about himself and his success: "His confidence in himself, that quality of 'whiteness' his brother commented on, had been diminished in some way" (106). Charlie's final acceptance of the botanica's presence (he had been ignoring it was there for months) and his entrance into the establishment reflect a certain unconscious need that Charlie has for the culture that he has "lost." Thus, his entrance and plea for help from the owner are a way for him to reappropriate a cultural identity that was denied to him—he must accept who he is in order to understand what he is.[34] He decides to become a tourist in his family's cultural and ethnic identity and finally immerses himself in what is immediately available to him. Rather than wanting to be recognized as Puerto Rican, or demanding that everyone accepts it, he instead accepts it himself and acknowledges this aspect of his personality, as seen at the end of the story when he visits his family, whom he had been avoiding in order to spend time with Brett, and joins a conversation about *"brujería."* By participating in this conversation, Charlie accepts his identity and begins to explore all its aspects in order to begin incorporating them into his already-stated and accepted identity. According to Cruz-Malavé, "Contemporary Puerto Rican cultural practices in the United States may be seen, then, to inhabit the space between these two implosions: that of origins and that of a certain future." At the end of the story, Charlie is emerging "from a space of double deterritorialization and banishment" that had been imposed on him by his family.[35]

What can be seen here is that instead of mimicry—seeking to establish a national identity within the diaspora—Diasporican homosexuals are affirming an ethnoracial identity that is more relevant to their experiences outside Puerto Rico, as seen in Vázquez-Pacheco's "Brujo Time." As Torres-Padilla states, "for Puerto Ricans in the United States there are obvious reasons behind the emphasizing of their ethnicity as opposed to nationality. Separated from their geographic base, 'their homeland,' and 'othered' by North Americans, it is not surprising that Puerto Ricans in the States will seek ways of recreating *puertorriqueñidad* for reasons of survival and political necessity."[36] However, rather than affirming an ethnic identity that is often expected to disappear through the process of assimilation and, hence, incorporation into the mainstream culture, what is affirmed by Charlie in Vázquez-Pacheco's story is in fact his sexuality. Whereas Hawley states that identities based on sexuality may not yet be accepted by societies, Charlie has in fact claimed his homosexuality and incorporated it in the same way an individual might claim ethnic affiliation. Thus, Vázquez-Pacheco plays with mainstream society's policy of "Don't Ask, Don't Tell," but applies that ideology to Charlie's Puerto Ricanness.

The moving away from Diasporican homosexuals as a marginalized group occurs because those seeking to modify *puertorriqueñidad* as a national identity do so by reappropriating a colonialist/neocolonialist model. For example, one of the models relevant to the discussion in this essay is the male/female dichotomy, which may take into account race and class but excludes sexual *otherness*. This particular model is relevant because, according to Kurtz, "[w]hile masculinities are certainly structured in relation to socially prescribed roles of women . . . masculinities serve, just as importantly, to structure power relationships between men."[37] The focus on this colonial/Western/patriarchal structure, or, as described by Francisco Valdes, "heteropatriarchy,"[38] keeps the Diasporican homosexual in the periphery while those in perpetual search for answers to questions such as "What is Puerto Ricanness?" and "What criteria should be used to define Puerto Ricanness?" continue on a quest for a "homogeneous" and uniform definition. This perception coincides with Stuart Hall's definition of "cultural identity," which he describes as the "terms of one, shared culture, a sort of collective 'one true self,' hiding inside the many other, more superficial or artificially imposed 'selves,' which people with a shared history and ancestry hold in common."[39] Therefore, to continue along these lines, according to Marina De Chiara, is to continue a model of "Westernization," of imposing an identity defined by others according to the ways that an individual, or an entire group of people, must conform in order to be accepted by mainstream society.[40]

The Puerto Rican image of identity in both Puerto Rico and the United States that has been imposed by neocolonialism and that "excludes" the Diasporican homosexual, because of its continued emphasis on a gender dichotomy that excludes "other" sexualities, goes against the notion that identity is transformative, ignoring the fact that it "is the way in which culture becomes significant to individuals and the way they define themselves. . . . it is also distinguished by its changeable and variable nature."[41] This conflict between how to define *puertorriqueñidad* forces the category of "otherness" on those individuals who do not fit within the definition being created.

Who, then, is the Puerto Rican sexual "other?" The Puerto Rican sexual other is that individual from the diasporic community who does not conform, based on positivist ideology, to the established and defined "U.S. Puerto Rican" ethnic identity. This Puerto Rican is "othered" because he is not within the line of vision of the constructivist process that seeks to acknowledge the importance of the Diasporican experience within the overall "definition" of what it means to be Puerto Rican on the island and in the United States.[42] Why is it important to take into consideration this Puerto Rican sexual other, and what makes this Puerto Rican different? It is necessary that those individuals who are othered, in this case Diasporican homosexuals, be acknowledged as both existing and adding their contribution to the betterment of the Diasporican experience. Can continuously modifying identity while excluding any segment of the diaspora differ from the colonial/neocolonial impositions already present in all aspects of Puerto Rican culture? The Diasporican homosexual community, marginalized by both the North American and the Puerto Rican system of "sexual meanings," compresses sexuality into a mold that segregates this already-peripheral group from the rest of society. Accordingly, how do gay Puerto Ricans "negotiate and contest" a gay identity with aspects of the larger Puerto Rican culture? Can a gay Puerto Rican be a Puerto Rican? "How do [Puerto Rican] homosexuals structure their sexual conduct, especially the sexual roles into which they enter?"[43] For instance, besides references to his own ethnic identity as a Diasporican/Latino gay man, Emanuel Xavier is very open about his sexuality and his life in the streets as a hustler and drug dealer, as detailed in his story "Banjee Hustler." Mikey, the protagonist and Xavier's "alter ego" in this story, sells drugs at "The Sanctuary," the most popular gay club in New York City. The following is a description of the protagonist's character: "A hundred bucks and Mikey would drop to his knees and feast on your supremacy with starving lips which, at the age of three, already knew hunger and submission thanks to older cousin Chino. Two hundred and the gates of Banjee heaven would spread wide open while you ripped through his soul like the needle on the record high above the altar from Dominick X's deejay booth."[44] It is important to note the reference to the penis as "your supremacy," which reflects the notion that heteropatriarchal societies place certain expectations on men based on each society's concept of maleness, masculinity, and machismo. "Oppression positions homosexual masculinities at the bottom of a gender hierarchy among men. Gayness . . . is the repository of whatever is symbolically expelled from hegemonic masculinity."[45]

Xavier's description of Mikey is also reminiscent of La Fountain-Stokes, who writes in "My Name, Multitudinous Mass" that "I fuck whomever I want (or so the people say) and let whoever wants to fuck me do the same, we look like mysterious knots, tied one to the other in strange contortions that only wizards can undo" (66). This exposed aspect of their sexuality, whether fictional or not, is a confirmation of a sexual identity that is not separate from their ethnic identity. It does not take away from asserting their Puerto Ricanness, but instead it is an acknowledgment of another aspect of that *puertorriqueñidad.* Thus, their inclusion of these particular descriptions, for them as writers, has to do with the fact that "[c]ultural representations by homosexual men and women have sought not only to deconstruct those signs of deviance but also to incorporate them and use them for a different purpose."[46] This claim by Montero is one of the narrative strategies employed by Vázquez-Pacheco, La Fountain-Stokes, and Xavier.

The scholarship pertaining to Puerto Rican homosexuality has generalized this group, placing on them labels that reflect "behavioral characteristics" based on sexual roles duplicated by other groups. This labeling also reflects the neocolonialist process of categorizing individuals into niches. Ramírez, for example, describes five categories of Puerto Rican men: straight, *entendido, ponca, bugarrón, and loca* (and within the *loca* category there are three subdivisions: *loca pasiva, loca activa,* and *vestida*).[47] Again, this form of labeling is a characteristic that is present in colonialist/neocolonialist models of identification, which have been adopted as well in *el ambiente.* As Hall affirms, homosexuals themselves "have often oppressed gender non-conformists within their own community."[48] The question that comes into play is, "Are [Puerto Rican] homosexuals structured along lines of power/dominance firmly rooted in a patriarchal [Puerto Rican] culture that privileges men over women and the masculine over the feminine?"[49] The answer must be yes if they are grouped into one of the two genders that Western societies recognize—and at the same time deny any deviation from. Thus, Robert Vázquez-Pacheco, Emanuel Xavier, and Larry La Fontaine-Stokes embark on a voyage of self-(re)discovery with the goal of reintroducing a "lost" or "denied" self to an entity that is in transition. And because identity cannot be defined but only interpreted, it will depend on their needs, experiences, and environment, as seen in Charlie and Mikey's cases, who do not claim one identity over another but instead go about their lives with the knowledge that they are who and what they are, which does not make either of them any less a man.

For Puerto Rican gay men, or the Diasporican homosexual, this search for the self has become a process of "imaginary reunification."[50] This reunification takes place as a new "breed" of Diasporican/Nuyorican writers make their way through the periphery, making their voices postcolonial, speaking for the first time, introducing the narrative and autobiographical "I" that has been denied in the past. As opposed to mainstream writers, they break with traditional forms of storytelling by avoiding mimicry and instead responding to a need to write their lives as detailed as they need to be—it is a reality that allows the peripheral Puerto Rican to voice his "existence." It is as Cruz-Malavé states: the Diasporicans "do not oppose dominant structures frontally, rather, they deploy themselves laterally, in a movement that, despite its fitful, disjunctive character, is more than an avoidance of dominant restrictive maneuvers. It is also a style, an art."[51] It is an interpolation into "mainstream" culture (North American, Puerto Rican, Diasporican) that allows them to ascertain, to reclaim, identities that until this point in time they have never been allowed to have.

NOTES

1. Judith Lorber, *Paradoxes of Gender* (New Haven, CT: Yale University Press, 1994); Annamarie Jagose, *Queer Theory: An Introduction* (New York: New York University Press, 1997); Donald E. Hall, *Queer Theories* (New York: Palgrave Macmillan, 2003).

2. Jagose, *Queer Theory*, 86.

3. Rafael L. Ramírez, *What It Means to Be a Man: Reflections on Puerto Rican Masculinity*, trans. Rosa E. Casper (New Brunswick, NJ: Rutgers University Press, 1999), 44–45.

4. Steven P. Kurtz, "Butterflies Undercover: Cuban and Puerto Rican Gay Masculinities in Miami," *Journal of Men's Studies* 7, no. 3 (Spring 1999).

5. Katherine Gatto, "Mambo, Merengue, Salsa: The Dynamics of Self Construction in Latina Autobiographical Narrative," *Philological Papers* 48 (Oct. 1998): 84.

6. Enrique Morales-Díaz, "Catching Glimpses: Appropriating the Female Gaze in Esmeralda Santiago's Autobiographical Writing," *Centro* 14, no. 2 (Fall 2002): 134.

7. Edna Acosta-Belén, "Beyond Island Boundaries: Ethnicity, Gender, and Culture Revitalization in Nuyorican Literature," *Callaloo* 15, no. 4 (Autumn 1992): 981–982.

8. Ibid., 980.

9. Arnaldo Cruz-Malavé, "Colonial Figures in Motion: Globalization and Translocality in Contemporary Puerto Rican Literature in the United States," *Centro* 14, no. 2 (Fall 2002): 4–25.

10. Larry La Fountain-Stokes, "My Name, Multitudinous Mass," in *Bésame Mucho: New Gay Latino Fiction*, ed. Jaime Manrique with Jesse Dorris (New York: Painted Leaf Press, 1999), 61. Hereafter cited in text.

11. Donald Hall, *Queer Theories*, 101.

12. Travis Montez, "Americano: An Interview with Emanuel Xavier," 2002, http://www.suspectthoughtpress.com/xavierinterview.html (accessed 2 Aug. 2003).

13. Donald Hall, *Queer Theories*, 46.

14. Ramírez, *What It Means to Be a Man*, 92.

15. John C. Hawley, ed., *Post-colonial Queer: Theoretical Intersections* (Albany: State University of New York Press, 2001), 20.

16. Acosta-Belén, "Beyond Island Boundaries," 989.

17. Ramírez, *What It Means to Be a Man,* 104.

18. Ibid., 89.

19. *El ambiente* is the Spanish equivalent to "in the life"—a way to refer to gay communities, lifestyles, and so on.

20. Oscar Montero, "The Signifying Queen: Critical Notes from a Latino Queer," in *Hispanisms and Homosexualities*, ed. Sylvia Molloy and Robert McKee Irwin (Durham, NC: Duke University Press, 1998), 161.

21. Hawley, *Post-colonial Queer*, 22.

22. José L. Torres-Padilla, "When 'I' Became Ethnic: Ethnogenesis and Three Early Puerto Rican Diaspora Writers," *Centro* 14, no. 2 (Fall 2002): 190.

23. Jaime Manrique with Jesse Dorris, eds., *Bésame Mucho: New Gay Latino Fiction* (New York: Painted Leaf Press, 1999), 60.

24. Ibid., 100.

25. Emanuel Xavier, *Americano* (San Francisco: Suspect Thoughts Press, 2002), 54.

26. Emanuel Xavier, "Banjee Hustler," in Manrique and Dorris, *Bésame Mucho*, 165.

27. Xavier, *Americano*, 54.

28. Ibid.

29. A *guayabera* is a type of shirt worn in tropical weather. It is originally from Cuba, where it was worn by peasants but later adopted by landowners. Today, many wear it in place of shirt and tie.

30. Acosta-Belén, "Beyond Island Boundaries," 981.

31. Robert Vázquez-Pacheco, "Brujo Time," in Manrique and Dorris, *Bésame Mucho*, 102. Hereafter cited in text.

32. Acosta-Belén, "Beyond Island Boundaries," 985.

33. Cruz-Malavé, "Toward an Art of Transvestism," 141.

34. Frances Negrón-Montaner, "Echoing Stonewall and Other Dilemmas: The Orga-

nizational Beginnings of a Gay and Lesbian Agenda in Puerto Rico, 1972–1977 (Part I)," *Centro* 4, no. 1 (Winter 1991–1992): 77.

35. Cruz-Malavé, "Colonial Figures in Motion," 8.

36. Torres-Padilla, "When 'I' Became Ethnic," 186.

37. Kurtz, "Butterflies Undercover."

38. Francisco Valdes defines "heteropatriarchy" as "the intertwining of androsexism and heterosexualism to validate malecentric and heterocentric biases." See his "Notes on the Conflation of Sex, Gender, and Sexual Orientation: A QueerCrit and LatCrit Perspective," in *The Latino/a Condition: A Critical Reader*, ed. Richard Delgado and Jean Stefancic (New York: New York University Press, 1998), 544.

39. Stuart Hall, "Cultural Identity and Diaspora," in *Colonial Discourse/Postcolonial Theory: A Reader*, ed. Patrick Williams (New York: Columbia University Press, 1994), 393.

40. Marina De Chiara, "A Tribe Called Europe," in *The Post-colonial Question: Common Skies/Divided Horizons*, ed. Iain Chambers and Linda Curti (New York: Routledge, 1996), 228–233.

41. Acosta-Belén, "Beyond Island Boundaries," 982.

42. Ibid., 984.

43. Tomás Almaguer, "Chicano Men: A Cartography of Homosexual Identity and Behavior," in *Social Perspectives in Lesbian and Gay Studies: A Reader*, ed. Peter M. Nardi and Beth E. Schneider (New York: Routledge, 1998), 357.

44. Xavier, "Banjee Hustler," 148.

45. R. W. Connell, *Masculinities* (Berkeley and Los Angeles: University of California Press, 1995), 78.

46. Montero, "Signifying Queen," 164.

47. Ramírez, *What It Means to Be a Man*, 95–98.

48. Donald Hall, *Queer Theories*, 97.

49. Almaguer, "Chicano Men," 357.

50. Stuart Hall, "Cultural Identity," 394.

51. Cruz-Malavé, "Colonial Figures in Motion," 10.

BIBLIOGRAPHY

Acosta-Belén, Edna. "Beyond Island Boundaries: Ethnicity, Gender, and Culture Revitalization in Nuyorican Literature." *Callaloo* 15, no. 4 (Autumn 1992): 979–998.

Almaguer, Tomás. "Chicano Men: A Cartography of Homosexual Identity and Behavior." In *Social Perspectives in Lesbian and Gay Studies: A Reader,* ed. Peter M. Nardi and Beth E. Schneider. New York: Routledge, 1998.

Balderston, Daniel, and Donna J. Guy, eds. *Sex and Sexuality in Latin America.* New York: New York University Press, 1997.

Connell, R. W. *Masculinities.* Berkeley and Los Angeles: University of California Press, 1995.

Cruz-Malavé, Arnaldo. "Colonial Figures in Motion: Globalization and Translocality in Contemporary Puerto Rican Literature in the U.S." *Centro* 14, no. 2 (Fall 2002): 4–25.

———. "Toward an Art of Transvestism: Colonialism and Homosexuality in Puerto Rican Literature." In *¿Entiendes?: Queer Readings, Hispanic Writings,* ed. Emilie L. Bergman and Paul Julian Smith, 137–67. Durham: Duke University Press, 1995.

———. "'What a Tangled Web!' Masculinity, Abjection, and the Foundations of Puerto Rican Literature in the United States." In *Sex and Sexuality in Latin America,* ed. Daniel Balderston and Donna J. Guy, 234–249. New York: New York University Press, 1997.

De Chiara, Marina. "A Tribe Called Europe." In *The Post-colonial Question: Common Skies/Divided Horizons,* ed. Iain Chambers and Linda Curti, 228–233. New York: Routledge, 1996.

Delgado, Richard, and Jean Stefancic, eds. *The Latino/a Condition: A Critical Reader.* New York: New York University Press, 1998.

Gatto, Katherine. "Mambo, Merengue, Salsa: The Dynamics of Self Construction in Latina Autobiographical Narrative." *Philological Papers* 48 (Oct. 1998): 84–90.

Hall, Donald E. *Queer Theories.* New York: Palgrave Macmillan, 2003.

Hall, Stuart. "Cultural Identity and Diaspora." In *Colonial Discourse/Post-colonial Theory: A Reader,* ed. Patrick Williams, 392–403. New York: Columbia University Press, 1994.

Hawley, John C., ed. *Post-colonial Queer: Theoretical Intersections.* Albany: State University of New York Press, 2001.

Jagose, Annamarie. *Queer Theory: An Introduction.* New York: New York University Press, 1997.

Kurtz, Steven P. "Butterflies Undercover: Cuban and Puerto Rican Gay Masculinities in Miami." *Journal of Men's Studies* 7, no. 3 (Spring 1999): 371–390.

La Fountain-Stokes, Larry. "My Name, Multitudinous Mass." In *Bésame Mucho: New Gay Latino Fiction,* ed. Jaime Manrique with Jesse Dorris, 61–67. New York: Painted Leaf Press, 1999.

Lorber, Judith. *Paradoxes of Gender.* New Haven, CT: Yale University Press, 1994.

Manrique, Jaime, with Jesse Dorris, eds. *Bésame Mucho: New Gay Latino Fiction.* New York: Painted Leaf Press, 1999.

Molloy, Sylvia, and Robert McKee Irwin, eds. *Hispanisms and Homosexualities.* Durham, NC: Duke University Press, 1998.

Montero, Oscar. "The Signifying Queen: Critical Notes from a Latino Queer." In *Hispanisms and Homosexualities*, ed. Sylvia Molloy and Robert McKee Irwin, 161–174. Durham, NC: Duke University Press, 1998.

Montez, Travis. "Americano: An Interview with Emanuel Xavier." 2002. http://www.suspectthoughtspress.com/xavierinterview.html (accessed 2 Aug. 2003).

Morales-Díaz, Enrique. "Catching Glimpses: Appropriating the Female Gaze in Esmeralda Santiago's Autobiographical Writing." *Centro* 14, no. 2 (Fall 2002): 131–147.

Nardi, Peter M., and Beth E. Schneider, eds. *Social Perspectives in Lesbian and Gay Studies: A Reader.* New York: Routledge, 1998.

Negrón-Muntaner, Frances. "Echoing Stonewall and Other Dilemmas: The Organizational Beginnings of a Gay and Lesbian Agenda in Puerto Rico, 1972–1977 (Part I)." *Centro* 4, no. 1 (Winter 1991–1992): 77–95.

Ramírez, Rafael L. *What It Means to Be a Man: Reflections on Puerto Rican Masculinity*. Trans. Rosa E. Casper. New Brunswick, NJ: Rutgers University Press, 1999.

Torres-Padilla, José L. "When 'I' Became Ethnic: Ethnogenesis and Three Early Puerto Rican Diaspora Writers." *Centro* 14, no. 2 (Fall 2002): 181–197.

Valdes, Francisco. "Notes on the Conflation of Sex, Gender, and Sexual Orientation: A QueerCrit and LatCrit Perspective." In *The Latino/a Condition: A Critical Reader*, ed. Richard Delgado and Jean Stefancic, 543–551. New York: New York University Press, 1998.

Vázquez-Pacheco, Robert. "Brujo Time." In *Bésame Mucho: New Gay Latino Fiction*, ed. Jaime Manrique with Jesse Dorris, 101–112. New York: Painted Leaf Press, 1999.

Xavier, Emanuel. *Americano*. San Francisco: Suspect Thoughts Press, 2002.

———. "Banjee Hustler." In *Bésame Mucho: New Gay Latino Fiction,* ed. Jaime Manrique with Jesse Dorris, 147–175. New York: Painted Leaf Press, 1999.

———. *Christ-Like*. New York: Painted Leaf Press, 1999.

15 MANUEL RAMOS OTERO'S QUEER METAFICTIONAL RESURRECTION OF JULIA DE BURGOS

BETSY A. SANDLIN

Manuel Ramos Otero (1948–1990) has earned considerable literary fame in Puerto Rico while remaining relatively unknown to many United States–based literary critics. Although he lived in New York for half of his life and wrote nearly all of his literature there, Ramos Otero only published works written in Spanish, thus complicating the traditional United States/island dichotomy by which many writers of Puerto Rican heritage have been categorized. Ramos Otero stressed that, for him, *brincar el charco* (jumping the puddle) did not provide a moment of cultural amnesia in which he forgot his "old" self and embraced the "new"; rather, it was only on the "other" side of the so-called puddle that he could analyze his *puertorriqueñidad*: "Esta ciudad [New York] me dio la distancia necesaria para entender a Puerto Rico y crecer políticamente. Aquí desarrollé mi identidad como puertorriqueño" (This city gave me the distance necessary to understand Puerto Rico and to grow politically. Here I developed my identity as a Puerto Rican).[1]

Ramos Otero's decision to move to the United States stemmed from the marginalization he felt on the island as a result of his homosexuality, making him what Manuel Guzmán has termed a "(s)exile."[2] Ramos Otero commented in an interview, "no aguantaba la atmósfera represiva de Puerto Rico. . . . En Puerto Rico sentía muchísima persecución debido a la apertura de mi sexualidad" (I could not bear Puerto Rico's repressive atmosphere. . . . In Puerto Rico I felt a lot of persecution due to my sexuality).[3] Although not perfect, New York became a space from which he could live and write with less social stigmatization. Nonetheless, Ramos Otero constantly negotiated tensions he felt between two of his "identities" (gay and Puerto Rican), which, although lived simultaneously, could not always be expressed as such: "Constantemente repito que para mí, en Puerto Rico siempre fue más fácil ser puertorriqueño que homosexual, y en Nueva York es más fácil ser homosexual que puertorriqueño" (I constantly repeat that for me, in Puerto Rico it was always easier to be Puerto Rican than homosexual, and in New York it is easier to be homosexual than Puerto Rican).[4] In "El cuento de la Mujer del Mar" from the eponymous collection of short stories published in 1979, a man simply called *el cuentero* (the storyteller) reflects on his multiple identities—as an immigrant and a (s)exile, a gay man, a writer, and a Puerto Rican. The storyteller's multiple identifications are embodied in the character Palmira Parés, who may be interpreted as a fictional version of poet Julia de Burgos (1914–1953), herself now a "fictionalized" historical figure from Puerto Rico's past. Parés, who mirrors Burgos, is constructed to further mirror *el cuentero*, who in turn could be interpreted as Ramos Otero's fictionalized double.

In Ramos Otero's short story, the queering[5] of his literary precursor, a woman who has been transformed into a mythic figure and cultural icon,[6] is an oppositional strategy that manipulates the past in order to infiltrate and critique dominant, homophobic notions of Puerto Ricanness and Puerto Rican literary history. Traditionally, both of these categories of identification have misrepresented, underrepresented, or failed to (re)present gay, lesbian, or otherwise queer perspectives. The storyteller's primary tactics, in the process of claiming his (and Ramos Otero's) right to define himself as a Puerto Rican author despite perceived "otherness," include retelling the story of Julia de Burgos by queering her into the abject character "Palmira Parés"; revalorizing her because of this queerness; and demonstrating how Julia/Palmira has transcended death, *olvido* (obscurity), and erasure, a feat the *cuentero* (and Ramos Otero) himself aims to achieve.

On a simplistic level, "El cuento de la Mujer del Mar" is a metastory, or a story about storytelling. The Puerto Rican *cuentero* and his Italian lover, Angelo, alternately take on the role of Scheherazade, maintaining their love affair through the nocturnal construction of the parallel stories of Palmira Parés and Vicenza Vitale, as New York City is converted nightly into their own private Arabia. In the words of the *cuentero*, "era necesario que Angelo siguiera siendo el amado, aún si para retenerlo a mi lado, hubiera tenido que contarle el cuento de una mujer que no existió" (it was necessary for Angelo to continue being the lover, even if to keep him at my side, I would have to tell him the story of a woman who didn't exist).[7]

Palmira is scripted as a well-known legend from the *cuentero's* homeland, whereas Vicenza is molded after Angelo's Italian immigrant grandmother. Through the men's storytelling, however, the two women blend together as one mythic character called "the woman of the sea," "la Mujer del Mar," or "la donna del mare" [*sic*]. Both men are immigrants in New York City, reviving and reconstructing images of women who represent their cultural pasts—retellings that often contain more fiction than fact, as the *cuentero* suggests—in order to confront the present:

> [L]a maldición de amor entre dos emigrados, yo buscándome en los versos viejos de Palmira Parés y la visión fantasma del pueblo costero, él regresando por la misma ruta de Vicenza Vitale a la playa frente al volcán, a la Napoli polvorienta de los cuentos frente al fuego en un sótano de Bayonne. Amándonos en la zona de un inglés callejero. (100–101)
> [The curse of love between two emigrants, me searching for myself in the old verses of Palmira Parés and the ghostly vision of a coastal town, him returning by Vicenza Vitale's route to the beach near the volcano, to the dusty Naples of stories in front of a fire in a basement in Bayonne. Loving each other in the area of street English.]

Palmira Parés may be understood as an easily recognizable yet fictionalized version of Julia de Burgos, who has become a mythic figure herself in Puerto Rican culture on and off the island. Burgos's life was infamously marked by tragedy, depression, and melancholia—epitomized by her mysterious death in New York City as she wandered the streets alone and without identification.[8] Similarly, Magali García Ramis describes Parés as "[a]n image of the kind of poet who, a failure before the world and bourgeois respectability, takes refuge in drugs, death, a needle, love, escape, a lethal move toward New York, the cold, work—the end."[9] As a (s)exile, Ramos Otero's protagonist is also a social outcast; both he and his precursor thus reside outside the parameters of "acceptable" behavior in their native Puerto Rico, compelling both to leave.

Regarding the life story of Palmira/Julia, the *cuentero* notes, "[h]ay versiones" (there are versions; 95). Ramos Otero's queer version of Julia de Burgos—reconfigured as Parés—emphasizes her as a *mujer mala* (bad woman): a heroin addict who spent time in jail and died of a drug overdose, a madwoman with syphilis, and (notably, something García Ramis does not mention) a lesbian or perhaps a bisexual. In resurrecting his precursor, the *cuentero* "exposes" (i.e., composes) rumors about her life that would not be accepted by dominant society, or by Puerto Ricans who would wish to promote a nostalgic, idealized picture of Julia de Burgos as a heroic symbol of *puertorriqueñidad*.

An example of the "desecration" of Burgos's image is a tale in which Palmira is interpreted by the police ("ellos")—enforcers of hegemony—as a violent hysteric and drug user while they uncover visual evidence of her *locura* (madness) in a hotel room:

> En vez de plumas de pavo real para rasgar la lira, encontraron las agujas rojas todavía y la jeringuilla de cristal. Encontraron el presentimiento de que la Mujer del Mar había asumido a plenitud la locura. Tal vez fue el miedo que sintieron cuando vieron las navajas yén clavadas en el espejo. (95–96)
> [Instead of peacock feathers to pluck the lyre, they found needles still red and the glass syringe. They found the premonition that the Woman of the Sea had gone completely mad. Perhaps it was the fear they felt when they saw the knives still stuck in the mirror.]

Not only do the knives thrust into the mirror visually represent Palmira's "madness," but one could also argue that the shattered, disrupted mirror symbolizes a rejection of her "self" as it is projected to the outside world.[10] Through her violent actions, Palmira instills fear in the representatives of dominant society, demonstrating that she is beyond their understanding and, as such, beyond their control. The storyteller seizes postmortem power over the poet's image, uncovering "truths" about her that mainstream mythification would scramble to conceal. The marginalized storyteller thus claims Julia de Burgos (disguised as Palmira) as one of his own, stripping her away from her status as a socially accepted/acceptable cultural symbol and converting her instead into a queer icon.

One way in which Ramos Otero deviates from Burgos's commonly told biography is in the portrayal of Parés's childhood. According to the narrator, "[s]u padre es Francisco Parés, herrero del Bitumur, hombre de complejo carácter donde se funde la soberbia, el ansia del mar y la vida aventurera" (her father is Francisco Parés, blacksmith from Bitumur, a man of complex character in whom pride, a yearning for the sea, and a life of adventure meld together; 91–92). In this sense, the father figure is similar to romanticized accounts of Burgos's father, who is often characterized as the cause of the poet's love of the sea and the Puerto Rican landscape, as well as the person who introduced her to tales of adventure, thus inspiring her to become a writer.[11] However, Ramos Otero's version eventually disrupts the traditional, triadic patriarchal family structure (husband, wife, and child), first by making the poet's mother a marginalized *mujer mala*, as Palmira herself will later become: "De la madre se sabe que los abandonó por un pescador y que murió de malaria en una casucha gris al margen de la desembocadura del río Manatí" (Of the mother, it is known that she abandoned them for a fisherman and that she died of malaria in a gray shack on the bank of the mouth of the Manatí River; 92). Ramos Otero then further queers the poet's upbringing by turning her into an orphan and disappearing the patriarch into the sea: "Todavía una niña, va a vivir al pueblo en el Orfelinato de la Inmaculada. Francisco Parés se va de marino mercante, nunca escribe ni regresa" (Still a child, she goes to town to live in the Orphanage of the Immaculate Conception. Francisco Parés leaves to become a merchant marine; he never writes or returns; 92). Thus, the paternalistic influence often ascribed to Burgos is dismantled. Parés's abandonment by her family is depicted as the cause of her "eterno peregrinar por las playas de la infancia" (eternal pilgrimage through the beaches of her youth) and the reason for her nickname "la Mujer del Mar" (92). In this way, heterosexual love and loss are stripped of their privilege as the basis for the poet's melancholia, a move that is particularly significant since one widely accepted version of Burgos's life story plots her as a romantic heroine who suffered from depression after being abandoned by her lover, leading to alcoholism and her eventual death.[12]

Ramos Otero's account of the Julia de Burgos story does not cast her as the tragic heroine of a traditional (heterosexual) romance plot. On the contrary, Palmira's most important intimate encounter comes from a same-sex relationship with Filimelé, an intertextual reference to a character who appears in two poems—"La búsqueda asesina" and "Puerta al tiempo en tres voces"—by Luis Palés Matos. In his study of the figure of Filí-Melé,[13] created by Palés Matos and re-created by contemporary Puerto Rican poet Iván Silén, Alfredo Villanueva Collado concludes that both poets script the character as an object of *machista* fantasies. In the case of Palés, he argues, the poet "rechazado por una Filí-Melé que ejerce su derecho de selección erótica, la transforma en una musa poética que no es sino un personaje creado por el artista y por lo tanto sometido a la mano moldeante de su fantasía" (rejected by a Filí-Melé who exerts her right to erotic choice, he transforms her into a poetic muse who is merely a character created by the artist and therefore subjected to the molding hand of his fantasy).[14] Ramos Otero's version of Filí-Melé not only rejects her male creators' sexual advances but also does so in favor of a female partner:

> A Filimelé la llamaron siempre la mujer de los Poetas. . . . En una casa de la Marina con balcones de hierro, ella fue la mujer de la Mujer del Mar. Ahora nadie dirá que fue cierto, Palmira Parés escandalizó el orden de su época. (102)
> [They always called Filimelé the woman of Poets. . . . In a house at the Marina with iron balconies, she was the woman of the Woman of the Sea. Now no one will say it was true, Palmira Parés scandalized the order of her time.]

He thus reveals Parés's queerness while also identifying with Palmira's same-sex desire on a personal level and uncovering and celebrating the "scandal" she caused.

The *cuentero* situates the love affair of Palmira and Filimelé at night in the ironically named "Hotel Central." The hotel, as a traditionally marginal space, and night, as a marginal time, may symbolize obfuscation, migration, homelessness, and (s)exile. In "El cuento de la Mujer del Mar," though, the darkness of night and the privacy of hotel rooms provide veils of protection for all the lovers—*el cuentero* and Angelo in the Hotel Christopher, as well as Palmira and Filimelé, whose love affair lives in the nightly, private narrations of the two men, is mirrored in the men's relationship, and is "resurrected" (i.e., invented) publicly in Ramos Otero's story. The men are sheltered by the safe spaces of storytelling, the night, and New York's Christopher Street alleyways, stoops, and shadows, which become sites of sexual freedom where "el miedo," or fear caused by socially imposed restrictions, disappears (94). Despite their seemingly abject nature, images of "calles abandonadas," "ruinas," "la negra intemperie," and "peldaños orinados" (abandoned streets; ruins; the black darkness; the urine-covered steps; 94) are positively reconfigured as sites of love and creativity. The sunlight that would expose the men and terminate their private, nocturnal storytelling is perceived as an unwelcome threat. Like vampires, the two men remain "cogidos por la mano para no ver el sol" (holding hands in order to not see the sun; 94). The sunlight, as a symbol of mainstream society, signals the end of their affair and of the "women of the sea":

> Sentados en los escalones de Christopher Street, casi abrazados pero nunca, casi sabiendo que lo nuestro no existiría cuando saliera el sol, a menos que la viéramos doblar una esquina y contáramos su cuento cuando sale la luna. (101)
> [Sitting on the stairs of Christopher Street, almost hugging but never, almost knowing that what was ours wouldn't exist when the sun came up, unless we saw her turn the corner and we told her story when the moon comes out.]

The characterization of the hotel in which one awaits his or her lovers as "uninhabited" and as located strategically on the "shores" of the sea highlights its marginality, its existence on the fringe, away from heteronormative society:

> Uno sabe que a veces, al mirarse al espejo, uno es una llaga de fuego. Uno sabe, que otras veces, uno es la Mujer del Mar, hambrienta del amor, buscando a todos los marineros de barbas rojas que alguna vez siguieron su rostro transformado por el azogue, en el espejo empañado de un hotel deshabitado, a la orilla del mar. (91)
> [One knows that sometimes, looking at himself in the mirror, he is a wound of fire. One knows that other times, he is the Woman of the Sea, hungry for love, looking for all the sailors with red beards that once followed his face transformed by mercury, in the steamy mirror of an uninhabited hotel, at the seashore.]

Here, the protagonist directly identifies himself not only with but also as the "woman of the sea" ("otras veces, uno es la Mujer del Mar"). Although Arnaldo Cruz-Malavé has discussed this strategy as cross-gender identification, or a type of literary transvestism, the strategic verb "es" suggests more than imitation; instead, there is a hermaphroditic melding of the two (or four) subjects: Palmira (Julia) and *el cuentero* (a thin disguise for Ramos Otero himself).[15] Negating the "logic" of gender and chronological boundaries, the protagonist later proclaims, as if pointing to a past life: "Es probable quen [*sic*] algún lugar del tiempo, yo fuera la Mujer del Mar" (It is probable that in some other place or time, I was the Woman of the Sea; 98).

Cruz-Malavé argues that Ramos Otero's protagonists willingly inhabit abject positions, finding power and a voice in "castration and gender-crossing, superfluidity and equivocalness."[16] He suggests that Ramos Otero's characters openly celebrate and flaunt their *locura* (both madness and queerness) in a campy, yet politically defiant, stance. In "El cuento de la Mujer del Mar," similarly, Ramos Otero crosses gendered, dualistic lines to identify and fuse with a female literary precursor (Palmira/Julia). Of this connection, Gelpí asserts: "En lugar de crear una genealogía literaria o de prolongar el logos paterno, se establece una alianza con una figura doblemente marginada por el canon: como poeta y como mujer" (Instead of creating a literary genealogy or extending the paternal logos, an alliance is established with a figure doubly marginalized by the canon: as a poet and as a woman).[17] In his alliance with Parés, one could also argue that the storyteller willingly self-identifies with what could be considered stereotypes: the gay man as feminized, and the "feminine" as prone to hysteria and irrationality. Significantly, the gay protagonist revalorizes Palmira's madness and thereby embraces his own affective self as fodder for his writing.

The *cuentero* most admires Parés's self-reflexive poetry, in which he claims she revealed her deepest and darkest (what he considers her truest) self. The story features eleven excerpts that were supposedly written by Parés, often about her relationship with Filimelé. Parés's titles—"Los espejos del tiempo" (The Mirrors of Time), "Los callejones del exilio" (The Alleyways of Exile), and "El mar" (The Sea)[18]—reflect thematic preoccupations of Burgos/Parés and the *cuentero*/Ramos Otero, including identity and self-reflection (reflective bodies of water that act like mirrors), recalling and rewriting the past, and the making visible of the marginal spaces that (s)exiles inhabit, represented by "alleyways of exile." The storyteller/Ramos Otero identifies with Burgos, re-created as Parés, on multiple levels: a self-reflexive interest in their craft, the experience of exile from the island, and metaphorical (s)exile within a patriarchal and heterosexual system and economy of emotions.

Through quoting her poetry in his retelling of the story of the "Mujer del Mar," the *cuentero* seeks to expose the "truth" of her life:

> Yo quería escribir la verdadera historia de Palmira Parés, oscura poeta de mi pueblo, sabiendo quel [*sic*] más nocturno de sus versos dice más del ser del mar que cualquier playa enlluvecida. Nadie comprenderá jamás que sus momentos más fantasmales fueron las madrugadas de heroína en el exilio. (107)
>
> [I wanted to write the true story of Palmira Parés, dark poet of my town/people, knowing that the most noctural of her verses say more about being from the sea than any rain-soaked beach. No one will ever understand that her most phantasmal moments were her early mornings of heroine/heroin in exile.]

The multiple meanings of "oscura poeta" ("dark poet," in reference to her morose themes, the color of her skin, and her obscurity to those outside Puerto Rico) and the dual meaning of "heroína" (heroin and heroine) illustrate not only admiration and valorization but also the refusal to reject the abject in his precursor, signaling an acceptance and celebration of his own social marginalities. Palmira is not completely idolized or idealized by the *cuentero* but is instead valued for her complexities, "imperfections," and notoriety. For the *cuentero*, Julia/Palmira's "momentos más fantasmales" ("ghostly" and thus strange or queer) are cause for commemoration.

Despite morbid images that would seem to indicate what Cañas labels "derrotismo" (defeatism) in Ramos Otero's literature, in "El cuento de la Mujer del Mar" death is not entirely negative.[19] While it could be a traditional metaphor for marginality, particularly in terms of the "social death" involved in being a (s)exile, in the poetry of Parés the very boundaries between life and death are blurred, as the *cuentero* remarks: "la vida es lo mismo quel [*sic*] crepúsculo, es lo mismo quel [*sic*] verano de Venus, la vida es, inevitablemente, lo mismo que la muerte" (life is the same as the twilight, it is the same as the summer of Venus, life is, inevitably, the same as death; 97). Death may be a path to transcendence, like the sexual release of "the little death," as the storyteller remarks: "Angelo y yo nos amaremos siempre, aunque las enfermedades incurables, como la sífilis o el cáncer, nos separen, quedan las miles de noches del amor *en busca de la muerte*" (Angelo and I will love each other forever, even though incurable diseases, like syphilis or cancer, might separate us, the thousands of nights of love in search of death remain; 94, italics added). Like craziness, darkness, hotels, and other sites of queerness, death and writing can be liberatory spaces. In praising Palmira's "libro más maravilloso: *El mar*," which the *cuentero* especially admires for its metapoetic nature, he comments:

> Es el acto de creación el que finalmente la libera para dejarla sola con la muerte, repitiendo el encuentro con la otra [Filimelé], múltiple, mar, marinera de la muerte. Entonces sus versos enloquecen fragmentando la realidad en suicidios sucesivos, como un eclipse. (108)
> [It is the act of creation that finally liberates her to leave her alone with death, repeating the encounter with the other woman, multiple, sea, mariner of death. Then her verses go mad fragmenting reality into successive suicides, like an eclipse.]

Again, for the storyteller, the fragmentation and madness that he finds in Palmira's last book increase its value and authenticity. Writing, or "el acto de creación," and death are forces that free Parés, and therefore the *cuentero*, from a repressive society, allowing them to be "múltiple," complex, contradictory.

Writing is also the way in which Palmira and the *cuentero* can achieve a sort of eternal existence. Just as Palmira lives on through her verses and in the ongoing cultural reconstruction of her image, the *cuentero* hopes to subvert his own physical mortality, since "[n]o hay cuentero que no muera, pero el cuento eterniza lo que contaron sus manos" (there is no storyteller who doesn't die, but the story eternalizes that which his hands told; 115). To protect himself from "olvido" after his physical body no longer existed, Cañas insists that Ramos Otero wanted to leave "una imagen, una máscara, que fuera lo suficientemente potente como para que perdurara más allá de su muerte" (an image, a mask, that was powerful enough to outlast death).[20] I contend that this is one of the motivations for his resurrection of a famous literary precursor—to show that such an eternal existence is possible through literature, storytelling, (self-)mythification, and the re-creation of one's image by the public. It was important for Ramos Otero to leave such an indelible mark so that his queer presence would continue to disrupt the patriarchal and heteronormative literary tradition and definitions of *puertorriqueñidad* that he inherited, even after his physical life was extinguished. Through the queering of Julia de Burgos, then, Puerto Rican literary history is placed under severe scrutiny. According to Rubén Ríos Ávila, "Ramos Otero has no nation to dismantle, no authoritarian father figure to debunk . . . in his case the target is the literary canon of Puerto Rican letters."[21]

In the metafictional story of the "Mujer del Mar," for instance, literary genre lines, Puerto Rican literary criticism, and the Puerto Rican "canon" are challenged. The story sometimes reads more like literary criticism, complete with "factual" footnotes, citations of her (fictional) poetry, and (fictional) bibliographic references. In one such moment, the storyteller lashes out at critics who have misunderstood Parés's poetry. After a fictional quote from an unnamed scholar who blamed Parés for "un libro desigual que carece de unidad temática y de enfoque" (an uneven book that lacks thematic unity and focus), the *cuentero* retaliates in a footnote: "Estos 'retazos críticos' nada añaden a la comprensión de su poesía. Se incluyen por el carácter anecdótico de sus palabras, como testimonio inmóvil de una 'crítica' que todavía los hispanistas cultivan" (These "critical fragments" add nothing to the understanding of her poetry. They are included for the anecdotal character of their words, as unwavering testimony to the "criticism" that Hispanists still cultivate; 107n9). In a recuperatory move that rescues Palmira/Julia from the grasp of such closed-minded literary "authorities," the protagonist revalorizes his precursor for breaking with tradition, much as he does:

> Palmira Parés es el poeta puertorriqueño más ignorado de su tiempo. . . . Rompe los ríos folklóricos que azotan entonces con fatal persistencia a nuestra lírica, para invadir el más intenso drama metafísico del hombre, en la zona del mar, invisible desde el exilio. Rechaza el lirismo lúbrico de muchos contemporáneos, persiguiendo en el ritmo agónico de su verso su propia palpitación. (108–109)
> [Palmira Parés is the most ignored Puerto Rican poet of her time. . . . She breaks the folkloric rivers that lashed with fatal persistence against our poetry, to overcome the most intense metaphysical drama of man, in the zone of the sea, invisible from exile. She rejects the lubricous lyricism of many of her contemporaries, pursuing her own beat in the moribund rhythm of her verses.]

He then praises the publication of "un estudio de su poesía [que] *la redime justamente del olvido: Palmira Parés: poeta de la esquizofrenia*, Oscar Azevedo, Revista de Artes y Letras, Universidad de la Habana, Número 7 de 1950" (a study of her poetry [that] justly redeems her from oblivion: *Palmira Parés: Poet of Schizophrenia*; 109, italics added). This bibliographic citation by the obtrusive narrator disrupts the "fictional" frame of the story, appearing in the main body of the text—not in the footnotes, as most of his citations do—to further emphasize the *cuentero's* own fixation on escaping oblivion/erasure. It also illustrates once again the "queerness" (schizophrenia) of Parés as seen in her verses and with which he identifies.

The eponymous collection in which "El cuento de la Mujer del Mar" was published begins with an epigraph from Palés Matos that expresses the idea that history and stories, which can both be translated as *historia* in Spanish, are one and the same:

> y en resumen, tiempo perdido
> que me acaba en aburrimiento.
> Algo entrevisto o presentido,
> poco realmente vivido
> y mucho de embuste y de cuento.
> [and in summary, time lost
> that ends in boredom.
> Something foreseen or foretold,
> little truly lived
> and many lies and stories.]

"Time lost"—that is, the past—does not inspire nostalgia or attempts to recuperate its loss but is, instead, the cause of "boredom" and an invitation for invention; unhindered by chronology, it also looks forward, being foreseen, predicted, guessed. Memory consists of lies, fibs, hoaxes, and stories. It is with these thoughts in mind that Ramos Otero seizes the "real" Julia de Burgos from Puerto Rico's (literary and cultural) history and turns her into Palmira Parés. For Ramos Otero, authoring a text is an opportunity to play with the past and subvert dominant cultural memories and myths.

Ramos Otero's resurrection of his literary precursor and transformation of her into a fellow (s)exile are undoubtedly metafictional meditations. While I have been unsuccessful in finding a clearly demarcated theory of what might be called "queer metafiction," the political transgression involved in feminist metafiction holds promise for authors whose metafictional projects involve not only homosexual identification but other markers of social "difference."[22] Clearly, feminist, gay, lesbian, and "queer" concerns should not be conflated, but the need for correcting and/or inserting such representations and perspectives into inherited literary traditions presents a similar metaliterary cause. While the issue of misrepresentation seems to be the focus of feminist metafiction, queer metafiction would deal mainly with erasure and negation, that is, the lack of openly queer issues, themes, and authors. This is particularly true in the case of Ramos Otero, who faced a literary tradition that, as Cruz-Malavé, Torres, and others have noted, was nearly devoid of queer voices before he burst onto the scene in the 1970s.

David William Foster has examined the connection between homosexuality and metafiction in repressive realities that exclude and/or misrepresent homosexuals. He argues that "[f]rom the point of view of the literary author, problems related to dealing with taboo and denigrated subjects can lead naturally to a metafictional interest in making the representation and narration of such subjects one foregrounded aspect of a text."[23] In other words, authors who deal with homosexual themes and live in societies that wish to silence and erase them may also self-consciously deal with the very issue of representation in their texts. According to Foster, gay and lesbian authors therefore have an urgent, and perhaps necessary, preoccupation with metafiction, and he lists one of the problems they address as "how to leave a record of personal experiences that seem to be illegitimate and insubstantial because they lack any confirming function within textual models available for reporting them."[24]

Foster's work provides an important stepping-stone, but it is too literally grounded in the heterosexual/homosexual binary to be labeled as a full theorization of what I would call "queer metafiction." Once again, DeGuzmán reminds us that the term "queer" goes beyond the literal designation of same-sex relations and instead serves as a transgressive adjective and verb "meaning to question, to puzzle, to put in doubt."[25] Michael Warner echoes this sentiment, insisting that "[t]he preference for 'queer' represents, among other things, an aggressive impulse of generalization. . . . For both academics and activists, 'queer' gets a critical edge by *defining itself against the normal rather than the heterosexual.*"[26]

Such an active questioning of the "norm," and the very category of "normal," runs throughout Ramos Otero's story. His metafiction is concerned with leaving a record of "difference" in various forms and expressions, not just the representation of homosexuality as an essential category of identity. Ramos Otero's spaces, characters, and themes are queer in many ways; he addresses marginalization in terms of not only homosexuality but also gender, madness, illness, drug use, profession, exile, and colonization. As these categories intersect, Ramos Otero's *cuentero* is able to imagine himself as and identify with a fictionalized version of Julia de Burgos beneath a broad rubric that we may label "queer." As Warner asserts, "'Queer' is also a way of cutting against mandatory gender divisions,"[27] and such a link between the male, homosexual poet and the famous, female, self-identified heterosexual poet—according to dominant labeling structures—is not only plausible but also politically successful in the *cuentero's* quest for visibility. In "El cuento de la Mujer del Mar," Ramos Otero represents queerness on two levels: first, on the metafictional level, within the story, as the *cuentero* contemplates his own craft and fights to define himself as a legitimate voice in the homophobic literary landscape he inhabits; and second, through the rewriting of Julia de Burgos, a dominant sign belonging to the literary and social spheres that repress him, transgressively recontextualizing her to (re)present his own (previously unrepresented) subjectivity.

Through the *cuentero*, Ramos Otero revives (remembers, recuperates) and radically re-visions (re-mythifies, re-cognizes) his literary precursor for his own metafictional survival. Laura Doan and Sara Waters argue that gay and lesbian authors often construct their own metaliterary genealogies, since it is difficult to find any in extant cultural texts. They illustrate this creative move with the recurrence of supernatural beings in lesbian fiction, which appear because of what they characterize as the "uneasiness" of the project of "making up lost time." Doan and Waters explain that ghosts like Julia/Palmira "occupy abject but troubling positions on the borders of dominant structures of knowledge; like legends, they function as the natural repositories of subversive secrets, offering those secrets for recognition and retrieval by the empathetic reader of historical texts."[28]

Aurea María Sotomayor insists that, for Ramos Otero, "[l]a genealogía en su narrativa funciona a manera de un estilete que rasga 'las quimeras del origen' que son la clase, el sexo, la familia, la nación" (geneology in his narrative functions as a stylus/dagger that tears "the chimeras of origin" that are class, sex, family, and nation).[29] In his quest to not only retrieve but reconstruct his genealogy, as Sotomayor suggests, markers of "identity" are fused together, interchangeable, and malleable; the *cuentero* is Palmira, who is Vicenza, who is Ramos Otero and at times Angelo; fiction is history, history is fiction, literature is criticism, poetry is prose. Sotomayor argues that, in Ramos Otero's literature, "El genealogista fragmenta, busca fisuras, descubre lo heterogéneo" (The genealogist fragments, looks for fissures, discovers the heterogeneous).[30]

I suggest that Ramos Otero's resurrection and reconstruction of a historical figure and, more importantly, a literary precursor focus on multiple layers of queer identification, self-reflection, and the revision of historical/literary record necessary for the survival of minoritarian subjects like the *cuentero* and Ramos Otero himself. He queers Julia de Burgos in part to validate his own subjectivity and to disrupt Puerto Rican literature and identity narratives with his own queer voice, celebrating the reality of social marginality while also questioning its very terms. What would be deemed by heterosexist society as the uncomfortable desecration of a revered cultural figure is a way for Ramos Otero to exact a metafictional revenge against a literary tradition that would historically reject and silence him and consign him to oblivion. By identifying with a Puerto Rican literary and cultural icon and reconstructing her as a (s)exile, Ramos Otero and his autobiographical *cuentero* are able to construct a liberatory, "queer metafictional" space in which the past is creatively manipulated to embrace so-called marginalized perspectives in definitions of *puertorriqueñidad* and, more specifically, Puerto Rican literature.

NOTES

1. Marithelma Costa, "Entrevista: Manuel Ramos Otero," *Hispamérica* 20, no. 59 (1991): 61.

2. The term "sexile" is used by Manuel Guzmán to describe those who leave their homelands primarily in order to flee persecution based on sexual orientation. See Manuel Guzmán, "'Pa' La Escuelita con Mucho Cuida'o y por la Orillita': A Journey through the

Contested Terrains of the Nation and Sexual Orientation," in *Puerto Rican Jam: Rethinking Colonialism and Nationalism*, ed. Frances Negrón-Muntaner and Ramón Grosfoguel (Minneapolis: University of Minnesota Press, 1997), 209–228.

3. Costa, "Entrevista," 59.

4. Ibid., 61.

5. I use the transitive verb "to queer" to connote the act of questioning, opposing, and defying patriarchal and heterosexist standards of "normativity." As María DeGuzmán explains, the term "conveys not merely same-sex object choice, but the activity of putting something taken for granted into question." She adds, "From the end of the eighteenth century onward, 'queer' was actually employed as a verb—'to queer'—meaning to question, to puzzle, to put in doubt. . . . 'Queer' as a verb and as an adjective marks a resistance to conventional social structures and business as usual." See her "Turning Tricks: Trafficking in the Figure of the Latino," in *Trickster Lives: Culture and Myth in American Fiction*, ed. Jeanne Campbell Reesman (Athens, GA: University of Georgia Press, 2001), 170.

6. The Julia de Burgos mythos has been discussed by Manuel de la Puebla and others. I examine her as a cultural icon in my dissertation: "Julia de Burgos as a Cultural Icon in Works by Rosario Ferré, Luz María Umpierre, and Manuel Ramos Otero" (PhD diss., University of North Carolina, 2003).

7. Manuel Ramos Otero, "El cuento de la Mujer del Mar," in *El cuento de la Mujer del Mar*, by Manuel Ramos Otero (Río Piedras, PR: Ediciones Huracán, 1979), 89. Hereafter cited in text.

8. Much has been written about Burgos's demise. See, e.g., Consuelo López Springfield, "'I Am the Life, the Strength, the Woman': Feminism in Julia de Burgos' Autobiographical Poetry," *Callaloo* 17, no. 3 (1994): 701–714; Manuel de la Puebla, *Julia de Burgos, amor y soledad* (Madrid: Torremozas, 1994).

9. Magali García Ramis, "Women's Tales," in *Images and Identities: The Puerto Rican in Two World Contexts*, ed. and trans. Asela Rodríguez de Laguna (New Brunswick, NJ: Transaction, 1987), 109–110.

10. In "A Julia de Burgos" from her *Poema en veinte surcos* (1938), the private "yo" is praised as the more liberated voice that finds self-expression in poetry; the public Julia ("tú") is criticized as a false, social construction that bows to the expectations of others.

11. For more on the romanticized portrait of Burgos's father, see López Springfield, "'I Am the Life, the Strength, the Woman.'"

12. For discussions of Burgos as a romanticized, tragic heroine, see María M. Solá, "La poesía de Julia de Burgos: Mujer de humana lucha," in *Yo misma fui mi ruta*, by Julia de Burgos, ed. María M. Solá (Río Piedras, PR: Ediciones Huracán, 1986), 7–48; Luz M. Medero-Díaz, "The Cultural Myth of Julia de Burgos" (MA thesis, Arizona State University, 1993).

13. I have maintained each author's spelling of the character's name.

14. Alfredo Villanueva Collado, "Filí-Melé: Símbolo y mujer en la poesía de Luis Palés Matos e Iván Silén," *Revista Chicano-riqueña* 10 (1982): 53.

15. Cruz-Malavé and Gelpí link the *cuentero*/Ramos Otero and Burgos/Parés based on biographical facts that overlap, like place of birth and the recurrence of autobiogra-

phy in Ramos Otero's work. See Arnaldo Cruz-Malavé, "Toward an Art of Transvestism: Colonialism and Homosexuality in Puerto Rican Literature," in *¿Entiendes? Queer Readings, Hispanic Writings*, ed. Emilie L. Bergmann and Paul Julian Smith (Durham, NC: Duke University Press, 1995), 137–167; Juan Gelpí, *Literatura y paternalismo en Puerto Rico* (San Juan: Editorial de la UPR, 1993).

16. Cruz-Malavé, "Toward an Art of Transvestism," 137. As Cruz-Malavé notes, for Antonio Pedreira and René Marqués—both of whom wrote about Puerto Rico's colonized status—Puerto Rico is negatively portrayed as "a male child who had to come to terms with his fallen national past before achieving manhood and independence" (ibid., 138). For Marqués, homosexuality is "the collective condition of all Puerto Ricans, indeed of all colonials [and] the central myth of the Puerto Rican nation—the myth that attempts to explain our inability to achieve nationhood as the story of the growing pains of a pato or maricón (faggot)" (ibid., 137). Cruz-Malavé suggests that Ramos Otero transforms Marqués's abject homosexual figure into a positive symbol, expanding definitions of "nation" to include the sexually marginalized.

17. Gelpí, *Literatura y paternalismo en Puerto Rico*, 149.

18. Burgos's works are *Poema en veinte surcos* (1938), *Canción de la verdad sencilla* (1939), and *El mar y tú; otros poemas* (published posthumously in 1954).

19. Dionisio Cañas, *El poeta y la ciudad: Nueva York y los escritores hispanos* (Madrid: Cátedra, 1994). Death is a leitmotif for Ramos Otero. Daniel Torres discusses the representation of HIV in Ramos Otero's books of poetry (*El libro de la muerte* and *Invitación al polvo*); it should be noted, however, that *El cuento de la Mujer del Mar* appeared before Ramos Otero was diagnosed with the virus. See Daniel Torres, "La metáfora silenciosa del sida en *El libro de la muerte*," *Cuadrivium* 2, no. 3 (1998–2000): 61–74; Daniel Torres, "Manuel Ramos Otero," in *Latin American Writers on Gay and Lesbian Themes: A Bio-critical Sourcebook*, ed. David W. Foster (Westport, CT: Greenwood, 1994), 346–349.

20. Cañas, *El poeta y la ciudad*, 130.

21. Rubén Ríos Ávila, "Caribbean Dislocations: Arenas and Ramos Otero in New York," in *Hispanisms and Homosexualities*, ed. Sylvia Molloy and Robert McKee Irwin (Durham, NC: Duke University Press, 1998), 102.

22. Feminist metafiction is defined by Gayle Greene as the revision of traditional literary plots that have been detrimental to women. It emphasizes women as readers and writers, placing them in charge of creating their own images and dismantling stereotypes in literary "canons." Challenging the literature of the past, feminist metafiction engages in an "analysis of gender as socially constructed and [the] sense that what has been constructed may be reconstructed." See her "Introduction: Feminist Metafiction as Re-vision," in *Changing the Story: Feminist Fiction and the Tradition* (Bloomington: Indiana University Press, 1991), 2.

23. David William Foster, *Gay and Lesbian Themes in Latin American Writing* (Austin: University of Texas Press, 1991), 5.

24. Ibid., 6.

25. DeGuzmán, "Turning Tricks," 170.

26. Michael Warner, introduction to *Fear of a Queer Planet: Queer Politics and Social*

Theory, ed. Michael Warner, Cultural Politics 6 (Minneapolis: University of Minnesota Press, 1993), xxvi (italics added).

27. Ibid.

28. Laura Doan and Sara Waters, "Making Up Lost Time: Contemporary Lesbian Writing and the Invention of History," in *Territories of Desire in Queer Culture: Refiguring Contemporary Boundaries*, ed. David Alderson and Linda Anderson (Manchester, UK: Manchester University Press, 2000), 16.

29. Aurea María Sotomayor, "Geneologías: O, el suave desplazamiento de los orígenes en la narrativa de Manuel Ramos Otero," *Nómada* 1 (1995): 92.

30. Ibid., 95, 105.

BIBLIOGRAPHY

Burgos, Julia de. *Antología poética*. Prologue by Yvette Jiménez de Báez. 5th ed. San Juan: Coquí, 1979. (Originally published 1967.)

Cañas, Dionisio. *El poeta y la ciudad: Nueva York y los escritores hispanos*. Madrid: Cátedra, 1994.

Costa, Marithelma. "Entrevista: Manuel Ramos Otero." *Hispamérica* 20, no. 59 (1991): 59–67.

Cruz-Malavé, Arnaldo. "Toward an Art of Transvestism: Colonialism and Homosexuality in Puerto Rican Literature." In *¿Entiendes? Queer Readings, Hispanic Writings*, ed. Emilie L. Bergmann and Paul Julian Smith, 137–167. Durham, NC: Duke University Press, 1995.

DeGuzmán, María. "Turning Tricks: Trafficking in the Figure of the Latino." In *Trickster Lives: Culture and Myth in American Fiction*, ed. Jeanne Campbell Reesman, 168–184. Athens, GA: University of Georgia Press, 2001.

Doan, Laura, and Sara Waters. "Making Up Lost Time: Contemporary Lesbian Writing and the Invention of History." In *Territories of Desire in Queer Culture: Refiguring Contemporary Boundaries*, ed. David Alderson and Linda Anderson, 12–28. Manchester, UK: Manchester University Press, 2000.

Foster, David William. *Gay and Lesbian Themes in Latin American Writing*. Austin: University of Texas Press, 1991.

García Ramis, Magali. "Women's Tales." In *Images and Identities: The Puerto Rican in Two World Contexts*, ed. and trans. Asela Rodríguez de Laguna, 109–115. New Brunswick, NJ: Transaction, 1987.

Gelpí, Juan. *Literatura y paternalismo en Puerto Rico*. San Juan: Editorial de la UPR, 1993.

Greene, Gayle. "Introduction: Feminist Metafiction as Re-vision." In *Changing the Story: Feminist Fiction and the Tradition,* 1–27. Bloomington: Indiana University Press, 1991.

Guzmán, Manuel. "'Pa' La Escuelita con Mucho Cuida'o y por la Orillita': A Journey through the Contested Terrains of the Nation and Sexual Orientation." In *Puerto Rican Jam: Rethinking Colonialism and Nationalism*, ed. Frances Negrón-Muntaner and Ramón Grosfoguel, 209–228. Minneapolis: University of Minnesota Press, 1997.

López Springfield, Consuelo. "'I Am the Life, the Strength, the Woman': Feminism in Julia de Burgos' Autobiographical Poetry." *Callaloo* 17, no. 3 (1994): 701–714.

Medero-Díaz, Luz M. "The Cultural Myth of Julia de Burgos." MA thesis, Arizona State University, 1993.

Palés Matos, Luis. *Obras (1914–1959)*. Río Piedras, PR: University of Puerto Rico Press, 1984.

Puebla, Manuel de la. *Julia de Burgos, amor y soledad*. Madrid: Torremozas, 1994.

———. "Julia de Burgos como mito." In *Julia de Burgos*, ed. Manuel de la Puebla, 81–91. Río Piedras, PR: Mairena, 1986. Reprinted from *Mairena* 20 (1985).

Ramos Otero, Manuel. *El cuento de la Mujer del Mar*. Río Piedras, PR: Huracán, 1979.

———. *Invitación al polvo*. Río Piedras, PR: Plaza Mayor, 1991.

———. *El libro de la muerte*. Río Piedras, PR: Editorial Cultural, 1985.

Ríos Ávila, Rubén. "Caribbean Dislocations: Arenas and Ramos Otero in New York." In *Hispanisms and Homosexualities*, ed. Sylvia Molloy and Robert McKee Irwin, 101–119. Durham, NC: Duke University Press, 1998.

Sandlin, Betsy A. "Julia de Burgos as a Cultural Icon in Works by Rosario Ferré, Luz María Umpierre, and Manuel Ramos Otero." PhD diss., University of North Carolina, 2003.

Solá, María M. "La poesía de Julia de Burgos: Mujer de humana lucha." In *Yo misma fui mi ruta*, by Julia de Burgos, ed. María M. Solá, 7–48. Río Piedras, PR: Ediciones Huracán, 1986.

Sotomayor, Aurea María. "Geneologías: O, el suave desplazamiento de los orígenes en la narrativa de Manuel Ramos Otero." *Nómada* 1 (1995): 92–106.

Torres, Daniel. "Manuel Ramos Otero." In *Latin American Writers on Gay and Lesbian Themes: A Bio-critical Sourcebook*, ed. David W. Foster, 346–349. Westport, CT: Greenwood, 1994.

———. "La metáfora silenciosa del sida en *El libro de la muerte*." *Cuadrivium* 2, no. 3 (1998–2000): 61–74.

Villanueva Collado, Alfredo. "Filí-Melé: Símbolo y mujer en la poesía de Luis Palés Matos e Iván Silén." *Revista Chicano-riqueña* 10 (1982): 47–54.

Warner, Michael. Introduction to *Fear of a Queer Planet: Queer Politics and Social Theory*, ed. Michael Warner, vii–xxxi. Cultural Politics 6. Minneapolis: University of Minnesota Press, 1993.

16 SUBVERTING THE MAINLAND

Transmigratory Biculturalism in U.S. Puerto Rican Women's Fiction

MARY JANE SUERO-ELLIOTT

The last several decades have witnessed the emergence of a distinct thematic trend in contestatory Latina literature. This trend is transnational and theorizes a new model of immigrant bicultural identity based on the transmigratory patterns of Latinos in the twentieth century, specifically Mexican Americans, Cuban Americans, and Puerto Ricans.[1] U.S. Puerto Rican women writers have been instrumental in transnationalizing literary resistance from their particular vantage point within the Puerto Rican diaspora.[2] The diaspora and its historical context make Puerto Rican transmigration and the psychosocial identity that develops from it—what I call "transmigratory subjectivity"—unique.

Transmigratory identity is a self-empowered subjectivity that emerges from the sociological phenomenon of transmigration. Explicitly theorized by Linda Basch, Nina Glick Schiller, and Cristina Szanton Blanc in *Nations Unbound,*[3] the concept of transmigration delineates a twentieth-century form of migration—one that differs fundamentally from the nineteenth- and early-twentieth-century model of European emigration to the "New World." In the traditional model, migration tended to be a single, unidirectional event, entailing permanent relocation to the United States as the host country. Because migration therefore meant irrevocably severing ties with the homeland, many immigrants in the United

States aspired to assimilation into the host culture. In the latter half of the twentieth century, Puerto Ricans who moved from the island to the mainland participated in another kind of migration, one called, in various scholarly contexts, reverse, return, circular, international, and transnational migration.[4] This kind of fluid, flexible, back-and-forth mobility between home and host countries was made possible by the advent of modern technology. Not only can immigrants fly home in a matter of hours, but they can establish "social networks" that span home and host cultures with the help of email, phone, fax, and even money wires.[5]

One of the most significant characteristics of transmigration for the analysis of oppositional Latina literature is the access to the originary culture it allows those who migrate. This cultural access, in turn, makes the goal of total assimilation obsolete for twentieth- and twenty-first-century immigrants. Puerto Ricans in particular have the benefit not only of modern technology but also of a political identity that renders official boundaries more permeable.[6] As members of a Commonwealth, Puerto Ricans do not struggle to obtain visas, passports, or permits to travel to the continent. This makes movement to and from the mainland for work, family, or pleasure relatively easier for Puerto Ricans than, for example, for Cubans and Mexicans (Duany).

The concept of transmigration therefore defines a new process of migration to the mainland and adaptation to dominant society, in which migrants establish social networks that keep them intimately connected with their home culture. The possibility of continuous access to a Puerto Rican cultural heritage facilitates the development of a new immigrant identity that is integrative rather than assimilationist or separatist. This identity is contestatory in its transformative properties; it has the potential to change the host culture proactively through home cultural influence. The potential for identificatory empowerment inherent in textual transmigration differs from the personal growth portrayed in the "ethnic bildungsroman" as described by Lisa Lowe, the "Chicana bildungsroman" theorized by Annie O. Eysturoy, the nineteenth- and early-twentieth-century European immigrant narrative of assimilation, and the minority coming-of-age narrative of alienation and assimilation within U.S. culture.[7] Several U.S. Puerto Rican women have thematized personal growth from victim to agent for their racial and gendered characters through the development of a transmigratory consciousness.[8]

This consciousness, in turn, is radical because of its intimate engagement with a Latino originary culture.

Alba Ambert and Esmeralda Santiago represent U.S. Puerto Rican Latinas who theorize the oppositional potential in a transmigratory subjectivity through their fiction. Ambert's *A Perfect Silence* and Santiago's *América's Dream* both depict the journey of a female protagonist from raced and gendered disempowerment to self-determined agency as a fully viable bicultural subject.[9] The completion of this trajectory is informed by the textual development of a transmigratory consciousness; in other words, bicultural viability depends on the protagonist's affirmative access to her Puerto Rican cultural legacy.[10] *Silence*'s Blanca and *Dream*'s América "return" physically and/or imaginatively to the island in order to form an agentive subjectivity in the socially and politically prejudicial context of the continental United States.[11] An intimate engagement with Puerto Rico as an originary nation defines the empowered subjectivity of these Diasporican protagonists.

The opposition inherent in a Puerto Rican transmigratory consciousness is its validation of a Puerto Rican cultural legacy when developing a successful ethnic American identity on the mainland. Because transmigration entails the active accessing of a home cultural heritage through the actual or imaginative return to Puerto Rico as the culture of origin, oppositional potential in these protagonists' transmigratory consciousness also embodies the subversion of the American Dream as exploitive ideology in an imperialist mythology. By "returning" to and thus affirming Puerto Rican culture in the face of the sociocultural denigration they experience in the United States as the putative utopia of immigrant desire, these Puerto Rican protagonists reject the seduction of the mythology of U.S. superiority, exposing its fiction as imperialist ideology.

Examining the history of the island's relationship with the continental United States helps define a particularly Puerto Rican form of transmigratory resistance as depicted in U.S. Puerto Rican women's novels. Puerto Rico's history—the 1898 annexation of Puerto Rican territory by the United States, the island's subsequent status as a colonial dependent, the 1917 Jones Act defining Puerto Rican citizenship, the aggressive United States–sponsored industrialization and urbanization of the island, the destructive militarization of Vieques in 1941, the exploitation and relocation of Puerto Rico's labor by U.S. corporate interests, the massive waves of migration in the 1950s and 1980s, the Americanization of

Puerto Rican culture, the lack of official borders between Puerto Rico and the United States—created a colonialist context for Puerto Ricans that resulted in the largest diaspora in recent history.[12] With almost half of its population living in the diaspora, Puerto Rico has an inordinately large number of cultural representatives on the mainland (Duany, 282).

As a result of this particular national and cultural history, I contend that Diasporican authors, as demonstrated by Ambert and Santiago, may figure resistance against U.S. involvement in Puerto Rican culture and exploitation of Puerto Rican economy specifically in the context of the mainland. The history of the relationship between Puerto Rico and the United States makes the oppositional potential in the Diasporican bicultural subjectivity unique. The experiences and realities of the diaspora complicate the idea of actual return as identificatory and cultural resistance. Puerto Rico's status as a "colonial dependency" since 1898 has defined island culture: "As an overseas possession of the United States, the Island has been exposed to an intense penetration of American capital, commodities, laws, and customs" (1). This status therefore affects any opposition to the United States as a colonialist force that involves the validation of the originary nation. What the fiction of U.S. Puerto Ricans like Ambert and Santiago demonstrates is that the resistance inherent in a viable biculturalism is sometimes most effectively deployed in a mainland context, within the continental United States. By accessing the originary culture and importing it, as it were, to the mainland, these Puerto Rican bicultural subjects change the cultural cartography of the imperialist nation, in effect undermining the colonialist "penetration" of Puerto Rican culture enacted by the United States on Puerto Rican soil.[13]

By emphasizing the U.S. mainland as the primary site of resistance, these texts both draw attention to the continued colonization of the originary nation and subvert the strategies of that colonization from its source. The magnitude of the diaspora and the realities of the diasporic condition create a context in which resistance is more effective from the mainland. Duany points out that "diasporic communities are an integral part of the Puerto Rican nation because they continue to be linked to the Island by an intense circular movement of people, identities, and practices." Therefore, "the Puerto Rican nation is no longer restricted to the Island but instead is constituted by . . . Puerto Rico itself and . . . the diasporic communities settled in the continental United States" (5). The sociopolitical motivators of the diaspora make subversive the development of an empowered bicultural subjectivity on the mainland. Although situated in the continental United States, this oppositional subjectivity is transnational in nature because of its intimate engagement with Puerto Rico as the home culture. Thus, we see Ambert's protagonist healing psychic fracturing by visiting the island but living her life as an integrated bicultural subject in the United States and teaching her "American" daughter by example a successful bicultural legacy. The protagonist of Santiago's novel explicitly engages in transforming the host culture by importing Puerto Rican cultural identity to the United States.

A Perfect Silence differs from *América's Dream* in that it figures actual return to Puerto Rico. Although return to the island marks a definitive epoch in the protagonist's life, it is not conclusive because it does not signify the culmination of a trajectory away from objectification toward self-empowerment. Yet this return has transmigratory effects because it ultimately allows the protagonist to learn self-determination—it is in Puerto Rico that she first acquires the tools for identity validation that she later accesses by "returning" to her culture of origin through her memories of a Puerto Rican past. In other words, although the protagonist migrates once more to the continent after returning to Puerto Rico, it is through imaginative return to her island culture that she recovers from the psychic fracturing she undergoes in the United States.

Ambert's novel, an extended bildungsroman, is framed by the trope of female madness, opening with the narrator in a private mental hospital in Boston after an attempted suicide and closing with her recovery and release. The text's central narrative depicts Blanca's migration to and from the United States; taken to the United States as a child, she later chooses to relocate to the continent as an adult. When she first returns to Puerto Rico with her grandmother, the novel associates Puerto Rico with warmth (of both climate and culture), with a heightened potential for happiness (after negative experiences in New York), with her mother (because her mother lives, gives birth to Blanca, and dies on the island), and with voice as an expression of the self (it is through an engagement with Spanish in Puerto Rico that Blanca experiences the self-validating potential of language as vocal expression). Although also the context of the continuation of abuse at the hands of her grandmother and later her husband, it is significant in terms of the development of a bicultural identity that Blanca first experiences happiness, learns to use her voice, and positively associates the island with her mother in Puerto Rico. In other words, within the narrative's metaphorical subtext, I read Blanca's character as transmigratory because it is through migration between home and host culture that the text develops her character—positing Puerto Rico as the culture of voice and therefore resistance, the culture of her loving mother and therefore a positive maternal legacy, and the culture of first happiness and therefore potential self-fulfillment.

Furthermore, cultural and personal validation occurs through a psychic recovery dependent on a return to a Puerto Rican past. Blanca's successful self-healing is founded on a return to Puerto Rico through her memories of its culture, language, geography, and climate. Although she chooses to migrate once again to the mainland after living in Puerto Rico, the text's conclusion gestures toward a transmigratory consciousness in Blanca by depicting a recovery from psychic disintegration dependent on return to a past constituted by Puerto Rican culture. Actual return to the island in order to heal is not as highly charged in a symbolic sense since it is relatively easy. Every instance of actual return in the text is figured as escape, mitigating the metaphorical resonance of physical return as an act of identificatory resistance. Moreover, the symbolic power of Puerto Rico as a national entity is corrupted by its colonialist status vis-à-vis the United States. Return, then, has particular implications within a text such as Ambert's, in which the originary culture has an adulterated national identity because of its relationship to the host country.

Rejecting actual return as an oppositional trope, however, does not serve to support the American Dream as imperialist mythology of nationalist superiority in Ambert's text. Instead, every description of mainland geography belies the idea of the United States as the focus of migrant hope. The negative physical depictions of the mainland serve to expose the illusory quality of the American Dream. The narrator describes New York as "a dark, dirty place, stuffed with tall houses with many windows and many doors. The doors were always locked. When Blanca peeked out the window, there was no brilliant sun that made her . . . skin lie still and quiet, drinking its heat. . . . It was dingy, the colors muted" (45). This kind of description differs from the geography of the island as experienced by Blanca, who "loved her island where the sun almost always shone and flowers peeked through stones. She ran about capturing the aromas of the barrio, the crows of roosters, the garrulous prattle of matrons" (128–129). In direct opposition to New York, Puerto Rico is "home" to Blanca: "The powdery sands of her island slipped away like a dream. Somewhere along the way, she lost the sweetness of ripe plantains on her tongue and the snap of tin roofs setting in the hot sun. . . . [S]he had lived a life of exile in gray cities of unforgiving geographies" (33). The descriptions of the different physical environments parallel the cultural geographies of the mainland and the island. Puerto Rico is the warm, sunny place in which Blanca first discovers a self-directed happiness. She experiences the continent, in contrast, as physically cold and culturally alienating: "Snow makes me melancholy. . . . It brings back images of my arrival in this stark land, farther north than I had ever been, where something inside me has died" (212). In opposition to her connection between island and mother, Blanca associates the U.S. mainland with psychological death.

The text cites racism as one of the major reasons why Blanca becomes disillusioned with her version of the American Dream as a Harvard student on scholarship. In Boston, she and her daughter "were considered less than white. . . . Blanca struggled to maintain her identity intact, not to fall into the madness of not being who she was" (216). Racism directly affects Blanca's sense of self as the progress she has made in Puerto Rico is eroded by the aggressive alienation of Puerto Ricans in the United States. When racism threatens Blanca's sense of identity, the promises of Puerto Rican citizenship are exposed as false. She reacts by "refus[ing] to assimilate into a foreign entity, although cultural invasion bludgeoned her mercilessly" (216). Blanca's refusal figures resistance as antiassimilation because it constitutes an attempt at self-preservation and an act of cultural agency.

Given the history of colonial dependency and the sociopolitical phenomenon of the diaspora, it is significant that Blanca both loses her sense of self and heals a fractured psyche in the cultural context of Anglo America. The central episode of psychic breakdown is triggered by anti–Puerto Rican prejudice. On the subway, soon after dealing with her daughter's experiences with violent racism at school, Blanca feels "disconnected from the packed bodies and crawled into a cocoon of alienation. . . . These were faces drawn by alien experiences. Indifferent faces" (219). She then realizes that "it was she who was foreign, alien, different. . . . She had lost her anchor in this disconcerting environment.

She had no key to let her enter into a world of definite identities. . . . She suffered a searing split" (219–220). That night "she decided to die" (220).

The most direct cause of Blanca's loss of self is the racist environment of the United States. The irony brought out by this association is that the hostile environment is her "own" country—Blanca's psychological reaction to racism exposes the corrupt history of deception and exploitation behind the conception and reality of Puerto Ricans' U.S. citizenship. It is crucial that Blanca succeeds in healing herself within the same context in which she suffered her psychic malady, because in this way she proves her entitlement to both political and cultural citizenship. The story ends with Blanca being released from the mental hospital in which she has been institutionalized, free to go home to her daughter. The text does not suggest, however, a future return to Puerto Rico. *Silence*, then, does not follow a pattern of physical return in which conscious choice validates the originary culture. Instead, the text legitimizes island culture more obliquely, through the nature of Blanca's recovery.

Blanca authors her own "cure," bypassing the Anglo-American male doctor's misdiagnosis: "'I think that maybe by going back, way back, to the beginning, and then working my way from there to the present, to what is, maybe I'll find a way of understanding who I am'" (17). She bases her successful self-healing on a return to a past constituted in large part by Puerto Rican culture and geography. I argue that because this text figures actual return as "escape" through portrayals of Blanca's grandmother's frequent journeys to the island, because Puerto Rico is a Commonwealth, and because Blanca experiences identity degradation and disintegration on the mainland, transmigratory resistance most effectively takes place within the continental United States. Rather than trying to escape her problems by returning to Puerto Rico, Blanca confronts these problems within the culture that contributes to them. In doing so, she redefines Puerto Rican cultural citizenship, "seizing" the American subjectivity to which Puerto Ricans are entitled by virtue of their political status.[14] I define this text as transmigratory both because Blanca learns of the potential for happiness and first finds her voice through physical return to Puerto Rico and because it is through a return to her past that she self-heals. Thus, transmigratory return plays a crucial part in the protagonist's move from victim to agent, object to subject, and disempowerment to self-validation.

Esmeralda Santiago's 1996 novel, *América's Dream*, more directly articulates racialized migrant resistance as Puerto Rican cultural influence on the mainland. The text theorizes oppositional Diasporican agency both through a metaphorical paralleling of geopolitical entities with specific characters and through the nature of the central protagonist's U.S. Puerto Rican subjectivity in New York. Santiago comments on the relationship between Puerto Rico and the United States by metaphorizing her central characters. As a domestically abused woman, América subtextually represents a colonized Puerto Rican identity, while her abusive boyfriend, who guards the beaches from Puerto Ricans for use by the U.S. military and tourist industry, embodies the colonialist domination of Puerto Rican territory and culture. When América escapes the abuse by moving to New York and subsequently developing an agentively raced and gendered subjectivity, the text metaphorically subverts the historical domination of Puerto Rico by the United States.

América's Dream differs from *A Perfect Silence* because it does not portray either actual return or imaginings desirous of actual return. At the center of my argument for reading this novel as representative of transmigratory sensibility is América's dissemination of a Puerto Rican cultural sensibility on the mainland. As a racialized migrant from a "peripheral" to a "core" culture, América embodies both individual and collective resistance through active and symbolic participation in the Hispanicization, to borrow Ilan Stavans's terminology, of the U.S. mainland.[15] With a broad definition of "return," I read América's relocation to the continent and the consequent transmission of her Puerto Rican–inflected values, habits, and desires as being equally subversive of U.S. sociocultural hegemony as the actual and imaginative returns depicted in Ambert's *A Perfect Silence*. I further suggest that Puerto Rico's history supports this interpretation of Santiago's novel. Through both direct articulation and analogic association, the novel defines Vieques (América's island home) and thus Puerto Rico in general as colonized by the United States.[16] The descriptions of an exploitive tourist industry and the militarized beaches in Vieques point to Puerto Rico's dependent colonialist status. The text's analogic paralleling of América as an abused and powerless woman with the small island and of her oppressive lover, Correa, with the U.S. government extends its depictions of Puerto Rico as a colonized territory.

The novel's contextualization of América's developing agency on the mainland begins with a detailed portrayal of her experiences of disempowerment in Vieques, where she works as a maid at a small hotel that caters to Anglo-American tourists. This contextualization serves to substantiate an interpretation metaphorically paralleling América and Correa with Puerto Rican culture and U.S. oppression. América's Puerto Rican life has never been under her control; she lacks personal agency in her relationships with her abusive lover, alcoholic mother, and rebellious teenage daughter. Santiago contextualizes this lack of agency in Puerto Rican culture, highlighting the mainland as the site of América's eventual development of an agentive subjectivity through a "seizing" of a specifically Diasporican cultural citizenship.

América herself realizes the extent of her powerlessness on the island: "My life is not really mine. . . . Correa rules every action I take. . . . Is that any way to live?" (68). Her acknowledgment of her impotence in the face of Correa's domination takes place in the context of U.S. Navy test bombings. As the navy uses "the beaches for target practice" (64), her question "hangs in the fragrant air . . . , punctuated by the flashing red sky, the thumps of bombs finding their target, the yielding earth quaking beneath her feet" (68). América's thoughts on her powerlessness are interrupted constantly by reminders of Puerto Rico's geopolitical subordination in its Commonwealth status to the United States, whose power is represented here by the aggressively destructive acts of its military. Santiago thus interrelates the violence of the bombing, representative of U.S. geopolitical power, and América's lack of agency in the face of Correa's violent abuse. This juxtaposition associates the central characters with national identities.

Red flashes, dull thuds, and trembling ground disrupt the "clear night" (64) and the "fragrant air of the garden" (68) as exploding bombs violate the natural peace of the island. In this case, Santiago deploys a Western imperialist symbolism equating femaleness with a passive and fertile earth and masculinity with an aggressively invasive force in order to critique both gender and colonialist oppressions.[17] The text sets up a comparison between América's powerlessness as a physically and psychically oppressed woman and the violation of the island's natural order and between Correa's abuse and the violent navy aggression manifested by its target practice. This analogic association is sustained by historical Western dualistic symbolism in which the female body is figured in the imperialist imaginary as the conquest. This imaginary conflates the raced other and the gendered other with its allegorization of newly discovered territories.

In historicizing European territorial conquests, Anne McClintock describes an imperialist symbolics that "feminiz[ed] . . . terra incognita" and amounted to a "strategy of violent containment."[18] I suggest that Santiago's characters enact the imperialist construct McClintock describes. América's maltreated and passive character metaphorizes a colonized land and culture in her association with the Puerto Rican island of Vieques. With his "violent containment" of his girlfriend's actions, Correa's abusive character mirrors the restrictive military practices of the U.S. government on the island. The relationship between América and Correa thus reflects a subtextual theorization of geopolitical relations; the novel's subtext defines the relationship between the United States and Puerto Rico as colonized through the deployment of the symbolics of a specifically imperialist imaginary. This interpretation defines *América's Dream* as a transmigratory text through a metaphorical reading of a conclusion that serves to both subvert the imperialist paradigm from which Santiago borrows and to propose an alternative paradigm for transnational relations. The text establishes this allegorical context in Vieques, reflecting an imperialist symbolic economy when it refers to Correa's initial seduction of the fourteen-year-old América as "La Conquista" (24) and his periodic raping of América as "the taking of América" (109). By the conclusion of the text, through América's developing agency, this same paralleled signification subverts the nationalist ideologies perpetuated by the mainland through mythologies such as the American Dream that cast the United States as a superior sociopolitical entity and Puerto Rico as the subordinated Third World in need of U.S. patronage.

Because América embodies this type of collective colonization through individual disempowerment, it is significant in terms of the novel's thematic framework that she simultaneously transmits her Puerto Rican culture and develops an agentive subjectivity on the mainland. The novel's definition of the originary culture as corrupted by colonialist exploitation renders return less effective as a resistive trope. Instead, América relocates to the continent, liberating Puerto Rican identity from its colonialist context. The portrayals of América's cultural influence in

New York work against the goal of homogeneity behind the assimilationist model. Because this model is intrinsic to the traditional American dreaming that has helped inspire Puerto Rican migration, the text also subverts the definitive ideologies of the American Dream while transforming the psychosocial character of the diaspora.

The text theorizes a new migrant model, one that redefines both separatist and assimilationist philosophies. América negotiates two cultures while her very presence as a successful Puerto Rican migrant on the mainland serves to reconfigure the U.S. cultural landscape. What distinguishes América from Blanca, however, is América's conscious influence on U.S. culture through her role as the nanny/housekeeper of an Anglo-American family in a wealthy suburb of New York. Thus, *Dream* theorizes a migrant identity radically resistive in its self-consciously transformative effect on a hegemonic host culture.

América's agency becomes directly transmigratory when she deliberately "Puerto Ricanizes" her employers' behavior. After the first few days on the mainland, "América sighs with satisfaction. She's learning their ways and is beginning to change them" (152). América accesses Anglo-American culture on an intimate level through her job. Traditionally devalued as women's work, and increasingly considered brown women's work in parts of the United States, domestic labor in this text becomes a site of resistance for a raced and gendered identity. Rather than passively obeying instructions, América chooses to transform the dominant Anglo culture her employers represent by introducing Puerto Rican values. She educates her charges in Puerto Rican culture, in this way indirectly counteracting the Americanization of Puerto Rican culture by the U.S. government.[19] After befriending other Latina nannies, América realizes their significant impact on their charges' lives: "All these Americanitos are learning about life from us. We're from a different country, we speak a different language, but we're the ones there when they're hungry, or when they take their first step" (228).

In addition to her Hispanicization of Anglo America, América is empowered personally by relocating to the continent, where her life is "different." She reflects, "For the first time I can remember I'm in control" (182). América's seizing of an agency defined by the text as raced and gendered, female and Puerto Rican, culminates when she ends Correa's abuse. Toward the conclusion of the novel, Correa surprises

América alone with the children. Finally, América is able to resist him, determining, "I won't let him. He won't kill me. He won't" (317). In the ensuing struggle, after he stabs her repeatedly, América kicks him, causing him to die instantly when his head hits a countertop. Although the police arrive almost simultaneously, it is América who defends and ultimately saves herself.

This moment in the text has thematic resonance on multiple levels. América's physical self-defense is the culmination of a psychological process that remains inchoate until her arrival on the mainland. Immediately before she learns of the employment opportunity in the United States, América has an epiphany: "I . . . let Correa keep me down. . . . I let him because he's a man. . . . But I'm smarter. . . . All women are stupid! We've let ourselves believe that men are better than we are" (114). In Vieques, however, she is unable to act on her epiphany. Instead, the author juxtaposes América's feminist realization with the opportunity to relocate to the mainland, indirectly associating América's embryonic feminist impulses with her future life in New York. It is only on the continent that América takes the first steps toward independence. She tells herself, "I'm going to worry about myself from now on, about what I want and what I need" (231). Signaling a newfound independence, América's focus on herself is a crucial stage in the development of an agentive subjectivity.

On a metaphorical level, América's resistance to Correa's final assault theorizes sociopolitical relations between the United States and Puerto Rico. As discussed above, the text indirectly associates América with a colonized Puerto Rico and Correa with the imperialist interventions of the United States. When América successfully resists Correa, the text metaphorizes the oppositional potential in América's developing transmigratory sensibility. The text thus posits an alternative transnational exchange, one that subverts both the history that colonized Puerto Rico originally and the U.S. nationalist ideologies that perpetuate mythologies of Puerto Rican subordination. The last paragraph of the novel substantiates this metaphorical reading of Santiago's characterizations: "Correa's woman was unscarred, but América González wears the scars he left behind the way a navy Lieutenant wears his stripes. They're there to remind her that she fought for her life, and that . . . she has a right to live that life as she chooses" (325).

In terms of individual identity, the concluding passage of the novel illustrates pride in a defended female subjectivity. América's experiences on the mainland teach her to value herself as a U.S. Puerto Rican woman. A metaphorical interpretation of the novel's thematic framework reads ethnicity as implicit in the concluding passage. The text's numerous references to the aggressive militarization of Vieques render thematically resonant the comparison between América's pride in her self-defensive actions and a navy lieutenant's pride in his stripes. I suggest that with this comparison, the novel's subtext continues to thematize Puerto Rico–United States relations, concluding with the metaphorical recuperation of an autonomous geopolitical and cultural identity for Puerto Rico. When América defends herself from Correa, she validates her identity in the face of potential annihilation. Metaphorical extension validates a cultural and political Puerto Rican identity in the face of U.S. interventions. The novel concludes with the culmination of a process in which dispossession and coerced subordination are subverted and in which self-determined independence is fostered for the protagonist and projected as future potential for Puerto Rico. Through the metaphorization of nationalist identities, the novel offers a model for future international exchanges that revisions colonialist and neocolonialist paradigms of global hierarchies. In this way, *América's Dream* embodies a radical critique of U.S. interventions in Puerto Rico as well as of the mythology of the American Dream. By the conclusion of the novel, "América's dream" becomes an alternative transmigratory paradigm for individual and cultural identities.

A Perfect Silence and *América's Dream* demonstrate how U.S. Puerto Rican women authors have played an important role in defining a shift in Latina discourse that moves beyond the idea of "border identity" to situate raced and gendered agency within a transnational context. This placement marks the development of a new theory of identity that has conceptual repercussions both for the personal and for the collective. Puerto Rican writing participates in Latina challenges to hierarchies within the "global village" and in Latina restructuring of transnational imaginaries. These contributions leave an indelibly Puerto Rican mark on the cartographies of culture and self continually being defined and redefined within the United States.

NOTES

1. My research focuses on Mexican American, Cuban American, and U.S. Puerto Rican writers' thematizations of migration as representative of the three major subgroups constituting the "Latino" identity in the United States.

2. According to Jorge Duany's *The Puerto Rican Nation on the Move: Identities on the Island and in the United States* (Chapel Hill: University of North Carolina Press, 2002), the Puerto Rican diaspora "has mobilized standard concepts of the nation, culture, language, and territory on the Island and elsewhere." As a result, "popular images of Puerto Rican identity have been thoroughly deterritorialized and transnationalized" (7). A Puerto Rican transmigratory consciousness thus necessarily emerges out of this diasporic culture. For other comprehensive discussions of the history of the diaspora, see also Lisa Sánchez González, *Boricua Literature: A Literary History of the Puerto Rican Diaspora* (New York: New York University Press, 2001); Robert Fernandez, *The Disenchanted Island: Puerto Rico and the United States in the Twentieth Century* (Westport, CT: Praeger, 1996); and Clara E. Rodríguez, "A Summary of Puerto Rican Migration to the United States," in *Challenging Fronteras: Structuring Latina and Latino Lives in the U.S.*, ed. Mary Romero, Pierrette Hondagneu-Sotelo, and Vilma Ortiz (New York: Routledge, 1997), 101–113.

3. Linda Basch, Nina Glick Schiller, and Cristina Szanton Blanc theorize transmigration through a sociological lens in *Nations Unbound: Transnational Projects, Postcolonial Predicaments, and Deterritorialized Nation-States* (Amsterdam: Gordon and Breach, 1994).

4. See Duany, *Puerto Rican Nation on the Move*. Hereafter cited in the text as "Duany."

5. See Basch, Schiller, and Blanc, *Nations Unbound*. Benedict Anderson also discusses the impact on current national identities and political subjectivities of the revolutions in transportation and communication, which include the invention and development of motor vehicles, commercial aviation, radio, telephone, film, television, video recording, and personal computers ("Exodus," *Critical Inquiry* 20 [1994]: 320–321). Capitalism's advancements result in a world order oppressively efficient in its exploitation of labor and lead to greater social, political, and economic inequalities (321), to which, according to Anderson, migrants can respond by refusing exclusive political loyalty and instead developing a more fluid idea of political citizenship. This flexibility, however, does not translate for him into any kind of liberatory methodology: "today's long distance nationalism strikes one as a probably menacing portent for the future. First of all, it is the product of capitalism's remorseless, accelerating transformation of all human societies. Second, it creates a serious politics that is at the same time radically unaccountable" (327). Unlike the Diasporican texts analyzed here, Anderson's "Exodus" does not allow for the possibility of a self-affirming subjectivity emerging from long-distance nationalism or predict the potential for liberatory consequences in the maintenance of transnational social networks.

6. In *American Dreaming: Immigrant Life on the Margins* (Princeton, NJ: Princeton University Press, 1995), Sarah J. Mahler writes, "Migration evolves through the devel-

opment of transportation and other social capital links from the host to the home country, links that open new opportunities for economic survival" (57). Despite island geography, Puerto Rico gained a kind of "proximity" to the United States with Commonwealth status and air travel. Duany explains how a migrant "flow" is "facilitated by the lack of formal political barriers between Puerto Rico and the United States. As they move between the Island and the mainland, Puerto Ricans need not carry travel documents or apply for visa permits; the frontier between the two places is more cultural than juridicial" (213).

7. See Lisa Lowe, *Immigrant Acts: On Asian American Cultural Politics* (Durham, NC: Duke University Press, 1996); and Annie O. Eysturoy, *Daughters of Self-Creation: The Contemporary Chicana Novel* (Albuquerque: University of New Mexico Press, 1996).

8. Judith Ortiz Cofer is another U.S. Puerto Rican author whose texts may be defined as transmigratory. In particular, her novel *The Line of the Sun* (Athens, GA: University of Georgia Press, 1989) parallels *América's Dream* in its theorization of a mainland bicultural identity oppositional in its dependence on Puerto Rican originary culture.

9. All references to *A Perfect Silence* and *América's Dream* draw from the following editions: Alba Ambert, *A Perfect Silence* (Houston: Arte Público Press, 1995); and Esmeralda Santiago, *América's Dream* (New York: HarperCollins, 1996).

10. Gloria Anzaldúa's theory of the new mestiza in *Borderlands/La frontera* (San Francisco: Aunt Lute Books, 1987) overlaps with my theory of literary transmigration in regard to the negotiation of two different cultures, the development of a bicultural subjectivity, and the contestatory potential in the raced and gendered subject. However, the concept of transmigratory identity differs from the theory of the new mestiza in its reliance on the originary culture for personal and collective agency. The new mestiza represents empowerment largely within a domestic context; literary transmigration deploys the trope of "return," both actual and imaginary, to represent the necessary access to the originary culture for the development of an agentive bicultural subjectivity.

11. In "Puerto Rican Literature in the United States: Stages and Perspectives," in *Recovering the U.S. Hispanic Literary Heritage*, ed. Ramón Gutiérrez and Genaro Padilla (Houston: Arte Público Press, 1993), 53–68, Juan Flores proposes a model of U.S. Puerto Rican identity that, although including the idea of return to the island, remains limited by nostalgia. The second of the four stages in his model, which are "the here-and-now, Puerto Rican background, reentry and branching out" (183), involves physical or imaginative return to Puerto Rico. This "passage" back to the home country is a form of cultural recovery that enables a more empowered "reentry" into New York. It differs, however, from the development of a transmigratory sensibility because of its nostalgic and utopian leanings. What defines transmigratory consciousness as oppositional is its emphasis on a return that signifies an access to the originary nation and culture as lived reality. This lived reality fundamentally informs the resistive nature of the transmigratory bicultural subject.

12. See Sánchez González, *Boricua Literature*; Fernandez, *Disenchanted Island*; Mario Murillo, *Islands of Resistance: Puerto Rico, Vieques, and U.S. Policy* (New York:

Seven Stories Press, 2001); Virginia E. Sánchez Korrol, *From Colonia to Community: The History of Puerto Ricans in New York City* (Berkeley and Los Angeles: University of California Press, 1994); and William V. Flores and Rina Benmayor, eds., *Latino Cultural Citizenship: Claiming Identity, Space, and Rights* (Boston: Beacon Press, 1997).

13. Research shows that Puerto Rican immigrants often make tangible the intimate connections between home and host cultures by reestablishing facets of island culture on the mainland. According to Sánchez Korrol, "Once in New York City, [Puerto Rican migrants] set about reconstructing neighborhoods solidly modeled on familiar institutions, similar to those they knew in Puerto Rico" (*From Colonia to Community*, 211). Flores and Benmayor write, "New York, loosely termed, is 'the other island' for Puerto Ricans and El Barrio the largest and oldest Puerto Rican community in that city" (*Latino Cultural Citizenship*, 7).

14. In *Women Singing in the Snow: A Cultural Analysis of Chicana Literature* (Tucson: University of Arizona Press, 1995), Tey Diana Rebolledo points to the necessity for Chicanas in the last few decades to "seize their subjectivity" in and through the development of their own gendered and racial discourse.

15. See Ilan Stavans, *The Hispanic Condition: Reflections on Culture and Identity in America* (New York: HarperPerennial, 1995).

16. As part of Puerto Rico, Vieques has been subject to U.S. colonialism. "In 1941 . . . the U.S. Navy took over seventy-two percent of the territory of Vieques" (Murillo, *Islands of Resistance*, 48), limiting the civilian population to a "narrow sliver in the middle of the island . . . surrounded by . . . the Navy's Atlantic Fleet" (55). Military activities have caused health problems and environmental degradation.

17. Anne McClintock quotes from Peter Hulme's "Polytropic Man: Tropes of Sexuality and Mobility in Early Colonial Discourse" (from *Europe and Its Others,* vol. 2, ed. Francis Barker, Peter Hulme, Margaret Iverson, and Diane Loxley [Colchester, UK: University of Essex, 1985]): "Land is named as female as a passive counterpart to the massive thrust of male technology" while theorizing the imperialist "feminizing of terra incognita." See her *Imperial Leather: Race, Gender and Sexuality in the Colonial Contest* (New York: Routledge, 1995), 26, 24. Both Hulme and McClintock refer to an imperialist symbolic economy in which land is feminized in metaphorical opposition to a masculinist conquering force.

18. McClintock, *Imperial Leather*, 24.

19. In the autobiographical *When I Was Puerto Rican* (New York: Vintage Books, 1993), Esmeralda Santiago details the aggressive Americanization of Puerto Rico's educational system attempted by the U.S. government.

BIBLIOGRAPHY

Ambert, Alba. *A Perfect Silence*. Houston: Arte Público Press, 1995.

Anderson, Benedict. "Exodus." *Critical Inquiry* 20 (1994): 314–327.

Anzaldúa, Gloria. *Borderlands/La frontera*. San Francisco: Aunt Lute Books, 1987.

Basch, Linda, Nina Glick Schiller, and Cristina Szanton Blanc. *Nations Unbound: Transnational Projects, Postcolonial Predicaments, and Deterritorialized Nation-States.* Amsterdam: Gordon and Breach, 1994.

Duany, Jorge. *The Puerto Rican Nation on the Move: Identities on the Island and in the United States.* Chapel Hill: University of North Carolina Press, 2002.

Eysturoy, Annie O. *Daughters of Self-Creation: The Contemporary Chicana Novel.* Albuquerque: University of New Mexico Press, 1996.

Fernandez, Robert. *The Disenchanted Island: Puerto Rico and the United States in the Twentieth Century.* Westport, CT: Praeger, 1996.

Flores, Juan. "Puerto Rican Literature in the United States: Stages and Perspectives." In *Recovering the U.S. Hispanic Literary Heritage*, ed. Ramón Gutiérrez and Genaro Padilla, 53–68. Houston: Arte Público Press, 1993.

Flores, William V., and Rina Benmayor, eds. *Latino Cultural Citizenship: Claiming Identity, Space, and Rights.* Boston: Beacon Press, 1997.

Hulme, Peter. "Polytropic Man: Tropes of Sexuality and Mobility in Early Colonial Discourse." In *Europe and Its Others,* ed. Francis Barker, Peter Hulme, Margaret Iverson, and Diane Loxley, 2:17–32. Colchester, UK: University of Essex, 1985.

Lowe, Lisa. *Immigrant Acts: On Asian American Cultural Politics.* Durham, NC: Duke University Press, 1996.

Mahler, Sarah J. *American Dreaming: Immigrant Life on the Margins.* Princeton, NJ: Princeton University Press, 1995.

McClintock, Anne. *Imperial Leather: Race, Gender and Sexuality in the Colonial Contest.* New York: Routledge, 1995.

Murillo, Mario. *Islands of Resistance: Puerto Rico, Vieques, and U.S. Policy.* New York: Seven Stories Press, 2001.

Ortiz Cofer, Judith. *The Line of the Sun.* Athens, GA: University of Georgia Press, 1989.

Rebolledo, Tey Diana. *Women Singing in the Snow: A Cultural Analysis of Chicana Literature.* Tucson: University of Arizona Press, 1995.

Rodríguez, Clara E. "A Summary of Puerto Rican Migration to the United States." In *Challenging Fronteras: Structuring Latina and Latino Lives in the U.S.*, ed. Mary Romero, Pierrette Hondagneu-Sotelo, and Vilma Ortiz, 101–113. New York: Routledge, 1997.

Sánchez González, Lisa. *Boricua Literature: A Literary History of the Puerto Rican Diaspora.* New York: New York University Press, 2001.

Sánchez Korrol, Virginia E. *From Colonia to Community: The History of Puerto Ricans in New York City.* Berkeley and Los Angeles: University of California Press, 1994.

Santiago, Esmeralda. *América's Dream.* New York: HarperCollins, 1996.

———. *When I Was Puerto Rican.* New York: Vintage Books, 1993.

Stavans, Ilan. *The Hispanic Condition: Reflections on Culture and Identity in America.* New York: HarperPerennial, 1995.

CONTRIBUTORS

FERDÂ ASYA is assistant professor of English at Bloomsburg University of Pennsylvania. She received her doctoral degree in American literature from Indiana University, Bloomington. She has taught English and American literature and French language courses in Canada and Malaysia and published articles and entries on the fiction of Edith Wharton, Nella Larsen, and Diane Johnson. Recent projects include research on American expatriate writers in Paris.

WILLIAM BURGOS is assistant professor of English at Long Island University, Brooklyn Campus, where he teaches European and American literature, African American literature, and Puerto Rican and Latino American literature. He is the coeditor, along with Carlos Antonio Torre and Hugo Rodriguez Vecchini, of *The Commuter Nation: Perspectives on Puerto Rican Migration* (1994).

ANTONIA DOMÍNGUEZ MIGUELA is assistant professor of English at the University of Huelva, Spain. She is the author of "Esa imagen que en mi espejo se detiene: La herencia femenina en la narrativa de Latinas en Estados Unidos" (2001) and "Pasajes de ida y vuelta: Narrativa puertorriqueña en Estados Unidos" (2005) and coeditor of *Evolving Origins, Transplanting Cultures: Literary Legacies of the New Americans* (2002). Her research interests are U.S. Latino/a narrative and ethnic women's writing.

VICTOR FIGUEROA received his doctoral degree in comparative literature from Harvard University in 2000. He is assistant professor of Latin American and Caribbean literature at Wayne State University, Detroit. His most recent publications include "Martí's Infanticides: Ismaelillo between the Pen and the Sword" (*Latin American Literary Review*, 2004) and "A Kingdom of Black Jacobins: Alejo Carpentier and C. L. R. James on the Haitian Revolution" (*Afro-Hispanic Review*, 2006).

TRENTON HICKMAN is associate professor of English at Brigham Young University, where he teaches courses in Latino/a literary history and literature, U.S. literature, and the novel. He has published essays in MELUS, *Studies in the Novel*, *Journal of Caribbean Studies*, and *Southwestern American Literatures*. He is also a poet and translator.

JOSÉ M. IRIZARRY RODRÍGUEZ is professor of American literature at the University of Puerto Rico, Mayaguez. He was a recipient of a grant from Recovering the U.S. Hispanic Literary Heritage Project for researching the life and works of Pedro Juan Labarthe in English. He is currently working on various projects on Puerto Rican and Afro–Puerto Rican identity construction and a critical introduction for the reprinting of Labarthe's first novel.

KELLI LYON JOHNSON is assistant professor of English at Miami University, where she teaches writing and literature. She is the author of *Julia Alvarez: Writing a New Place on the Map* (2005) and several essays on U.S. Latina and Caribbean women writers, including the fiction of Achy Obejas, Edwidge Danticat, and Demetria Martinez. Her current research explores collective memory in Chicana literature.

JOANNA BARSZEWSKA MARSHALL is associate professor of English at the University of Puerto Rico, Cayey. Her most recent work focuses on Caribbean women writers and food. She has published an article on Merle Hodge's *Crick, Crack Monkey*, "Resisting the Attempt to 'Civilize' Family and Appetite," in *Sargasso Journal*; her essay "Pride, Shame, Food, and Hunger in the Memoirs of Esmeralda Santiago" is being prepared for publication in *MELUS*.

ENRIQUE MORALES-DÍAZ is associate professor of Spanish and the coordinator of the U.S. Ethnic Studies Program at Hartwick College. He specializes in contemporary Latin American literature, U.S. Latino/a cultural studies, and gender and postcolonial studies. He has published essays on Esmeralda Santiago (*Centro Journal*) and on Reinaldo Arenas (*Postcolonial Text*). He is working on his manuscript, "Farewell Master, Farewell: Reinaldo Arenas' Postcoloniality," which will be published by Cambria Press in 2008.

SOLIMAR OTERO is assistant professor of English at Louisiana State University. She is a Cuban/Puerto Rican American scholar of African diaspora studies with a specialization in religious folklore and Latino Caribbean literature. She has conducted ethnographic research in Havana, Cuba, and in Lagos, Nigeria, as a Fulbright Researcher. Her work has appeared in *Africa Today, The Black Scholar,* and *Atlantic Studies.* She recently edited a special issue of *Western Folklore* dedicated to Afro-Carribean religions.

CARMEN HAYDÉE RIVERA is associate professor of English at the University of Puerto Rico, Río Piedras. Her teaching and research in U.S. literatures focus especially on Latina/o literatures and diasporic Puerto Rican writers. Recent publications have appeared in *Sargasso Journal* and *Dialogo*. She also has contributed to Alan West-Duran's collection *Latino and Latina Writers.*

LISA M. SÁNCHEZ GONZÁLEZ is associate professor of English at the University of Connecticut. She is the author of *Boricua Literature: A Literary History of the Puerto Rican Diaspora*. Her work has appeared in various journals and anthologies, including *American Literary History*, *Cultural Studies*, and *Recovering the U.S. Hispanic Literary Heritage.*

BETSY A. SANDLIN is assistant professor of Spanish at Sewanee, the University of the South. Her teaching and research interests include gender and sexuality in Latin American, Caribbean, and U.S. Latina/o literatures. Her most recent publications include "'*El hombre teje cuentos*': Manuel Ramos Otero's Queer Metaliterary Spiders," in *Revista Monográfica/Monographic Review*; "Julia de Burgos as a Cultural Icon in Luz María Umpierre's *The Margarita Poems*," in *Bilingual Review/Revista Bilingüe*; and "'Poetry Always Demands All My Ghosts': The Haunted and Haunting Poetry of Rane Arroyo," in *Centro Journal.*

MARITZA STANCHICH is associate professor of English at the University of Puerto Rico, Río Piedras, where she teaches U.S., Caribbean, and

Latina/o literatures. Her work on literature of the Puerto Rican diaspora and on Faulkner has appeared in the journals *Sargasso* and *Mississippi Quarterly*. She has also contributed to the collection *Prospero's Isles: The Presence of the Caribbean in the American Imaginary* (2004). She was an award-winning journalist and has also worked for academic unionization.

MARY JANE SUERO-ELLIOTT has taught at the University of Washington, Antioch University, and Seattle University. Currently an independent scholar, she focuses her research on Chicana, Puerto Rican, and Cuban American writing and theories of transnationalism and globalization. Upcoming publications include "Challenging Catholicism: Hagar vs. the Virgin in Graciela Limon's *The Memories of Ana Calderon*." She has recently completed a book on transmigration and oppositional identity as theorized in Latina women's literature entitled *Transmigratory Subjectivity in Contemporary Latina Fiction*.

JOSÉ L. TORRES-PADILLA is associate professor of English at the State University of New York, Plattsburgh, where he teaches U.S. literature, ethnic literatures, and creative writing. He has published several essays on multicultural literature in journals and anthologies, including *Centro Journal*, *MELUS*, *Race and the College Classroom*, and *Complicating Constructions: Race, Ethnicity, and Hybridity in American Texts*. He is a poet and writer, and his creative work has appeared in many literary journals and magazines. He is working on a book on the Latino short story, a project for which he received a grant from the Recovering the U.S. Hispanic Literary Heritage Project. He is the managing editor of the *Saranac Review*, a literary journal, and is the cofounder and codirector of the North Country Institute for Writers of Color.

JOHN WALDRON is assistant professor of Spanish at the University of Vermont, where he specializes in Latin American and U.S. Latino literature and culture. He recently coedited a special issue of the journal *Discourse* entitled "Mexican Cinema from the Post-Mexican Condition." He is currently working on how cultures "on the move" challenge Western notions of citizenship and knowledge.

INDEX